# Saving America's Countryside

# Saving America's Countryside

## A GUIDE TO RURAL CONSERVATION

BY Samuel N. Stokes WITH A. Elizabeth Watson

AND CONTRIBUTING AUTHORS

*Genevieve P. Keller and J. Timothy Keller*

FOR THE NATIONAL TRUST FOR HISTORIC PRESERVATION

The Johns Hopkins University Press
BALTIMORE AND LONDON

*This book has been brought to publication with the generous assistance of the Fowler Fund. The project was supported in part by grants from the Cecil Howard Charitable Trust, the Eva Gebhard-Gourgaud Foundation, the Richard King Mellon Foundation, and the National Endowment for the Arts.*

The Johns Hopkins University Press
701 West 40th Street, Baltimore, Maryland 21211
The Johns Hopkins Press Ltd., London

The paper used in this publication meets the minimum requirements of American National Standard for Information Sciences—Permanence of Paper for Printed Library Materials, ANSI Z39.48-1984.

*The National Trust for Historic Preservation is the only private, nonprofit national organization chartered by Congress to encourage public participation in the preservation of sites, buildings, and objects significant in American history and culture. Support is provided by membership dues, endowment funds, contributions, and grants from federal agencies, including the U.S. Department of the Interior, under provisions of the National Historic Preservation Act of 1966.*

*The opinions expressed in this publication are not necessarily those of the U.S. Department of the Interior.*

Library of Congress Cataloging-in-Publication Data

Stokes, Samuel N., 1940–
    Saving America's countryside: a guide to rural conservation / by Samuel N. Stokes with A. Elizabeth Watson and contributions by Genevieve P. Keller and J. Timothy Keller; sponsored by the National Trust for Historic Preservation.
        p.    cm.
    Bibliography: p.
    Includes index.
    ISBN 0-8018-3695-6 (alk. paper). ISBN 0-8018-3696-4 (pbk. : alk. paper)
    1. Historic sites—United States—Conservation and restoration. 2. Landscape protection—United States. 3. Conservation of natural resources—United States. 4. United States—Rural conditions. I. Watson, A. Elizabeth. II. National Trust for Historic Preservation in the United States. III. Title.
E159.S76   1989
333.7'2'0973—dc19                                                           88-19941

*Title page illustration:* USDA—Soil Conservation Service, Gene Alexander

# Contents

# Case Studies

*The locations of case studies are denoted by black dots on the accompanying maps.*

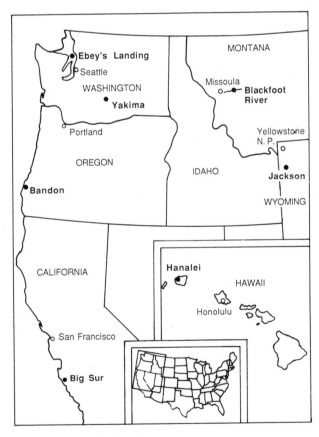

**Western case study locations**

**Midwestern case study locations**

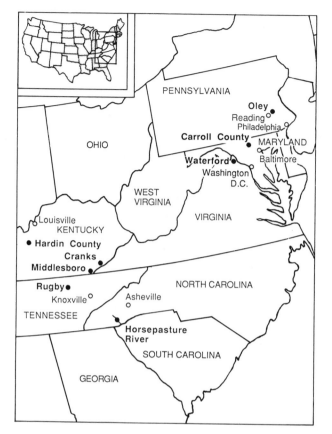

Southeastern case study locations

Northeastern case study locations

# Foreword

This call-to-action book, prepared under the auspices of the National Trust for Historic Preservation, is long overdue. During the great surge of urbanization in the past four decades the nation has turned its back on small-town America and the rich legacy concentrated in America's countrysides and rural communities.

Thomas Jefferson would surely deplore our tendency to ignore the importance of country things. Always worried about the corrupting influence of large cities, Jefferson held an almost mystical political conviction that the republic he helped found would be sustained in the long run by cohesive communities of yeoman farmers. "The small landholders," he wrote, "are the chosen people of God . . . whose breasts He has made His peculiar deposit for substantial and genuine virtue."

Even as the twentieth century winds to its close, many of us who were nurtured in rural surroundings share Jefferson's beliefs about the contributions small communities make to our national life. And our concerns are intensified as the experts inform us that by 1990 75 percent of the U.S. population will reside in urban areas that lie within fifty miles of the nation's shorelines in a burgeoning megalopolis that will soon swallow most of the remaining rural areas along our coasts.

Written both for people who live in communities that lie in the path of this coastal juggernaut and for small-town Americans everywhere who want to preserve the environmental attributes that make their communities distinctive, this handbook is more than a how-to manual for environmental activists. It describes the dynamics of conservation action for

*We owed it to do, not what was to perish with ourselves, but what would remain, to be respected and preserved into other ages.*

Thomas Jefferson

all levels of community leaders by combining case studies of successful conservation/preservation programs with general information about environmental design, historic preservation, land-use planning, and existing government programs designed to help communities create life-giving environmental plans. Its most powerful message appears in the sections that present detailed information concerning action plans already executed by counties and communities from Maine to Hawaii. The very names of these communities dramatize the wide range of conservation opportunities outlined in this volume:

| | |
|---|---|
| Oley, Pennsylvania | Horsepasture River, North Carolina |
| Bandon, Oregon | Ebey's Landing, Washington |
| Cranks, Kentucky | Dubuque County, Iowa |
| Big Sur, California | Jackson Hole, Wyoming |
| Cranbury, New Jersey | McHenry County, Illinois |
| Waterford, Virginia | Carroll County, Maryland |
| Hanalei, Hawaii | Blackfoot River, Montana |
| Wells, Maine | Brattleboro, Vermont |
| Rugby, Tennessee | Eaton County, Michigan |
| Cazenovia, New York | Guilford, Connecticut |

*Saving America's Countryside* tells the story of how concerned rural people in each of these communities became environmental pioneers by taking action to fashion plans and programs that enhanced the environment and the economic values of their towns and regions. Some organized in order to stop unwanted highways or dams. Some developed innovative strategies to protect irreplaceable open space or stream valleys or farmlands. Others generated a consensus for conservation action by initiating inventories of their communities' natural and cultural resources. And still others learned how to reach out to state and federal agencies and private nonprofit organizations to marshall the additional financing—or the outside intervention—needed to save crucial lands or historic buildings or to implement environmental improvements desired by their communities. These case studies offer a road map for citizens in rural America who want to protect and enhance the livability and appeal of their communities and valleys.

The book's exquisite timeliness lies in the fact that it is being published at a juncture when the nation appears ready for a new wave of conservation action. There are good grounds for optimism that Congress will soon enact legislation to create an American Heritage Trust (funded by federal receipts from oil leases on the continental shelf) to provide dollar-for-dollar matching funds for communities that have conservation/preservation projects that are ready to be implemented. The Heritage Trust will offer federal incentive funding for programs ranging from the acquisition of open space to the creation of greenways (conceived as "fingers of green" encompassing networks of walkways, bicycle trails, and refuges for wildlife interwoven with forestlands or river corridors) to the preservation of prized historical and cultural assets. The Heritage Trust will provide a potent incentive for local and regional groups who want to augment their economies by enhancing their overall environments.

As this volume suggests, there are many paths to rural renewal. Every town or region can initiate programs that will make it a more attractive place to live and visit. Many small towns thrive today as "gateways" to parks or wildlife sanctuaries or historic places—and many communities have yet to discover and exploit the economic potential of natural or cultural assets that lie on their doorsteps.

As a result of citizen initiatives of the past three decades, hundreds of new park, wildlife, and historic areas have been identified and developed by our national and state governments. Today, for example, one can stop and visit the Derry, New Hampshire, farm where Robert Frost wrote some of his finest poetry, because that state purchased and preserved a site that was being used as an auto junkyard. And tourists can now visit new national park areas in such out-of-the-way towns as Flat Rock, North Carolina (Carl Sandburg's last home), Fort Davis, Texas (a well-preserved cavalry post), and Pecos, New Mexico (the ruins of the easternmost outpost of the Pueblo Indians).

New Mexico, a state which has an array of small towns with fascinating histories, is a case study all by itself. In the process of according belated recognition to the contributions made by Spanish and Indian pioneers, New Mexicans are perceiving that tourism linked to their archeological and cultural assets can be magnified many times. The Espanola valley, for example, is the locale where, in 1598, a party of Spanish pioneers became the first European families to settle permanently on U.S. soil. The history of this western Plymouth Rock has never been fully told, and now local citizens are building facilities where the story can be acclaimed and interpreted. And New Mexico's Zuni Indians have recently asked Congress to provide a new focus for archeological preservation by creating the nation's first Indian national park where young Zuni men and women will interpret their own culture to incoming tourists.

As the homogenization of urban America accelerates and vacationers grow wary of the moneychangers who operate our ever-present tourist traps, the lure of attractive small towns may increase as places to live and to visit. Rural areas that raise funds to preserve distinctive architectural and cultural qualities are making investments that will assuredly enhance the future of their communities. Moreover, every small town can plant trees and flowers—or preserve a marsh or forest or riverside park—that will add to its appeal. Kansas is a case in point. Ninety percent of Kansas towns have volunteer tree boards who serve as green-wardens of their communities.

This book suggests that towns at the edge of suburbia should fight for managed-growth policies that respect nature's limits and exhibit reverence for the human environment created by earlier generations. I believe such rural areas can profit by studying the decisions made by modest-sized cities in their regions that have relied on a conservation/preservation ethic to guide their development within municipal boundaries. Among the cities that come to mind as models are Lowell, Massachusetts, Boulder, Colorado, Santa Fe, New Mexico, Madison, Wisconsin, and Eugene, Oregon.

The authors of this work offer the wise counsel that communities should begin with inventories of their assets and should be assiduous in using a total environmental approach in developing their plans and projects. It is a good guess that some towns and counties that conduct such surveys will discover they have overlooked segments of their history that could serve as building blocks for vital projects. I suspect that some communities have buildings or trails or nature sanctuaries where they could recount the stories of explorers who first trod parts of the American earth. Perhaps others have overlooked opportunities to interpret nearby ruins, or to commemorate the lives and work of memorable literary figures such as Ernest Hemingway, Sinclair Lewis, and Willa Cather.

My own experience growing up in a rural area tells me this country needs small towns. We need close-knit communities because they are excellent places to rear children. We need them as slow-lane refuges where people overwhelmed by urban stress can find quietude and peace of mind. We need them as an antidote that dramatizes the failures and shortcomings of American urbanization. We need them as laboratories of cleanliness where we can gather baseline data about environmental health. And we need the diversity they provide, as a reminder of the lifestyles and values of an older, perhaps saner, America.

This work reminds us that each generation has its own rendezvous with the land, its own opportunity to make history by creating lifegiving environments for its children. It is time for a new wave of conservation action in rural America. We must act—and learn to cherish and live in harmony with our past—because that is the only way truly civilized people can live.

Stewart L. Udall, *Phoenix, Arizona*
*December 1988*

# Preface

Our love of America's countryside motivated us to write this book. We find many attractions in rural America: certainly they include streams to canoe, mountains to hike, productive farmland to behold, and historic small towns to explore. But more important, rural America has been home for significant periods of our lives, and it is where many of our relatives and friends reside. We feel privileged to have been able to work for its conservation.

As have many Americans, we have become increasingly concerned about the many threats to the rural environment we cherish and have puzzled over how to protect it. There are excellent publications on land trusts, zoning, historic preservation, and farmland conservation, but none gives an overview of all the techniques that can be used to protect the rural environment, particularly if one is concerned not about just one resource, but about all the resources that make a rural community unique. It was out of this concern that this book was born.

It was out of this same concern that one of the authors, Samuel N. Stokes, urged the National Trust for Historic Preservation to establish its Rural Program in 1979. The program has focused national attention on the importance of America's diverse rural historic resources, including the environments of which they are a part, and forged new alliances among organizations concerned with the protection of historic, natural, and agricultural resources. The program staff, which for several years consisted primarily of Samuel N. Stokes and A. Elizabeth Watson, advised rural communities, wrote publications, and led workshops on the techniques for protecting rural areas. The program started in the Trust's Mid-Atlantic Region and is now a national program, coordinated from the organization's headquarters.

Two major components of the Rural Program were demonstration projects in Cazenovia, New York (Case Study 6), and Oley, Pennsylvania

(Case Study 1), designed to show how rural communities could protect their natural, historic, and agricultural resources by working through both local government and nonprofit organizations. The two communities, chosen competitively, had outstanding resources and, most important, a strong local commitment to protect what they had. In collaboration with the College of Environmental Science and Forestry of the State University of New York at Syracuse (in the case of Cazenovia) and the Berks County Conservancy (in the case of Oley), the Rural Program staff worked with these communities intensively from 1980 to 1984, advising them on the range of techniques described in this book. Although the National Trust and other outside advisors were much involved in these protection efforts, the leadership for the projects was always at the local level and the Trust benefited from the collaboration at least as much as did the communities.

This book would not have been possible without the assistance of numerous individuals. First, we would like to thank the residents and leaders of Cazenovia and Oley who allowed the National Trust to work in their communities. Without this first-hand experience and the insights they provided, we could never have written this book. In Cazenovia, we are particularly indebted to Don R. Callahan, Andrew F. Diefendorf, Faith T. Knapp, Terry R. LeVeque, James D. Mietz, and Dorothy W. Riester; in Oley, to E. Garrett Brinton, Dennis G. Collins, Hilda S. Fisher, Andy Glick, Phoebe L. Hopkins, Jane Levan, Duane E. Pysher, and Donald Shelley. In addition to these individuals, volunteers too numerous to name devoted many hours to filling out inventory forms, taking photographs, preparing maps, checking well gauges, and performing many other essential tasks.

Much of the inspiration for this book has come from the leaders of local and state conservation organizations and from local and state officials across the country. They patiently described protection programs in their communities, and the case studies are the result of their contributions. In particular we would like to thank the following leaders of nonprofit organizations: Mark C. Ackelson (Iowa Natural Heritage Foundation), Thomas C. Bailey (Little Traverse Conservancy, Michigan), Richard W. Carbin (Vermont Land Trust), Constance K. Chamberlin (Waterford Foundation, Virginia), Doug Cheever (Heritage Trail, Iowa), Carolie Evans (Guilford Land Trust, Connecticut), Joseph M. Getty (Historical Society of Carroll County, Maryland), Hank Goetz (Lubrecht Forest, Montana), Ralph H. Goodno, Jr. (Housatonic Valley Association, Connecticut), Samuel M. Hamill, Jr. (Middlesex-Somerset-Mercer Regional Study Council, New Jersey), Robert J. Hammerslag (Essex Community Heritage Organization, New York), Jean W. Hocker (Jackson Hole Land Trust, Wyoming), Robert J. Kiesling (Nature Conservancy, Montana), Randi S. Lemmon (Housatonic Valley Association, Connecticut), Frederic L. McLaughlin (Citizens Concerned about I-69), Morton K. Mather (Laudholm Trust, Maine), Richard M. Monahon, Jr. (Historic Harrisville, New Hampshire), Robert Myhr (San Juan Preservation Trust, Washington), William H. Schmidt (Vermont Land Trust), Marc Smiley (Yakima River Greenway Foundation, Washington), Barbara Stagg (Historic Rugby, Tennessee), Brian L. Steen (Big Sur Land Trust, California), Bill Thomas (Friends of the Horsepasture, North Carolina), Gary Werner (Ice

Age Trail Council, Wisconsin), Frank A. Wright (Cranbury Housing Associates, New Jersey), and Martin E. Zeller (Colorado Open Lands).

We are also most grateful to the following local and state officials: Stephen E. Aradas (McHenry County, Illinois), Catherine W. Bishir (North Carolina State Historic Preservation Office), K. Marlene Dorsey Conaway (Carroll County, Maryland), Daniel R. Cowee (Teton County, Wyoming), Arthur A. Davis (Pennsylvania Department of Environmental Resources), Dennis A. Gordon (Hardin County, Kentucky), and Charles E. Roe (North Carolina Heritage Program).

We have been assisted by many other conservationists and preservationists who inspired us and freely contributed ideas and suggestions. In particular, we would like to thank Joe Belden (Housing Assistance Council), Norman A. Berg (American Farmland Trust), Kathleen A. Blaha (Trust for Public Land), Christopher N. Brown (American Rivers), David Cottingham (Washington, D.C.), G. Ken Creighton (Nature Conservancy), Janet Diehl (Trust for Public Land), Ben Drake (Highlander Center), Benjamin R. Emory (Land Trust Exchange), Lynne Espy (North Yarmouth, Maine), Robert J. Gray (American Farmland Trust), Richard Hawks (State University of New York at Syracuse), Robert G. Healy (Conservation Foundation), John Jakle (University of Illinois), Mark B. Lapping (Kansas State University), Stanford M. Lembeck (Cooperative Extension Service, Pennsylvania), Stephen U. Lester (Citizen's Clearinghouse for Hazardous Wastes), Chester H. Liebs (University of Vermont), Richard A. Liroff (Conservation Foundation), Jim Lyon (Environmental Policy Institute), Edward T. McMahon (Coalition for Scenic Beauty), Margaret S. Maizel (American Farmland Trust), Robert Z. Melnick (University of Oregon), Erik J. Meyers (Environmental Law Institute), James F. Palmer (State University of New York at Syracuse), Caroline Pryor (Land Trust Exchange), Thomas W. Richards (Arlington, Virginia), Nobby Riedy (Wilderness Society), Frederick Steiner (University of Colorado, Denver), Robert E. Stipe (Chapel Hill, North Carolina), Isaac N. P. Stokes (Jericho, Vermont), Thomas E. Waddell (Conservation Foundation), and Warren Zitzmann (Falls Church, Virginia).

Numerous federal officials took time to explain their programs and review drafts of what we wrote. In particular we would like to thank Ty Berry (U.S. Fish and Wildlife Service), Gary R. Evans (U.S. Department of Agriculture), John J. Fay (U.S. Fish and Wildlife Service), Cathy A. Gilbert (National Park Service), Robert A. Hoppe (U.S. Department of Agriculture), Alan Jabbour (American Folklife Center), Robert J. Karotko (National Park Service), Don L. Klima (Advisory Council on Historic Preservation), Linda F. McClelland (National Park Service), Donald E. McCormack (U.S. Soil Conservation Service), Hugh C. Miller (National Park Service), Carol D. Shull (National Park Service), William S. Sipple (Environmental Protection Agency), LaVerne Smith (U.S. Fish and Wildlife Service), and Richard C. Spicer (National Park Service).

The book would not have been possible without a great deal of assistance and understanding from several staff members at the National Trust (both past and present), notably Greg Coble, Bonnie Cohen, Paul W. Edmondson, Marilyn Fedelchak, William B. Hart, Peter Hawley, Mary M. Humstone, Russell V. Keune, Mary C. Means, Elizabeth S. Merritt, Stefan Nagel, Charles F. Rotchford, and J. Jackson Walter. Douglas R. Horne designed the demonstration programs in Cazenovia and Oley; Susan Kidd did extensive research for Chapter 6; and Diane Maddex, director of the Preservation Press, provided guidance and assistance from the beginning and arranged for the book's publication. Monica B. Rotchford, the Rural Program secretary from its inception, typed and retyped the manuscript, made numerous suggestions to improve it, and cheerfully put in long hours on its final production.

Many others too numerous to mention helped us immeasurably in providing information, reviewing drafts, and obtaining illustrations.

We are also most grateful to George F. Thompson and his colleagues at the Johns Hopkins University Press, and Carolyn I. Moser, our copyeditor. They made numerous helpful suggestions to improve the text and illustrations.

We are particularly grateful to the Cecil Howard Charitable Trust, the Eva Gebhard-Gourgaud Foundation, the Fowler Fund, the Richard King Mellon Foundation, and the National Endowment for the Arts for their generous support of this book. We also wish to thank the Geraldine R. Dodge Foundation and the J. M. Kaplan Fund for their generous assistance in helping establish the Rural Program.

Many of the drawings were prepared especially for this book. For the maps in Chapter 3, we gratefully acknowledge the contributions of the volunteers and staff of the Cazenovia Community Resources Project, the students and faculty of the State University of New York at Syracuse, and Land and Community Associates of Charlottesville, Virginia. Special thanks are due to Frederick Schneider, AIA, Shaun Eyring, and W. Thomas Ward of Land and Community Associates, who, under the direction of J. Timothy Keller, prepared many of the drawings.

Each author has worked in rural conservation and contributed ideas to the entire manuscript. Samuel N. Stokes developed the concept of the book and was its editor and principal author. He was the primary author of Chapters 1, 3, 6, and 7 and wrote portions of the other chapters. A. Elizabeth Watson was the primary author of Chapters 2, 4, and 5 and the Conclusion. Genevieve P. Keller wrote portions of Chapters 1, 2, 3, and 7. J. Timothy Keller contributed to the sections on scenic areas and design guidelines and Case Studies 7, 14, and 24.

Finally, we wish to thank our families and friends for their inspiration, encouragement, patience, and support over the years it has taken to make this book a reality.

Samuel N. Stokes, *Washington, D.C.*
A. Elizabeth Watson, *Harrisburg, Pennsylvania*
Genevieve P. Keller, *Charlottesville, Virginia*
J. Timothy Keller, ASLA, *Charlottesville, Virginia*
*January 1989*

# Saving America's Countryside

# Rural Conservation

Rural Americans protect their communities for a variety of reasons. Some begin because of a burning issue—a dam proposed for a scenic stream, a shopping mall planned on prime farmland, or the imminent demolition of the last one-room schoolhouse in the county. Others become involved because they sense a general threat—often increased or unplanned development—and believe that existing efforts are inadequate to counteract it. Some are interested in protecting natural areas; others want to save farmland or historic buildings; a few have a concern for the total environment. They may be elected officials, members of a community group, old-timers, or newcomers. Their livelihoods may be farming or ranching, or they may work in a local business or in the nearest town. Whatever your interests, whoever you are, this book is intended for you, the rural citizen who wants to take action locally to protect and conserve your community's heritage and resources.

If you are already part of a group, so much the better. Although it is true that one person can make a difference, group action (which in this context includes government) is more effective than one person working alone. Organizing to protect the countryside often follows a typical process: a small group of people get together, outline the problems they see, conduct research on the needs of the community, define a mission, develop a strategy and program, and begin the long, hard haul to make it all work. From holding meetings to buying land, group action can help you accomplish dozens of tasks. You need people, knowledge, money, and access to the media and public officials—frequently all at once and in a hurry. This book helps you to divide the process of organizing and taking action into a manageable number of steps.

*My state will undergo overwhelming changes that will alter the whole landscape irretrievably in the next generation. Change is accelerating beyond my ability to imagine its impact by the end of this century. How we are going to hang onto some vestiges of the hundreds of years of rural life that have passed, damned if I know. It will take powerful thought and powerful effort.*

Catherine W. Bishir
*North Carolina State Historic Preservation Office*

1

Before going further, let us discuss definitions. Few people, whether scholars, citizens, or public officials, agree on what, precisely, is "rural." "Rural," in our book, is up to the reader to decide. Generally, we expect the place where you live to be a relatively sparsely populated area that lies beyond the city and its suburbs; it should be a place where natural resources are the basis for at least some of the residents' livelihoods—farming, ranching, fishing, timbering, and mining, among others.

What we mean by "rural conservation" is more important. The word *conservation* means, in the traditional sense imparted by Gifford Pinchot, the turn-of-the-century founder of the U.S. Forest Service, the wise use and management of natural resources to achieve the greatest good for the greatest number of people for the longest period of time. Conservation as Pinchot knew it was a rather utilitarian attitude; he had little use for the concern of his contemporary, John Muir, for places of wild beauty. Today, however, the idea of wilderness preservation is regarded by conservationists as one kind of "use" or "management." Our own, expanded concept of conservation not only acknowledges this more modern attitude but also embraces the idea of the *community* as a resource, from individual farms or landholdings, to social institutions, to the local economy as a whole. The rural communities that people have managed to build over the years, using both the natural resources at hand and their own talents and traditions, represent a substantial investment. That investment deserves our respect and creativity as we protect it and build upon it. Rural conservation, then, includes protecting natural and scenic resources, preserving buildings and places of cultural significance, and enhancing the local economy and social institutions.

Rural America has never been static. We recognize the inevitability, and desirability, of change. Rural conservation calls for the foresight to manage change: to minimize its negative effects and to use it to improve the community's economic vitality, employment and educational opportunities, municipal services, and civic amenities. We believe change can occur while respecting natural areas, retaining agriculture, and preserving diverse cultural and historic resources. Indeed, rural communities should demand no less.

Many forces are at work against rural conservation, however often directed with the best of intentions, and are frequently outside your community's control. Contaminated wells may lead local authorities to extend water and sewer lines to deal with residents' health needs, but water and sewer lines characteristically lead to development pressures on farmland or denser population growth than existing roads or schools can handle. An example of well-intended actions outside your community's direct control may be the decisions of the state highway department: rural communities traditionally have needed better roads to get their goods to market; now, however, those same roads may bring increased development. Similarly, decisions to change federal farm policy or tax policy may have an enormous effect on a farmer's decisions about what to plant and how much, or whether to plant at all, or on a real estate developer's expectation than an office building at the new highway interchange miles outside the city limits will be a success.

Still other obstacles to rural conservation lie within the community. Most property owners are reluctant to accept regulation of changes to their properties. Likewise, many developers do not wish to incorporate

desirable but unprofitable features into their designs to counteract noise, traffic problems, storm-water runoff, or other unhappy impacts of new development. Convincing both owners and developers to act in the interests of the community at large, for the "common good," is a difficult challenge. Simply stating that well-planned development enhances everyone's property values is hardly enough when the benefits are long-term and the profits short-term. Even those who are anxious to pursue rural conservation may find a problem within their ranks. Too frequently, those working to protect various rural resources have pursued separate strategies. Moreover, rural communities frequently lack the funds and knowledge necessary to deal firmly with development pressures or to deal creatively with problems of declining population. In the latter situation, a community may feel compelled to welcome any kind of development offering taxes and employment no matter what the trade-offs. This book suggests ways for you to help your community to develop a rural conservation program in spite of the obstacles.

Although the issues and the solutions can differ greatly from community to community, we believe there are some common principles to be found in most successful rural conservation programs:

*Rural conservation should integrate natural resource conservation, farmland retention, historic preservation, and scenic protection.* Rural conservation offers an opportunity for people with a broad range of con-

Rural conservation combines a concern for natural, historic, agricultural, and scenic resources. The combination of such resources makes scenes like this agricultural valley in Vermont universally attractive.

cerns to work together to protect and improve their communities. While there may be good reasons in some instances for those concerned with protecting wildlife habitat, for example, to organize separately from those concerned with preserving farmland or historic buildings, joining forces may make more sense. Seemingly different concerns are often, in fact, closely linked. The windbreak, which is designed to prevent soil erosion, also provides habitat for wildlife and is a scenic element in the landscape. The historic farmhouses and barns prized by the local historical society are far more interesting if they are still used by farm families and surrounded by active farmland. In addition, most of the techniques designed to protect these resources are the same. If a new zoning ordinance or easement program is proposed for a community, it will be more effective—and easier to marshal public support for—if it addresses all of a community's threatened resources, not just one or two.

*A successful rural conservation program is linked to the social and economic needs of the community.* A program that does not take into account social and economic needs is unlikely to gain wide community support. Such concerns as inadequate low-income housing, joblessness, or the problems of minorities and single-parent families may be beyond our capacity as conservationists for direct action, but we should at least make sure that our programs do not create problems for those attempting to address those concerns. Moreover, there may indeed be opportunities to combine rural conservation with the advancement of other community interests: Conserved resources can attract tourists and new employment opportunities, and historic houses can be rehabilitated for low-income housing, to mention but two examples. By the same token, social service organizations should not ignore conservation issues. Rural conservation is important to everyone, whatever their circumstances.

*Rural conservation programs will be more successful if local governments and private nonprofit organizations cooperate.* Local governments and private nonprofit organizations each have their strengths and weaknesses. Working together in a rural conservation effort ensures that each will do what it does best while making up for each other's disadvantages. Some activities, such as environmental inventories, can be undertaken cooperatively. Other projects are best handled by one or the other, but preferably in complementary ways. For instance, local government can regulate the use of private land in a way that a nonprofit organization obviously cannot. On the other hand, nonprofit organizations can undertake more controversial programs, are less bound by rules, and generally can act faster when speed is important. If a key parcel of lakefront property, the ideal site for a much-needed county park, suddenly comes on the market, a nonprofit organization may be able to buy it quickly. The local government, on the other hand, may be required to get approval from the voters, by which time the property may have been sold to another party or become too expensive to acquire. Yet, the private nonprofit organization can subsequently sell the lakefront site to the local government, which may have the long-term resources to develop and maintain the park.

*Rural conservation programs will be more successful if they rely on more than one technique.* If successful rural conservation calls for the cooperation of local government and nonprofit organizations, it follows that a strategy of using multiple techniques to protect the character of rural

4

communities is also desirable. For example, you can seek to protect wet-lands by simultaneously educating the public about their importance, reg-ulating their exploitation through ordinances, and acquiring them by donation.

*The public should be involved at all stages.* The more you inform the public about your plans and the more you adapt your strategies to the con-cerns you encounter, the better are your chances for success. You cannot alienate or exclude any group—farmers, newcomers, public officials, or the press—and expect to succeed.

*Rural conservation requires a long-term commitment.* Although you may solve an immediate crisis—whether it is a water pollution threat or a proposed demolition of a historic bridge—other threats undoubtedly will occur in the future. If conservation programs are in place, the community will be better able to deal with future challenges. It takes time to reveal to a community the benefits of protecting its farmland, its wetlands, or its historic mills. It also takes time to persuade landowners that implement-ing soil conservation plans or donating easements can be wise economic and environmental decisions.

No one book can cover all the conservation issues facing rural commu-nities or describe all of the available protection techniques. *Saving Amer-ica's Countryside* concentrates on those issues and techniques that apply at the local level to a large number of communities. It introduces you to the basic techniques necessary for a comprehensive rural conservation pro-gram. *Saving America's Countryside* is a "how-to" manual designed to be read in its entirety, but not everyone will use it that way. It should also work as a reference book, to return to for ideas, information, and encour-agement. You will find additional information, both on subjects that are covered and on related topics, in the suggested reading sections for each chapter.

In a capsule, here is what this book is about: Chapter 1, which covers most of the conservation issues faced by rural communities, should be helpful both in deciding what issues you wish to address and in marshaling arguments to use in discussing the importance of protecting your commu-nity's resources. Chapter 2 describes the basic principles of organizing a rural conservation effort through local government and nonprofit orga-nizations. Chapter 3 shows you how to gather and evaluate information about significant resources. Chapters 4 and 5 outline the specific tools that local governments and nonprofit organizations can use to protect a com-munity's resources. Chapter 6 explains how to obtain help from the many national and state agencies and organizations that are prepared to assist your community. Chapter 7 discusses educating your community about the importance of its resources and of implementing protection programs.

Although we will give you an overview of many rural conservation techniques, you will need to decide which ones will work in your commu-nity. Some techniques may be politically unacceptable, cost too much, or lack the necessary enabling legislation. Addressing the issues in your com-munity requires you to understand what is unique about your community and to develop a strategy that best fits it. This book suggests how you can build that understanding, what processes might work as you take action, and which ideas you should consider in tailoring programs to your community. Regretfully we remind you of a platitude that is all too true here: there are no easy answers. While uncomplicated boosterism sometimes goes a surprisingly long way—any place looks better without litter, or with trees planted along the village sidewalks, or with a welcome sign at the entrance to the community—other more challenging programs will be needed as well. While other communities that have tried rural conservation can provide some of the answers, ideas that work in one place generally need adaptation to be grafted onto another. Our concept of rural conservation calls on you to provide not only motivation and determination, but also creativity and a "can-do" attitude. We hope that you will take the ideas in this book and make them work, or even develop new ways to conserve resources. Along the way, you are likely to experience frustration or delay, opposition, or just plain stubbornness. It is not easy to gain the political cooperation or team spirit so necessary to your long-term success.

Also along the way, we expect that you will gain personal satisfaction from organizing a rural conservation program. Perhaps that satisfaction will come from associating with fellow residents and sharing information about and hopes for your community. Or perhaps that satisfaction will come from implementing a new program and seeing it gain widespread support within the community. At the very least you will know that the things you care for in your community stand a better chance of being enjoyed by future generations because you cared enough to participate in a protection program. The dividends are well worth the effort it will take.

# Rural Concerns

## I. INTRODUCTION

**W**hat makes *your* community special? Clean water? Rich farmland? A dramatic coast? Historic sites? Opportunities to hike and fish? The willingness of neighbors to help one another? No doubt there are a number of resources and less tangible values that have made you decide your community is a place worth protecting. No doubt you also have a number of concerns about the future of your community. Is the groundwater being polluted? Are farmers being forced out of business by mounting debts or encroaching development? Are vacation homes cluttering the waterfront? Are historic farmsteads falling into ruin? Are "no trespassing" signs blocking access to a favorite trail? Do you no longer know your neighbors? Or perhaps your worries have to do with a vision of the future based on what is happening to a nearby community. "Do we want McHenry to look like Cook County?" asked conservation leaders in neighboring, and still-rural, McHenry, Illinois (see Case Study 9).

Identifying community values and concerns such as those mentioned above is a good way to start the rural conservation process; it can be enjoyable, too. For instance, the arts council of Harrison County, Iowa, located in the loess hills along the Missouri River, sponsored a day-long bus trip around the county. Participants observed, sketched, and mapped the natural and built environment and ended the day with a group discussion on the county's problems and potentials. The day's activity resulted in an increased commitment to improving the appearance of the towns and enacting conservation measures to protect the fragile bluffs overlooking the river.

While we can describe national trends, you have to decide what applies to your community. Obviously, each county and town has its own particular character and needs. A community in the West may have a water short-

## Questions for a Rural Conservationist

*Alan Gussow, artist and author, suggests that rural conservation leaders start by asking themselves the following questions:*

**1.** *If you took a visitor around your community, what places would you be certain to include?*

**2.** *Where would you get out of the car and walk around? Why those places?*

**3.** *What are the recurring events, both natural and human, in your environment? Are they marked or observed? How?*

**4.** *Small towns and their surrounding countryside interact with each other. What indicators, if any, do you find in your town which reveal the beneficial effects of being in a rural setting? Can you think of any good qualities in the countryside which result from the nearness to a town?*

**5.** *What part of the environment in which you live is most likely to change? Is this change for the better? If not, why not; and what could you do to prevent or lessen the impact of this change?*

**6.** *If you could change one thing about your community, what would it be? Most importantly, what would be the first step to take in order to work toward that change?*

*(Alan Gussow to author, 6 May 1986.)*

age and controversy over its allocation, while a community in the Midwest may have abundant water but be worried about its pollution; a county in the Rockies may consist primarily of public land managed by the U.S. Forest Service and be particularly concerned about federal land-management policy, while a county in the South may be more concerned about the actions of private landowners. The needs of communities that are losing population or watching their economies decline, as is the case in much of the Great Plains, are very different from those of communities with rising populations and booming economies.

Fortunately you can protect many resources—such as wetlands, fertile soils, and cultural resources—at the community level. Other resources are more difficult to protect locally or are best addressed at the regional, state, national, or even international level. Watersheds, for instance, typically cross political boundaries. While a community can do much to protect the quality of its water, it probably will need to cooperate with neighboring jurisdictions as well. Although you can do a great deal to promote farmland retention, escalating land values in the region or declining commodity prices may force farmers out of business nonetheless. A problem such as acid rain requires not only federal action, but also international cooperation. In this chapter we concentrate on those rural conservation issues that can be addressed, at least in part, at the local level.

## II. ECONOMIC, DEMOGRAPHIC, AND SOCIAL ISSUES

Inseparable from issues concerning the protection of the environment—broadly defined to include natural, agricultural, scenic, and historic resources—are economic and social issues relating to the growth and decline of communities and the livelihood of individual citizens. Although the causes and the symptoms may differ, both those communities that are growing and those that are declining face environmental degradation.

### A. Growing Rural Communities

All Americans are familiar with the sprawl that has grown up around American cities and towns since World War II. As better roads have made it easier for people to commute longer distances to jobs, development has been pushed to the point that corridors of development now link many cities, such as the Boston to Washington, D.C., corridor on the East Coast, or the Los Angeles to San Diego corridor on the West Coast. In many parts of the country, a driver leaving a city is hard pressed to say where the city ends and the country begins. Piecemeal strip development of houses, stores, service stations, and fast-food restaurants along country roads accounts for the loss of much farmland and gives many rural areas a cluttered appearance.

In addition to the growth adjacent to towns and cities, many more remote rural areas are gaining in population. During the 1970s, for the first time in America's history rural areas as a whole grew faster than urban. The rural growth rate has been particularly high on the West Coast, in northern New England, and in parts of the South and the upper Great Lakes.

There are many reasons for this trend. Some people believe that rural areas are healthier and more pleasant places to live and work. For others

This house in Purcellville, Virginia, will soon give way to a shopping center. Loss of familiar landmarks and landscapes prompts the start of many rural conservation programs.

Population during the 1970s increased in most rural areas, although certain counties, notably in the Plains states, experienced population decline. These trends have continued in the 1980s. While most counties with increasing population are losing farmland and natural areas to new construction, counties with declining population often face severe economic problems.

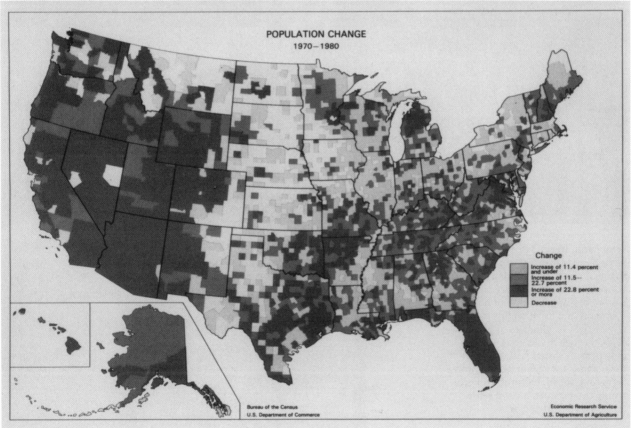

POPULATION CHANGE
1970–1980

Change

Increase of 11.4 percent and under

Increase of 11.5–22.7 percent

Increase of 22.8 percent or more

Decrease

Bureau of the Census
U.S. Department of Commerce

Economic Research Service
U.S. Department of Agriculture

the motivation to move stems from a desire for less expensive housing and lower taxes. For corporations locating new plants in rural communities, the impetus is often cheaper land or labor, which in turn can lead to greater residential growth nearby. Others move to rural areas at retirement.

Templeton, Iowa. The farms and natural areas that traditionally surrounded towns created sharp edges between town and country and enhanced our appreciation of both. The sight of a town's lights from a nearby field or glimpses of planted fields through a village street not only provide visual links between town and country, but also reinforce the strong social, cultural, and economic ties between a rural settlement and its outlying area.

Change has always been a part of rural America. Here a farmer in New Lenox, Illinois, describes to a Soil Conservation Service District Conservationist how this round barn used to house fifty-six cows.

10

Whether rural growth is the result of urban sprawl or is taking place in more remote rural areas, it is having a profound influence on the environment. Some of the changes that accompany increased population are clearly beneficial: for instance, increased employment opportunities and more services for rural residents, such as better schools, health care, and roads. Unfortunately, growth usually brings problems as well. Some of the more general problems created by development are described below.

*Inability of local governments to cope:* Many rural governments are run largely by unpaid officials and part-time staff. They often are ill-equipped to deal with the increasing complexity of governing a larger population. Rural governments frequently do not have professional planners to help them manage growth and ensure that new development does not adversely affect the environment.

*Increased cost of services:* Many rural community leaders believe that more development will increase the real estate tax base and hence help them to balance municipal budgets. While additional tax revenues certainly will be generated, the cost of new services demanded by new residents often outstrips the new revenues. This is particularly true in communities where new businesses attract families with school-age children. New residents may also demand improvements that natives found unnecessary, such as paving roads, adding special school programs, and increasing police protection.

*Increased social tensions:* Many rural communities have a close-knit character, and new residents may never be accepted totally by natives. The newcomers may have different social, cultural, or educational backgrounds from those of the existing population. They may have more money and different tastes. Charles F. Cortese has noted that "in Wyoming, the most predominant demand of newcomers is for more trees. Long-time residents often find the new demands expensive and balk at bearing the cost for things that they never needed before the new people came" (Weber and Howell 1982, p. 126).[1] The inmigration of wealthy outsiders (sometimes referred to as "gentrification") stimulates the local economy and sometimes means that key properties are preserved, but it may substantially alter the traditional social and cultural character of a rural community. The gentrification of a rural town may affect the agricultural economy if agricultural businesses are displaced by antique shops and boutiques, for example.

*Changes in land values:* As new residents buy homes or build new ones, property values are likely to rise. This will certainly be welcome news for many landowners. For others, however, it will cause problems, particularly for young families who may find they can no longer afford to buy a place of their own. The problem can be particularly acute in agricultural areas, where the price of land for farming may become prohibitive because of its value for development.

*Loss of rural character:* If it is the character of the rural environment that attracted many urbanites to move there in the first place, then the more of them who settle in a rural community, the more urbanized it becomes. Ironically, many new homeowners in rural areas are among the most vocal in arguing for curbs on further development.

The amount of new growth that rural communities can accommodate varies. In some instances, where finite resources are at stake, almost any growth may cause problems. The community's water supply may already be stretched to the limit, or it may be that new construction can take place only on a dwindling supply of prime farmland, threatening the future viability of agriculture in the community.

Fortunately, in most cases growth can be accommodated, and as described in subsequent chapters, a community can do a lot to ensure that any new development is well-planned. Development can be channelled into those sections of the community that are best equipped to deal with it—for instance, areas that are adjacent to existing towns or villages; areas that are not environmentally, historically, or visually significant; and areas where utilities and other community services can be offered at a reasonable cost. Rural communities should also ensure that, insofar as possible, developers pay for the added costs of the development to the community. For instance, they can be asked to pay for environmental studies of the sites they are proposing, for road improvements, for school buildings, and so forth. Finally, rural communities should, where appropriate, encourage developers to build in an architectural style that is compatible with existing buildings in the community and the natural setting (see *General Design Guidelines,* pp. 156–60). If done well, new construction can enhance a rural community rather than detract from it.

### TOURISM AND RESORTS

Developments associated with tourism and recreation are increasingly common throughout the country. Some, such as Steamboat Springs, a ski resort in Colorado, or Sea Pines on the coast of South Carolina, are large-scale operations that create whole new communities consisting largely of second homes.

Attracting visitors is a high priority for many rural communities. Tourism and resort development can stimulate the local economy and provide new jobs without creating some of the obvious environmental problems that a polluting industry might. Moreover, visitors do not require expensive public schools for their children, and so local governments are likely to collect more revenue than they spend for added services.

There are problems with tourism, however. On Tangier Island in the Chesapeake Bay, for example, watermen rolling wheelbarrows full of crab pots at the end of a workday often find the community's narrow streets choked with day-trippers who come by ferry for an afternoon visit. Residents of the Amana Colonies, Iowa's leading visitor attraction, complain that visitors pick their apples, peek in their windows, and block their driveways. Scenic Napa Valley, California, and its famous wineries receive more than half a million visitors each year. The visitors were initially welcomed because they brought in additional income and helped to publicize the wines. Now, however, the boom in tourist-related development threatens the valley's primary functions of growing grapes and making wine.

Ironically, visitor-oriented businesses and developments often destroy the cultural, scenic, and natural qualities that attracted visitors in the first place. Many tourist sites are noted for their adjacent long stretches of fast-food restaurants, motels, campgrounds, gift shops, and gas stations.

Resorts can create environmental problems, particularly when they are built in fragile ecosystems such as barrier islands and the steep slopes of

Tourism and recreation generate visitor dollars, but can also lead to excessive development. Telluride, Colorado, is a former mining town and designated National Historic Landmark. The adjacent ski resort has resulted in economic revival, but new development could overwhelm the community's historic and scenic qualities.

mountains. Several towns in Vermont, for instance, are concerned about water pollution resulting from condominium development at ski resorts, where the steep mountain slopes cannot absorb the waste water generated.

Since it is often the aesthetically pleasing environment that attracts visitors, it is in the self-interest of most communities with resorts and visitor attractions not to kill the goose that lays the golden egg. It makes good economic sense to plan for tourism and to regulate development in order to assure that the environment remains attractive. While some individual property owners may be able to make more money in an unregulated community, the population as a whole should benefit economically from reasonable environmental controls. "It's a whole new way of looking at our resources," says a Colorado senator. "People see that you can make more money by leaving the forest alone and letting people hike through it than you can by cutting down the trees and shipping out timber."[2]

## B. Declining Rural Communities

While many rural communities are dealing with the problems of growth, many others are struggling to escape the grip of economic stagnation and decline. The decline may be caused by local problems, such as the bankruptcy of a major business, the closing of a rail line, or the construction of an interstate highway bypassing the community, or by national or international economic trends, such as a drop in commodity prices. Rural communities tend to be more vulnerable to such changes than cities because they are often dependent on a single business or commodity for their economic well-being. Particularly hard hit in the 1980s are communities in the Great Plains, where rising interest rates for farmers, lower commodity prices, mechanization, and consolidation have led to a drop in population (see illustration, p. 20). As farmers go out of business, so do the businesses they patronize. According to one study, for every five farmers who leave an area, one small-town business fails.[3] Vacant stores, abandoned gas stations, and gaping holes where buildings once stood are visual evidence of the major impact that economic decline has had.

Small towns and crossroads communities such as Lima, Montana, were once the economic and social centers of rural America. Today, many are dying because of competition from regional shopping malls, loss of farm population, and school consolidations.

Many small towns, including Hillsboro, Texas, are working to enhance their downtown businesses to compete with regional shopping malls and to stem sprawl in rural areas. Here, an architect working with the Texas Main Street Center points out possible facade improvements to a store owner.

While there are many possible solutions for communities that wish to manage growth, finding solutions for communities that are losing population poses a greater challenge. Some have managed to create new jobs by attracting new businesses; others, blessed with attractive scenery, have been able to promote tourism. Clearly, more needs to be done to help rural communities diversify their economies and find new sources of income. Some rural organizations concerned with historic preservation have assisted in the revitalization of declining communities by promoting new uses for old buildings or by actually rehabilitating old buildings. They have found that they have a particular opportunity to help provide better housing and promote economic development, since much substandard housing and unused commercial property are also of historic interest (see illustrations, pp. 15 and 201).

## C. Revitalizing Small Towns

Small towns are the economic, cultural, social, and political centers in much of rural America. For centuries, the rural town has been the meeting place where stores, schools, doctors, farm-equipment dealers, and grain buyers have most often located. A rural town may also be the county seat, the home of a college, or the location of an industry.

Some rural settlements are hamlets consisting of fewer than a dozen structures. Often such settlements are located at a crossroads or near a boat landing or railroad depot. They may be dominated by a church, school, post office, diner, grain elevator, general store, gas station, or other local institution.

Few rural towns and hamlets are the diverse, largely self-sufficient communities they were when settled, or even twenty-five years ago. Rural Americans are increasingly making their purchases in regional shopping malls or in larger towns. As a result, many smaller towns and crossroad communities have suffered. Not only have businesses gone under, but also key social institutions, such as the local school, church, or post office, have

often become the victims of consolidation in the name of cost-effectiveness. With the loss of their stores, schools, post offices, cafes, and gas stations, many villages survive as little more than a collection of houses, alone and out of context.

As retail business grows, developers often choose to build new shopping facilities on the outskirts of towns, where there are larger lots and cheaper land. Not only can malls and commercial strips result in more development on farmland and natural areas, but they can also often lead to a loss of business for downtown merchants and store owners. Many towns are now working to enhance their downtown businesses to compete with the malls by taking advantage of attractive historic store fronts, finding new uses for vacant and underutilized buildings, providing better parking, and assuring a full range of stores and services. (For further information, contact the National Main Street Center, National Trust for Historic Preservation.)

Rural conservation leaders often find that they have good reason to work with those who are concerned about the economic vitality of nearby towns. Rehabilitation and new construction downtown not only enhance the town but also protect the countryside. When the Pyramid Company proposed a major new mall in rural Williston, Vermont, environmentalists allied themselves with businesses in the neighboring city of Burlington to fight the proposal.

Preservationists have played constructive roles in the economic revitalization of small rural communities such as Harrisville, New Hampshire. When the company that owned the village mills went bankrupt in 1970, community leaders interested in protecting the historic buildings and revitalizing the village's economy established Historic Harrisville. With funds raised locally and nationally, the nonprofit organization purchased six commercial buildings in the village core and rented them to a variety of new tenants, including a manufacturer of wooden looms, an engineering firm, and a day-care center. This venture into real estate not only saved historic buildings, but also created new jobs for residents.

Many mining towns are subject to cyclical "booms and busts" (see p. 17). Mercur, Utah, for example, was a boom town in 1910 when gold ore was reduced at the Golden Gate Mill (*top*). By 1971, the town was abandoned and only ruins remained (*bottom*).

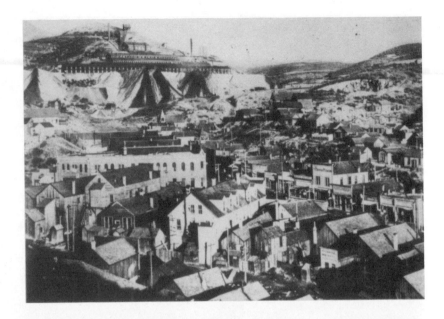

While towns and cities have developed successful strategies to promote their downtown businesses, the smaller crossroad settlements have received less attention and an increasing number of their merchants are going out of business.

## D. The Residents of a Rural Community

A rural community's people are its most important asset. As each community was settled and developed, its residents gave it a unique character based on their ethnic, religious, and occupational backgrounds. Human commitment and energy created rural communities; their vitality today still relies on people. Some rural conservation organizations will decide that it goes beyond their scope to address social and economic concerns directly. Others may find they have an opportunity not only to protect the environment but also to improve the economic well-being of their community's residents.

There are social and economic problems that cannot be ignored in rural America. Rural poverty is at least as big a problem as its urban counterpart, but it gets less attention. The signs of urban poverty—dilapidated tenements, scattered trash, and the homeless—are often more visible than rural poverty, which may be hidden from view on little-traveled back roads. A natural setting may make the scene of an unpainted farmhouse, outdoor privy, gullied fields, and barefoot children appear picturesque.

While rural poverty knows no boundaries, much is concentrated in certain areas such as Appalachia and the Ozarks. Rural poverty, like urban, is also more prevalent among blacks, Hispanics, American Indians, and migrant farm workers. Inadequate housing is a particularly serious problem for these groups. Some rural poor live in large houses with no insulation and exorbitant heating costs, while others are crowded into rented shacks with no plumbing. Rural water supplies are more likely to be contaminated, and health care, when available at all, may be inadequate and far away.

Local governments usually provide rural residents with fewer services, whether they be police, fire protection, public transportation, municipal water, or social services. In some cases there may be less need for these services than in cities. In others, it may be prohibitively expensive to offer them to widely scattered rural residents. While most communities provide public education, rural school children often have long bus rides and may have fewer opportunities to participate in remedial programs, advanced classes, and extracurricular activities. Many businesses also offer fewer services to rural communities: bus service to rural communities is declining, and rural electric companies sometimes charge high installation fees to customers in remote locations.

Each year many rural Americans move to town. Some may be forced to move because of increasing age, poverty, unemployment, or the lack of services. For others, there may be the lure of greater opportunities in the city. Those who are leaving the countryside—whether dairy farmers in

## Boom and Bust

*Some communities, particularly those near large-scale mining or construction projects, go through periodic cycles of "boom and bust." Many new workers may be needed today because the price of the ore being extracted is high. But once the price of the ore goes down, or the vein runs out, there may be little need for miners. Towns such as Crested Butte, Colorado, have been through several cycles of boom and bust. Often boom towns have to absorb large numbers of workers quickly, without time to plan adequately or to provide for new housing and community services.*

*Local governments sometimes support mining and energy development, despite the potential problems, because of expectations of new jobs and economic development. Although initial construction projects employ local rural workers, many mining and energy development operations bring in specialized workers instead of hiring local people.*

**In many hamlets such as Waterford, Virginia, the post office is one of the few remaining local services. In addition to providing an important function, it is a place where neighbors exchange greetings and news.**

## Water Contaminants in Rural Areas

*Sediments. Sediments released into surface waters through erosion result in cloudy water that threatens both plant and animal life by reducing the amount of light and, hence, photosynthesis in water. Once they settle, sediments can smother life on the bottom and decrease the capacity of reservoirs. Sedimentation is a particular problem near plowed fields and construction sites.*

*Nutrients and oxygen-reducing wastes. Elevated concentrations of nutrients such as phosphates and nitrates from waste water and fertilizers promote the growth of algae and seaweed, which take the place of other aquatic plants that fish and wildlife prefer for food. Decomposing aquatic plants, sewage, and animal manure use up oxygen as they decay, depriving fish and other animals of the oxygen they need to survive. The excessive decay speeds up eutrophication in lakes (the natural enrichment process that, over geologic time, causes lakes to fill in). The discolored, eutrophic water has an unpleasant odor that reduces its appeal for recreation.*

*Salts. Water salinity is a major problem in irrigated areas of the West. For example, the soils of the upper Colorado River Basin naturally contain a high concentration of salt. Water taken out of the Colorado for irrigation in this area is returned with such high salinity levels that it hampers downstream agriculture in the southwestern United States and northern Mexico. Also, groundwater overdrafts in coastal areas can cause seawater to enter an aquifer. In southeastern Georgia, for example, several aquifers have such high concentrations of salt that they are no longer dependable for fresh water*

Wisconsin or ranchers in Montana—may be replaced by newcomers, but in the process much of what makes Wisconsin Wisconsin and Montana Montana is lost. Saving land, water, wildlife, and historic buildings is indeed important, but if these resources are preserved while the existing population leaves, the success may be a hollow one. Conservationists should help make it possible for those who have traditionally lived in rural communities to continue to do so if they wish.

We now move on to specific environmental concerns, concerns which are in most cases closely related to the economic, demographic, and social issues already discussed. While we examine environmental resources individually, it is important to remember their interconnections. Water pollution may result not only in unsafe drinking water but also in declining fish population and species diversity. Removing trees along streams may lead not only to increased soil erosion on farmland but also to stream siltation, degradation of wildlife habitat, and loss of scenic quality.

## III. WATER AND RELATED RESOURCES

Sufficient water of high quality for domestic consumption, agriculture, industry, recreation, and wildlife is among a community's most important assets. Water supply directly affects the economic value of land, and as anyone who has tried to buy waterfront property can attest, water has both economic and scenic value. Water-based recreation, including boating, fishing, and swimming, is the most popular form of outdoor recreation in the United States.

### A. Water Supply

Surface water—streams, rivers, lakes—is the major source of water used in this country. It is replenished by rainfall and drainage from the surrounding watershed (the land area draining into a stream or other body of water). Groundwater is the other important source of water. Most rural Americans depend on groundwater for drinking, and about 40 percent of irrigation water is from the ground.[4] Although some groundwater is renewed by rain or melted snow that is absorbed into soil, most groundwater has accumulated over centuries and cannot be replenished easily. Geologic formations called aquifers store groundwater, while the area of land that contributes water to an aquifer is called its recharge area. A recharge area may be quite distant from the place where the water is withdrawn (see illustration, p. 20).

Water use in the United States increases each year. Many communities allow more construction of homes, industries, and irrigation systems than their water supplies can support. They may eventually be forced to purchase water from other areas at considerable expense. Farmers are the biggest users of water, with irrigation accounting for 81 percent of total water consumption.[5] Most irrigation is in the West, where per capita water consumption is twelve times that of eastern states (Conservation Foundation 1982, p. 91).

Many parts of the United States have abundant rainfall to replenish water supplies; others with little rainfall find water in short supply the year round. In the arid areas of the Southwest some rivers have had so much water removed that the flow is inadequate for boating, generating electricity, and the survival of aquatic life. The Colorado River, for instance, is usually dry by the time it reaches the Gulf of California. Although the most severe water shortages are in the Southwest, periodic shortages occur in most regions.

Depletion of groundwater is particularly serious in some areas. As water is withdrawn, the land often subsides, diminishing its storage capacity. In some areas along the Texas coast as much as 77 percent of the water removed is not replenished. As groundwater reserves are depleted, irrigation users dig deeper, more expensive wells. Irrigation costs have increased so dramatically in parts of Nebraska and the San Joaquin Valley in California that they threaten the future of agriculture in these major food-producing areas (Conservation Foundation 1982, p. 109).

There is much that rural communities can do to assure an adequate supply of water. Besides the obvious and important step of encouraging conservation, communities can identify the locations of their watersheds and aquifers on maps, establish a system to monitor water quantity, and limit development if it will endanger the supply of water. Measuring groundwater availability was an important aspect of the Oley Resource Project in Pennsylvania (Case Study 1). Also, communities can limit the location, density, and type of development through zoning to assure that the community's water capacity is not exceeded.

A community's water quality depends largely on land use and waste disposal practices. Water quality can also be affected by air pollutants (1.VII.D).[6] In some communities industry is the major source of pollution, while in others agriculture or runoff from urban areas may be the major contributor. Sources of water pollution may include inadequate septic systems, mining, agriculture, seepage from landfills, leaking underground storage tanks, and runoff from roads. Since rivers may carry pollutants long distances, the source of the problem may be in a neighboring community or even another state.

Water-pollution sources are frequently categorized as "point" or "nonpoint," depending on whether the pollution comes from a specific source or point, such as a storm sewer or industry, or a land area, such as runoff from farmland and construction sites. Most pollution-abatement programs have focused on point-source pollution. Nonpoint-source pollution is often just as serious but is more difficult to identify and regulate.

The chairman of a Virginia water authority remarks, "People have this feeling that water in the ground is good—they don't realize there is a possibility it is not."[7] Although pollution of any water source is serious, groundwater contamination is particularly alarming since it is very difficult and costly to correct. Pollutants tend to degrade slower in subsurface environments where there is no sunlight and microbiologic activity. In addition, water often moves so slowly through an aquifer that contaminants can remain long after the source of pollution has been eliminated. Determining the extent of groundwater pollution may be difficult, since one area may be polluted while another nearby may not be.

Major improvement in water quality has been made since the early 1970s, when increasing concern over pollution prompted the passage of the federal Clean Water Act (6.VI.A). Although there is still a great deal of contaminated water, deterioration in much of the nation's water supply has been checked. There has been more progress on checking point pollution than nonpoint and in protecting surface water than groundwater.

*(Conservation Foundation 1982, p. 109). Salts used to treat icy winter roads may also enter water supplies through runoff.*

***Disease-producing contaminants.*** *Contaminated water spreads disease when the bacteria, viruses, and parasites found in sewage, animal manure, and food-processing waste find their way into water supplies. In the Southeast, where many rural residents obtain their drinking water from shallow wells too close to septic systems and privies, water-borne disease is a particular problem.*

***Toxic chemicals.*** *Many chemicals used in industry and agriculture are toxic. Pesticides and nitrates from fertilizer frequently find their way into rural water supplies. In a national survey of over 45,000 wells, pesticides were detected in the water of close to 25 percent of them. (American Land Resource Association,* Land Report, *March/April 1987). Some industrial chemicals are toxic at levels of one part per billion, the equivalent of four drops in a large swimming pool. Seepage into groundwater from landfills, impoundments for industrial wastes, and leaking underground gasoline tanks is particularly dangerous, since many of the chemicals are not filtered out by soil and rock and are not biodegradable. The Environmental Protection Agency estimates that 100,000 underground storage tanks are leaking gasoline or other chemicals (Conservation Foundation 1984, p. 128). Since no one monitors most underground storage tanks and chemical dump sites, citizens are often unaware that chemical concentrations in their drinking water have reached hazardous levels.*

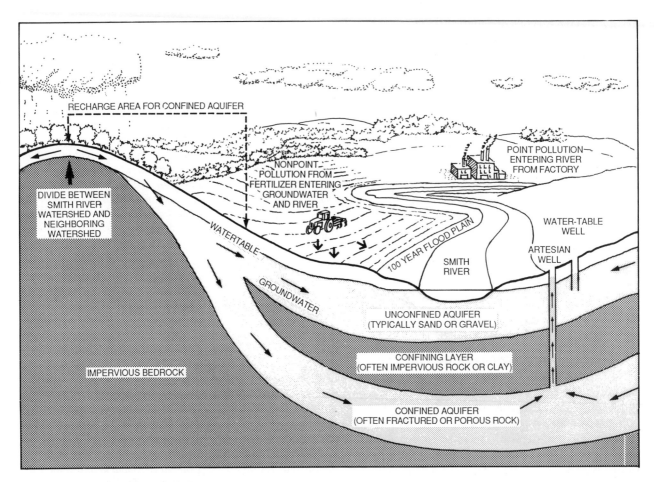

RECHARGE AREA FOR CONFINED AQUIFER

POINT POLLUTION ENTERING RIVER FROM FACTORY

NONPOINT POLLUTION FROM FERTILIZER ENTERING GROUNDWATER AND RIVER

DIVIDE BETWEEN SMITH RIVER WATERSHED AND NEIGHBORING WATERSHED

WATERTABLE

GROUNDWATER

100 YEAR FLOOD PLAIN

SMITH RIVER

WATER-TABLE WELL

ARTESIAN WELL

IMPERVIOUS BEDROCK

UNCONFINED AQUIFER (TYPICALLY SAND OR GRAVEL)

CONFINING LAYER (OFTEN IMPERVIOUS ROCK OR CLAY)

CONFINED AQUIFER (OFTEN FRACTURED OR POROUS ROCK)

The flow of water. This drawing is a simplified illustration of watersheds, water tables, groundwater, aquifers, aquifer recharge areas, flood plains, point-source pollution, and non-point-source pollution. The arrows indicate the direction of water movement. Rain and pollutants flow into surface water and groundwater. Pollution of groundwater, particularly in confined aquifers, is very difficult to correct.

Groundwater is the major source of water for many communities. In many parts of the country, it is withdrawn from aquifers that cannot be recharged or is withdrawn more quickly than it can be renewed. Here groundwater overdraft (water removed minus water returned) is shown for 38 of 106 regions in the United States in 1975.

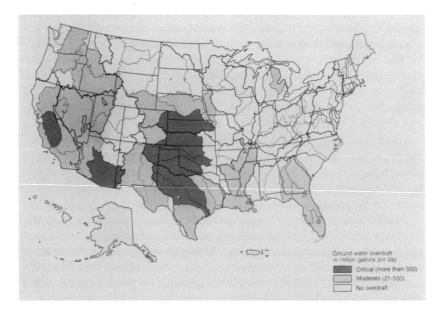

Ground water overdraft in million gallons per day

Critical (more than 500)
Moderate (21-500)
No overdraft

SAVING AMERICA'S COUNTRYSIDE

Zoning ordinances can limit the use of septic systems in poorly percolating soils, over aquifers that supply the community's water, or in watersheds draining into reservoirs (4.III). Zoning can also be used to prohibit or restrict agricultural practices that may contribute to water quality problems—feedlots or destruction of vegetation along streams, for instance. Finally, communities can acquire easements on land that is important for the maintenance of water quality, as described in Chapter 5.

## B. Rivers

Free-flowing streams and rivers have obvious aesthetic, recreational, and ecological values. Unfortunately, dams, water diversion, and stream channelization have frequently destroyed these values. Entire human settlements have also been submerged under reservoirs. Moreover, dams, diversion, and channelization generally result in changes in water depth, velocity, and temperature that in turn cause marked and undesirable changes in flora and fauna. Most large-scale projects are financed by the federal government (see *Federal Agencies Responsible for Dams*, p. 216); many smaller projects, such as small-scale hydroelectric power dams, are financed by individual investors. In recent years there have been fewer of the large-scale federal projects and more of the small-scale ones, particularly as federal subsidies for domestic energy production have created incentives for small-scale hydroelectric development.

Stream channelization (moving, deepening, and straightening stream beds), while protecting adjacent land from flooding and erosion, often creates more problems than it solves. During floods, downstream velocity increases, causing more destruction; also more silt and pollutants are car-

A Soil Conservation Service District Conservationist examines the soil in an irrigated field of the Imperial Valley in California. Here, salt buildup, caused by long-term irrigation, is restricting crop growth, a major problem in much of the West.

Feedlots are a source of water pollution in many rural areas. The owner of this Arkansas farm has dealt with the problem by building a "debris basin" with help from the Soil Conservation Service. Solids remain in the basin while liquids are strained out and used to fertilize fields.

ried down to lakes and estuaries where they cause additional problems. Channelization also results in the loss of riparian habitat for wildlife.

In addition to flood control, power generation, and water supply, dam builders often tout the recreational benefits of the reservoirs they will create. While they do allow for increased use by lake fishermen and the owners of large boats, they remove recreational opportunities for white-water boaters, river fishermen, and those who simply find a free-flowing river aesthetically pleasing.

The principal federal legislation protecting scenic rivers is the Wild and Scenic Rivers Act of 1968 (6.VI.B). Communities can protect rivers through zoning and subdivision controls restricting inappropriate uses on adjacent land and through land acquisition or easements along the banks.

## C. Wetlands

Wetlands are transitional areas between terrestrial and aquatic environments where the water table (the level of groundwater) is at or near the ground surface or the land is covered by shallow water. About 4 percent of the land area of the United States (exclusive of Alaska and Hawaii) consists of wetlands. Wetlands are a diverse lot, ranging from tidal flats, salt-hay marshes, and mangrove swamps on the coast, to prairie potholes, peat bogs, and cypress swamps inland, to name just a few.

Wetlands provide habitat for numerous fish, waterfowl, and other wildlife, many of which have economic value. Some animal species spend their entire lives in wetlands, while others use them primarily for breeding and raising young. Many salt- and fresh-water fish depend on wetlands for at least a part of their life cycles. Numerous reptiles and amphibians depend on wetlands, as do many mammals, including mink and muskrat. In short, given the great variety of species that depend on wetlands directly or indirectly, there are few ecosystems that are more important.

In some communities wetlands are the primary water-supply or recharge areas for aquifers. Wetlands also help to purify the water passing through them by filtering out silt and nutrients. Additionally wetlands, acting as sponges, absorb quantities of floodwaters, protecting downstream communities. Along coasts, they act as barriers to damaging storm waves. Finally, wetlands have high recreational value for hunters, fishermen, boaters, and many others who enjoy observing the scenery and wildlife.

The importance of wetlands was poorly understood until recently, and more than half of the wetlands in the United States (exclusive of Alaska and Hawaii) have been destroyed since the arrival of Europeans. Historically, drainage to create more land suitable for agriculture has been the greatest cause of destruction. By 1981, 94 percent of Iowa's wetlands had been drained, primarily for agriculture.[8] Destruction also continues in areas such as the Southeast, where forested bottomlands are being clearcut and drained for soybean production. Other causes of destruction include adding fill to create sites for housing, industry, and highways; dredging to aid navigation; reservoir construction; pollution; and waste disposal.

## D. Flood Plains

Water, in the form of floods, can cause tremendous damage. Flood plains—land that is subject to periodic flooding—serve a vital function

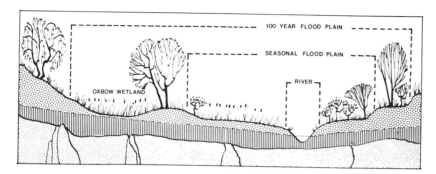

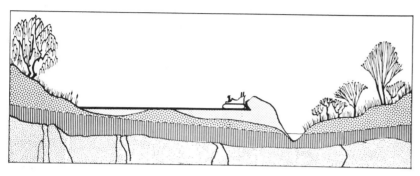

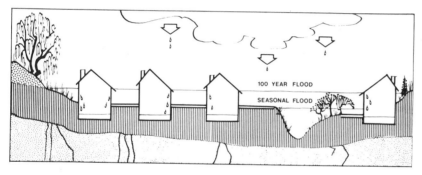

The impact of development in flood plains.

by reducing the height and speed of spreading flood waters (see illustration, above). Flood-plain vegetation slows flood water and allows some of it to be absorbed by the soil. Approximately 7 percent of the United States is within one-hundred-year flood plains (land that has at least a 1 percent chance of flooding in any given year) (Conservation Foundation 1982, p. 105).

Flood plains have frequently been used for settlement, industry, and agriculture despite their vulnerability. The soil is often excellent for agriculture, since floods periodically deposit soil washed off lands upstream. Flood plains are relatively flat, a characteristic that facilitates construction of roads and railroads; and they have good access to water for irrigation, industry, and transportation. Because of these advantages, people are willing to risk floods.

Construction on flood plains not only endangers life and property, but also increases the severity of floods by reducing the land's ability to store and buffer flood waters. Removing vegetation and paving over permeable soils increases runoff and results in intensified flooding downstream.

Flood plains are not completely unusable by people. They are often quite appropriate for agriculture and recreational facilities, such as playing fields, that do not require extensive, impermeable surfaces. Flood plains can easily be identified so local governments can zone them to prevent inappropriate development. There is also assistance available from the federal government in the form of flood-plain identification and federal flood insurance for property owners in communities with appropriate controls on flood-plain development (6.VI.D).

## E. Coasts

Coasts are among America's most spectacular scenic and recreational resources. They also have great biological diversity and productivity. Coastal wetlands and estuaries are vital habitats for many fish and shellfish valued by people. Since most of America's population is concentrated along coasts, many are under considerable development pressure and have suffered environmental degradation. Bay and ocean waters are threatened by pollution from municipal sewage, dumping, oil spills, and pollutants coming down the rivers that empty into them. Estuaries (partially enclosed water bodies such as the Chesapeake Bay, where fresh water mixes with sea water) and their associated wetlands are particularly vulnerable to pollution.

The barrier islands of the Atlantic and Gulf coasts are among the least stable of environments, being formed and destroyed by waves, tides, and ocean currents at relatively rapid rates. The cities and vacation homes built on them are particularly vulnerable. Unfortunately, approximately 40 percent of America's twenty-seven hundred linear miles of barrier islands have already been developed (Conservation Foundation 1984, p. 195).

The principal federal laws protecting coasts are the 1972 Coastal Zone Management Act and the 1982 Coastal Barrier Resources Act (6.VI.E). Local controls and land acquisition can also help.

## IV. THE LAND

## A. Soil

Composed of disintegrated rock, water, air, decaying organic matter, and microorganisms, soil is the critical link between rocks and plants. Soils vary greatly in their composition, and different soils best support different types of vegetation. Deep, well-aerated soils that retain sufficient water, contain a high percentage of nitrogen and organic matter, and are not too acidic are generally the most suitable for agriculture. The ability of soils to support building foundations, septic systems, roads, and structures also varies greatly. Most soils with a high clay content, for example, drain poorly, causing problems for septic systems. Such soils also frequently swell when wet, causing building foundations to crack.

The major threat to soils is erosion, a process that occurs naturally but which can be greatly accelerated through human activity. Most soils in their natural state are protected from wind and rain by vegetation, which may range from grasses to dense forests. When vegetation is removed, fertile topsoil, which may only be a few inches thick, is the first to erode. Topsoil generally has more capacity than the subsoil to hold the moisture

Topsoil erodes quickly if land is farmed without conservation measures. Erosion is particularly severe in the wheat fields of the Palouse area of eastern Washington State.

Wind erosion became a national crisis during the Dust Bowl years of the 1930s and remains a problem where farmers do not practice proper soil conservation. Here a field in Cascade County, Montana, is literally blowing away.

necessary for plant growth, supplies more nutrients, and more readily allows plants to establish root systems.

Topsoil erodes quickly if land is farmed without conservation measures. The result over time is less favorable growing conditions, reduced crop yields, and decreased livestock productivity. Fall plowing, a common practice that allows harsh winter winds and rains to move the bare topsoil, exacerbates the problem. Soil on farmland is eroding far faster than it is being replaced. It can take one thousand years to form one inch of topsoil, yet at an erosion rate of five tons of soil lost per acre per year—a rate the Soil Conservation Service generally considers to be tolerable—it takes just thirty-three years to lose an inch (Conservation Foundation 1982, pp. 236–37). Nationwide, more than a million acres of cropland go out of production every year owing to loss of topsoil from water erosion.[9]

Erosion rates depend on soil conditions and the type of agriculture practiced. Certain parts of the country are much more vulnerable than others.

**Average Annual Cropland Erosion**

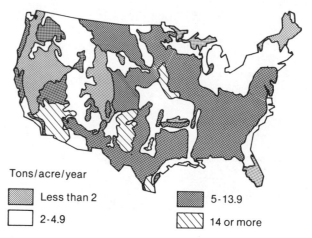

Tons/acre/year

| | | |
|---|---|---|
| Less than 2 | | 5-13.9 |
| 2-4.9 | | 14 or more |

1982 data. Includes sheet, rill, and wind erosion on cropland.

Erosion occurs in all regions, but it is a much greater problem in certain parts of the country, such as the Corn Belt and the Palouse area of eastern Washington and northern Idaho. Some 210,000 acres of the Palouse, excellent land for growing wheat, have lost all their topsoil.[10] The Conservation Foundation estimates that Iowa lost five tons of soil for every ton of corn it produced in 1977 (Conservation Foundation 1982, p. 234).

Erosion problems are not limited to farmland. Construction, mining, logging, and other activities destroy protective vegetation. The rates of erosion from such operations may be even more dramatic than that resulting from agriculture. For example, highway construction in Virginia resulted in two hundred times the erosion that occurred on undisturbed adjacent lands. Surface mining near Sheridan, Wyoming, has increased erosion eleven times the normal rate. Logging operations have washed five times the normal amount of sediment into creeks near Newport, Oregon.[11] Landslides caused by disturbing the vegetation on steep slopes result in the destruction of numerous homes, highways, and other structures every year (see illustration, p. 141).

Although the actual losses of topsoil and the impacts on agricultural production are alarming in themselves, the damage caused by washing, blowing, or dumping soil into other places is also a concern. Wind-blown soil can choke crops, suffocate livestock, and sandblast buildings. Moreover, runoff water carrying silt, fertilizer, pesticides, and herbicides can pollute water supplies and threaten aquatic life.

Fortunately, a great deal has been learned about the soils of the United States since the Dust Bowl years of the 1930s. The Soil Conservation Service, which was formed in response to those problems, has established a number of programs to protect soil (6.VII.A).

Good methods have been developed to control erosion both on the farm and off. Leaving vegetation along streams, contour plowing (plowing across the slope), and terracing (building terraces on slopes) decrease the speed of runoff and allow more water to soak into the soil. More recently,

No-till farming is becoming increasingly popular because it requires less labor and decreases erosion. Unfortunately, it requires more use of herbicides, which raises pollution and health concerns. Here in Montgomery County, Kansas, soybeans have been planted in wheat stubble.

These grass backslope terraces, which decrease erosion, were the first to be installed in southwestern Iowa.

many farmers have adopted "conservation tillage" and "no till" farming methods. In the former, some or all of the residue of the previous crop is plowed into the soil. In the latter, new seeds are planted in a slit in the midst of the last crop's stubble with little or no plowing. These techniques, while very effective in combatting erosion, depend on herbicides to control weeds, which can cause water pollution and health problems. Off the farm, runoff from construction sites can be controlled by such measures as temporary dams and reseeding; in logging operations, erosion can be controlled by assuring that heavy equipment does not make ruts that water can readily follow.

While these techniques unquestionably conserve soil, they can be expensive and thus reduce short-term financial returns for farmers, builders, and loggers. In many areas contour plowing and terracing are being dropped because the width of the big new farm machinery makes it difficult to plow on the contour or over the terraces. This heavy equipment also causes soil compaction that results in less water being absorbed—and hence, in more runoff and erosion. Many farmers engage in poor conservation practices when they need a quick return on their investment to pay off debts. Leased farmland is more likely to be abused, since the farmer has less long-term incentive to practice conservation on someone else's land.

In addition to what individual farmers, builders, and loggers can do, local governments can protect soils by regulating construction sites and prohibiting agricultural practices that lead to excessive erosion. The Soil Conservation Service's soil surveys should be of great assistance to communities interested in developing appropriate regulations to protect soils (3.III.C).

## B. Farming and Farmland

America's farms are diverse: Iowa corn and soybean farms, Washington apple orchards, North Dakota wheat farms, cranberry bogs in Massachusetts, Wisconsin dairy farms, poultry operations in Maryland, citrus groves in Florida, and California vineyards are all part of American agriculture. The owners and operators of these farms are as varied as the types of farms. There are full-time and part-time farmers, family-owned and -operated farms, and those owned by absentee landlords or international corporations. For some, farming is a livelihood; for others it is a hobby or a tax shelter. Americans engaged in agriculture may be fifth-generation farmers living on the land of their ancestors, back-to-the-land counterculture farmers, affluent gentlemen-farmers, or subsistence "dirt farmers." Some farm thousands of acres, while others make a living intensively cultivating ten acres.

American agriculture produces food and fiber for this country and much of the world. In 1986, agricultural products accounted for 13 percent of all American exports.[12] Although only 2.5 percent of the American work force is directly engaged in agriculture,[13] many other industries and businesses, including the manufacturers of farm equipment and the distributors and processors of food products, are based on agriculture.

Farmland has an inherent aesthetic appeal for many people. The seasonal changes of growing crops, the colors and textures of fields, and livestock grazing in pastures provide visual enjoyment. Farms also provide incidental recreational opportunities. Many farm owners allow access to

An abandoned farmstead makes way for more wheat in North Dakota. With increased mechanization, there are fewer farmers on the land, and many farm structures are abandoned or demolished.

their noncultivated land for hunting and other recreational activities. Agriculture has also been associated with a particular way of life that has contributed to American folk traditions, literature, music, dance, and other arts. Technology and economics, however, are radically reshaping life in farming areas.

Growth in rural areas over the last decade does not mean more farmers; in fact, the proportion of farmers in American society is smaller than ever before. In 1985 only 2.2 percent of Americans lived on farms, as compared to 44 percent in 1880.[14] There are also fewer farms today, but the ones that remain are larger. The average farm in 1986 was about 455 acres, more than three times larger than the average farm in 1880.[15]

Farming methods and farms have changed dramatically since World War II. Until the 1950s most farmers, in addition to raising a variety of cash crops, engaged in general farming to meet family and community nutritional needs. They planted vegetable gardens and orchards and raised livestock to produce milk, eggs, and meat. Many modern farming practices require increased acreage. Consequently, farmers often feel forced to buy or lease more land, plow marginal soil, or pull down obsolete structures on land that can be cultivated.

A *Newsweek* article on the changing appearance of American farms lamented that "country doesn't look like country anymore."[16] The startling visual impacts of farm modernization indicate the profound changes in the way crops and livestock are produced. Agriculture has become increasingly mechanized and less diversified in crops and livestock. Bigger and different machinery and the obsolescence of draft animals has resulted in a need for larger yet simpler outbuildings and an abundance of obsolete farm structures on most farms.

Monoculture (the exclusive planting of one crop) is the rule on many farms today. Although monoculture may be more efficient, it makes a farmer more vulnerable to problems such as pests and declining prices that might affect a single crop. Consequently Extension Agents are increasingly advising farmers to diversify. Farmers close to urban markets, where the demand for local produce has increased, are finding diversified agriculture profitable, particularly when they can sell their produce di-

An auction marks the close of another family farm. An increasing number of farmers are being forced out of business by declining prices and rising debt.

rectly to consumers through farmers' markets (see *Farmers' Markets*, p. 262).

Many American farms have multimillion-dollar capital investments in land, buildings, equipment, and livestock. Wealthy farmers may be a reality, but their assets are usually tied up in the land and equipment they need to make a living. Moreover, the risks are high: crops can be destroyed by drought, floods, or pests, or their value may plummet because of fluctuations in commodity prices. Recently many farmers have been forced to quit farming or have lost their land to foreclosure because of high interest payments for mortgages taken out when land values and agricultural commodity prices were higher than they are now. When crops fail or prices drop unexpectedly, farmers may lose their farms, their homes, their livelihoods, and their way of life. As farmers fail, their farms are usually consolidated with other holdings, bringing about a reduction in the number of family-owned farms.

It is often the medium-sized farms that have suffered the most. They do not have big enough operations to justify much of the efficient but expensive new machinery. The smaller farms have fared better because their owners often have the option of working on a second job off the farm.

Some one to two million acres of agricultural land are converted to urban uses each year.[17] Much of this land is considered prime farmland—land that has the best combination of physical and chemical characteristics, growing seasons, and moisture supply needed to produce sustained high yields with proper management. Unfortunately, prime farmland is often very desirable for development, since it tends to be flat and well-drained. Although development on prime farmland occurs in every section of the country, most of the concern has been in the Northeast, in the Sunbelt, and along the West Coast.

The various causes of the loss of farmland—whether it is lost to development, mineral exploitation, or destructive farming practices—can usually be traced to a single factor: farmland is an economic asset. Farmers' land is not only their primary asset, but also their life insurance and retirement fund. A disproportionately high percentage of American farmers are approaching retirement: in 1982, the average age of American farmers was fifty and climbing.[18] Their land is the final cash crop to sell at retirement to buy a house in town, a condominium in the Sunbelt, or a place in a nursing home. Few younger farmers, except for those fortunate enough to inherit a farm, can afford to purchase the land and equipment necessary to get started.

Farms adjacent to towns and cities are the ones most likely to become victims to creeping urbanization. Strip development along roads in agricultural areas diminishes the viability of remaining interior properties by reducing farm acreage, fragmenting farms into noncontiguous parcels, and creating nonagricultural neighbors. Suburban living and farming usually do not mix well, often resulting in tensions between farmers and non-farming neighbors. Thoughtless trespassers frequently trample crops, damage fences, leave litter, and allow their dogs to chase livestock.

Farmers often lose political control of local government as population changes occur. Local governments dominated by nonfarmers sometimes enact ordinances that discourage farming operations—by prohibiting, for example, the driving of slow farm machinery on highways, the operation of agricultural machinery at night, and the use of manure as fertilizer.

SAVING AMERICA'S COUNTRYSIDE

Urbanization in rural areas discourages agricultural activity even before the bulldozers arrive. As development moves closer, farmers may be unwilling to make improvements to their land and buildings. This attitude sets an "impermanence syndrome" in motion: Farmers cease to invest in new equipment; this reduces the level of farm business for distributors of agricultural supplies and equipment. As these suppliers go out of business, there are fewer convenient, nearby places for farmers to buy farm implements and have them repaired; purchase fertilizers, pesticides and seed; and obtain veterinary and other services. This further discourages the remaining farmers, who must travel great distances to obtain the goods and services they need.

A related development is the "farmette" or "ranchette": in many rural areas exurbanites are purchasing tracts of farmland that are bigger than typical suburban lots but smaller than the minimum size for a farm that could support a family. The new gentlemen-farmers or hobby-farmers may be protecting some farmland but are generally not a part of the agricultural economy.

The increase in value of land, the departure of lifelong friends, and the proximity of new neighbors with suburban lifestyles all hasten the selling-out process. Farmland conversion feeds on itself: each lost farm brings not only new houses with nonfarm families, but also stimulates more farmers to develop their land.

The need to protect farmland did not become a national concern until the late 1970s, when the federal government established the National Agricultural Lands Study (6.VII.B). Although subsequently enacted federal laws provide a measure of protection, most of the burden to preserve farmland is on state and local governments. Increasingly, local governments—using their power to regulate subdivisions, enact zoning ordinances, offer real estate tax relief, and purchase development rights—are attempting to protect farmland. The record, unfortunately, is spotty.

## C. Forests

Forests cover approximately one-third of the total American landscape. Lumbering has been a major industry since the earliest colonial times. The first settlers quickly saw the great profits that could be made by shipping lumber—particularly white pine for ships' masts—back to England, where wood was in short supply. Extensive precolonial forests fell as the demand for cleared farmland and wood for construction grew. Actually, much of the land that was cleared for agriculture in the East has since reverted to forests, as anyone who has come across stone walls while walking in New England woods can observe. The descendants of the original settlers learned that the soils of the Midwest were generally better for agriculture and moved west, leaving their old farms to grow up in trees.

The greatest period of American forest exploitation was during the second half of the nineteenth century, when a growing population and industrialization created many demands for wood. During this period, most lumbering was done without concern for environmental consequences. There was little effort to protect the forest's soil from erosion, and forest fires were common. It was largely Theodore Roosevelt's concern for the rapidly diminishing American forest that led to the establishment of the U.S. Forest Service in 1905.

Aside from their economic importance, forests provide habitat for many wildlife species. The importance of forests in protecting watersheds has long been recognized: by slowing runoff they allow rainwater to soak into the ground, recharging aquifers and reducing the potential for floods. Finally, forests are a source of enjoyment for many. The giant redwoods of the West and the fall foliage in the Upper Midwest, Appalachian Mountains, and New England draw visitors from afar. Throughout the nation forests have high recreational value as a setting for hiking, skiing, camping, nature study, hunting, and other outdoor pursuits.

Approximately 27 percent of productive forests are publicly owned,[19] principally by the Forest Service and the Bureau of Land Management. The balance is owned by individuals and corporations. How privately owned woodland is treated varies greatly. Many small lots are left alone, their owners being primarily interested in their aesthetic, wildlife, and recreational values. Other small lots are harvested haphazardly, with the owners cutting firewood as needed or removing saw logs when lumber prices are high. Most lumber companies and an increasing number of individual owners now manage their forests for long-term sustained yields. The Forest Service and other agencies are prepared to advise private owners and conservation organizations on wise forest management (6.VII.C).

Although environmentally sensitive management of private forests is much more common than it once was, abuses still occur. Small-scale owners are not always careful to design the skid roads needed to get logs out of forests in ways that prevent erosion. Trees along streams that shelter wildlife and provide shade for trout are sometimes removed. Large-scale owners often rely on spraying pesticides from the air, a practice that may harm wildlife and water quality. Monoculture has taken over commercial forests as it has cropland in some areas. In parts of the South, acres of fast-growing loblolly pines have replaced diversified oak-pine stands. In addition to being aesthetically less pleasing to most people, monoculture provides less diverse habitat for wildlife and invites pests that can multiply more rapidly on a single species.

## D. Rangeland

Rangeland is land on which the vegetation is predominantly native grasses, grasslike plants, or shrubs and it covers more than one-third of the nation. Most rangeland is located in the West, with states such as Wyoming and Nevada composed of more than three-fourths range. To many people the range is synonymous with cowboys and the wide open spaces "where the deer and the antelope play." While this image does apply in some instances, rangeland also includes Alpine meadows and fenced pastures that are carefully managed for maximum production of grasses. What constitutes rangeland is difficult to estimate precisely, since there is often no sharp line between range and forest or range and cropland. In addition to supporting cattle and wildlife, rangeland often contains large aquifer recharge areas and has many recreational uses.

Rangeland or prairie once extended much farther east than it does today, including much of the midwestern farmbelt. As settlers moved west, they settled the tall-grass prairie of the eastern plains first. The agricultural potential of these soils was and remains tremendous. However, as they moved farther west into the more arid short-grass prairie, roughly west of the 100th meridian that runs from central North Dakota to central Texas, where average rainfall is typically under twenty inches a year, settlers found themselves in areas where agriculture was increasingly marginal. In good years, when rainfall was abundant, crops did well. But in bad years, when rainfall was less than twenty inches—generally the minimum required for agriculture—crops failed. To make matters worse, when the crops failed, wind carried off much of the topsoil, culminating in the infamous Dust Bowl years of the 1930s.

The response to lack of rainfall in many areas has been to irrigate. Modern technology allows farmers to bring water from farther away and deeper under the surface than used to be possible. Much of the prairie is underlain by huge aquifers containing water trapped since the Ice Age. Today's powerful pumps can bring this water to the surface and distribute it on fields by center-pivot irrigation systems. But irrigation is generally a short-term solution, since the aquifers generally cannot be replenished.

Center-pivot irrigation has become a familiar landscape feature— particularly to air travelers crossing the Plains. This system covers 40 acres of a Nebraska cornfield. Although irrigation allows greater crop production, underground aquifers are being depleted.

Here in Nevada, overgrazing, which makes it difficult for beneficial grass species to regenerate, has damaged the rangeland to the right of the fence, making it less attractive for both livestock and wildlife.

Much of the West, particularly the more arid regions, is devoted to livestock rather than crop production. Overgrazing, however, principally by cattle, has been a major problem. When too many cattle are allowed to graze, they tend to graze favored species to the point where those species cannot easily regenerate. Shrubs like sagebrush and mesquite that have little value for cattle then take their place. Overgrazing also results in soil compaction and erosion, which further reduce range productivity. Also, cattle frequently compete directly with wildlife for forage. The Soil Conservation Service (SCS) estimates that more than 60 percent of American rangeland is in poor or fair condition (Conservation Foundation 1984, p. 172). The Bureau of Land Management (BLM), which manages 40 percent of the rangeland in the United States, has been criticized for permitting too much grazing. Ranchers who lease land from the BLM have less incentive for protecting that land than the land they own themselves.

Concern about overgrazing began in the late nineteenth century. The Forest Service set limits on grazing in national forests shortly after its establishment in 1905. The Taylor Grazing Act of 1934 gave the federal government the authority to control grazing on the public domain. Today the Forest Service and the BLM control range use on public land, while SCS advises private owners on range conservation (6.VII.C).

Overgrazing is not the only threat to rangeland; it can also be overused for recreation. Off-road vehicles and trail bikes have resulted in soil compaction, elimination of native grasses, and erosion.

## V. WILDLIFE AND ENDANGERED SPECIES

It is a rare rural community that does not value its wildlife—at least some of it. Farmers may consider deer pests if they trample corn crops; gardeners may object to groundhogs nibbling away in vegetable patches; and ranchers may wish to exterminate coyote that kill sheep. Yet, hunting,

The furbish lousewort, *Pedicularis furbishiae*, is found only in northern Maine and New Brunswick. Much of its habitat would have been destroyed had the Dickey-Lincoln Dam on the St. John River been built. The project was canceled in part because of concern for this endangered species.

trapping, fishing, and observing wildlife are major recreational activities for large numbers of rural residents, and these pursuits provide supplementary food and income for others. Moreover, the economies of many communities are heavily dependent on income from visiting hunters and fishermen. In a 1980 survey, the U.S. Fish and Wildlife Service found that 83 million Americans observed wildlife, 42 million fished, and 17 million hunted (Conservation Foundation 1982, p. 273).

Fortunately, Americans are becoming increasingly aware of both the value and the interconnectedness of wildlife and plants. We now realize that protecting habitat is the key to the survival of most endangered species. The habitat needs of wildlife vary tremendously. Some, such as the grizzly bear, require large areas of undisturbed land. Others require much less space or are more adaptable to human activities. Deer, for instance, thrive on a combination of second-growth forest and adjacent fields, a condition that is far more prevalent today than it was before European settlement. Consequently their numbers have increased markedly.

Many rural property owners place a high premium on making appropriate habitat for wildlife available through such activities as leaving dead trees favored by woodpeckers and eagles, creating wetlands by preventing runoff from fields, and encouraging the growth of shrubbery that shelters and provides food for small mammals and game birds. Unfortunately, other rural property owners destroy wildlife or their habitat by such activities as poisoning prairie dogs, draining wetlands to create more cropland, and removing hedgerows, which are excellent wildlife habitat but get in the way of efficient plowing.

Concerns about protecting wildlife started with game hunters, who became alarmed in the late nineteenth century at the disappearance of such species as the buffalo and the passenger pigeon. Traditionally most efforts to protect wildlife, particularly by state fish and game departments, were focused on species that are hunted and fished. Great progress has been made in their protection. Hunters who realize the importance of protecting breeding grounds and other habitats are often active conservationists.

Since the 1960s there has been growing interest in the protection of nongame and endangered species as well. More than one hundred species of vertebrate animals alone have become extinct in the continental United States since the arrival of Europeans. An even higher number of invertebrates and plants have become extinct, but an exact number cannot be determined since there is only incomplete information on what existed before. Relatively little is known about the habitat requirements of many species that might be endangered, particularly amphibians, invertebrates, reptiles, and plants (Conservation Foundation 1984, p. 174).

The Fish and Wildlife Service is the principal federal agency responsible for wildlife protection; a number of nonprofit organizations are involved as well. The Endangered Species Act of 1973, which the service helps to administer, is one of the strongest environmental laws (6.VIII.B).

## VI. SPECIAL RESOURCES

### A. Historic and Cultural Resources

Rural America has a wealth of historic resources—not only outstanding landmarks like Thomas Jefferson's Monticello, but everyday places as

Rural adobe mission churches are religious and social centers and important Hispanic contributions to American architecture. Traditionally, the earthen plaster was periodically renewed by the community, but many churches are falling into disrepair. The New Mexico Community Foundation is assisting communities in preserving historic churches like San Rafael, pictured here. The church is located within the La Cueva National Register district in Mora County.

Polish Catholic roadside shrine, Portage County, Wisconsin. Each region has characteristic landmarks that help make it special. Over forty ethnic groups left their mark on the rural Wisconsin landscape.

well: buildings and land that have been in use for many years and give a community its identity. Rural historic resources are varied: while farmsteads, mills, one-room schoolhouses, covered bridges, and rural churches are important, there are many others that should not be ignored, including general stores, Grange halls, the trails used by pioneers, and even early gas stations and diners.

Each rural area has groups of buildings and landscapes its residents consider important because they are pleasant to look at, because they have been an integral part of a rural way of life, or because they evoke familiar

Historic resources take many forms. Here, wagons traveling the Oregon Trail near Guernsey, Wyoming, left deep ruts in the sandstone. Trail remnants, many of which are on public lands, present a major preservation opportunity in the West.

and comforting associations of family and community. Protecting these buildings and landscapes conserves tangible and visible links with a community's past, preserves places that are important parts of a community's identity, and retains important resources that may provide historical information about how an area was settled, developed, or declined.

The agricultural landscape is particularly rich. Historic resources on American farms may include houses, barns, springhouses, smokehouses, root cellars, corn cribs, silos, windmills, and family burial plots. In addition, how farmers laid out their fields and manipulated the land through terracing, contour plowing, and drainage systems not only add interest to the landscape but also provide tangible evidence of a community's agricultural history. So do fencing materials, ranging from split-rail fences and Osage orange hedgerows to barbed wire. The agricultural landscape is constantly evolving as it reflects a changing economy as well as the needs, aspirations, and traditions of generations of farm families. It is not simply the individual farm building, but the grouping of buildings on the land and the repetition of farmstead after farmstead that give significance to an agricultural landscape. The farm complex takes on a significance that any one building alone lacks; viewed as a group, these buildings tell the changing story of agricultural life.

The juxtaposition of building shapes and forms, the mix of architectural styles and building materials, and the color and texture of the land itself give diversity to the rural landscape. Frequently in rural communities the harmonious relationship of buildings and their natural or agricultural settings is of special appeal to residents and visitors alike. A beautiful barn in the midst of a subdivision or a covered bridge adjacent to an interstate overpass loses much of its integrity and appeal.

The particular arrangement of buildings on the land makes each community unique. Historic communities such as Cranbury, New Jersey; Bishop Hill, Illinois; and Lodi, California, remain distinctive, and their

Hedgerows such as these in Mecklenberg, New York, tell us much about how fields were laid out and how land was divided. In addition to curbing erosion, they add visual interest to the landscape and provide habitat for wildlife.

SAVING AMERICA'S COUNTRYSIDE

Archeological resources may be dramatic like the cliff dwellings at Mesa Verde National Park in Colorado. More often they look like this cellar hole, which is all that remains of a late-seventeenth-century house at the Jefferson Patterson Park in Maryland. Archeological sites can tell us much about Indian and early European settlement.

preservation is very important to their residents. On the other hand, modern subdivisions or shopping centers in New Jersey, Illinois, and California may have little to distinguish them from each other.

Not all historic resources are visible above ground. Many communities also possess significant archeological resources that contain evidence about the way the land was used previously and about the lives and occupations of earlier residents. Archeological resources may be either historic—from the period since European settlement—or prehistoric—from earlier Indian and Eskimo settlements. Many archeological sites are revered by the descendants of the people who occupied them, and their protection from souvenir hunters as well as developers is of great importance.

Folklife traditions are as important to protect as more tangible reminders of our past. The ethnic diversity of Americans means that we have a tremendous wealth of traditions, folk tales, arts, and crafts. Culturally distinct rural areas usually have had unique ways of building, laying out farms, and creating furnishings and foods. As rural life styles and the old and no longer cost-effective ways of doing things die, the varied legacy of traditional cultural heritage is in danger of extinction in all regions of the country.

There are fewer people each year who have the skills and time for traditional crafts, or can remember old place names and customs, identify historic photographs, and tell and retell the folk tales of rural communities. The older residents of most rural communities—the people who have this knowledge and these skills—are untapped cultural resources. They are often pleased to be interviewed and pass on craft techniques to young people who will keep a tradition alive (3.IV.A).

Historic buildings and structures often fall victim to abandonment or obsolescence. A vast number of rural buildings stand vacant or are used only marginally. Since few farmers engage in general farming in the 1980s, chicken coops, sheep sheds, and small granaries are useless on many large

Stacking hay with a beaver slide is a fast-disappearing tradition in Montana, and the skill is as important to preserve as is the artifact. The American Folklife Center of the Library of Congress has documented this tradition along with many other rural traditions.

farms today. The slatted corncribs that stored feed corn on the cob, for example, are obsolete on most farms since modern equipment harvests corn by the individual kernel. The result is the loss of the corncrib—once a traditional element on American farms. Such historic resources have been lost almost universally and without much notice.

Surplus barns are a preservation problem in every region of the country. The condition of many barns today contrasts sharply with that of the general farming era, when a well-kept barn was the symbol of successful farming. Our magnificent barns were often built to house machinery, animals, and hay. But today's combines do not fit through the barn doors, livestock live in feedlots, and hay stays outside in compact one-ton bales.

There are other threats to historic resources. Development, of course, is a major cause of destruction. Individual buildings may survive—as in the case of a barn in the midst of a subdivision—but stripped of their natural or agricultural context. Moreover, the same dam that floods a scenic river may engulf historic mills, canals, farmsteads, burial grounds, and even entire villages.

Also, as farms consolidate, farmers frequently remove fences and hedgerows, no longer useful as boundary markers, that make the efficient use of large machinery more difficult. The result is an expansive landscape with fewer subdivided fields and diminished historical associations.

SAVING AMERICA'S COUNTRYSIDE

The Emminger round barn near Watertown, South Dakota, was built in 1910 and is listed in the National Register of Historic Places. Its current owner renovated it for continued use in his dairy operation.

Declining farm populations have resulted in consolidations that leave surplus church and school buildings in the countryside. Although many are historically and architecturally significant, they may be left to deteriorate or be demolished. Population declines also threaten the preservation of buildings in small towns that traditionally served the needs of farmers.

Another handicap to preservation of historic resources in rural areas comes from the commonly held belief in many communities that "old" means "poor," while "new" means "prosperous." Farm families—especially those who may have had to make do at times with outdated farm equipment, antiquated household appliances, second-hand trucks, and hand-me-down clothes because of the economic conditions of farming—are not always sympathetic to historic preservation.

The many farmers who would like to preserve their historic buildings and structures face frustrations and expenses. Maintenance and energy costs may be prohibitive or the necessary restoration skills unavailable. Not many people today, for example, are experienced at building stone walls or split-rail fences. Also, real estate taxes and liability insurance on unused or underused buildings may be too high for some to justify keeping them.

There has long been an interest in protecting outstanding monuments important in American history such as Mount Vernon and the Alamo. The National Park Service, state park agencies, and numerous nonprofit organizations own thousands of historic buildings throughout the United States. Widespread interest in the protection of nonmuseum buildings for their architectural or scenic qualities is more recent, dating from the late 1960s. More recent still has been the growth of interest in protecting whole districts. Preservationists have established Main Street projects to enhance older deteriorating commercial areas, and neighborhood conservation efforts have brought new life to numerous declining residential areas.

Historic preservation in rural areas, however, has often lagged behind such work in cities. Rural historic preservation programs have tended to

The National Trust and *Successful Farming* magazine recently sponsored a "Barn Again" competition. Over 500 farmers from 34 states submitted examples of successful barn rehabilitations.

Hillsboro, Virginia. Owners of rural buildings of architectural or historic interest are showing increased interest in rehabilitation.

focus on the protection of individual buildings, often as museums. Much more needs to be done to protect rural historic structures that are still lived in and worked in. New uses can often be found for buildings of historic or architectural interest if they are no longer needed for their original uses. Farm buildings can often be repaired or adapted to store new equipment and different crops. Throughout the country mills, schools, and other rural structures have been adapted for a variety of uses, including residences and stores. Fortunately an increasing number of local governments and nonprofit organizations are working to protect historic buildings that are still in use, as explained in the following chapters.

## B. Scenic Areas

No matter how important such resources as prime agricultural soil, clean water, and wildlife habitat may be, they rarely have the emotional appeal of a beautiful countryside setting. A love for scenic beauty often provides the common bond among people who work for the protection of wetlands, historic houses, and farmland. A community leader may strive to protect the economic well-being of local farmers, realizing that this is the key to farmland retention, but may be motivated—consciously or not—by the pleasure of observing scenic farmland and farming activity.

Many people appreciate and enjoy the countryside for its natural beauty. A 1986 survey showed scenic beauty to be the most important criterion Americans use in choosing parks and recreation areas (President's Commission on Americans Outdoors 1987, p. 40). The high automobile counts on scenic highways such as the Blue Ridge Parkway in North Carolina and Virginia attest to the popularity of visiting beautiful areas. Scenic beauty not only gives people pleasure, but also reduces stress and promotes mental health (ibid., p. 23).

Most natural and cultural resources have scenic value. Clear and unpolluted water, a pheasant poised in a meadow at the edge of a country road, field patterns accentuated by fences and hedgerows, a well-kept farmstead, a hardwood forest ablaze in fall colors—all are visual delights. Resource misuse has serious visual implications. Cloudy and stagnant water, channelized streams that no longer meander, bare fields scarred by erosion, mountains left pocked by strip mining, straight lines of look-alike houses, and muddy feedlots in the half shadow of a tumbled-down barn are visual symbols of a threatened rural landscape. In addition, there are problems that are primarily visual such as billboards and automobile graveyards.

Of course not everyone agrees on what constitutes scenic beauty. We have all heard that "beauty is in the eye of the beholder." Nor is there universal agreement that strip development, billboards, and automobile graveyards are blight that should be removed from the rural landscape. Some observers find such landscape elements interesting to observe for what they teach us about ourselves and our society (Jackson 1984). Moreover, visual preferences change with time. Wetlands would not have been considered beautiful a generation ago, and in the colonial era wilderness was more an object of fear than of beauty. Nevertheless, there is more agreement on how people rate scenery than is commonly thought. For instance, views incorporating water are universally popular (Sally Schauman in Smardon, Palmer, and Felleman 1986, p. 107).

The first step in protecting scenic resources is to establish community consensus on which scenery should be protected (3.IV.B). Communities can then use the results to designate areas to be protected through local controls and voluntary agreements. Specific visual blight problems such as billboards and junkyards can be regulated through ordinances.

## C. Outdoor Recreation

Interest in outdoor recreation has increased greatly during the twentieth century, particularly since 1960. Although some outdoor activities such as hunting, fishing, walking, ice skating, and boating were popular in the last century, others such as skiing and white-water boating for sport were practically unheard of. Increased leisure time and greater disposable income have increased interest in recreation. Furthermore, improved transportation has made it possible for most Americans to travel to a wide variety of places for recreation.

Americans participate in outdoor recreation for enjoyment and health. According to a 1983 survey, some of the most popular outdoor recreational activities (along with the percentage who participated) were swimming (53%), walking for pleasure (53%), picnicking (48%), driving for pleasure (48%), sightseeing (46%), fishing (34%), bicycling (32%), boating (28%), jogging (26%), camping (24%), and team sports (24%).[20]

Demands for outdoor recreation have been the impetus for protecting many environmental resources. In addition to land that is set aside for parks, land originally intended for other purposes is now used for recreation. For instance, some national forests, particularly in the East, are now used more for recreation than for logging. Much of the effort to clean up water supplies has been a result of pressure from water-sports enthusiasts and fishermen. But outdoor recreation can also result in environmental degradation—when too many people visit a park, use a campground, or paddle a river. For certain recreational areas it has become necessary to limit visitation. Environmental problems also result from inappropriate use—for instance, when trail bikers crush fragile desert vegetation or when boaters discard plastic waste that snares mammals or is eaten by fish.

Outdoor recreation can cause problems when it becomes too concentrated or damages fragile resources. Here, trail-bike riders have formed gullies on Idaho rangeland.

Providing outdoor recreation opportunities for profit and pleasure is a concern for many rural communities, particularly those that are far from publicly owned land. Traditionally much recreational activity has taken place on private land, either one's own or a neighbor's. In many communities it is traditional to permit people from the community to use private land for recreation if they do no harm. "No trespassing" signs are becoming more common, however, as demands for outdoor recreation increase and as more people leave the city looking for recreational opportunities. Many landowners are becoming concerned about vandalism, about the number of people using their land, and about potential liability for injuries.

Rural conservation leaders can play a role not only in protecting land for the enjoyment of community residents but also in working out agreements with property owners for responsible use by area residents. Trail clubs in particular, such as the Ice Age Trail Council in Wisconsin (Case Study 23), have been active in working out such agreements.

## D. Public Lands

Virtually all communities contain government-owned land, if it is only the land around schools and municipal buildings and along road rights-of-way. Particularly in the West, large proportions of some communities' land are owned by the federal government or, to a lesser extent, by state or local governments. The biggest federal land managers are the Bureau of Land Management (BLM), the Forest Service, the National Park Service, the Fish and Wildlife Service, and the Department of Defense. The land may be directly managed by the federal government or leased to individuals and corporations.

BLM is the largest of the federal land managers, overseeing many types of public land including rangeland, forests, watersheds, wilderness areas, wildlife habitats, recreation areas, and historic sites. All told, it is responsible for 473 million acres of public lands. BLM rangelands are often leased for long terms to ranchers, while lands containing fossil fuel and mineral reserves are leased to private corporations for exploitation.

There are many issues related to the appropriate uses of federally owned land, with logging companies, mining companies, ranchers, outfitters, and other businesses often lobbying for more intensive use while conservationists decry overuse. BLM and the Forest Service are committed by law to the concepts of "multiple use" and "sustained yield" (ensuring that the timber, grasses, and other resources on their land will be available for generations to come). Many conservationists argue, however, that BLM allows overgrazing and does not charge enough for its leases. Conservationists also argue that the Forest Service builds too many roads and allows too much cutting in areas that should be designated for wilderness and that the income received from timber sales does not equal the expense to the government of administering the cutting program.

Communities with significant public lands within or along their boundaries need to deal with the responsible officials in their conservation efforts (6.IX.E). Activities on public lands will have a major impact on adjacent communities and vice versa. For instance, development adjacent to Yellowstone National Park makes it difficult to protect the grizzly bear, whose range includes land outside the park. Conversely, the popularity of the park means there is great pressure to develop land in communities near the park. Such pressure in Jackson Hole, Wyoming, for instance, makes it difficult for conservationists there to protect that community's scenic ranch land (Case Study 2).

## VII. POTENTIAL PROBLEMS

### A. Highways

Highway construction is an issue that frequently pits neighbor against neighbor and community against community. "Yes, we need the road, but not through my back yard," goes the familiar refrain. Highway construction is closely related to rural growth issues. Clearly, construction provides jobs and roads lure new business. Unfortunately, employment projections often do not consider the lost jobs of farmers and others whose livelihood depends on a rural environment. Furthermore, cost-benefit analyses can never adequately put a price tag on such aesthetic values as a historic farmstead or a valley without development.

Although good roads are undoubtedly needed in many areas, they have sometimes been built where the need for them is questionable or along alignments that destroyed more resources than necessary. Most such problems occurred in the twenty-five years following World War II. The same road that brought inappropriate development to rural areas frequently drained needed development from a nearby downtown. Doughnut-shaped cities, with parking lots at the center and sprawling development on the periphery, were frequently the result. Highway construction is an issue that can unite rural conservationists and urban preservationists.

New highway construction and improvements to existing roads continue to be a leading cause of lost farmland, historic sites, wetlands, wildlife habitat, scenic areas, and many of the other resources that rural communities care about. But there is hope. The process of deciding which highway projects get funded is more open to the voicing of community concerns than it once was, and alternative solutions, such as improved public transportation, are more likely to be explored today than in the past (6.X.A).

## B. Surface Mining

Surface mining—of coal, iron, gravel and sand, peat, uranium, and other minerals—is important to the economies of many rural communities. It is also one of the most challenging and potentially devastating environmental problems. Not only does it scar the landscape, but it also can destroy people's homes and livelihoods. Some of the most serious problems are in the coal-mining areas of Appalachia, where farmers sold their mineral rights to absentee mining companies, little realizing the ultimate impact. When the companies eventually exercised their rights, they were able to do pretty much as they pleased with the land, regardless of the impact on the surface. By dumping mine tailings down mountain sides as they stripped off the coal, miners have created enormous problems downstream. Sulfuric acid draining from coal mines and tailings has killed aquatic plants and fish. Tailings washing into streams have raised stream beds, flooding communities such as Cranks Creek, Kentucky (Case Study 25). In communities such as Oley, Pennsylvania, quarrying has resulted in the draining of an aquifer on which farmers depended (Case Study 1).

Responsible mining practices followed by reclamation is possible (see illustrations, p. 234). Some communities have made good use of reclaimed land. Such land may even support rare plant species, as is the case for reclaimed limestone tailings in Michigan.[21] All told, however, the record on reclamation has not been good, and mine operations have left a legacy that will cost a great deal to correct. The Department of Agriculture estimates that about 2.7 million acres of mined land in the United States is in need of reclamation.[22] Until the passage of the 1977 Surface Mining Control and Reclamation Act, there were few controls on mine owners and few requirements that they restore the land after they cease to mine it (6.X.B).

## C. Toxic Waste

In recent years, toxic dumps like the one along Love Canal in Niagara Falls, New York, have captured headlines. Many others, however, still go unnoticed. Toxic chemicals pose obvious health hazards when they are indiscriminately dumped onto the land or flushed into municipal sewer systems ill-equipped to deal with them, as was the case in Middlesboro, Kentucky (Case Study 19). They pose even greater problems when they are dumped in unknown locations. Even homeowners may unwittingly add to the problem: many household chemicals—such as rodent baits, drain cleaners, and spot removers—are toxic and should not be sent to a landfill with other trash (see *Special-Purpose Ordinances,* pp. 164–65). In many cases there are significant concentrations of toxic wastes in municipal dumps that can seep into aquifers supplying drinking water.

The Environmental Protection Agency (EPA) estimates that 264 million tons of toxic waste were generated in the United States in 1981 (Conservation Foundation 1984, p. 69), or more than one ton per citizen. EPA also estimates that as much as 90 percent of these wastes may have been improperly disposed of in more than 34,000 dump sites and in over 180,000 pits, ponds, and lagoons.[23]

Major industries have improved their handling of toxic wastes in recent years. Furthermore, the technology for dealing with toxic waste has greatly improved. In many cases waste can be incinerated, treated to reduce its toxicity, reduced to smaller quantities, or recycled into useful products. Enormous problems remain from past unregulated dumping practices, however, and are still being caused by smaller, less scrupulous or knowledgeable manufacturers. Although EPA now regulates dumping, the laws have not always been effectively enforced (6.X.C). Moreover, there is mounting concern that many legal dump sites, such as deep wells and surface impoundments, have inadequate capacity and will eventually leak.

## D. Air Pollution

Air pollution is frustrating for many rural communities, since the major sources of air pollution are not generally within the jurisdiction of the local government. Given the ease with which airborne pollutants travel great distances, controls usually need to be imposed at the regional, national, and international levels to be effective.

Air pollution certainly causes health problems, and its role in respiratory ailments, heart disease, and cancer is well-documented. Air pollution can also have long-term adverse impacts on the environment. Sulfur dioxide and nitrogen dioxide, emitted primarily from coal- and oil-burning power plants and industries, combine with water in the atmosphere to create acid rain, which has a potentially devastating effect on lakes, rivers, and forests. As acidity increases, fish and some tree species are dying. There may also be adverse effects on human health (Conservation Foundation 1982, p. 67). Acid rain is also causing damage to stone buildings and monuments. Particularly affected are many rural areas in the East, downwind from midwestern industrial areas. Air pollution can also diminish part of the appeal of rural areas by eliminating clean air and the ability to see great distances.

As a result of the 1963 Clean Air Act, air quality does seem to be improving in most parts of the country for most pollutants (6.X.D). Some problems, however, such as acid rain are getting worse, since the effects of many pollutants are cumulative. Along with relying on federal and state air pollution laws, communities can regulate some causes of air pollution locally (see *Special-Purpose Ordinances*, pp. 164–65).

## VIII. CONCLUSION

This chapter has probably covered many potential problems in your community. However, you should not feel discouraged. There is much that rural leaders can do to deal with environmental problems, as we describe in the chapters that follow. Moreover, we hope this chapter has helped you to discover underappreciated assets in your community, assets that can be used in developing a rural conservation program.

Change is a common thread in many of the concerns we have discussed. Rural America has always experienced change, but its scale and pace are accelerating. Large residential subdivisions, shopping centers, superhighways, resort complexes, and mining operations are increasingly common in many areas. In others, farmers are leaving the land, and merchants the small towns, in increasing numbers.

Opinions on whether change is good, bad, or a mixed blessing are sure to vary in your community. The conflict over change is often between rich and poor, native and newcomer, young and old, but not always. Rising land values may mean profit for the retiring farmer who wants to sell land to a developer but spell bankruptcy for a neighboring farmer in need of increased acreage to make a living. Locating a manufacturing plant in a rural county may provide employment opportunities for some but ruin the countryside for others. Building a consensus for your rural conservation program on what change is needed and how it should be managed will no doubt be one of your greatest and potentially most rewarding challenges.

# Initiating and Managing
# a Rural Conservation Program

## I. INTRODUCTION

Why organize? Although you as an individual can accomplish much, your efforts can be far more effective when you are part of an organized group. An emotional appeal for support may be successful in initiating a conservation effort during a crisis; it is rarely enough to sustain a long-term effort, solicit funds, influence legislation, or support legal action. By spreading responsibilities and providing different outlets for different talents, an organized group is able to take maximum advantage of individual talents. Moreover, a group can grow and change over the long term by taking on new members, new leaders, new issues, and new programs. There are other important reasons to organize: to help you to gain credibility and clout in the community, and to allow you to meet legal requirements for raising funds and owning property.

Rural residents often have a tradition of organizing both to benefit their community and to help their neighbors. This "barn-raising" spirit is a definite advantage in getting things accomplished. Moreover, in stable communities with a number of long-time residents, most people already know their community and their neighbors well, making it easier for you to tap the best sources of support and knowledge. Says one experienced organizer, "Learn to turn to friends and associates for help—people will surprise you at times with their ingenuity. *Allowing* people to help is as important as wanting them to help."[1]

Both local governments and nonprofit organizations engage in rural conservation, and most of the techniques described in this chapter apply to both, as do many of the techniques described in Chapter 7, which addresses educational activities in more detail. Many rural citizens are active in local government and such private organizations as service groups,

Rural Americans have long cooperated to build their communities or carry out seasonal activities such as haying and harvests. Top, neighbors help a farm family near Millerstown, Pennsylvania, rebuild their dairy barn after a fire. With inadequate insurance to cover the loss, the family would have quit farming without such encouragement from the community. Bottom, ranchers and neighbors work to brand, castrate, ear mark, dehorn, and vaccinate calves at the Circle A Ranch near Paradise Valley, Nevada.

churches, and youth clubs, and thus can choose to work through either governmental or private action, or both. Materials written for grass-roots organizers sometimes assume that government is not responsive and that private action is the only route to follow. While this may be true in some communities where rural conservation is a concern, in others local government may support or even initiate rural conservation efforts.

That said, however, you may still find it necessary to confront governmental entities from time to time. Moreover, this chapter's measured tone in discussing the many aspects of organizing does not reflect the passion some issues generate. When all else fails, it is time to fight—as the farmers in Eaton County, Michigan, learned in opposing a highway through their lands (Case Study 4).

## II. DETERMINING AN ORGANIZATIONAL APPROACH

Should a formal organization be incorporated, or is an informal group sufficient? Should an effort be sponsored by the local government or by a private, nonprofit organization? Over time, should the form of the group change? Is some middle ground or cooperative approach possible, such as working with an established nonprofit organization or collaboration between nonprofit and government entities? This section explores these alternatives and their implications.

# Oley, Pennsylvania:
# Organizing for the Long Haul

Communities organize for rural conservation in a variety of ways. Oley Township in Pennsylvania (1987 pop. 3,345), where conservationists decided to work through both local government and nonprofit organizations, illustrates several of these ways. The efforts of Oley's conservationists began with a demonstration project involving the National Trust for Historic Preservation.

The heart of a prosperous farming area known as the Oley Valley, some ten miles from Reading, Oley has always cherished its heritage. Most of the township's twenty-four square miles are rich, rolling grain fields outlined by mature hedgerows, dotted with eighteenth-century stone farm buildings. Agrarian traditions based on the Pennsylvania German culture are still strong, and the valley is home to dozens of farm families whose roots reach back to Oley's first European settlers, who arrived in the early eighteenth century. The oldest family farm in Pennsylvania, farmed by the same family for eleven generations, is located in the township. Oley is, in fact, remarkable for its farms and villages (Oley and Pleasantville, both unincorporated) that strongly evoke the eighteenth and nineteenth centuries, when they were built. Outbuildings on many farmsteads retain distinctive handmade tile roofs dating from the eighteenth century, two covered bridges are still in use, and one of Oley's eight mills still produces stone-ground feed.

Oley's residents rely on local government for basic services—roads and schools, plus water and sewer in some areas—and little else. Zoning and subdivision regulation at the time the project began were similar to those found in many rural communities, with a presumption toward uniform residential development everywhere. Many months into

A side view of the house, stone barns, and other outbuildings of the Kaufman homestead. The locust trees surrounding the large barn at right are common to hedgerows and woodlots throughout the area.

the project, a lengthy comprehensive plan dating from the 1960s was unearthed in the municipal building's attic—telling evidence of a long-ago failure to connect the idea of planning with the township's real needs. A seven-page "policy statement" adopted as the township's comprehensive plan in 1971 stated an intent to retain the "rural-like identity" of Oley. Nowhere, however, was this goal equated with preserving agriculture and historic sites, the two central elements of that identity.

Oley Township's proximity to Reading (and to Philadelphia for more determined commuters) plus its attractive environment had encouraged some residential construction. Over the years, such development had been gradual; starting in the late 1970s, though, some residents began to view it as a threat.

Oley's most bitter experience with land-use conflicts, however, had come not from housing developments but from quarries. Oley's prime agricultural land (the word "prime" comes from the Soil Conservation Service's highest rating) is underlain in part by high-calcium limestone bedrock much in demand for cement and crushed stone. The first large-

Cemeteries can yield a wealth of historical information. The Hoch family cemetery is one of many to be found in Oley. It is on Pennsylvania's oldest family farm, now in its eleventh generation. Note the roofed stone wall and Germanic inscription, both familiar sights in Pennsylvania German areas.

SAVING AMERICA'S COUNTRYSIDE

Oley's fair logo, designed in 1972, commemorates the valley's heritage as well as its agricultural productivity.

scale quarry opened in the 1950s; two more companies came to the area soon after. Together, the three quarry companies own more than eight hundred acres in the township—not much in terms of land area, but plenty in terms of impact. For years residents endured in silence the blasting, the heavy truck traffic, the visual blight of mountainous wastes, and the companies' neglect and destruction of historic buildings on the properties they bought. But in 1978, the suspicious coincidence of the opening of a new quarry hole and the disappearance of a stream and several springs in the vicinity provoked an outcry from neighboring farmers, one of whom relied on the stream to water his dairy herd. When the landowners were given no assurance by quarry representatives that anything could be done about this, they formed a concerned citizens group. The group later urged the township government to create the Oley Resource Conservation Project.

In early 1979, the director of the Berks County Conservancy—a nonprofit organization concerned with protecting the county's farmland, natural areas, and historic sites—encouraged Oley to apply to become a demonstration community for the National Trust for Historic Preservation. When the trust accepted the township's application later that year, the township's supervisors appointed a four-member subcommittee of the planning commission. With the help of representatives from the trust, the subcommittee designed a three-year work program calling for (1) resource identification; (2) resource analysis, including research into protection methods; and (3) resource protection. The subcommittee was chaired by Hilda Fisher, a farm wife and retired schoolteacher from a widely respected family descended from the valley's original settlers. Other members over the life of the project included a social worker, a retired museum administrator, a farmer, a banker, and a realtor.

The mountainous tailings of high-calcium limestone quarrying operations exist side by side with corn-fields and historic buildings in Oley. Concern about quarrying prompted rural conservation efforts in the township. The highest tailings pile shown is higher than state regulations now allow: the new piles are much lower, and thus less visible, but cover more prime farmland.

Each member of the subcommittee became responsible for a group of volunteers. Three took responsibility for the three main areas of the inventory (historical, land use, and agricultural), and the fourth produced a newsletter. Like many rural communities, Oley has a variety of news sources, but none covers the entire township, making a uniform news source about the project a necessity. Moreover, publishing a newsletter was a concrete, short-term accomplishment that helped volunteers see quick results for their efforts.

After an initial period when it seemed as though there were too many things to do all at once, the subcommittee settled down into a routine of monthly meetings held a week in advance of the planning commission's scheduled date. Volunteer activities tended to revolve around producing results in time for the subcommittee meeting. In turn, the subcommittee's monthly reports to the planning commission assured commissioners and supervisors that their many activities indeed were part of a larger picture. The workload for the subcommittee soon became enough that it saw the need for a part-time coordinator. After advertising the position nationally, the subcommittee members chose one of their cohorts, Phoebe Hopkins (2.VI.E).

Resource identification took the greatest amount of time to accomplish during the first two years of the project and meant assembling a long list of outside advisors. For example, given the township's continuing concern over the effect on groundwater by the quarries, the subcommittee persuaded the U.S. Geological Survey (USGS) to cooperate on an eighteen-month "water budget" study. (A water budget measures how much water goes in and out of an area, and by what means. Fortunately, the fact that the township's political boundaries virtually coincide with the watershed made it feasible to conduct the study largely within a single jurisdiction.) The USGS agreed to use volunteers in reading the stream and rain gauges placed around the township, and to count the value of the volunteers' time toward the township's half of the costs. The township also received a Community Development Block Grant (see *Federal Economic Assistance*, p. 237) toward its participation. The study yielded valuable data for both water quality and quantity that will provide a basis for comparison with data collected in the future. And while it did not directly provide an answer as to why the stream and springs dried up, USGS geologists speculated that an impervious layer of rock supporting a high, or "perched," water table was irreparably cracked during blasting for the new quarry.

Analysis of the resources, research into protection methods, and establishing some protection took place as the inventory progressed. For historic resources, this happened quickly. In 1983, the National Register of Historic Places (6.IX.B) accepted Oley Township in its entirety as a historic district, one of the largest ever listed. A consultant experienced in architectural history and the National Register process helped the subcommittee submit the application. With her guidance, volunteers organized records, completed historical research on the land and its settlement, and assessed the relative historical and architectural merit of the township's many rural structures.

In the meantime, an agricultural survey revealing that the average age of Oley's ninety farmers was well over the national average had raised fears that widespread turnover in farm ownership was imminent and that key parcels might fall prey to development. An immediate step open to the township and cooperating farmers was the designation of an "agricultural security area," or an agricultural district (4.VI.B). Thus, only a few months after designation of the National Register district, a second major step toward protection of the township's resources was completed: designation of more than 8,000 acres of farmland as a security area.

In 1984, toward the end of the National Trust's involvement, it became apparent that achieving local protection required still more analysis and public education. Two things happened at this point: the establishment of another governmental task force and the creation of a nonprofit organization. The subcommittee itself disbanded, with members going on to participate in both the new task force and the new organization.

In answer to the subcommittee's recommendation that any efforts to change the township's planning and land-use regulation needed broader official representation, the township established a task force to conduct a "planning study." Officials named a committee of twenty township residents, including representatives of the board of supervisors, the planning commission, the water and sewer authority, and the new heritage association described below. The committee was asked to update the comprehensive plan, articulate a clear commitment to the township's agriculture and historic character in all township policies, and decide how best to deal with demands for development. To provide technical guidance to the committee, the township engaged the Brandywine Conservancy, a nonprofit land conservation organization with an extensive advisory service for municipal governments in Pennsylvania.

Such a study required substantial funding. At the same time, the National Register listing was a source of community pride, and residents felt it deserved a celebration. Thus was born in 1984 the Oley Valley Heritage Association. Its first activity was a "heritage festival," complete with a ceremony celebrating the register listing attended by Pennsylvania's Secretary of Agriculture. The festival raised seven thousand

dollars toward the planning study and was repeated in subsequent years. The association has also conducted other educational activities to persuade township residents to provide special care for the area's historic buildings. For example, tours of selected homes in the valley in 1987 helped raise funds toward a project to record Oley's unusual outbuildings through measured architecture drawings.

For eighteen months the planning study committee wrestled with ways to address the community's most important concerns. What emerged was a plan for new policy initiatives, including agricultural zoning, new subdivision controls, regulations to minimize damage to the limestone bedrock found in much of the township, and an ordinance delaying any demolition of historic buildings. The political commitment necessary to convert these ideas to township policy, however, has been slow in evolving. An effort in 1986 to enact "sliding-scale" agricultural zoning (4.III.D), the top priority of the committee, met with considerable landowner opposition and was turned down by the supervisors. The critical need for a sewage plan revision, including a second water-quality study, was addressed early in 1987. Finally, nearly three years after the planning study, the town supervisors adopted a comprehensive plan based on committee recommendations.

According to Phoebe Hopkins, now the director of historic preservation for the Berks County Conservancy, "The maps and data generated by the project proved invaluable in facilitating planning activities. Without the information, the initiatives, and the community education that the project fostered, Oley Township would be easy prey for inappropriate development. With this strong foundation for future action, the citizens of Oley have a fighting chance of preserving their heritage."

## A. Working with Local Government

By getting involved in local government, rural conservation leaders may be able to affect legislation and influence appointments to boards that can help their cause. It is often necessary to work with more than one level of government (see *Collecting General Information,* pp. 86–87). For example, some government services, such as sewer service, may be a function of county government or an independent authority, while other government activities, such as zoning, may be a function of the township.

Local government involvement is useful because attention from elected officials adds credibility to rural conservation activities. Moreover, governments can appropriate funds and pass bond issues to support programs or acquire property. And, of course, decisions by local government have the force of law.

Citizens may participate in local government in both informal and formal ways. Establishing an informal dialogue with local officials is the first step in educating them about rural conservation. Visiting, telephoning, and writing letters to local officials keep them aware that rural conservation issues are important to constituents. In both Cazenovia, New York, and Yakima, Washington, informal meetings with local officials were the first step toward full-fledged programs (Case Studies 6 and 27). Establishing communication with and enlisting support from government staff are also important. Such staff members as planning directors, zoning administrators, or building inspectors can become valuable allies if they sympathize with rural conservation concerns—or formidable foes if they do not. Adds one community organizer, "Be prepared to allow them to take credit for your ideas; credit almost always adds up to more than 100 percent."

Individuals can also work more formally with local government as members of commissions or elected officers. Citizens wishing to be appointed to a board should express an interest to their elected officials, or attend meetings and express opinions. Rural communities sometimes have a shortage of people interested in government service; consequently, those who attend meetings and offer good ideas are likely to be considered when a vacancy on a committee occurs.

Establishing a task force to deal with rural conservation concerns—the approach used in both Cazenovia, New York, and Oley, Pennsylvania (Case Studies 6 and 1)—is an effective way to organize. Local government may also establish other decision-making and advisory groups such as environmental commissions, planning boards, and historic district commissions.

## B. Establishing a Nonprofit Rural Conservation Organization

An incorporated nonprofit organization established especially for rural conservation is another way to focus community attention on the issues.

### *Establishing a Nonprofit Organization*

*Laws governing the establishment of nonprofit organizations vary from state to state. The advice of an attorney is important to assure that all steps are followed correctly. Here are the basic requirements.*

• *Deciding on the purposes and the powers of the organization;*
• *Deciding whether to invite members of the general public to join and, if so, what privileges they should have, such as electing the board;*
• *Drafting and filing (with the appropriate state office) articles of incorporation, the document that sets forth the decisions regarding how the organization will be run;*
• *Drafting and adopting bylaws, which include the number and types of officers and committees; and*
• *Authorizing officers to sign checks and make contracts.*

## Tax Exemption

*Qualifying for gifts that can be deducted from federal income taxes is essential for most nonprofit organizations. (If, however, a substantial portion of an organization's activity, as defined by the Internal Revenue Service, will consist of lobbying, it cannot qualify for tax exemption.) Many individuals and most foundations and corporations will give only to an entity that is considered a publicly supported, tax-exempt organization. In order for the IRS to recognize an organization as tax-exempt—that is, a "501(a)(3)" or a "501(c)(4)" organization as described in the Internal Revenue Code—the organization must file an application with the IRS. A similar designation from the state government may provide for exemption from state income and sales taxes, or local property taxes. Like incorporation, obtaining tax-exempt designation calls for an attorney's assistance (National Trust for Historic Preservation, Information Series, no. 14).*

There are four basic advantages to creating a nonprofit organization. First, nonprofit organizations can act more quickly and with less "red tape" than government can. This is true especially in real estate transactions, where private organizations may be more trusted by property owners who dislike government's taxes, land-use controls, and bureaucratic procedures. Second, while nonprofit organizations operate in the public interest, they need not obtain widespread voter approval, as government officials must do in creating rural conservation programs. Third, in most communities a nonprofit organization can obtain donations more easily than can local government (2.VII; see also *Tax Exemption,* left). Fourth, the corporate entity in itself provides certain protections for the organization's volunteers and staff from liability and will help the organization to obtain financing for real estate transactions.

Deciding on the purposes of the organization and its membership policy is particularly important in establishing a nonprofit organization. Many nonprofit organizations state their purposes broadly so they may expand their activities in the future even if they are being organized to deal with a single issue. The purposes of the organization also suggest what powers should be specifically mentioned in its articles of incorporation. For instance, if an organization might some day acquire property, the right to engage in such activity should be stated in its powers clause.

The issue of whether to seek members from the general public is a major one for a new organization. A large membership base may mean more income and volunteers, and creates within the community a core of people knowledgeable about rural conservation issues. Organizations with large memberships may be able to convince elected officials to pay more attention to their concerns, since their members potentially could influence the outcome of an election. If members are needed primarily to show community support, nominal dues encourage more people to join. Even if the primary purpose of membership is fundraising, most organizations feel some responsibility to provide services for members. These services may include a newsletter, advice on land stewardship, and discounts on admissions and items offered for sale.

A large membership base can, however, be a disadvantage. Serving members can divert resources from an organization's mission. Also, a group that needs to conduct confidential real estate transactions is often better off without public members. Moreover, organizations with only a board of directors involved in decision-making can usually move more swiftly than organizations where the members at large must be consulted.

Although most nonprofit rural conservation organizations invite members of the public to join, such very effective organizations as the Jackson Hole Land Trust in Wyoming (Case Study 2) and Colorado Open Lands (5.VIII.B) do not. In other instances, membership organizations are closely affiliated with a nonprofit entity without public members that is empowered to carry out land transactions. For instance, the Philadelphia Conservationists invites public membership and raises funds to acquire land, while the Natural Lands Trust (see illustrations, p. 202) manages land and does not have public members. The two organizations share the same office space, board, and staff. Organizations that decide not to have members may still have subscribers, donors, "friends," or other categories of supporters who make donations and receive newsletters or other benefits.

## Jackson Hole, Wyoming:
## Two Nonprofit Organizations
## and a Local Government
## Complement One Another's Work

Jackson Hole, Wyoming, a scenic valley named for an early trapper in what is now Teton County (1984 pop. 11,122), has a long history of protection efforts by an assortment of federal agencies, national and local nonprofit organizations, local planning officials, and philanthropists. This case study concentrates on the achievements of the Teton County Planning Commission, the Jackson Hole Alliance for Responsible Planning, and the Jackson Hole Land Trust.

Anyone who has seen Jackson Hole's spectacular scenery would understand why so many conservationists over the years have wanted to protect the valley and the dramatic Tetons rising above the valley to the west. In the summer, millions of vacationers pass through on their way to and from Grand Teton and Yellowstone National Parks. Jackson Hole's wildlife rivals its scenery. The 24,300-acre National Elk Refuge is the wintering ground for 7,500 elk, an impressive sight when they are concentrated in the refuge, where visitors can ride horse-drawn sleds out to see them.

Efforts to protect Jackson Hole and its environs date to the early days of the conservation movement. Yellowstone, to the north, was the world's first national park, established in 1872. The elk refuge was established in 1912; the Izaak Walton League purchased a major addition in the 1920s for donation to the federal government. Congress established Grand Teton National Park in 1929. Starting in 1927, John D. Rockefeller, Jr., began purchasing much of the adjacent private land, eventually donating it to the federal government to expand the park. The county also contains portions of three national forests.

With all but 3 percent of the land in Teton County in federal ownership, one might think Jackson Hole was well protected. Yet, development has boomed since 1965, when the construction of a major ski resort made Jackson Hole a year-round resort. By 1986 the population had soared to more than 10,000, compared with only 2,500 in 1950. In addition, a staggering two million people visit the county each year. The pressure on private land has been tremendous. Ranchland that sold for $500 an acre in 1950 has gone for as much as $15,000 in recent years. In the heyday of such prices, affordable housing for low- and middle-income families shrank to a dismaying degree.

As a result of these problems in the 1970s, conservationists in the county became increasingly concerned. Although the major assets of the community were protected by the federal government, private land—much of it important wildlife habitat and scenic ranches—was in danger of becoming a strip of development from the southern approach to Jackson all the way to Grand Teton Park to the north.

Spectacular as Wyoming's Grand Tetons are, their drama is increased by a view across the level lands of Jackson Hole. Privately owned ranches such as the one pictured here are under increasing development pressure throughout the valley. The barn, fences, and other structures are typical of the West.

The attitude of many local property owners, according to one conservationist, is "Look, 97 percent of the county is owned by the federal government already. We ought to be allowed to do what we like with 3 percent even if we do screw it up." Fortunately, much private land was and still is protected by families—many the descendants of homesteaders—who want to stay in ranching even though there is currently little profit in it.

Although there has been a planning commission in the county since 1968, active planning did not get under way until the mid-1970s. With the help of consultants, the county began to prepare its first land-use plan. There was considerable controversy surrounding the plan and much vociferous opposition to it, particularly from the construction industry and some ranchers. However, the county commission approved the plan, which incorporated a zoning ordinance, in 1977.

The "Teton County Comprehensive Plan and Implementation Program" called for the protection of critical natural resources and established environmental criteria that developers must meet to obtain development permits. The ordinance implementing the plan set residential lot sizes ranging from a minimum of three acres for most of the land in private ownership to twenty acres for the most critical environmental areas, mostly steep hillsides. The ordinance has a generous cluster provision (4.IV.B), allowing developers who place conservation easements (5.V) on at least 50 percent of their parcel to receive a density bonus up to 100 percent. For instance, the owner of a 300-acre parcel zoned for one unit per three acres who gives an easement on 150 acres to the county can build 200 units on the remaining 150 acres instead of the 100 normally permitted. A few large-scale developers have taken advantage of the cluster provision to build resort developments.

As part of the planning process, the county commission appointed a study group to recommend new approaches to protection. The group suggested the establishment of a national scenic area, in which the federal government would purchase easements on private land. The group's plan, which had the support of the county commission, was incorporated into legislation for a Jackson Hole Scenic Area introduced in Congress in 1977. The Izaak Walton League and other national conservation organizations urged its passage, as did many local residents. The bill passed the House of Representatives but died in the Senate after intensive lobbying by some county landowners and developers who opposed an increased federal role in the community.

After the 1978 loss in Congress and the election of an antiplanning slate to the county commission that same year, local conservationists decided that the days of federal solutions to land conservation issues in Teton County had ended for the foreseeable future. They decided to devote their attention to making the county plan work and to obtaining voluntary controls on property, through two new nonprofit organizations.

Story Clark and other conservationists established the Jackson Hole Alliance for Responsible Planning in 1978 as a membership and advocacy organization. Its purpose is to protect Jackson Hole's "wildlife, scenery, and open spaces through land use planning and an involved citizenry." The principal role of the alliance, according to Clark, its first director, has been to make sure that the county's plan is followed and to suggest new environmental protection measures the county commission should consider.

"Our approach since 1978 has been low key," says Clark. "We've tried to avoid the pendulum swings of the past in public sentiment about planning." Fortunately, much of the furor over planning in 1977 and 1978 has since died down. According to Clark, "People thought the plan would cut off growth and depress land values. When this didn't happen they became less concerned."

The alliance considers its most important role that of keeping the attention of county leaders focused on long-range planning for the county. It comments on major development proposals brought before the planning commission and advises developers on conservation concerns before they present their plans to the commission. The alliance is also concerned about public lands and design issues and about historic preservation in the town of Jackson. Its leaders have advocated the protection of wilderness areas in national forests and commented on federal land management plans.

The alliance's message—that a scenic community that protects its environment attracts more visitors and hence brings in more income—seems to be getting through. The organization now has more than one thousand members, including many county leaders. The alliance's staff places a heavy reliance on membership involvement in its programs. According to Clark, "We didn't just want to collect ten dollar dues. We wanted to keep people in the community involved. We think continuously about how to involve volunteers and to reward them for their work." The alliance's annual art auction, for instance, not only raises

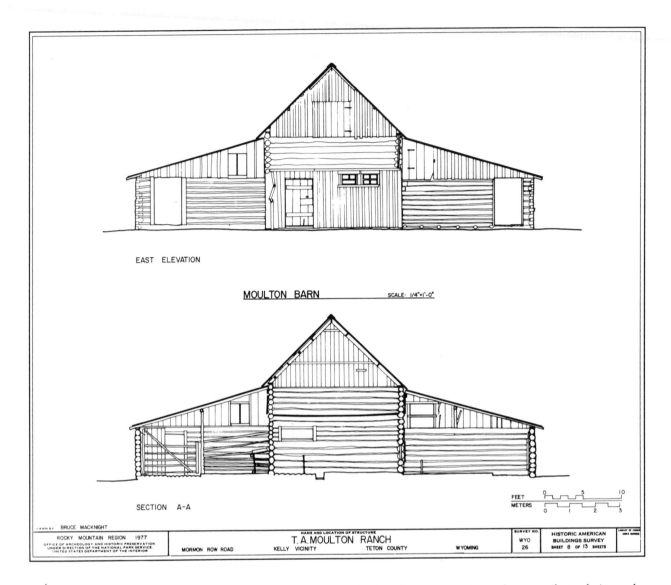

EAST ELEVATION

## MOULTON BARN

SCALE: 1/4"=1'-0"

SECTION A-A

FEET
METERS

DRAWN BY BRUCE MACKNIGHT

| ROCKY MOUNTAIN REGION 1977 OFFICE OF ARCHEOLOGY AND HISTORIC PRESERVATION UNDER DIRECTION OF THE NATIONAL PARK SERVICE. UNITED STATES DEPARTMENT OF THE INTERIOR | NAME AND LOCATION OF STRUCTURE T. A. MOULTON RANCH | | | | SURVEY NO. WYO 26 | HISTORIC AMERICAN BUILDINGS SURVEY SHEET 8 OF 13 SHEETS | LIBRARY OF CONGRESS INDEX NUMBER |
| --- | --- | --- | --- | --- | --- | --- | --- |
| | MORMON ROW ROAD | KELLY VICINITY | TETON COUNTY | WYOMING | | | |

T. A. Moulton homesteaded in Jackson Hole in 1908. In 1960 the National Park Service purchased his 160-acre ranch to add it to Grand Teton National Park. The Historic American Buildings Survey division of the Park Service documented the ranch through measured drawings.

needed money but also involves area artists, who contribute their work and in the process become more committed to the organization and its goals.

The Jackson Hole Land Trust, established in 1980, grew out of a recommendation in the county plan encouraging the donation of conservation easements. The Izaak Walton League provided support to help launch the land trust. In June 1980, the alliance and the league cosponsored a workshop on land conservation, inviting a representative of the Trust for Public Land to lead it. Several participants then established a local steering committee that met at weekly breakfasts during the summer to develop an organizational plan and recruit a board of trustees. A local foundation and several residents gave money to get the land trust established, and Jean Hocker, who had lobbied for the federal scenic area legislation while working for the league, was hired as its first director in 1982.

Since it wants to be able to work with all landowners in the community regardless of their positions on such controversial issues as plan-

SAVING AMERICA'S COUNTRYSIDE

ning, the land trust does not take positions on issues. Unlike the alliance, the land trust is not a broad-based membership organization; instead, it relies on its board and small staff to carry out its program. By early 1988, the land trust had acquired 2,110 acres of land plus easements on a further 3,229 acres, in thirty-nine separate transactions. In accepting land and easements, the land trust is primarily concerned about protecting scenic views and wildlife habitat.

At first the alliance and land trust shared office space and a secretary. They soon decided they could be more effective by reinforcing their separate identities with separate facilities. If the land trust was to be successful in working with conservative ranch families, it needed to be entirely separate from the alliance, which might advocate land-use controls the ranchers would oppose. According to Hocker, "Although the two organizations grew out of the same antecedents, they fill different niches and have grown in different ways."

Although the county government and the two nonprofit organizations are completely independent from each other, they bring three complementary and effective approaches to rural conservation in Jackson Hole.

## C. Informal Private Group

Most local nonprofit organizations have their origins in small, informal groups that arise out of concern for one or more community issues—as happened in Oley, Pennsylvania, and Jackson Hole, Wyoming. Although incorporated nonprofit organizations or officially sanctioned governmental committees are often more effective, informal groups may also contribute to rural conservation, as was demonstrated in the case of the Eaton County, Michigan, highway fight (Case Study 4). Organizers may decide they want to remain an informal group that meets to discuss issues from time to time, influences local policy, and mobilizes support in times of crisis or concern. The organizers may not want to be troubled with incorporating as a formal organization or take the time to meet on a regular basis or keep official records.

## D. Working through an Existing Nonprofit Organization

Sometimes, the initial organizers in a rural conservation effort already belong to the same existing organization—perhaps a nature club, historical society, garden club, or Grange. In such a case, that organization can lead the effort, on either a permanent or temporary basis. For example, the Amana Heritage Society, an established nonprofit organization in Amana, Iowa, created a temporary landmark committee that coordinated local conservation activities and directed the preparation of the community's historic preservation plan. The landmark committee took advantage of the society's ability to accept deductible donations and a state grant to fund its work. Later, the committee formed the nucleus of the board of directors of a new organization, the Amana Preservation Foundation.

Some rural communities already have a number of nonprofit organizations. There is usually considerable overlap of officers and members. A new organization might be the last thing anyone wants, since many people already have too many meetings to attend. In such a case, working through an existing organization may be preferable. A pitfall, however, to working with an existing organization is that it already may have a long agenda. Making rural conservation a priority may require so much time and effort that starting a new organization would be more efficient.

## III. GETTING STARTED

In the initial stages of organizing, two factors are important: a general recognition that the time is ripe for rural conservation action, and satisfactory individual involvement. Furthermore, it is important to begin building a strong base of leadership for the organization's long-term benefit.

### A. Timing

In organizing, timing is key. If there is no sense of urgency or widespread feeling that new issues need addressing, even a well-conceived proposal may fail. A crisis is perhaps the easiest way to spur action, despite the high potential for failure once a threat is on the doorstep. Threats may be less immediate, however. Perhaps a past crisis was resolved unsatisfactorily, perhaps it is time to fine-tune previous policies, or perhaps it seems that little things are adding up to major change, even if only a few people are doing the arithmetic. With appropriate education of the community, seemingly minor changes or past problems and decisions can become the kind of issues needed to inspire action.

---

CASE STUDY 3
_____

## Dubuque County, Iowa: Capitalizing on a One-Time-Only Chance to Create the Heritage Trail

Not every urgent reason to organize needs to be a threat. In the case of the Heritage Trail in Dubuque County, Iowa (1984 pop. 91,737), the Dubuque County Conservation Board and a nonprofit, all-volunteer organization, Heritage Trail, Inc. (HTI), capitalized on a unique opportunity to acquire a 25-mile railroad right-of-way in the rugged and picturesque Mississippi River valley. In 1979 when plans for the abandonment of the rail line became known—six years after a county plan had recommended its acquisition should the opportunity ever arise—the county government faced financial limitations because of a depressed local economy and could not assure funds for both acquisition and development of a public recreational trail. HTI arose to lead a seven-year effort to acquire and build the trail, in the beginning over the active opposition of adjacent landowners fearful of the adverse impacts

Norma Cade, a founding board member of Heritage Trail, Inc., is shown with a trail neighbor crossing a newly rebuilt railroad trestle. The bridge, one of more than thirty along the trail, was decked by volunteers just two months after title to the corridor was secured from the railroad. Visitors flocked to the trail from the beginning, when only a few miles at a time could be opened because of burned bridges and title questions.

of public use—vandalism, for example. "We were a buffer for the conservation board and handled most of the confrontation," comments Doug Cheever, HTI president and one of the organization's founders.

Key to the success of the fledgling organization was breaking down a seemingly overwhelming task into discrete, achievable projects. "We got started by asking people whom we thought might be interested in the trail to give us five hours a week for six months to get us off the ground," recalls Cheever. Step by step, with an eye to successful projects elsewhere in the Midwest and the help of the Iowa Natural Heritage Foundation (a statewide nonprofit land conservancy), HTI obtained the necessary approvals and opened sections of the trail to public use. As the trail grew, public awareness and support from trail users mounted. By the time that all but a short segment at the Dubuque end of the trail was completed in 1987, local businesses and more than 1,200 individuals had paid for more than half the cost of the trail—$235,000 for acquisition by the conservation board, and approximately $5,500 per mile for fencing and surfacing supervised by HTI volunteers. The volunteers donated an estimated 45,000 hours of work toward trail improvements and promotional activities over the five years it took to create the trail.

Today, an estimated 50,000 visitors use the trail each year, primarily for biking and hiking, offering a significant boost to the local economy. A modest fee supports one trail ranger and operational expenses. Says Art Roche, HTI's publicity chairman: "By far the most notable achievement is the preservation of this complete cross-county conservation corridor at a time when the 'window of opportunity' for accomplishing this was rapidly closing. The linear park is rich with human history, geological interests, and botanical delights. . . . Heritage Trail merges delicate prairie with rugged woodlands, public access with minimal disturbance, and private initiative with public ownership."

## Nuts and Bolts

*Meetings. Meetings should have a specific purpose and agenda, communicated ahead of time to participants. The person chairing the meeting should solicit questions and opinions from participants and clarify decisions that are made or deferred for further discussion. Participants should leave knowing what tasks they need to accomplish before the next meeting. A regular meeting time is useful so that participants can plan ahead.*

*Scheduling. A group's schedule of activities should be compatible with the rhythm of the community. In farming communities, winter may be the time for holding meetings or scheduling intensive projects. Expect to take a break during planting and harvest. "We sell a lot of cucumbers to pickle companies so everything else stops when we have to get the cucumbers out in June," reports a North Carolina county historic preservation leader. Beware of local pitfalls: only three people showed up in an Iowa community for a talk on rural conservation that was scheduled for the same night the local basketball team played its archrival.*

*Work space. Buy, rent, share, or borrow—someone's home, space at the town hall, a schoolroom, a restaurant, a church basement. Remember that an office is more than simply a place to meet and work: it is a symbol of the organization. Meetings may appropriately be held in private homes for the sake of convenience, but public meetings should take place in public spaces where no one would feel uneasy about attending.*

*Equipment and supplies. An organization's needs may be as modest as stationery and stamps. In most rural conservation organizations a typewriter and camera are used regularly, but even these often can be*

## B. Initial Organizers

The initial nucleus of people interested in organizing for rural conservation may be small and informal—perhaps only a few neighbors concerned about protecting the area where they live. In other communities, the initial impetus may come from government officials; two or three members of the planning board, for instance, may be concerned about community problems and want to enlist citizen support.

A small group of dedicated individuals can be particularly effective in the initial stages of organizing. A group of, say, five to fifteen means that everyone has a high level of participation. Members of a small group are likely to enjoy a personal sense of accomplishment when tasks are completed, strong group loyalty, and a sense of belonging. Such feelings are essential to sustain the group's momentum.

Early organizers are most effective if they draw allies from a cross-section of the community. It is natural for organizers to call on friends and neighbors for help. The danger is that such a group may be regarded as a social or political clique that does not represent the entire community. The failure of a rural conservation organizing attempt in a New Jersey township was largely the result of not including a broad enough cross-section of residents. Some of the more vocal farmers were not invited to the initial meetings for fear they would object to such an initiative. Once they learned about the proposed program, they lobbied energetically and successfully against it. Some of these same farmers later became leaders of a countywide effort to protect farmland, using many of the same techniques they had earlier opposed. The difference was that in the countywide effort they were invited to participate from the beginning.

A coalition of both old and new residents may result in a group with a variety of backgrounds and skills helpful to a rural conservation effort. In some communities, the initial organizers may be newcomers who moved to the community because of its rural character. They may realize the need to organize for rural conservation first because they have experienced the results of poorly planned change in other communities where they have lived. Those regarded as newcomers may include long-term residents who are not natives. Dorothy Riester, who chaired the Cazenovia Community Resources Project in New York, notes that even after living in the community for twenty years, she is still considered a newcomer (Case Study 6).

Successful organizers enlist people who reflect the different occupational, economic, educational, ethnic, religious, and age groups found in the community. In many rural areas, older residents own much of the land and are politically influential. Members of a prominent family, the school principal, or the president of a local company may be useful allies as well. After all, the intention of the group is to foster communitywide involvement in determining the future of that community.

## C. Leadership

Any successful organization needs leaders. Different organizations need different kinds of leaders, and often more than just one. Congenial mediator or articulate spokesperson, able coordinator or idealistic visionary, such individuals are the "sparkplugs," as one community organizer has put it. "Without able, dedicated, competent mobilizers," she says, "it's not likely that things will coalesce."[2]

In many groups, the work always falls on the same shoulders (as an old saying goes, "If you want to get something done, find a busy person"). All the same, it is wise to pass positions around, in order to develop the leadership skills of members and to encourage "informal leaders" to take on formal responsibilities. Many organizations have been left floundering when a key individual has resigned, moved away, or died. One staff member of a local nonprofit organization observes, "We have a 10 to 20 percent annual turnover in our trustees that needs to be planned for. We strive to have qualified replacements trained and waiting." Anyone with vision, tact, time, and commitment is potentially a leader, but he or she may need opportunities to gain community respect and to develop or refine skills such as public speaking. Presidents and board members need not possess professional experience in business, real estate, banking, or law. Hilda Fisher, for example, taught in the elementary school and became a leader in her church and a volunteer for the annual Oley Fair. These experiences made her a well-known and respected person in the community with a number of skills to bring to a leadership position in Oley's rural conservation project (Case Study 1).

*borrowed. More sophisticated equipment such as photocopiers, computers, or projection equipment for slide shows, films, or videotapes may come in handy. Consider buying used equipment or, better yet, obtaining donations of equipment from local businesses.*

*Transportation. Members can use their own cars to conduct inventories, attend conferences, and visit other communities, for which they may receive tax deductions. Check out using a vehicle owned by local government. The Big Sur Land Trust in California accepted the donation of a good used car that the executive director uses for organization business.*

## IV. DEALING WITH CONFLICT

Rural conservation is not without controversy, certainly. While much of a rural organization's work should be in support of its own proposals, the group may have to take a concerted stand against other proposals as well. Besides confrontation, lobbying, and litigating, techniques for dispute resolution may help in dealing with conflict and solving problems.

## A. Confronting a Crisis

One of the most frequent motivations for organizing is the eleventh-hour protest in a time of crisis. A rezoning controversy or a school closing are common examples. Angry and concerned, citizens band together to take action. Such a crisis can quickly mobilize many people, including those who might not otherwise become involved.

Though it may be easy to mobilize opposition in a crisis, it may be more difficult to reach a consensus quickly on a course of action. As one organizer has put it, "You get a group of people in a room; some want to sue; some want to form a citizens' group; some want to hire their wife's nephew who is a planner to do an impact statement to refute the existing impact statement. How is a group going to sift through all of these ideas and figure out what's going to work?"[3]

Whether a group has two weeks, two months, or two years to deal with a crisis, the odds of success are better if the group approaches the problem systematically. When a crisis develops or a potential problem is forecast, it is important for the group to meet with the concerned parties to explore all of the options and to seek possible solutions. Environmental conflict management techniques, described below, may offer alternatives to outright confrontation.

There are many reasons why last-minute efforts often fail. In many instances, the sponsor is already organized and has a paid staff to combat any opposition; in some cases, a political deal has already been struck before plans are made known to the public. To fight such opponents may require going to court—or the classic last-ditch demonstration in front of the bulldozer.

Win or lose, a crisis may stimulate a community's awareness and not only prompt action on related issues but also provide a basis for organizing a long-range effort. In Cazenovia, New York, for example, an unsuccessful attempt to prevent construction of a subdivision on a wetland was later helpful in gaining support for improved protection for other areas (Case Study 6). Once a crisis is over, it is important to evaluate the effort to determine what went right or wrong and why, to thank supporters and contributors, and to assess the group's strengths and talents to learn from the experience. Reflecting on her experience as part of the successful effort to stop the damming of the New River on the North Carolina–Virginia border, one organizer says:

> After you win, keep working. Old dams never go away; old water projects never go away. They're going to come back at you a couple of years later, or some other issue is bound to affect you. While you have power, while you've got people geared up, get them to keep going and do something positive to permanently protect it. It also makes you look better. Otherwise, you're just obstructionists or you're just anti-progress. Instead, get your group to be *for* something. Start saying "We don't just want to stop things; we want people to know that our area is a special place."[4]

Another valuable result of fighting a crisis is learning how to avoid other crises in the first place. Once organized, a group should develop an "early warning system" for discovering potential problems before project proponents have successfully made their way through the various stages of approval that usually are required. Monitoring the public notice section of local newspapers and attending governmental public meetings are generally useful steps. Many states have "sunshine" laws preventing closed-door meetings of elected officials where decisions are made, and citizen participation in the form of public hearings and comment periods for proposals often are mandated.

CASE STUDY 4

## Eaton County, Michigan: Fighting a Highway—and Winning

Sometimes an informal unincorporated group works best, and sometimes organizing around a single issue rather than rural resources in general works best. Citizens Concerned about I-69 is a case in point on both counts. This is also the story of a group that went beyond efforts to persuade and decided to lobby and litigate as well.

Eaton County, Michigan (1984 pop. 88,292), is largely agricultural, with much of it prime farmland. Farmers make their living from dairy products, livestock, corn, and wheat. However, the growth of nearby Lansing plus the construction of highways in the county have put considerable pressure on agriculture in recent years.

When, in the early 1970s, the Michigan Department of Transportation (MDOT) proposed connecting Charlotte and Lansing by a new sixteen-mile section of Interstate 69 that would sweep through much of the remaining agricultural land and encourage increased sprawl from Lansing, many of the county's farmers objected. The Eaton County Planning Commission and several township boards expressed concern as well. The proponents of farmland preservation recommended that the new interstate be placed alongside U.S. Route 27, an alignment that would use much less agricultural land. However, MDOT argued that the Route 27 alignment would destroy more wetlands (which proved not to be the case) and that the dogleg alignment (see illustration, p. 70) would serve anticipated development to the west of Lansing. In 1976, MDOT approved an environmental impact statement (EIS) (see *Environmental Impact Statements*, pp. 208–9) for the dogleg alignment.

In May 1976, Fred McLaughlin, a Lansing architect, read about the controversy in a local paper. McLaughlin, who was raised in rural Eaton County, sympathized with the farmers and decided to investigate. After studying the EIS and meeting with MDOT officials, he became convinced that the new interstate was not needed, or at least that the dogleg was not justified. With the support of several farmers in the area, McLaughlin set out to see what could be done.

In January 1977, McLaughlin met with several aides to the governor. "Their reaction was: 'You are right; we've got to call the chairman of the state transportation commission and tell him to put a hold on this project until we can look into it.' Well, my jaw fell. I could not believe I was getting that kind of reaction." The aides asked the Michigan Environmental Review Board to investigate. In April, however, the board concluded in a report to the governor that proper procedures had been followed and that there was no justification for changing the alignment. The governor concurred. Although McLaughlin and his colleagues lost this round, they learned an important lesson: They could make top officials pay attention to their concerns, but they were also going to need grassroots political support for their cause.

In early 1977 McLaughlin and a half dozen farmers established Citizens Concerned about I-69 (CCAI) as an ad hoc unincorporated group. They purposely chose a name that did not express a point of view so as to generate broad support in the affected communities. The group never had regular meetings or launched a formal membership campaign. However, it developed a highly effective informal network to get timely information to the people who needed it by telephone and newsletters. According to McLaughlin, the group did not need a high degree of organization. The meetings were usually held in someone's home and started with coffee and doughnuts and talk about crops and weather.

CCAI prepared a resolution calling for rerouting I-69 out of prime farmland. They avoided questioning the need for I-69 and avoided the obvious recommendation that it should parallel Route 27. CCAI had a reason for being vague: They did not want to appear to be telling MDOT where or how to build a highway because that would give MDOT the opportunity to marshal specific arguments against the resolution.

In 1978, CCAI took the resolution to most of the township and municipal boards in the county. The group planned each meeting carefully, deciding which members would make the best impression. According to

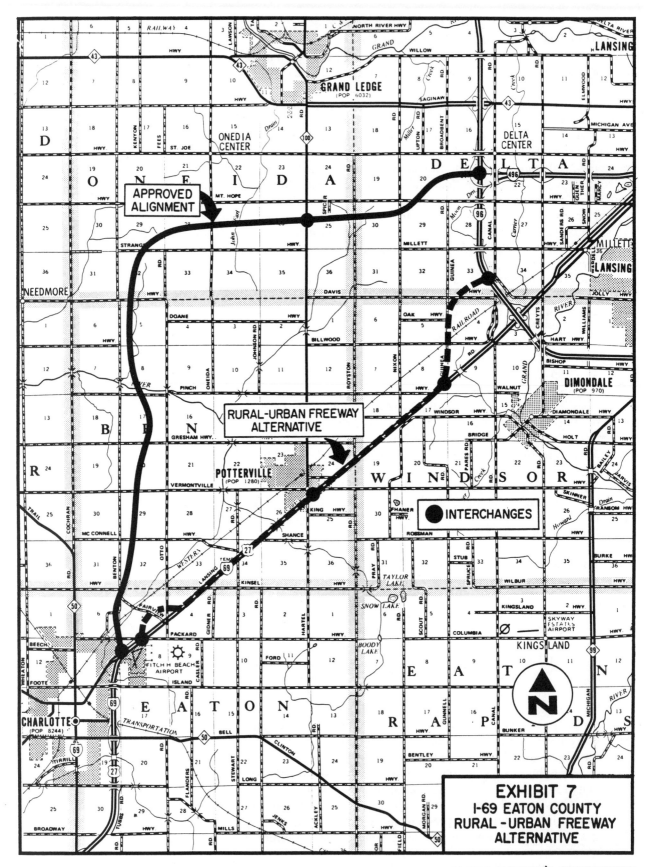

APPROVED ALIGNMENT

RURAL-URBAN FREEWAY ALTERNATIVE

● INTERCHANGES

EXHIBIT 7
I-69 EATON COUNTY
RURAL-URBAN FREEWAY
ALTERNATIVE

SAVING AMERICA'S COUNTRYSIDE

McLaughlin, "We were fortunate in having people in our group who were very well regarded in the area—through family and business ties. We made a real effort to be credible and we handled ourselves responsibly. Even MDOT staff said privately that we had been very fair in our dealings with them."

The boards of twelve of the sixteen townships in the county supported the resolution, as did key municipal councils, planning commissions, and the Eaton County Farm Bureau. This led to a turnaround vote of support for the resolution by the Eaton County Board of Commissioners, which had earlier agreed with MDOT's proposed alignment.

In addition, the press was supportive. Several editorials in the *Detroit Free Press* supporting CCAI's position, written after CCAI members met with the editor, were particularly helpful.

The group's members also contacted their congressman and senators. Howard Wolpe, who ran Senator Donald Riegle's Lansing office, listened sympathetically and gave them much good advice on strategy, on occasion assisting in making key contacts in the federal bureaucracy. Wolpe was himself elected to Congress in 1978 and continued to help.

In 1979 the group filed suit against MDOT, seeking an injunction against further development of the road, claiming that EIS procedures had not been followed and that inadequate attention had been given to farmland retention. Although the court dismissed the suit in August 1980, the litigation further delayed MDOT.

Disappointment over the lawsuit was overshadowed by great news from Washington. Wolpe's office called to say that a rider could be placed on the 1981 U.S. Department of Transportation (USDOT) and Related Agencies Appropriations Act to halt all work on I-69 for ninety days to allow for federal review and a new public hearing. A few weeks later several CCAI members drove to Washington for a meeting, chaired by Wolpe, with several top USDOT officials. A number of issues were discussed, but the meeting did not seem to be getting anywhere until one of the Eaton County farmers made an emotional appeal for immediate action. He predicted that if the road went through, it would spell the end of agriculture in the I-69 area within twenty years. According to McLaughlin, he told the officials to get serious and act, or he might as well head home to get on with his farming and watch Eaton County agriculture dwindle quickly to nothing. That simple statement seemed to have a greater impact on them than all the reports and figures. Later that day, USDOT staff called Wolpe to say that they favored reopening the issue. The rider on the appropriations bill passed the Congress.

The USDOT public hearing was held in November 1980. Most of the testimony and most of the witnesses, including CCAI's own highway and environmental consultants, supported the Route 27 alignment. In December, the U.S. Secretary of Transportation recommended that the highway alignment be moved to Route 27 in order to conserve farmland. Bowing to the pressure, MDOT reluctantly reopened the EIS process and finally, in December 1981, approved the Route 27 alignment.

Although CCAI no longer exists, it has left an important legacy. In addition to having achieved their goal, the former members now know they can have a say in their community's future. More tangibly, several were appointed or elected to positions of civic authority in the county.

*Opposite:* This page out of the environmental impact statement for rerouting Interstate 69 in Eaton County, Michigan, shows why the dogleg "approved alignment" of 1977 stirred such opposition. Ultimately, opponents to the alignment, who had coalesced around a concern for the impact on farms in the area, were successful in obtaining approval for an alternative alignment along an existing route. (Note the grid settlement pattern of the Midwest as reflected by secondary roads. Each section is one square mile.)

## What Does a Mediator Do?

## B. Resolving Disputes

Implementing cooperative approaches to problem-solving and to resolving disputes can make a rural conservation organization more effective in dealing with an immediate crisis. These approaches can help an organization to be creative in resolving the conflicting priorities inherent in land use and resource protection, whether or not a crisis is involved. Mediation is perhaps the best-known among techniques the Conservation Foundation has categorized as "environmental dispute resolution," all of which are voluntary and "involve some form of consensus building, joint problem solving, or negotiation" (Bingham 1986, p. 5).

Dispute resolution is characterized by a series of steps: mutual education of the interested parties, generation of options for resolution based on a jointly acceptable description of the issue and its potential impact, bargaining over the acceptability of the options, and, finally, agreement. A continuing relationship among the parties to implement the agreement may also result (Bidol, Bardwell, and Manring 1986, p. 13). For example, mediation involves someone without a stake in the issue who assists those with conflicting interests in exploring differences and discovering where they agree. A negotiated settlement meeting each party's most critical objectives is achieved by accommodations on lesser concerns; the mediator's objective is to identify an outcome in which each party could declare a partial victory. Dispute resolution, unlike binding arbitration or litigation, allows the parties to remain in control in reaching any terms or settlement.

Situations where dispute resolution can be used involve parties whose stake in the issue can truly be affected by the actions of the other parties; as one manual puts it, "If you could win in court, why talk?" (Bidol, Bardwell, and Manring 1986, p. 14). These situations also involve some amount of urgency and some room for bargaining even if the parties' values differ markedly. Using dispute resolution techniques without some sophistication in negotiation and ability on the part of the negotiator to assert the organization's interest, or without the guidance that a mediator can provide, could endanger the organization's effectiveness and public support (ibid.). On the other hand, these techniques can markedly enlarge an organization's options for achieving its aims beyond lobbying and litigating.

CASE STUDY 5

## Appalachian Trail, Connecticut: The Housatonic Valley Association Becomes Part of the Protection Solution

Sometimes a local organization may be able to provide a key role in resolving an impasse by adding its own thoughts to the dialogue or by committing itself to becoming part of the solution, or both. In 1983 the Housatonic Valley Association, a watershed conservation organization, ventured into a standoff among a landowner, the federal government, and local residents to help provide information, ideas, and finally a local commitment to protecting a portion of the land in dispute.

The issue involved protecting a 5-mile segment of the Appalachian Trail running through a tract of more than 2,000 acres in the northwestern hills of Connecticut. The corporate owner insisted on selling all or none of the tract to the National Park Service, which had authorization only to acquire a 1,000-foot-wide corridor, or some 300 acres. Even if it were to obtain congressional authorization to acquire the whole tract, the Park Service quickly learned that local sentiment was adamantly opposed to such extensive federal ownership in the three affected towns.

With approval from the three towns, the Housatonic Valley Association enlisted a state-sponsored environmental review team advising western Connecticut towns on the effects of proposed land-use changes. For this project, the team was composed of representatives from federal, state, and local agencies and the association, plus representatives from the Appalachian Trail Club and the Appalachian Mountain Club, voluntary groups responsible for trail management. Both the team and the association embarked on studies of the tract, the team to provide baseline information and preliminary maps and the association to refine the team's studies and inject ideas for resolution.

Federal ownership was of special concern to area residents. Farmers took a dim view of abandonment of prime farmland; wildlife and forestry managers worried that nuisance species would get out of hand with prohibition of timbering and hunting; and owners in the affected area feared recreational overuse and increased traffic. Moreover, one town's landfill and sand and gravel pit were located on the tract, which the Park Service stated should be terminated. The same town opposed removal of hundreds of acres of land ripe for development from its tax rolls.

With study and accommodation, a resolution of these competing and conflicting interests began to emerge. First, visible land along the trail was defined as a visual buffer area for permanent protection by the Park Service and the towns, leaving the way open for negotiation on exactly what that protection might entail. The company relented on its all-or-nothing stance.

The solution involved the acquisition by the Park Service of only scenic easements in much of the area under dispute, allowing continuation of forestry, farming, hunting, and even the landfill and sand and gravel operations (under strict screening and reclamation requirements). The corporate owner, working in conjunction with the association, will complete the master plan developed through the project by undertaking limited residential development on 200 acres and conveying more than 20 acres to expand a popular nearby state park.

---

## V. DEVELOPING A PROGRAM

Once the initial stages of organizing (and, perhaps, dealing with a crisis) are over, it is time to consider the long term. Where does the organization intend to concentrate its efforts, and what are those efforts to be?

The boundaries of the Waterford National Historic Landmark in Virginia include much of the land visible from the village, as illustrated by the topographic map (*right*). This is also the primary area of concern for the Waterford Foundation (Case Study 28). The delineation was intended to protect not only the village, but also its pastoral setting, shown in the aerial photograph (*opposite*). As development around Washington, D.C., spreads further into the countryside, the open land around the village has come under increasing pressure. In 1986 a developer proposed a major subdivision in the fields to the east of the village (see arrow), which could have jeopardized the integrity of the rural landmark. The developer eventually agreed to limit construction to the least visible areas of his parcel.

## A. Defining Boundaries

Among the initial tasks of organizing is determining a geographic area of concern. Often, the area can be defined by political boundaries—township or county lines, for example. If the organizers are concerned about a natural resource, such as their water supply, they might designate the watershed as their area of concern. Other factors such as property ownership, cultural characteristics, and economic conditions can also influence decisions about boundaries. The Chester-Sassafras Foundation began with a group of citizens concerned about quality of life in Kent County on the Eastern Shore of Maryland. They soon realized that the opposite shores of the Chester and Sassafras rivers, which defined the south and north boundaries of the county, were just as important as the county itself. They reached out to residents of both shores of both rivers as well as Kent County, and named their organization accordingly. In another case, the Waterford Foundation in Virginia used visual criteria to define its boundaries, including all of the land that was visible from the village (Case Study 28). In some regions of the country where rural populations are quite small and widely scattered, it may make better sense to work at the state level, as does the Montana Land Reliance, a land trust based in Helena.

## B. Assessing Community Needs

Along with an environmental inventory (Chapter 3), proof of a community's needs can be invaluable in building local support and in setting goals and objectives, as they are described below. Kim McAdams, director of the Brazoria County Park Commission in Angleton, Texas, says that assessing a community's needs can "eliminate the unknowns and get a true picture of the public you're serving. . . . The effectiveness of a needs as-

sessment is well worth the time investment. You'll learn things about your public you don't know, and be able to justify project proposals and funding requests."[5]

In Brazoria County, a survey of randomly selected residents, designed with the help of staff at a local university and assisted by volunteers, was conducted by telephone over a period of two months. The county learned that, contrary to popular belief, the beach was more popular than athletic fields and sports complexes; that water-oriented recreation was preferred over other types of recreation; and that residents were often unaware of what recreational opportunities were available. The county used its new knowledge to create a plan for a countywide park system to be developed through user fees and bonds and to sponsor the formation of the Cradle of Texas Conservancy, a private nonprofit organization designed to work with the county in the acquisition of the "unique areas with wide open spaces" valued by the survey's respondents.[6]

On the other hand, a show of modest support for rural conservation should not discourage organizers. Says a nonprofit organization director,

## Preparing a Budget

*Even an organization with very modest needs should prepare an annual budget that shows estimated expenditures by category and revenues by source. Making a realistic budget forces an organization to establish its priorities, provides a financial planning tool that reduces the time devoted to money spent at each meeting, and establishes fiscal accountability for all of the organization's decisions.*

*A budget can include the following categories:*

*Staff (salaries and fringe benefits)*
*Consultants*
*Office space (rent and utilities)*
*Equipment (e.g., furniture, computer, typewriter, and camera)*
*Telephone*
*Supplies (e.g., stationery, film)*
*Printing and photocopying*
*Postage*
*Publications (books and periodicals)*
*Travel (local and out-of-town)*
*Insurance*
*Special projects*
*Contingency (to meet unexpected needs)*

"There does not have to be unanimous agreement within a community for conservation to take place. There are always going to be some people who are not in favor of it."[7]

Setting priorities is a vital part of needs assessment. One helpful exercise for identifying issues and setting priorities is a brainstorming session, in which a group leader guides a discussion focusing on issues the group might address. Using a blackboard or large sheets of paper, someone records ideas as they are raised. Each participant then ranks each issue, assigning points as to its level of importance (Connecticut Trust for Historic Preservation 1982, p. 7). Another method of identifying issues and priorities was used in Thomas County, Georgia, where residents selected at random were asked to answer open-ended questions. Those interviewed were asked to discuss their concerns under each of four topics: social issues, jobs, governmental relations, and land use.

## C. Developing Goals and Objectives

Sometimes organizers are so anxious to get on with a program that they are reluctant to spend much time developing clearly stated goals and objectives. Yet, the investment of a group's time and energy in refining their vision and philosophy can result in more consensus in the initial stages, more efficiency as the program is being carried out, and more satisfaction at the end for having achieved "winnable" targets.

Goals are the link between the purpose of the organization and its activities or program. They are targets to work toward, such as "protecting the recreational opportunities that make our community special," "preserving our historic architecture and cultural identity," "making attractive, affordable housing available to all our residents," "assuring a future for agriculture in our community," or "assuring a safe water supply." Goal-making is the place to be ambitious, idealistic, and eloquent.

Objectives, however, are the specific outcomes the group needs to achieve to meet its goals. Objectives should be realistic and precise and help a group to measure its effectiveness in meeting its goals. They are usually stated in such terms as "to establish twenty-five miles of public hiking trails in this decade," "to conduct three educational tours of our historic areas each year," "to make thirty units of low-income housing available within five years," "to develop and enact an agricultural zoning ordinance within three years," or "to establish a monitoring system for wells in all parts of our community over the next year." Classifying the objectives as urgent, necessary, or desirable may help an organization establish its priorities.

After defining goals and objectives an organization needs to develop a work program or action plan that identifies those activities required to achieve the organization's objectives. Among other benefits, the work program defines the organization's financial needs, which in turn can lead to preparing a budget (see *Preparing a Budget,* left) and a fund-raising plan (2.VII). In a work program, each objective is broken down into a reasonable number of tasks that can be accomplished according to a specific timetable. For example, a new organization whose highest priority in its first six months is recruiting members must identify and assign all of the tasks associated with recruitment: designing and printing brochures; developing a list of potential members and contacting them; collecting, re-

Board members of the Madison County Heritage Foundation of Georgia hold a one-day retreat with a representative of the National Trust to discuss the needs of their rural county and set goals for the future of the organization.

cording, and depositing dues; setting up membership records; and acknowledging the new members.

The development of goals, objectives, and a work program are akin to the process a local government uses in developing a comprehensive plan (4.II). In either case, it is important to maintain flexibility. An organization or government should be willing to change its objectives and work program to become more effective in achieving its goals, or even to change its goals in light of a reassessment of community needs.

## VI. GETTING PEOPLE TO DO THE WORK

Once an organization knows what it wants to accomplish and has outlined its work program, it requires people to get the jobs done. Even small organizations need to decide who will do what: who will determine policy, type the minutes, collect the mail, speak to the press, and notify members about meetings. Each supporter brings certain skills, talents, and interests to the organization; the trick is to use them well. Establishing committees is an effective way to delegate authority and to divide the work. Volunteers can do much of the work required, but sometimes the most efficient means of getting things done is to hire someone to do the work.

### A. Volunteers

Every organization needs volunteers; at the very least the board members are usually volunteers. The extent to which a nonprofit organization or local government is able to enlist volunteers with various skills and backgrounds has considerable impact on its effectiveness and reputation. Quite apart from the service they perform, volunteers strengthen an organization by learning more about its goals and operations from their work. If members feel their involvement is vital to an effort, they are more likely to retain interest over a longer period of time and have a stronger sense of

## Looking a Gift Horse in the Mouth

*While many local groups have benefited from aid offered by other nonprofit organizations, whenever a nonprofit organization offers services that may be helpful, it is a good idea also to consider the organization's motivation. Universities, for example, provide excellent research, but it may be more extensive than necessary, tangential to the community's real concerns, and more academic than practical. Professors may be hoping for a stimulating educational experience for their students or may need to conduct field work for a research paper. In either case, while they no doubt also have the interest of the community at heart, and the community may indeed benefit, the project design may be dictated more by the academic calendar or by preconceived research considerations than by the community's specific needs. As another example, if a national organization offers its assistance in litigation, its interest may be setting a national legal precedent, whereas the local interest may evolve to the point where settling out of court may be preferable to preserve the ability of opposing parties to work together in the future.*

commitment to the organization's goals. They may also have a significant impact on public opinion. Just from numbers alone, it is easy to see that in Oley, Pennsylvania, volunteers have strengthened rural conservation's long-term credibility in the community. Of a population of three thousand, 7 percent, or more than two hundred voting-age residents, were involved.

Volunteers can perform routine tasks, such as making telephone calls or stuffing envelopes, but they may also be able to perform skilled tasks such as making maps, tracing deeds, or conducting tours. Occasionally, an organization's supporters donate professional services: a local attorney might be willing to draft articles of incorporation and by-laws; an accountant may audit financial records or administer grant funds; an art student might design a poster; a retired newspaper reporter might be willing to write press releases. Many rural areas have a number of retirees with a lifetime of experience to apply and enough leisure time to donate their services. Retired people who have moved to a new community often see volunteer work as a good way to become acquainted with new neighbors while making a contribution to their chosen community.

A Virginia group, the Friends of Staunton River, found that one of its members had worked as a nuclear power specialist for more than twenty years and could "run circles around" the local power company at public hearings by challenging their projections on demand for power generation. The Cazenovia Community Resources Project in New York was fortunate to have a professional geologist residing in the community who volunteered to map geological and water resources. Such informed volunteers provide a local group with invaluable assistance that is normally available only from paid consultants.

Keeping a file of members' or residents' skills and of who is willing to do what prepares an organization to use volunteers effectively. Some organizations distribute questionnaires asking members to volunteer for a variety of services. The actual request for each volunteer's help, however, is usually made in person once the volunteer coordinator or committee chair has verified that the volunteer is equipped to do the job. One of the most ticklish situations in coordinating volunteers is turning down a volunteer who is not capable of performing the task at hand.

Service organizations and youth clubs can often assist rural conservation programs. In Washington, the Yakima Valley Council of Camp Fire has adopted the Yakima River Greenway Foundation as one of its projects (Case Study 27). These girls earned badges by planting and maintaining trees in one of the Greenway parks.

Most volunteers appreciate being given a choice of tasks. People volunteer for a variety of reasons; knowing their motivations and using this information to assign them appropriate work is essential. Someone who volunteers in order to keep busy may enjoy an ongoing task such as compiling the group's scrapbook or heading the telephone committee. A new resident who sees community service as a way of becoming integrated into the community might be happiest working on a large committee with an assignment that will allow contact with a number of people.

Although volunteers are not paid, their work is important and they should be accountable for their actions. Volunteers who collect information or write reports need to be just as accurate as paid professionals. Volunteers who meet the public are official representatives of the organization; their behavior and ability to explain the organization's purpose and accomplishments reflect on the organization's reputation.

A group's leaders and staff should regularly acknowledge and thank all volunteers for their efforts. Publicizing the extent of volunteer services in an annual report, recognizing volunteers at the annual meeting, or holding a reception in their honor are good ways to let volunteers know they are important.

## B. Enlisting the Support of Other Local Groups and Agencies

It is important to work with other local organizations to develop cooperative approaches to local problems and to avoid duplicating efforts. Even the smallest rural community can call on a number of agencies and organizations for assistance. Local organizations such as the Rotary, Ruritans, Lions, or Home Demonstration Club may be valuable sources of labor in rural conservation programs (7.V.E).

There may be several local governmental agencies whose help can be enlisted. The sewer authority, for instance, may employ an engineer who can identify sources of groundwater pollution. The county planner may be able to identify areas where development pressures are anticipated. In addition, there may be local representatives of agencies who can be of assistance. In Oley, Pennsylvania, for example, the District Conservationist trained volunteers to use the Soil Conservation Service's soils inventory to produce drafts of the natural resource maps needed. The State University of New York, in another example, provided invaluable assistance to the Cazenovia Community Resources Project. Universities, along with their allied research institutes or Cooperative Extension Service offices, frequently offer their services to communities, often at no charge or at low rates.

## C. Outside Experts

Outside experts can provide information on a variety of matters ranging from fund-raising to zoning. A planner from another township can be invited to show slides at a public meeting to illustrate the impact of uncontrolled growth in order to help citizens envision the future consequences of continuing unrestricted growth in their community. Agricultural preservation proponents in Brattleboro, Vermont, for example, asked speakers from other places to visit and discuss successful projects. While outside

## *Orienting Professional Visitors*

*The following suggestions should help make the visits of those who visit your community more productive:*

*• Before the visit, provide visitors with previous reports, such as the comprehensive plan or a summary of goals and objectives, plus copies of the local newspaper and the organization's newsletter, so that visitors gain a sense of the community before arriving.*

*• Be honest about any opposition to an outsider's involvement in the program. Warn a speaker if a challenge is anticipated at a public gathering.*

*• Be candid about community problems. If certain controversial issues are not discussed publicly in the community, say so.*

*• Let visitors know what to expect. Will boots be needed for a visit to a dairy farm, or will a warm jacket and hat make a day's outing more comfortable?*

*• Provide visitors with a map and a tour of the entire community. Don't focus only on what is unique and overlook the everyday, characteristic features of the area.*

*• Introduce visitors to a cross-section of the community—including farmers, nonfarmers, and business people.*

*• Visit places where local people go; suggest morning coffee with farmers at the local diner. Don't just go to the chic new restaurant.*

*• Invite visitors to attend community events such as fairs, church services, and public meetings and make them feel welcome. Participating in local events will give outsiders an opportunity to know the community better.*

# A Conservation Handbook
## For Amana Villages

Cover of the handbook prepared for residents of the Amana villages in Iowa to advise them on appropriate techniques for the restoration and maintenance of their buildings and land.

professionals can supplement local efforts with information or guidance, they cannot make up for a lack of local interest or leadership.

A number of state, regional, and national groups have professional staffs who are available to give lectures, help brainstorm, and offer advice (Chapter 6 and Appendix). For example, when Amana, Iowa, first became interested in preparing a historic preservation plan, it sought the assistance of the Iowa State Historic Preservation Office in developing a scope of services and in identifying prospective consultants. The agency not only supplied half of the funding for the project but also advised the steering committee on questions to ask prospective consultants and helped to evaluate the consultants who were interviewed.

Outside experts are sometimes mistrusted. Local leaders should therefore choose the outside professional with the most appropriate credentials and empathy for the particular community and consider carefully who introduces the visitor to the community. For instance, farmers may listen with more interest to a visiting landscape architect who is introduced by the county Extension Agent rather than by the president of a garden club.

### D. Paid Consultants

If the amount of work to be done is limited, it is usually simpler to contract with a consultant than to hire an employee who may require not only a salary but also benefits, office space, and assurances of continued employment. Hiring a consultant also encourages a group to accomplish its work within a set amount of time, and a paid expert can give the group clout: often, the word of an outsider carries more weight.

Before a group decides to hire a consultant, it should know what specific tasks it wants the consultant to perform. Establishing a steering committee is an effective way to begin the process of hiring a consultant. This committee sets the project's goals and objectives and develops a detailed work program or outlines the scope of the needed services. The steering committee may find it helpful to investigate similar projects in other areas to develop a list of potential consultants, determine the going rate for such work, and set a realistic calender in which to complete the project.

If the project is relatively large, then the committee may decide to issue a request for proposals (often called an RFP), inviting prospective consultants to bid for a contract by outlining their approach and cost of services. For a small job, the committee may wish to retain the services of a consultant already known to the group without going through the more time-consuming RFP process.

Once the consultant is chosen, both the organization and the consultant should develop a contract or letter of agreement. The contract should be as specific as possible, covering the work to be done, responsibilities of the organization, due dates, payment schedule, and provisions for amending or terminating the contract. The steering committee should designate one of its members as the official contact for the consultant.

Consultants can either be paid a fixed fee for portions of the work as they are completed or by the hour. A fixed-fee contract reduces the chance for unpleasant surprises—if, for example, the work takes longer to complete than expected. On the other hand, an hourly fee may work best if it is difficult to estimate how long a project will take or to know at the beginning what all of the tasks may be. If a consultant is paid by the hour, then it is wise to agree beforehand on the maximum number of hours that are needed. Having several phases allows for a periodic review of the work, promotes regular communication, and helps to assure that the project stays within budget.

The organization is ultimately responsible for the work produced on its behalf and has the right to question the consultant's work and recommendations until all is understood. Likewise, the group should be sufficiently flexible to revise its contract if conditions change or the services are too complex to complete in the time allowed.

## E. Paid Staff

Making the decision to hire staff is a big step for nonprofit organizations and many local governments. Accordingly, many start small. When volunteers can no longer do the job, a part-time secretary may be the most efficient use of scarce funds. Much of what applies to retaining consultants applies to hiring staff. A written job description ensures that the applicant, the group's board, and any existing staff know what is expected.

In searching for staff members, organizations should not overlook candidates within the community. Just as there are many skilled volunteers in rural communities, there may be residents who can apply a variety of work and life experiences to a new career in rural conservation. Phoebe Hopkins, for example, started out as a steering committee member for the

### Choosing a Consultant

*An interview gives the steering committee and the prospective consultant an opportunity to get acquainted. Three consultants are usually a good number to interview. An effective way to start is to ask consultants to explain their approach and relevant experiences. Interviewers should ask consultants to talk about similar projects and note how well they seem to understand other communities. It is often helpful to ask why a consultant wants to do the work and which aspects of the project would be most stimulating or challenging. The prospective consultant's attitude, understanding of the community, and ability to communicate ideas are important things to consider. A good consultant will use the interview to ask questions about the community.*

*The interview, the quality of the proposal, recommendations from previous clients or other professionals, and price should be the basis for choosing a consultant. It is not always a bargain to accept the lowest bid: if a higher one comes from a more qualified candidate and is still within the group's financial means, it could be a good idea to accept it.*

*An intern—either paid or volunteer —can often fulfill some of the functions of a consultant or a staff member. Some schools and professions require internships for degrees and licensure. Interns can be used most effectively in the following circumstances:*

*• When their work is supervised by a professional who is qualified to advise in the subject;*
*• When they work on a specific, well-defined project;*
*• When they have sufficient time to devote to a project to assure its completion; and*
*• When the project is straightforward. Controversial or sensitive projects are probably beyond students' capabilities.*

*Interns may also be available through nonprofit organizations, such as the National Trust's Yankee Intern Program, sponsored for the northeast states by the magazine of the same name, and the Center for Environmental Intern Programs Fund.*

Oley Resource Conservation Project before she became the project's single paid staff member. Her knowledge of the community as well as her background in environmental education made her a good choice for a staff position. Even if residents have less professional experience than outsiders, they may more than make up for it in commitment and firsthand knowledge of the community.

## VII. FUND-RAISING

Of all of the tasks confronting the Oley Project, fund-raising was the most daunting. Yet, Phoebe Hopkins recalls, "It was easier to raise money than I thought. Knowing exactly what the money was to be used for and having a list of groups and individuals to ask for a donation really helped. It got easier each year, too."[8] The development of a realistic fund-raising plan is the first hurdle. The plan should identify both the amount of money to be raised in a set period of time and potential sources of funds.

In most communities a nonprofit organization can obtain donations more easily than can the local government. Although donations to both may be tax deductible, many residents are reluctant to contribute funds to a local government that is also taxing them. If a local government needs voluntary contributions for a rural conservation effort, it may be more successful if it raises the necessary funds through a cooperating nonprofit organization.

Individual contributions, both large and small, are the best sources of funds in most communities. Local businesses and corporations, or national corporations with local facilities, are also good bets. When looking outside the community, the organization will usually have more success starting with regional or state sources. Gifts from national foundations, for all of the publicity they generate, are the least likely sources of funding, particularly the kind of steady, year-to-year unrestricted contributions that keep an organization running. Success in fund-raising on the national level generally requires resources or issues of national significance and evidence of successful local fund-raising. There are also, of course, grants from state and federal agencies (Chapter 6).

Most organizations find it more difficult to raise money for general operating expenses than for special projects. People like to see specific results from their money. Helping to buy an endangered property is more exciting than donating money for office rent and telephones. There are, however, several effective ways to generate operating expenses. Membership dues are a prime source. Sometimes a local government might contribute, especially if the rural conservation effort is organized as a governmental committee. Many communities rely on an annual event or benefit, such as a festival or crafts fair, to raise a substantial portion of their expenses (Case Study 28). Sale of publications or other items can also help.

For special projects that may ultimately yield a financial return, it may be possible to persuade a foundation to make a "program-related investment," or PRI. Most foundations make grants out of income earned from investing their principal. Federal rules governing foundations, however, permit the investment of principal (that is, making loans) in projects related to the foundation's program—hence the name. Generally, the rate of interest and other terms on such a loan are more favorable than commercial loans, but few foundations have taken advantage of PRIs, as it is often difficult for recipients to identify income-producing activities that could repay such loans. The Gates Foundation made a PRI loan to Colorado Open Lands for its limited development project for Evans Ranch. The loan aided in the purchase of the ranch, and the land trust was able to repay the loan through selective sales of the land (5.VIII.B).

## VIII. EVALUATION

Every organization, no matter how successful, needs to take stock of its activities, ponder the future, and consider possible changes in its structure, approach, and outlook. Evaluation can help an organization to face new circumstances, whether those circumstances are a dramatic increase in members or a failure to achieve an important objective. Each year the board, other leaders, and staff of an organization should reserve time to reflect on their efforts. This questioning process may encourage a group to end programs that have achieved their primary objectives and to consider new programs. At the end of its first year, the Amana Preservation Foundation in Iowa instituted a series of Saturday morning breakfast meetings to review its accomplishments and to make plans for the future. The breakfast meetings, in contrast to monthly board meetings on Thursday evenings, allowed the board to concentrate on the organization's needs when they were more relaxed. At one of these meetings the board decided it lacked the visible projects needed to increase local support. Consequently, the foundation undertook several activities that it could accomplish in a relatively short time and could involve other constituencies. With the assistance of school children, Boy Scouts, and others, it planted an orchard, reconstructed historic fences and lanterns along one village street, and began enhancement of the community's lily lake.

Those who are deeply involved with a group may miss strengths and weaknesses in their own program. Bringing in an outsider to help evaluate programs may be useful in gaining a fresh perspective. For instance, the regional offices of the National Trust for Historic Preservation offer assistance to groups developing goals and evaluating programs, as do the community development agents of the Cooperative Extension Service. Of course, the experience and sensibilities of the individual providing the outside perspective are of paramount importance. For several years, the Piedmont Environmental Council of Warrenton, Virginia, invited a British planner, who had advised it on the establishment of the organization, to spend a week annually helping the staff and board to evaluate the past year's program and to plan for the next.

Some groups find that getting away from home helps the evaluation process. Isolation from everyday concerns and a change of environment, plus recreation and socializing, can promote a more creative and objective examination of the organization. Participants usually return from such retreats with renewed interest and enthusiasm.

## IX. CONCLUSION

Effective organizing is more an art than it is a science, but it is hardly a mysterious art. The skills you bring to initiating and managing your rural conservation efforts are the same skills you use at home, on the job, and in your leisure-time activities. Many of these are "people" skills: learning to

## Hints on Fund-Raising

*Here are a few suggestions for getting your organization's fund-raising off to a good start:*

• *Develop a positive public image before trying to raise money.*
• *Use every contact imaginable— neighbors and friends of board members, officers of local corporations and civic groups, wealthy people who grew up in the area but moved away, people owning second homes in the community.*
• *Make personal contact with a prospective donor. If the person making the visit or telephone call or writing the letter knows the donor, personal contact should be even more effective.*
• *Talk or write about the program before requesting a donation. Why is it needed? How will it benefit the community? What will it cost? Be brief, be direct, and don't be embarrassed by having to ask for money.*
• *Ask for specific amounts or items. Judge in advance what a donor can afford.*
• *Keep records of volunteer time as an indication of one form of community support. Occasionally, volunteer time can be used as an in-kind match for grants.*
• *Don't give up in the face of delays and rejections. Fund-raising requires patience as well as energy.*
• *Keep people informed of the organization's progress and invite them to events. Once people have given money, they have a vested interest in its success.*

## Recovering from Failure

*Rural conservation organizations do suffer setbacks. Such setbacks may not be all bad, as one nonprofit director, Dennis Collins, says: "The most important thing about a failure is, you never fall back to square one. It's never a total failure because you've changed the perceptions of people whether you got what you wanted or not" (telephone conversation with author, August 1986). Even so, dealing with discouragement and a loss of income following a poorly attended event, or a defeat on an important zoning issue, is difficult. To make an effective comeback, the group needs leaders determined to accomplish the group's goals in spite of the setback.*

*An organization can learn from what went wrong by asking: Where did our strategy fail? Did we need more resources—more money, people, information? Did we fall short on publicity? Were we too dependent on one or two individuals who did not help as we had expected? Were communications weak among our members? Do we need more programs to be of real service to the community? Once a group knows what its problems are, it can begin to solve them. One nonprofit management consultant has this encouragement for organizations facing difficulties: "Emphasize that the purpose of looking at problems is to find ways to make the organization* better. *It is not to cast blame or wallow in guilt. The Greek philosopher Heraclitus said, 'You can't step in the same stream twice.' . . . Learn from your mistakes, but do not dwell on them. . . . The secret is to keep trying" (Flanagan 1981, pp. 271–72).*

judge people and situations and to apply the right amount of persuasion and incentives to bring about the best possible outcomes. Still other skills are managerial: determining how you can best organize your time and resources (including people) to get the work done. Like any art, however, learning to organize well takes practice: to learn and improve on the skills you need to be successful in rural conservation, you need to plunge in.

**Hilda Fisher (third from left) meets with other members of the Oley Resource Conservation Project's steering committee to plan activities and evaluate progress. Meetings around her kitchen table often ended with a glass of mint tea and home-baked desserts, and time to chat.**

3

# Analyzing the Rural Community

## I. INTRODUCTION

Learning about your community is an important and enjoyable part of a rural conservation program. To implement a rural conservation program and persuade fellow residents of the need for protection, you need both general information about your community (see *Collecting General Information*, pp. 86–87) and specific data about natural, historic, and agricultural resources in your community: what they are, where they are located, and how they are threatened or can be enhanced. This detailed information is often called an environmental inventory (or an ecological or natural resources inventory). Many environmental inventories do

Stow Witwer reminisces about ranch life. His barn is virtually a museum of Weld County, Colorado, history. Older residents can provide a community with invaluable information for an environmental inventory.

## Collecting General Information in a Community

*Community leaders embarking on a rural conservation program should be able to answer basic questions like the following:*

- *What is the history of our community? When did most of the settlement take place and why? How have land uses and the local economy changed over the years?*
- *What level of local government most directly affects decisions about rural resources in our community? The county? The township?*
- *Are there other local government entities, such as water or school authorities, that influence the fate of our community's resources?*
- *Who are the key officials in our community? What are their names, titles, and responsibilities? Are they elected? Appointed? Salaried? Full-time? Does their influence go beyond their official responsibilities? Where does their support come from in the community? Who are the un-official leaders? How do they exert their influence?*
- *What does the latest census reveal about our community? What are the statistics on population, age, sex, race, education, housing, occupation, and income? Have there been major changes since the last census? Is the population growing or declining? Getting richer or poorer?*
- *What are the principal businesses in our community? How many people do they employ? To what extent are residents employed in the community?*
- *Is there an official comprehensive or master plan for our community? How helpful is it? Is it used as the basis for decision-making? Does it take rural conservation issues into account?*
- *What ordinances and regulations affect private property? Is there a*

not include cultural, historic, and scenic resources. We believe this is a mistake.

An environmental inventory usually consists of a set of maps showing the location of resources and problem areas and a companion report describing the resources, how they were identified, why they are important, what threats they face, and how they can be protected. An inventory may also include drawings, photographs, lists of species, statistics, and the like.

The last step in an inventory, the analysis of the data, is probably the most important. The analysis should provide both local governments and nonprofit organizations with an objective basis for selecting the most important environmental issues to address.

Unfortunately, once completed, many inventories sit on the shelf, particularly if they are done by outsiders with little community involvement. You can guard against this by considering from the start how the inventory will be used and organizing the data for easy retrieval by your community's decision-makers. Knowing what information you need and how it will be used will help you to guard against the twin dangers of collecting too little or too much data. Too little makes it difficult to reach wise decisions about land use—decisions which will be accepted in the community and which, if necessary, will stand up in court. On the other hand, collecting too much data, in addition to wasting time, can result in missing the forest for the trees.

Your community's environmental inventory should provide the information necessary for making sound decisions on land use. It should be the major source of information used by local government in land-use planning and in designing ordinances to guide development. Using the inventory, planning boards can steer development away from such important resources as wetlands, prime farmland, easily erodible slopes, scenic vistas, and historic sites, or require appropriate adjustments to developments that will affect these resources. Property owners, too, can use the inventories to determine the appropriateness of their land for specific uses.

An inventory also establishes base-line data, allowing a community to monitor the effects of future changes on clean water, wildlife, prime farmland, and other quantifiable resources. For instance, a major aspect of the inventory in Oley, Pennsylvania, was the mapping of groundwater and measuring stream flow. As a result of the inventory, Oley can monitor the effects of future limestone quarrying on the water table and hold the quarries' owners accountable for changes (Case Study 1).

Finally, an environmental inventory has educational value: it can be used to inform fellow citizens about the environment and to build consensus for a protection program.

The environmental inventory conducted by the Cazenovia Community Resources Project (CCRP) in New York illustrates the inventory process throughout this chapter. Cazenovia's inventory convinced many Cazenovians that their town is a very special place that should be protected from uncontrolled development. It has also resulted in the creation of effective new ways to guide the community's future.

## II. PREPARING AN INVENTORY

Preparing an inventory entails first deciding what information to include and then marshaling the necessary resources to accomplish it.

# A. What Information to Include

The information included in an environmental inventory depends upon the type and number of resources present and the threats to those resources. Almost all communities need to know about such basic resources as soils, water, habitat for valued wildlife, and significant historic buildings. Most communities also have more specialized needs. A county in Nebraska, for instance, might identify the location of segments of the Oregon Trail that should be protected, while a Michigan county might map abandoned railroad rights-of-way as potential recreation trails and sanctuaries for native grasses. A county in California may have an urgent need to identify hillsides prone to mud slides, or a county in South Carolina might wish to pinpoint the nesting sites of bald eagles.

Ideally an inventory will be comprehensive and identify all of the community's significant resources. The more comprehensive the inventory is, the more likely it is that a community will discover potential problems or opportunities. For instance, a community may already know that a proposed dam will flood prime farmland, but a comprehensive inventory might also show that the impoundment will also destroy habitat for valued game and a prehistoric Indian burial ground.

A community should guard against collecting and mapping too much data: potential users may become overwhelmed by the detail and fail to take into account the most important findings. The inventory need only contain sufficient information to raise the necessary questions about proposed changes to the community's environment. Mapped data on soil types, for instance, does not have to be accurate to the foot, but it should delineate general areas where different soils are located. If a subdivision is proposed in an area where clay soils might cause foundations to crack and prevent adequate percolation from septic systems, the planning board can insist that the developer pay for a more detailed, site-specific study to demonstrate that the actual building and septic system sites are not on such soils.

Although a comprehensive inventory may at first seem expensive, it is usually more cost-effective to conduct an inventory all at once than to inventory separate categories over a long period of time. Much of the information collected for one aspect of the inventory is necessary for others. Some communities, however, do not have the financial resources, personnel, or governmental commitment needed to undertake a comprehensive inventory at one time. Others may urgently need information about a particular resource. Such communities may concentrate on one or more resources of immediate concern in the community, such as wetlands, historic sites, or prime farmland. In such instances, the inventory may be expanded as changing circumstances demand or as additional time and money become available.

There are a variety of ways to record inventory information. They typically involve the use of forms, maps, and photographs. Inventories for certain resources should follow standard formats. For instance, the Soil Conservation Service has a specific format for soil surveys, and most states use a particular format for historic-building inventories. For other resources, where there may be no standard formats, the community must decide how to organize the information it collects.

*zoning ordinance? A subdivision ordinance? How effective are they? What state laws affect private property?*

*• What state and federal regulations directly affect our community? For example, are there properties in the National Register of Historic Places? Are there wetlands or coastal zones regulated by state law? What land is owned by the federal or state government?*

## Resources Inventoried and Mapped in Cazenovia

*Geological Resources:*
  *Surficial geology*
  *Sand & gravel deposits*
  *Unique geological areas*
*Soil Resources:*
  *Soil type*
  *Slope*
  *Depth of bedrock*
  *Depth to seasonal high water
    table*
  *Permeability*
  *Soil erosion potential*
*Water Resources:*
  *Groundwater resources*
  *Aquifer recharge areas*
  *Surface water*
  *Wetlands*
  *Flood hazard areas*
  *Cazenovia Lake watershed*
  *Surface water drainage*
*Habitat:*
  *Woodlots*
  *Deer winter shelter areas*
  *Fish spawning areas*
*Agricultural Resources:*
  *Prime agricultural land*
  *Farmer-owned & -leased land*
  *Agricultural districts*
*Architectural & Historic Resources:*
  *Historic buildings survey*
  *National Register nominations*
*Recreation Resources:*
  *Recreation areas*
  *Recreation activities*
*Visual Resources:*
  *Visual inventory*
  *Viewsheds*
*Composite analysis maps:*
  *Critical resources*
  *Sensitive resources*
  *Residential suitability*
  *Industrial & commercial suitability*
  *Critical farmlands analysis*

*(Town of Cazenovia, N.Y., Land-Use Guide: A Report of the Cazenovia Community Resources Project [Cazenovia: Town of Cazenovia, 1984], pp. 47–48.)*

Even if some resources require special formats, the community can ensure compatibility of the different parts of its inventory so that various types of information can be compared and analyzed. For instance, maps should generally be prepared at the same scale. All maps, photographs, and other documentation should also be labeled and numbered so they can be used and stored in a systematic manner. Investigators should always note the source and date of any information. The community should establish a single place to file all recorded information and assemble a library containing reports and reference books used in compiling the inventory.

## B. When to Conduct an Inventory

Conducting an inventory at the beginning of a rural conservation effort provides a sound basis for decision-making and is an effective way to ensure that proponents can back up their positions. Early publication of the inventory findings can build support for a newly organized rural conservation program. Since properly conducted environmental inventories are usually not controversial, they are good initial projects. Other logical times to conduct an inventory are prior to developing or amending a master plan or land-use ordinance.

## C. Who Conducts the Inventory

Local governments, which need the information for preparing comprehensive plans and land-use ordinances, usually sponsor environmental inventories. Although some rural counties and townships have staff planners who can conduct inventories, most rely on consultants. Volunteers from the community are frequently overlooked as a source of assistance. Using a combination of local government staff, consultants, and volunteers and designating one person as the inventory coordinator usually produces the best results. The coordinator can assure that the work gets done, that the format for data is consistent, and that the information collected is accurate and unbiased. The coordinator should have training and experience in ecologically based planning. Many, but not all, graduates of university programs in landscape architecture, planning, geography, and environmental science receive this kind of training.

STAFF

Many counties have full-time planners, although few rural townships can afford them. In addition to preparing a county inventory and plan, or contracting for their preparation, a county planner may be able to assist townships in preparing theirs. In many states, counties are not broken down into townships (Virginia, for instance), or, if they are, planning may not be a function of township government (Illinois, for instance). Regardless of the availability, dedication, and skills of staff planners, they seldom have all of the skills necessary to complete a comprehensive environmental inventory alone. In New York the Cazenovia Community Resources Project (CCRP) received considerable advice from Madison County's planner. Since he was the only planner for the county, the amount of time he could devote to Cazenovia, one of sixteen townships in the county, was necessarily limited.

## Cazenovia, New York: Using an Inventory to Build Consensus for Rural Conservation

Cazenovia is typical of rural communities just beyond the fringe of metropolitan areas—but more beautiful than many, and therein lies the problem. Its rolling farmland, historic village, wooded ridges, large lake, and clean streams attract many who would like to settle there. Cazenovia, with a population of 5,997 (1984) and an area of 50 square miles, has a full range of retail services and recreational opportunities, a library, a newspaper, a small college, and good schools—with the added benefit of Syracuse just down the road providing city conveniences. Until the 1970s, the community was far enough from Syracuse— a 20-mile drive—to have preserved a distinct sense of place and to have escaped the suburbanization that was the fate of towns nearer Syracuse.

**Residents in most communities can identify views that make their hometowns distinctive. For residents of Cazenovia, New York, the dairy farms and wooded ridges make their community a special place worth protecting.**

This lithograph provides a bird's-eye view of Cazenovia in 1890. Today, most of the structures are still standing, although the railroad no longer exists, and most of the elms have succumbed to Dutch elm disease. Old views are of great assistance in tracing architectural and landscape history.

But as thoughtful town residents watched homes on 1-, 2-, and 3-acre lots sprout up around the village and the lake they asked, How many more and how long before Cazenovia becomes just another Syracuse suburb? They knew that Cazenovia's historic character, lake, and farmland might not survive the growth such assets attract. When the National Trust for Historic Preservation announced its demonstration program for rural communities in 1979, Cazenovians saw a possible fit with their needs.

The township's history of successful conservation efforts appealed to the National Trust: an informal citizens group—later incorporated in 1969 as the Cazenovia Preservation Foundation—had been working since the early 1960s to document and protect historic buildings in the village. As a result of the group's successful campaign to revitalize Albany Street, Cazenovia's main street, a number of downtown businesses voluntarily restored their storefronts and replaced unattractive signs. The foundation had also protected the banks of Chittenango Creek within the village and established a trail along it. Furthermore, the Cazenovia Advisory Conservation Commission, established by the town board in 1974 to advise the township on environmental protection, had identified the township's significant wetlands and was ready to take on new responsibilities. Above all, a number of Cazenovians were con-

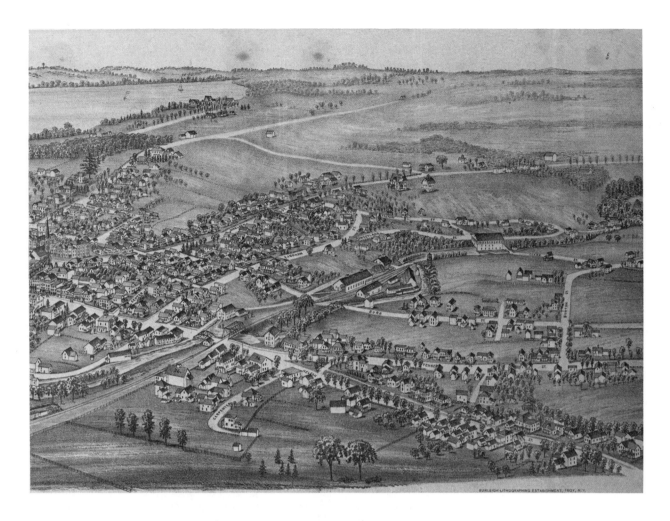

cerned about their community, had conservation experience, and were willing to devote time to the protection of their town.

While there had been efforts to protect historic buildings, wetlands, and the creek, less had been done to protect other resources, particularly farmland and the lake. Although dairying is still a major occupation in Cazenovia, farmland is threatened by development. Subdivisions of the large estates surrounding the lake not only mar the scenic views of the lake but also threaten water quality as increased quantities of lawn fertilizer and effluent from septic systems find their way into it.

A lawsuit over drainage problems made many township leaders realize that the town needed to pay closer attention to conservation. In 1967 the state district health officer gave approval for septic systems for twenty units to be built on fill over a wetland at the northern end of the lake. As one might expect, problems soon developed with the septic systems. The residents of the subdivision sued the developer, the state, and the township. By approving the subdivision, they argued, the state and township were partly responsible for the problem. The township eventually agreed to put in a drainage system, and the state put a moratorium on further development in the area. The suit forced township leaders to realize that inappropriate development threatened not only

The village of Cazenovia was laid out in 1794. In the 1960s, conservation leaders initiated a successful program to help businesses on Albany Street preserve their historic storefronts. This experience helped to prepare conservationists for the broader goal of protecting environmental resources throughout the township.

their environment but municipal coffers as well. The town passed a new subdivision ordinance that addressed the worst problems, but many residents believed that they also needed a more comprehensive approach to environmental protection.

In 1980, the National Trust selected Cazenovia as a demonstration community, and Don Callahan, the town supervisor—the elected chief administrator of the town—appointed representatives of key municipal and service organizations to a committee to oversee what became known as the Cazenovia Community Resources Project (CCRP). Callahan asked Dorothy Riester, a noted artist and leader of the Cazenovia Preservation Foundation, to chair the committee. The town board, the planning board, and the conservation commission were all represented on the committee. There were also representatives of the separately incorporated village of Cazenovia, the unincorporated hamlet of New Woodstock, the farmers, and the businessmen.

The Faculty of Landscape Architecture at the State University of New York (SUNY) in Syracuse was a major source of technical advice throughout the project. Richard Hawks, an associate professor of landscape architecture at SUNY, specializing in communitywide environmental planning, provided guidance to the steering committee from the outset. Hawks saw an opportunity not only to put into practice new mapping techniques but also to provide experience to his landscape architecture students.

Hiring a part-time staff to supplement and coordinate the work of the community volunteers was essential to the success of CCRP. Terry LeVeque, a landscape architecture graduate student at SUNY, was hired as a graduate assistant in the summer of 1980 to help with the environmental inventory. She later became project director, working under the supervision of the steering committee.

The CCRP steering committee decided to follow a four-step process:

1. Define the assets of Cazenovia to be protected and learn about threats to them;
2. Study techniques that could be used to protect those assets;

Cazenovia conservationists were particularly concerned about the protection of their lake and wetlands. A connecting portion of these wetlands (not visible here) was filled in and built upon in the 1960s, resulting in drainage problems and community commitment to environmental protection. These wetlands are also visible in the aerial photograph on p. 106.

3. Recommend specific actions for the town, village, and private groups to undertake; and

4. Assist in the implementation of the recommendations.

The steering committee then established six task groups to focus on Cazenovia's agricultural, historic, environmental, municipal, recreational, and visual resources. The committee invited additional volunteers with appropriate skills and backgrounds to join the task groups.

The task groups, whose activities are described throughout this chapter, set out to inventory community resources. The volunteers and LeVeque collected information in a variety of ways: by studying maps and other documents in town, village, and county offices; asking farmers to fill out questionnaires; interviewing hunters about wildlife habitat, and hikers and cross-country skiers about recreation trails; and documenting every pre-1930 building in the town. Volunteers also sought information on population trends, the agricultural economy, the needs of small businesses, and potential threats, such as sewer lines planned by the Madison County Sewer District. Most of the volunteers regarded the inventory as an exciting opportunity to learn about their community. Some commented that they traveled back roads they did not know existed.

LeVeque and the volunteers recorded much of the information they collected on maps. These maps became the basis for analyzing both resources and problems and were used in CCRP's public presentations (see *Resources Inventoried*, p. 88). The conservation commission still uses the maps for its review of subdivision requests.

Education was an important ingredient of the project. In December 1980, each task group made a report at a major public meeting in the village hall. As a result of the meeting, Cazenovians became more aware of just how special their community was, and more people began to volunteer their services. LeVeque periodically prepared press releases on CCRP, and the weekly *Cazenovia Republican* covered many of the project's activities. In the summer of 1982 the paper ran a popular series of articles on the township's assets (see illustration, p. 245). Each article was written by a CCRP volunteer and highlighted a different resource. Moreover, information from the inventory was used to prepare pamphlets for owners of historic houses on how to preserve them and for residents of the lake watershed on how to protect its water quality.

When the inventory was completed in the winter of 1981, the CCRP steering committee started the second step in the process, namely, analyzing the community's resources in relation to the techniques that could be used to protect them. To conduct this analysis, SUNY students supervised by Hawks prepared a series of overlay maps that made possible the comparison of resources (see illustration, p. 125). CCRP also recommended to the town board that it establish an ad hoc planning commission that could receive the recommendations of CCRP and consider new ordinances. Although the town already had a planning board, it had enough to do reviewing applications for subdivisions. The planning commission was able to spend its entire time considering new ordinances without other pressures.

The final major CCRP activity was the preparation of its *Land Use Guide* (Town of Cazenovia 1984), which summarized the CCRP's work and presented its recommendations. The *Guide* makes recommendations for the protection of each natural resource, cultural resource, and "character zone." (The report divides Cazenovia's landscape into six character zones—areas such as the lake watershed and the farmland which have similar physical and cultural characteristics.) The *Guide* assigns responsibility to specified governmental groups and nonprofit organizations for follow-up to assure implementation. In 1987, both the town and village boards adopted the *Guide* as their official plans.

The conservation commission now uses the list of "critical" and "sensitive" resources identified in the *Guide* for environmental reviews of proposed developments prior to making recommendations to the town and village planning boards. The identification of these resources has helped to provide an objective basis for the commission's work and strengthened its role.

The Cazenovia Preservation Foundation has used the environmental inventory to identify important properties that should be protected through acquisition. It has already acquired an abandoned railroad right-of-way for a trail and two properties on the outskirts of the village to help establish a proposed greenbelt. One of these will have covenants placed on it to protect open space and historic buildings prior to resale.

Most importantly, community leaders now believe they are in a much better position to make wise decisions about land use in Cazenovia. Professional planning help will certainly be needed in the future, but the data they have collected and the skills they have developed will make it possible for them to better evaluate proposed developments and make better use of outside experts.

---

## CONSULTANTS

A community can either retain a consulting firm to undertake an entire environmental inventory or retain individual consultants with skills in particular fields unavailable within the community. If the community foresees a possible lawsuit—perhaps by a developer whose subdivision application may be denied on the basis of environmental data collected for the inventory—it is a good investment to retain a consultant with unimpeachable credentials to conduct the inventory, or at least review and endorse its findings. The consultant may do the work alone or supervise and coordinate the work of volunteers. CCRP retained a consultant to help to design the scenic resources portion of the environmental inventory (Case Study 8).

Assigning a member of the staff or a volunteer resident to work closely with any consultant is essential. A consultant working without community involvement can easily miss features that residents can point out.

## VOLUNTEERS

An inventory done with volunteer labor is usually less expensive and more sensitive to the community's needs than the typical inventory conducted solely by staff or consultants. A major advantage of volunteer involvement is that citizens become more knowledgeable about inventory techniques and their own community; this knowledge stays in the community long after the inventory is completed. Few communities, however, can rely entirely on volunteers, since they will probably lack essential skills and sufficient time to complete all the tasks required.

A staff coordinator or consultant may be able to give volunteers on-the-job training. Also, some universities, nonprofit organizations, and state agencies offer short courses on techniques for inventorying certain resources. Cazenovia's inventory was accomplished by a combination of volunteer and staff work. CCRP was fortunate to have the volunteer talents of such residents as Andy Diefendorf, a professional geologist who mapped the geology and groundwater, and Faith Knapp, a landscape architect who gathered information on wetlands, wildlife habitat, and woodlots. Both were also leaders in the conservation commission. In all, some two hundred volunteers were involved in the inventory. In addition to providing a valuable service, the volunteers became more committed to conservation because they had a personal stake in assuring that the data they collected were reliable and used.

Work can be divided in many ways depending on the scope of the task, the budget, the calendar, and the skills, knowledge, and interests of the citizen volunteers. Separate task groups for each resource worked well in Cazenovia. In some communities, volunteers are able to make maps, type reports, take photographs, or accomplish other necessary tasks. In other communities, volunteers may only have the time to serve as advisors and informants to consultants.

## OTHER ASSISTANCE

Communities conducting environmental inventories can also get free assistance from a number of sources. The Soil Conservation Service's (SCS) District Conservationists, for instance, can provide invaluable assistance. The SCS District Conservationist for Madison County gave extensive help to CCRP in mapping soils and wetlands. He also helped the agricultural task group to survey farmers' needs for land.

High schools, colleges, and universities can assist in inventory projects and, in the process, enrich the curriculum for students in biology, geography, geology, history, landscape architecture, architectural history, planning, wildlife ecology, and other courses (2.VI.B).

## D. Maps

Maps are the principal means of storing and presenting much of the data collected during an environmental inventory. They are the most effective medium to show the locations of community resources at a single glance. A reproduceable base map includes the standard information that the surveyors wish to have appear on all of the individual resource maps, such as contour lines, surface water, roads, and buildings.

For CCRP, a State University of New York (SUNY) landscape architecture student prepared a base map by splicing together U.S. Geological Survey (USGS) maps. Project volunteers used aerial photographs and their own observations to update the map. Volunteers were especially interested in locating their homes and understanding resources present on their properties. Working on inexpensive paper maps was a valuable learning experience for Cazenovia's citizen volunteers. They did not worry excessively about mistakes, knowing they could make more finished copies later.

The appearance of maps can affect the acceptance of the inventory. Even if a community group conducts its own inventory and makes its own maps, its final maps should be of professional quality. A cartographer, drafting teacher, landscape architect, engineer, geologist, or land-use planner can offer advice on graphics and format and review the maps for accuracy and appearance.

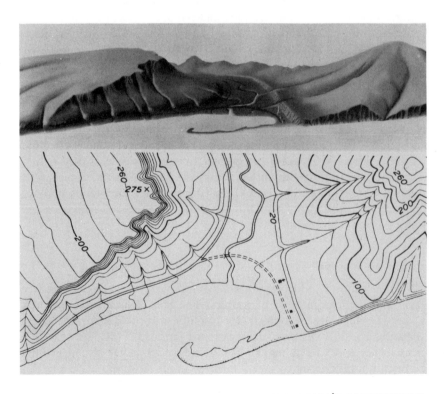

The relationship between topography (*top*) and contour lines (*bottom*).

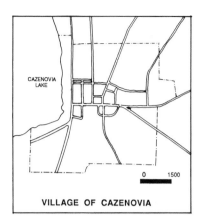

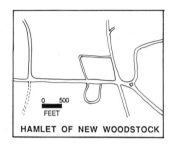

VILLAGE OF CAZENOVIA

0    1500

HAMLET OF NEW WOODSTOCK

0    500
FEET

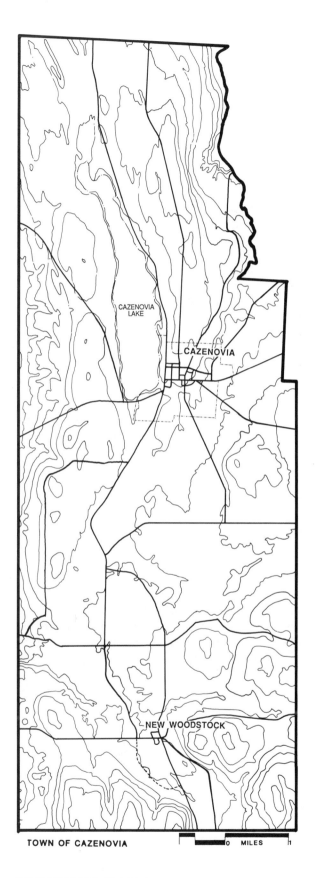

CAZENOVIA
LAKE

CAZENOVIA

NEW WOODSTOCK

TOWN OF CAZENOVIA

0    MILES    1

CAZENOVIA
COMMUNITY
RESOURCES
PROJECT

## Preparing a Base Map

*Base maps for rural areas are usually made from U.S. Geological Survey (USGS) topographic maps, available for the entire country. In addition to topography, the maps show the location of surface water, major wetlands, roads, buildings, and other features. The most detailed topographic maps measure 7.5 minutes of latitude and longitude on a side. These quadrangles (or "quads") cover fifty to seventy square miles at a scale of 1:24,000—that is, one inch on the map equals 24,000 inches (2,000 feet) on the ground. Topographic maps in the 7.5-minute series are available for most of the United States and are the ones most frequently used for base maps. For areas not covered by the 7.5-minute series, less detailed smaller-scale topographic maps are available.*

*You will probably need to use several USGS maps. The relevant portions can be pieced together and the resulting collage photographically reproduced on Mylar to make a base map. Mylar, the trade name for the most commonly used material for making high-quality, durable maps, is a transparent plastic sheet that can have information transferred to it photographically or by pen, stencils, and ready-made "transfer letters" that stick on. Photographic techniques may also be used to expand or reduce the size of the preliminary base map.*

*You can add the following to the base map:*

*• Buildings and roads constructed since the USGS maps were made;*
*• Up-to-date municipal boundaries;*
*• Some adjacent areas, since some resources in need of protection, such as aquifers, may extend beyond the community's boundaries;*
*• Title block with the name of the community and state, the name of*

## E. Sources of Data

Once a community has a base map, it should decide which individual resources to inventory and then collect the data. Data can be collected from a number of sources. Much of the information should be readily available in previous studies done by local, state, or federal agencies and nonprofit organizations, but it is wise to make sure those studies are reliable. In Cazenovia, CCRP found that SCS had completed the county soil survey and had studied the lake's watershed; the Cazenovia Preservation Foundation had also inventoried historic buildings in the village; and the conservation commision had surveyed wetlands. For much of the data all that was needed was updating and adjusting the scale of existing maps to make them consistent with the new ones.

Each community needs to decide how many maps to prepare. Some, like Cazenovia, prepare a large number (see *Resources Inventoried,* p. 88), but others might combine several features and produce far fewer maps. A minimum number of maps might be three: one that shows land use; a second that shows the most important resources (such as historic sites, prime farmland, and wetlands) and constraints (for example, steep slopes and high water table); and a third that shows the suitability of land for development (3.VII).

EXISTING SURVEYS AND MAPS

The soil surveys prepared by SCS are often the single most useful source of information for an environmental inventory. The survey maps and explanatory text contain information on much more than agricultural potential, indicating slope, wetness, depth to bedrock, and other valuable information. The SCS District Conservationist can provide great assistance in understanding soil survey data.

USGS has maps, publications, and services that can be helpful to many aspects of the inventory, including topography, geology, and water resources. Maps can be ordered from USGS or, in many areas, purchased at local stores.

In addition to USGS and SCS maps, there are many others that may prove useful. Some states, such as Iowa and Massachusetts, have general-purpose maps showing a variety of environmental information. Tax maps generally show property lines and are available for most communities. Cazenovia, for example, used tax maps to record information about the ownership of individual farms. Of course, the scale of these maps may not be the same as the community's base map, and so they may require enlargement or reduction, but many printing and engineering firms have the necessary photographic equipment to accomplish this.

AERIAL PHOTOGRAPHS

All rural communities have been photographed from the air by USGS, the Agricultural Stabilization and Conservation Service, or other agencies. Used to produce most maps, these photographs are also valuable in developing resource maps for a community. They can be used to identify such features as land use, new construction, drainage patterns, types of vegetation, wetlands, landslides, and forgotten historic ruins. Some older aerial photographs can be particularly useful in identifying past land uses and historic sites.

USGS is preparing "orthophotoquads," which are aerial photographs that correspond to the topographic quadrangles. They are available for many communities. Unlike most other aerial photographs, orthophotoquads are corrected for the distortion present in all photographs.

Color and infrared photographs are available from USGS for many areas. Infrared photographs, using special film and filters, highlight certain features, such as water, wetlands, and certain types of vegetation, even when they are printed in black and white. USGS also sells satellite photographs, which are particularly helpful when large areas are being surveyed. However, the Landsat photographs currently available to the public do not have sufficiently high resolution to be useful for most county and township environmental inventories.

With the aid of an inexpensive stereoscope, overlapping aerial photographs can be used as stereoscopic (or stereo) pairs to create dramatic three-dimensional images similar to the commercially produced photographic pairs our great-grandparents enjoyed on their hand-held stereoscopes. Stereo pairs can be helpful in identifying such features as stone walls, trees, rock outcroppings, and buildings, as well as problems such as erosion. An inventory team studying historic resources in remote parts of the U.S. Virgin Islands used stereo pairs to identify sugar-plantation ruins lost in tropical forests.

OTHER SOURCES

State natural resources departments, regional planning commissions, and numerous other agencies and organizations can help. State offices responsible for coastal management are good sources of data. Most coastal states received grants under the Coastal Zone Management Act (6.VI.E) to undertake comprehensive inventories in the late 1970s. State transportation departments often have detailed environmental information and aerial photographs prepared as part of the highway planning process. Universities may have valuable reference materials as well as personnel who can provide assistance. Local boards of health, watershed associations, and sewer authorities are other potential sources of information. Previous studies by consultants, students, universities, government agencies, or nonprofit organizations may also prove helpful. If a federal or state environmental impact statement has been prepared for a nearby project, it may contain useful information about environmental resources and sources of data (see *Environmental Impact Statements,* pp. 208–9).

Engineering, planning, landscape-architecture, and other area firms may have maps or data and be able to recommend other sources. Not all firms, however, are willing to share the information they have collected; others may expect to be paid for their time or at least reimbursed for such out-of-pocket expenses as map reproduction, telephone calls, and postage.

Residents, too, may have valuable information to contribute to an inventory. A farmer may know a great deal about soil and other resources; local hunters may be able to provide information about wildlife habitat; and an elderly resident, whose family has saved letters, diaries, farm journals, and photographs, may have an attic full of historic resource materials.

*the inventory project or plan of which the map is a part, the name of the group that made the map, the date it was made, a legend that defines symbols, indication of scale, and a north-pointing arrow;*

*Once all the desired information is on the Mylar base map, you can reproduce as many inexpensive paper copies as you need.*

Slope is usually described as percentage. Ten percent slope, or a "one in ten slope," means that the ground rises one foot in elevation for every ten feet of horizontal distance. Slope information can be determined from USGS topographic maps using a special ruler that measures the distance between contour lines and gives a reading in percentage of slope. It can also come directly from SCS maps, where the range of slope percentages is noted for each soil type. Most communities find the slope information from SCS maps satisfactory for their purposes. An SCS District Conservationist, a landscape architect, or a land-use planner can assist in analyzing slope information.

## F. Field Work

Although data can be obtained from maps, aerial photographs, and other reports, there is no substitute for information collected in the field to verify and supplement existing sources. Field checks should always be made before important decisions on sites are made. In many cases, the sharp divisions between different resources or conditions shown by lines on maps do not exist on the ground. Soil types, for example, tend to grade from one to another. Winter—if there is not too much snow—is often the best time to conduct field work, since the leaves are off deciduous trees and there is less vegetation to hide conditions. A camera (see *Photographing the Countryside,* pp. 246–47), notebook, and map are essential equipment; a tape recorder may be useful.

Field work can be fun, and it provides volunteers with the opportunity to get to know their environment first-hand. There are risks, however: Field surveyors should be informed about any residents (or their animals) likely to be unfriendly, trespassing laws, and natural hazards such as poison ivy, ticks, and snakes. They should also consider such seasonal activities as hunting, and plan their visits accordingly. To reduce the suspicion that often greets surveyors, the sponsoring organization should publicize the inventory, make advance arrangements for visits, and keep the authorities informed (see *Assuring a Good Reception,* p. 102). If possible, surveyors in rural areas should work in pairs; using a "buddy system" is safer, more enjoyable, and more efficient. For example, one person can photograph a property while the other records on a map where the photograph was taken; one can drive while the other takes notes.

The following sections describe how to inventory specific features, resources, and problems. Communities do not need to inventory all of these; each community needs to decide its own priorities.

## III. INVENTORYING NATURAL FEATURES

## A. Relief

Relief is the most basic feature mapped by any community. Since most of the work has already been done by USGS and SCS, it is the easiest feature to map. It is important to identify steep slopes, where loose soils and light vegetative cover may be prone to erosion or landslides. Slope information, available on topographic and soil maps, is essential in identifying areas appropriate for development and those best left alone. Slope is usually described as a percentage (see illustration, below) and is usually mapped in ranges, such as 0 to 8 percent, 8 to 15 percent, and so forth. The percentage at which a slope becomes too great for safe construction varies depending on soil conditions, climate, bedrock geology, vegetation, and construction technique.

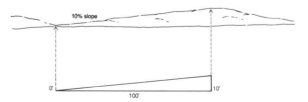

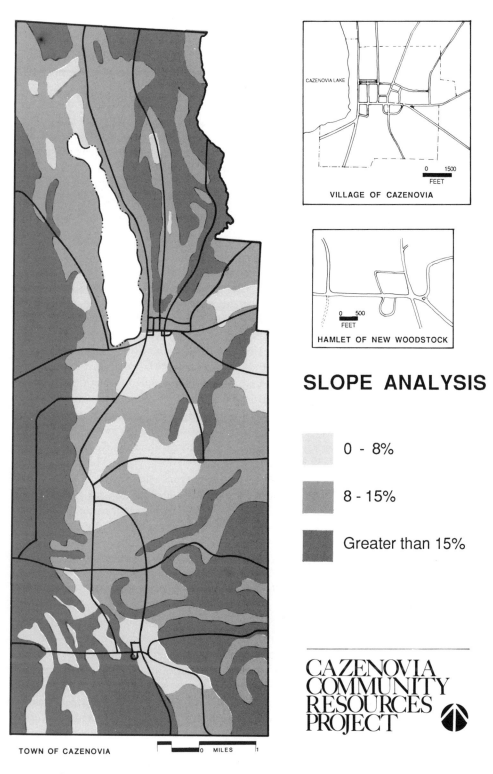

VILLAGE OF CAZENOVIA

HAMLET OF NEW WOODSTOCK

## SLOPE ANALYSIS

0 - 8%

8 - 15%

Greater than 15%

CAZENOVIA
COMMUNITY
RESOURCES
PROJECT

TOWN OF CAZENOVIA

## B. Geology

Geology is the key to understanding why the land is shaped the way it is, why some areas have abundant groundwater and others none, and why

## Assuring a Good Reception

*To assure that field surveyors have a good reception, the sponsoring organization may find the following steps advisable:*

- *Arrange for introductions from friends and neighbors where possible.*
- *Make appointments in advance to visit at times convenient for the property owner.*
- *Publish a notice of the inventory with the names and photographs of the recorders in the local newspapers or send notices to property owners.*
- *Supply surveyors with a letter of introduction on the letterhead of the local sponsor verifying the project.*
- *Supply the police or sheriff with the names of surveyors, the license numbers of the automobiles they are using, and the field work schedule, in case residents complain about suspicious people taking notes and photographs or driving slowly past their homes.*

some have rich topsoil and others poor. The geological inventory provides information about a community's soil, vegetation, and water resources, and also points to such potential problems as earthquakes, sinkholes, landslides, and aquifer contamination. A study of a community's geology also determines the location of sand, gravel, stone, clay, coal, peat, and other useful minerals.

Although some communities may need a professional geologist to conduct an inventory, most can rely on geology maps prepared by USGS, state geological surveys, universities, and other sources. Unfortunately, USGS geological maps are not as extensive as the topographic maps. Assistance in interpreting information and in mapping data is often available from the SCS District Conservationist, a high school earth-science teacher, or a geologist at a nearby college. Much information about such geological features as sand and gravel deposits and depth to bedrock can be obtained from SCS maps.

### C. Soil

Many people mistakenly assume that soil surveys are useful primarily for agriculture. In fact, they provide vital information on the suitability of soils for construction, recreation, water impoundment, and many other land uses. Because of soil's interrelationship with so many other natural features and processes, soil often reveals more about an area than any other single resource. Many soils with an abundance of clay, for example, drain poorly, shrink, and swell, presenting problems for both agriculture and construction. Other soil characteristics—such as depth of topsoil, susceptibility to flooding, and potential for erosion—can also limit an area's usefulness.

Communities generally do not need to conduct their own soils inventory because the SCS surveys cover most of the country. The quality of the surveys varies with their age. The more recent ones are more accurate and thorough, and include more information on soil characteristics for land uses other than farming. The SCS District Conservationist can assist citizens in interpreting the soils data and understanding soil properties.

Soil scientists have developed a system for identifying soils and assigning them to "soil series" on the basis of such factors as particle size, mineral composition, organic content, and degree of acidity. More than fifteen thousand soil series have been identified in the United States. Each series is given a name, usually derived from the name of the location where it was first identified. A single township may have twenty or more soil series; in Cazenovia there are forty-six. Each series is further subdivided into phases, based on percentage of slope, depth, and other features.

A soil survey consists of maps, descriptions of each soil phase, and charts that describe the best uses and limitations of each. A typical survey rates each soil phase for its suitability for different crops, trees, wildlife habitat, construction, septic systems, and water management.

Soil scientists make use of topographic maps, geological maps, and aerial photographs to prepare soil surveys. They also conduct extensive field work, studying vegetation and digging pits to analyze the soil's depth, texture, acidity, and wetness. Their maps, superimposed on aerial photographs, delineate boundaries between soil phases, although in many areas soil phases grade from one to another gradually.

A section of the Madison County soil survey map showing soils found near Cazenovia Lake. The first two letters for each area refer to the soil series and the third letter refers to the slope class. "HnB," for instance, refers to Honeoye silt loam, with a slope class of B, or 3 to 8 percent. The description of HnB in the survey reveals that this series is well-suited for a variety of crops, but only moderately well-suited for construction, because the substratum does not drain well. "Ce" refers to the Carlisle muck series. As the name implies, it represents wetland.

Environmental inventories require extensive field work. Here an SCS soil scientist delineates soils information on an aerial photograph as part of a complete soil survey in Pottawattamie County, Iowa. The soil auger in the foreground is used to take subsurface samples.

If SCS has completed its soil survey of the county, the main task is transferring the information from the SCS maps onto the community map. Although one SCS map incorporates all of the information about soil for a given area, it may be more useful for the community to record different characteristics on different maps. CCRP, for instance, chose to make separate maps for soil groups (series with related characteristics), slope, depth to bedrock, depth to seasonal high water table, permeability, and soil erosion potential.

In addition to soil surveys, SCS has prepared farmland maps for many counties confronting development pressures. These maps show prime farmland (land that has the best combination of physical and chemical characteristics, growing season, and moisture supply needed to produce sustained high yields with proper management), unique farmland (land used for specialty crops such as cherries and cranberries), and farmland of state and local importance.

## D. Water and Related Resources

A study of water resources is a basic component of any environmental inventory. An inventory of water resources can identify locations of both groundwater (water found underground) and surface water (such as streams, ponds, and estuaries); water quantity; current uses and future needs; existing and potential threats to water quality; wetlands and flood plains; and scenic areas. The inventory can also establish base-line data on water quantity and quality that can then be compared with data collected in the future to measure deterioration or improvement in the community's water supply.

With professional supervision, volunteers can collect and map much of the data. Since setting up a water study and analyzing the data require professional expertise usually not available in rural communities, it may be necessary for a community to seek assistance from a regional, state, or federal agency or a professional consultant. The SCS District Conservationist can assist a community in compiling and analyzing much of the available water-related data. State agencies responsible for health, natural resources, and geological surveys, regional planning commissions, watershed associations, water and sewer authorities, and health boards can also provide data, assist in mapping water resources, and help to monitor water quantity and quality.

Water quantity can be determined by estimating the volume of surface water and groundwater reserves, studying stream flow, and surveying yields from municipal and residential wells. Such studies, which often require extensive drilling, can be expensive. Sometimes valuable information can be obtained from the logs of commercial well drillers. For a fee, USGS can assist a community in analyzing its water resources. Oley, Pennsylvania, for example, contracted for such a study (Case Study 1).

The USGS Hydrologic Atlas series includes maps of groundwater and surface water for parts of the country. In addition to identifying water supply, the maps indicate such potential problems as floods, sedimentation in streams, and salinization of aquifers in coastal areas.

SURFACE WATER AND WATERSHEDS

Identifying watersheds lets a community know what runoff water drains into which streams, lakes, wetlands, and reservoirs. Watershed boundaries (see illustration, p. 20) are generally defined by the highest points of land between bodies of water. USGS topographic maps help in making these determinations. A community can use watershed maps to keep polluting activities off land draining into reservoirs and other waters that should be kept clean.

Maintaining the water quality of Cazenovia Lake was a concern of CCRP. For a lake of its size, its watershed is unusually small, resulting in a slow turnover of water and making the lake vulnerable to pollution from septic systems, lawn fertilizers, and sedimentation. CCRP mapped the lake's watershed and recommended stricter land-use controls within it.

## GROUNDWATER

Groundwater comes from aquifers, geologic formations that yield water in usable quantities. The aquifer can be bedrock or unconsolidated sand and gravel. An aquifer recharge area is the surface area where rainfall or runoff seeps through the ground into the aquifer. Protecting aquifers and their recharge areas from pollutants is especially important for a community dependent on groundwater for human consumption or irrigation. The geological inventory should indicate the location of aquifers, aquifer recharge areas, and land uses that may contaminate aquifers.

## WATER QUALITY

Keeping water supplies free of pollution is essential for every community. Unfortunately, many communities do not realize a problem exists until water quality is monitored. Although there have long been programs which monitor water supplies for waterborne diseases, many communities have not tested for chemical pollutants, such as gasoline leaking from deteriorating underground tanks.

State health or environmental departments routinely test water quality and may be able to do all of the necessary monitoring for a community. In some cases, however, a community may need more intensive monitoring than the state is capable of providing. Water pollution is generally classified as point source (coming from a known source, such as a storm sewer or discharge from a factory) and nonpoint source (coming from a general area such as farm fields or a subdivision with septic systems). Potential sources of pollution, such as landfills, feedlots, and gas stations, should be mapped.

## SEASONALLY HIGH WATER TABLES

The water table is the level below which the soil is saturated with water. Some areas with high water tables during certain times of the year have periodic problems with septic systems and wet basements. These areas can be identified through the soil survey. CCRP mapped seasonally high water tables and recommended that areas with water seasonally within two feet of the surface not be built upon.

## WETLANDS

A map of wetlands shows a community and property owners the locations of these vital resources. There can be considerable controversy over what areas should be classified as wetlands, since the controls on their use may be quite restrictive. Many can be identified through soil surveys, which indicate poorly drained soils. Vegetation is also a useful indicator:

Aerial photographs are invaluable aids to environmental inventories. In addition to showing land use, they make possible the identification of such resources.as wetlands, which are important for maintaining a community's water quality and protecting wildlife. This aerial photograph of Cazenovia shows a wetland extending from the north end of the lake to the upper edge of the photograph. The subdivision to the east of the wetland (see arrow) was built on fill over what was once part of the wetland.

many plants prefer wetlands or can exist only on them. Infrared aerial photographs can help to distinguish between wet and dry areas.

The U.S. Fish and Wildlife Service, which is conducting a National Wetlands Inventory that includes all of the nation's coastal and inland wetlands, is an excellent source of assistance. Wetlands are classified on the basis of hydrologic, geomorphologic, chemical, and biological factors. About 40 percent of the United States (exclusive of Alaska and Hawaii) has now been mapped. Information on the inventory is available from wetland coordinators in the regional offices of the service.

FLOOD PLAINS

All communities should identify flood plains so that construction on them can be avoided or controlled. The Federal Emergency Management Agency has mapped flood plains for some seventeen thousand communities. These maps are designed to be used by communities in developing protection programs. USGS is also in the process of mapping flood plains, but these maps are less detailed. Federal flood plain and flood hazard maps are more usually available for communities with larger populations at risk from flooding. Information on precipitation, topography, land use, and past floods is used to prepare flood plain maps. Soil surveys note alluvial deposits, which indicate the location of past floods. Typically, communities map one-hundred-year flood plains, which are areas that have at least a one in one hundred chance of flooding in any given year. Flood plains can be subdivided into flood ways—where flood waters are generally deepest and fastest—and flood fringe areas—where the dangers are less severe. CCRP mapped flood plains and identified them as critical resources that should not be developed in any way that would impair their ability to retain flood waters.

## E. Vegetation

Vegetation, both natural and planted, is a significant resource to include in any comprehensive inventory, yet it is often overlooked or treated only briefly. An inventory of vegetation indicates the presence of such resources as trees for timber and wildlife habitat. Certain plant species are characteristic of wetlands or certain soil types. Others may indicate disturbed areas, loss of topsoil, or the presence of pollutants. Vegetation can reveal past land use: a stand of white pine may mark the place where a farmer's field once lay, and daffodils may indicate a former house site. Since vegetation usually provides visual amenity in a community, mapping it can help residents to identify some of the special attributes of their community.

CLASSIFICATION SYSTEMS

Several classification systems can be used in inventorying vegetation. A community may choose a system based on the nature of its vegetation and the purposes of the inventory.

The most basic classification system is based on structure, or the overall assemblage of plants in an area. William M. Marsh defines the following eight classes: forest, woodland, orchard or plantation, brush, fence rows, wetland, grassland, and field (see illustration, p. 108). This classification system is often sufficient. A community that wishes more detail could subdivide these classes. For instance, forests can be classified as deciduous, evergreen, or mixed and wetlands as forested or not forested.

The next level of sophistication is to identify plant "communities" or "associations," which are assemblages of plants typically found together. A forest community in Virginia might be termed Oak-Hickory or in Idaho, Ponderosa Pine–Douglas Fir, indicating which species are "dominant" (i.e., exert the greatest influence on other plants in the community).

The most sophisticated vegetation inventory entails making a list of all of the species found in a given area and noting their relative abundance. Although this degree of detail usually is not necessary, rare species or exceptional occurrences of common ones, such as particularly fine specimens or old-growth timber stands, should be included. (If rare or endangered species are found, it may prove counterproductive to publicize their location, since excessive visitation or destruction could result.)

More specialized inventories may be appropriate in some communities. For example, a county in Utah might wish to study the health of its rangeland, a county in Indiana might note the locations of undisturbed prairie, and a town in North Carolina may want to note the location of shade trees along public rights-of-way. Such information, for example, can help to mount a program to protect range from overgrazing, native grasses from herbicides, or street trees from road widenings. It can also be used to ad-

Surveyors studying a community's vegetation can adapt William M. Marsh's structural inventory categories or develop their own.

**Level I**
**(vegetative structure)**

Forest
  (trees with average height greater than 15 ft with at least 60°₀ canopy cover)

Woodland
  (trees with average height greater than 15 ft with 20–60°₀ canopy cover)

Orchard or Plantation
  (same as woodland or forest but with regular spacing)

Brush
  (trees and shrubs generally less than 15 ft high with high density of stems, but variable canopy cover)

Fencerows
  (trees and shrubs of mixed forms along borders such as roads, fields, yards, playgrounds)

Wetland
  (generally low, dense plant covers in wet areas)

Grassland
  (herbs, with grasses dominant)

Field
  (tilled or recently tilled farmland)

vise property owners about plantings that are most appropriate in preserving the community's historic appearance.

## WHO CONDUCTS INVENTORY

Personnel needs depend largely on the scale of the inventory. An inventory of plant structure can be carried out largely by knowledgeable volunteers with access to topographic maps and recent aerial photographs. In more intensive surveys volunteers can identify plants and map findings, but may require the assistance of someone trained in biology, ecology, forestry, horticulture, or landscape architecture. Among sources of assistance are biology teachers, who may assign a vegetation inventory as a student project; a garden club; scientists working in the area for the U.S. Forest Service, the National Park Service, the Soil Conservation Service, or the Bureau of Land Management; and the Nature Conservancy. Many communities also have nature centers and state or local parks with trained naturalists who may be eager to assist with communitywide projects as a way of increasing public interest in their facilities. Nearby parks and public lands may already have species lists that can provide a basis for community surveys.

The Nature Conservancy, through its Natural Heritage Program, is working with more than forty state natural resource agencies to inventory natural resources that are exemplary, rare, or endangered. The resources can be an endangered plant or animal species, a community of plants and animals, habitat for an endangered species, or other natural features. Data is recorded on each resource's occurrence, number, condition, and degree of endangerment.

There are many useful field identification guides. Some are national in their coverage and others regional or local. A local botanist can advise which are the best for a particular area. Aerial photographs can be used not only to identify structure but also to make finer distinctions. For instance, the texture of the tree tops in the photographs can be used to tell mature stands from younger ones; infrared photographs can help distinguish between coniferous and deciduous trees; and stereo pairs can indicate relative tree height and hence maturity.

## F. Wildlife

Although relatively few communities inventory their terrestrial and aquatic wildlife or assess the health of wildlife populations, there may be good reasons to do so. Wildlife is a major asset in most rural areas. Many people enjoy observing wildlife. Hunting and fishing may also be important food sources, popular forms of recreation, or significant occupations in a rural community.

Since many animal species range over a wide area, it can be difficult to count them. Wildlife biologists count some species through the use of aerial photographs or tag birds or mammals to monitor their movements. Wildlife biologists frequently estimate wildlife populations by counting individual animals, droppings, burrows, or nests in a sampling area. The degree to which foliage or grasses have been eaten is also a good indication of wildlife populations. Estimates of age and sex distribution indicate whether a population of a particular species is healthy.

For most communities the best approach to wildlife protection is to identify and protect habitat, including nesting grounds and spawning areas. Fortunately, considerable information exists concerning favorable habitat for many species. Plant species preferred by wildlife can also be noted for protection. For instance, retaining trees that shade streams assures the cool water temperatures trout require. Consequently, the conservation commission in Cazenovia concluded that the best approach to pro-

Communities interested in wildlife protection may wish to develop a species-habitat matrix similar to this one, which was developed for Albion, Washington. Matrices can be prepared for other resources as well.

| SPECIES | ANIMAL HABITAT | | | OCCURRENCE | | | | | COMMENTS |
|---|---|---|---|---|---|---|---|---|---|
| | BREED-ING | LIVING | EATING | COMMON | UN-COMMON | RARE | MIGRANT | RESI-DENT | |
| American Robin *Turdus migratorius* | W | W | G S | ● | | | ● | | |
| Barn Owl *Tyto alba* | W | W | W S | ● | | | | ● | |
| Mourning Dove *Zenaida macroura* | G S | G S | G S C | ● | | | | ● | |
| Red tailed hawk *Buteo jamaicensis* | W | W | G W S C R | | ● | | | ● | |
| Porcupine *Erethizon dorsatum* | W | W | W | | | ● | | ● | |
| Norway rat *Rattus norvegicus* | G S | G S | G S C | ● | | | | ● | |
| Beaver *Castor canadensis* | W R | R | W R | | ● | | | ● | |
| White tailed deer *Odocoileus virginianus* | W | W S | W S G C | ● | | | | ● | |

tecting trout in the township's streams was to monitor and control adjacent land use. The commission also mapped fish spawning areas in the township. Deer in upstate New York require the shelter of forested areas to protect them from winter storms and prefer southern and western facing slopes, where snows melt earlier. Therefore CCRP mapped areas where deer habitat was most favorable.

Depending on the needs and skills available in the community, inventories of wildlife or wildlife habitat can be conducted by either community volunteers or outside professionals. Most communities have a number of amateur bird watchers, naturalists, and hunters who are skilled at animal identification. If they are organized in a club, such as a chapter of the National Audubon Society or a rod and gun club, their group may be willing to take on a wildlife inventory as a project. Local amateur naturalists may already participate in wildlife censuses, such as the Audubon Society's annual Christmas bird counts.

Additional information and assistance are available from the same sources as for vegetation inventories (3.III.E). In addition, state fish and game agencies can be of assistance for game species, and many now maintain information on nongame species as well, especially if they are endangered or threatened. Biologists working at national wildlife refuges or field offices of the U.S. Fish and Wildlife Service can give advice. For coastal communities, the service has prepared comprehensive inventories and maps of fish, wildlife, and plant species.

## G. Climate

Data on microclimates—the climates of small, distinct areas—may be particularly important for communities where conditions vary greatly from one part of the community to another, as they frequently do in mountainous and coastal areas. A microclimate, because of its particular exposure, elevation, or vegetation, may have warmer or cooler temperatures than adjacent areas, different average wind velocity, more or less precipitation, or a greater likelihood of fog. Such conditions may affect the suitability of a site for construction or agriculture. Temperature and precipitation records for many communities are available from the National

Oceanic and Atmospheric Administration. Additional weather information may be available from the Cooperative Extension Service and the Soil Conservation Service.

## IV. INVENTORYING SPECIAL RESOURCES

### A. Historic and Cultural Resources

Conducting a historic inventory helps a community to identify and understand the economic, geographic, environmental, social, and cultural forces that shaped its development. An inventory establishes where and why settlement occurred; traces transportation networks such as roads, canals, and railroads; identifies agricultural patterns and practices; outlines the development of commerce and industry; and identifies ethnic and other influences on the community's environment. Such information can be used in preparing nominations to state and national registers (6.IX.B) and in developing a local ordinance to protect resources (4.V.C).

An inventory should not record simply the oldest or the finest examples of architecture, or only the homes and gardens of the rich and famous. It should include a wide range of buildings, landscapes, and archeological sites; to be thorough, the rural inventory should address all of the components of the rural landscape and include land as well as buildings. A farmhouse, for example, should not be considered as an isolated architectural landmark, but rather as part of an agricultural complex that has evolved over time.

The degree of detail for a historic resources survey will vary with the community's needs. If a nomination to the National Register is contemplated, considerable information is required. If the purpose, however, is to note the location of potential resources that can be studied later in greater detail should demolition, alteration, or adjacent new construction be proposed, then a less detailed study may be appropriate. The location of unprotected archeological sites should be kept confidential to protect them from unskilled amateur archeologists and souvenir hunters.

Most state historic preservation offices (SHPOs) (6.IX.B) supply inventory forms for recording data. Unfortunately, most state forms have been developed for use in urban areas and may therefore not be well suited for recording landscape features and rural structures. Rural communities may thus find it necessary to develop their own supplemental forms to record this information.

The surveyor should take enough black-and-white photographs to record all aspects of a property's character. There should be at least one overall landscape view, showing the property in its environmental context, as well as photographs of all the associated structures and landscape elements. Late fall, winter, and early spring, when there are few leaves on deciduous trees and few crops in the fields, are usually the best times to take photographs that show landform, extent of the property, and architectural details (see *Photographing the Countryside,* pp. 246–47).

The final step in conducting the historic resources inventory is to evaluate significance. The criteria developed by the National Park Service for the National Register should be helpful in this regard (see *Evaluation Criteria,* p. 115).

# Hanalei, Hawaii: The Cultural Landscape

Although many historic preservation organizations have inventoried historic structures, only a few have surveyed the cultural landscape. A Hawaiian organization, 1000 Friends of Kauai, with the assistance of the state historic preservation office, undertook such a survey of the Hanalei Valley on the island of Kauai in 1986 and 1987. The survey identified significant existing landscape components and was seen as the first step in understanding these resources so that new growth can be encouraged to be in harmony with local values and agricultural practices.

The surveyors identified ten components that occur in most landscapes. The components, described in Figures 1–10 and originally developed by Robert Z. Melnick for the National Park Service, can be used to compile a checklist of historic landscape elements to investigate. This list can be adapted to reflect local conditions and resources. USGS topographic maps and aerial photographs are often helpful in such a survey (McClelland, Keller, Keller, and Melnick forthcoming).

Ten common landscape components illustrated in Hanalei: (1) *Spatial organization patterns.* Natural boundaries, road systems, and field patterns organize the landscape. In Hanalei, the pattern is defined primarily by taro fields. (2) *Land use.* Farming, mining, ranching, fishing, recreation, industry, and forestry leave their imprint on the land. Growing taro is a major land use in Hanalei. (3) *Response to natural features.* Mountains, rivers, forests, and other natural resources influence

the location of structures and fields and provide building materials. Hanalei's irrigation system depended on water diverted by this remnant of a stone dam. (4) *Circulation networks.* Footpaths, livestock trails, roads, railroads, and canals link elements of the landscape. The Hanalei Bridge connects Hanalei to other communities. (5) *Boundaries.* They may be streams, ridges, fences, stone walls, or hedgerows. In Hanalei, earthen dikes separate one taro field from another. (6) *Vegetation.* Characteristic vegetation could include orchards, wood lots, windbreaks, and ornamental plants. In Hanalei, banana trees along dikes prevent erosion and provide shade and fruit. (7) *Cluster arrangement.* The arrangement of buildings, fences, and paths may reveal a property's historical use. The dwellings and sheds clustered close to the taro fields are characteristic of Hanalei. (8) *Structures.* All structures, including barns, sheds, schoolhouses, canals, windmills, and mine shafts should be inventoried. Board and batten farmers' cottages are traditional in Hanalei. (9) *Small-scale elements.* Often overlooked are such features as fence posts, abandoned farm machinery, road markers, and foot bridges. This wooden aqueduct is a small-scale element in Hanalei. (10) *Historical views.* They are reminders of the way in which past inhabitants experienced the landscape. This view of the Hanalei Bay and pier varies little from the historical view.

ANALYZING THE RURAL COMMUNITY

## Sources of Information for Historic Inventories

*The following are good sources for inventories of historic resources:*

- *State historic preservation office*
- *State and local libraries and archives*
- *State and local historical societies and preservation organizations*
- *Census reports and homesteader records*
- *Architectural history and history faculty at area schools*
- *Family letters, papers, and Bibles*
- *School, church, and business records*
- *Books on local history and accounts of travelers*
- *Historic photographs, maps, and engravings*
- *Cemetery inscriptions and burial records*
- *Deeds and wills*
- *Newspaper archives*

*In addition, surveyors need to make contact with local-history, genealogy, and architecture buffs as well as with older people who have good memories and have lived in the community a long time. Older citizens often know which buildings are the oldest, who lived in them, and what crops were planted in which fields in the past.*

**Each community undertaking a historic inventory needs a data sheet. In some instances, the state historic preservation office issues a standard form. In others, the local organization develops its own to reflect local conditions, building practices, and terminology. This form, developed for Hanalei, Hawaii, includes all of the basic information needed.**

To conduct a historic resources inventory, a community needs persons with a knowledge of archeology, architectural history, and landscape history; an understanding of the local history and land use; and experience in doing inventories. Although some of the skills should be available locally, most communities need professional assistance as well. Many communities combine the services of a paid consultant with those of local volunteers. The SHPO can often provide names of qualified individuals or firms to conduct historic inventories.

Regardless of who conducts the inventory, it should be done in cooperation with the SHPO. That office can provide useful guidance and possibly some funding. Since an important reason for undertaking an inventory is to nominate properties to state and federal registers, thereby affording them a measure of protection, it is essential that the information be recorded in an approved manner.

---

**HANALEI PROJECT: HISTORIC STRUCTURES DATA SHEET**
**1000 Friends of Kauai and Land & Community Associates**

Tax Lot Number:_____

1. Site name (if applicable or N/A):_____

2. Address or location:_____

3. State zoning:_____County zoning: _____Use permit:_____

4. Field recorder(s):_____

5. Date(s) recorded in field:_____

6. Owner's name:_____

7. Owner's address:_____

8. Use: Original: Agricultural Residential   Non-Agricultural Residential   Store   Mill/Warehouse

        Institutional (specify)_____   Other _____

      Present: Same   Part-time Residential   Vacation Rental   Retail and General

9. Condition:   Excellent   Good   Fair   Deteriorated   Ruin

10. Threats to structure:   None/ Not Known   Abusive Alterations   Neglect   Road Construction

        Private Development   Government Activity

11. General style groups:_____

12. Height:      1 Story   1 1/2 Story   2 Story   More than 2

13. Facade width:   1 Bay   2 Bay   3 Bay   4 Bay   More than 4 Bay

14. Wings and additions:   Rear   Side   Front   (Show location on attached grid sheet)

15. Principal Roof configuration:   Gable   Hipped   Shed   Other_____

16. Roof materials: Orignial (if known)_____Existing_____

17. Exterior wall materials:   Original (if known):_____

        Existing:_____

18. Principal lanai type: Engaged   Attached   Location: Front   Side   Rear

19. Principal lanai integrity:   Original   Screened Enclosed   Other Alteration   Removed   Unknown

20. Foundation treatment:   Slab   Elevated   Other_____

21. Foundation materials:_____

Volunteers can trace deeds, read old newspapers, and scan past census reports (although nonprofessionals have a tendency to collect more information than necessary). A local historical society may be able to help. Local volunteers may be more likely than outside consultants to recognize kinship links and historic place names used in boundary descriptions in deeds. In Cazenovia, Terry LeVeque and Dorothy Riester coordinated and supplemented the work of the volunteer surveyors.

FOLKLIFE TRADITIONS

Communities concerned with protecting their folklife resources and traditions may wish to conduct a folk-arts inventory. Also, traditional ways of siting, building, and furnishing buildings are of interest in a historic resources survey. A folk-arts inventory can include listings of which people in the community still practice such traditional crafts such as

---

22. Other distinguishing features:(Describe)

    Windows:_____

    Porch Details:_____

    Other:_____

23. Outbuildings:_____

            Commercial  Agricultural-related Commercial  Other (specify)_____

    (Attach additional form for each pre-1946 outbuilding and show location on attached grid sheets.)
           Auwai  Other
24. Distinguishing site features:   Walls   Fences   Plant Materials  Gardens   Walkways   Ponds
    Describe_____

25. Site integrity:   Original    Moved    Distance moved: <1/2 mi  1/2-2  2-4  More than 4

    Original location, if known _____

    Original occupants:_____

26. Cultural/ethnic affiliations:

    Native Hawaiian  Chinese  Japanese  Filipino  Causacasion  Unknown  Other_____

    Cultural/ethnic affiliations of subsequent occupants:_____

27. Persons or events of significance associated with structure (if known):

    Owner/Occupant:_____

    Event:_____

    Architect/Builder:_____

    Date(s):_____

28. Quad map used:_____

29. UTM Data:  Zone:_____  Northing:_____  Easting:_____

30. Direction building faces:   N   S   E   W   NE   NW   SE   SW

31: Comment:_____
_____
_____
_____
_____
_____
_____
_____
_____
_____
_____

---

## Evaluation Criteria for the National Register of Historic Places

*Once you have completed a historic resources inventory, you may wish to evaluate the significance of the inventoried properties. The National Park Service has developed the following criteria for evaluating properties nominated to the National Register of Historic Places:*

*The quality of significance in American history, architecture, archeology, and culture is present in districts, sites, buildings, structures, and objects that possess integrity of location, design, setting, materials, workmanship, feeling, and association, and:*
**A.** *that are associated with events that have made a significant contribution to the broad patterns of our history; or*
**B.** *that are associated with the lives of persons significant in our past, or*
**C.** *that embody the distinctive characteristics of a type, period, or method of construction, or that represent the work of a master, or that possess high artistic values, or that represent a significant and distinguishable entity whose components may lack individual distinction; or*
**D.** *that have yielded, or may be likely to yield, information important in prehistory or history.*

*(Code of Federal Regulations, vol. 36, pt. 60.)*

Documenting folklife is an important part of gaining community understanding. Here a member of the Montana Folklife Survey team interviews Agnes Vanderburg on the Flathead Reservation about her method for baking wild camas roots. Vanderburg instructs children about tribal traditions at a summer camp on the reservation.

building stone walls or split-rail fences. It can identify extant examples of such community folk arts as basketmaking or rug weaving and document the practitioners' techniques and the history of their crafts. It can also include recordings or videotapes of folk musicians or storytellers relating local folk tales and legends.

Volunteers can conduct much of a folk-arts inventory. Such a project is often a good way to involve both senior citizens and schoolchildren. A nearby university or the state government may have a folklife program with a folklorist on staff who can offer assistance in locating a qualified person to help organize the inventory and assist in choosing the appropriate type of documentation. The Folk Arts Program of the National Endowment for the Arts and the American Folklife Center of the Library of Congress may also be able to assist a community.

## B. Scenic Areas

An inventory of scenic resources can be an important component of an environmental inventory. The results of a scenic inventory can be used in developing comprehensive plans, land-use ordinances, and design guidelines; determining the potential visual impact of a proposed development (see *Visual Simulations,* p. 162); educating community residents; deciding what properties to acquire or protect through easements; and determining locations for new developments, roads, trails, or utility lines.

During the past two decades, landscape architects have pioneered a number of methods for assessing visual quality in a community. Some methods rely primarily on the skills of expert landscape architects; others place heavy emphasis on a community's participation; many by their very nature include a degree of subjectivity. The approach chosen should depend largely on how the inventory information will be used. If a zoning ordinance is going to be based in part on a survey of citizens' preferences, for example, a statistically sound system of sampling public opinion is necessary. On the other hand, if the primary objective is to increase a community's awareness and to demonstrate to community residents that there is much agreement on what is beautiful in the community, a less comprehensive (and less expensive) approach may be appropriate.

An inventory of scenic features should not be limited to what is "beautiful." Scraggly hedgerows or a dilapidated store, while not scenic, may be prominent visual features that serve as major points of identity in a com-

Rating criteria for the scenic quality inventories conducted by the Bureau of Land Management are used to identify areas of public land that should be protected.

## Scenic Quality Inventory/Evaluation Rating Criteria and Score

| Landform | Vegetation | Water | Color | Adjacent Scenery | Scarcity | Cultural Modifications |
|---|---|---|---|---|---|---|
| High vertical relief such as prominent cliffs, spires or massive rock outcrops; or severe surface variation or highly eroded formations including major badlands or dune systems; or detail features dominant and exceptionally striking and intriguing such as glaciers. **5** | A variety of vegetative types in interesting forms, textures, and patterns **5** | Clear and clean appearing, still, or cascading white water, any of which are a dominant factor in the landscape. **5** | Rich color combinations, variety or vivid color; or pleasing contrasts in the soil, rock, vegetation, water or snow fields. **5** | Adjacent scenery greatly enhances visual quality. **5** | One of a kind; or unusually memorable; or very rare within region. Consistent chance for exceptional wildlife or wildflower viewing. **6** | Free from esthetically undesirable or discordant sights and influences; or modifications add favorably to visual variety. **2** |
| Steep canyons, mesas, buttes, cinder cones and drumlins; or interesting erosional patterns or variety in size and shape of landforms; or detail features present and interesting though not dominant or exceptional. **3** | Some variety of vegetation, but only one or two types. **3** | Flowing or still, but not dominant in the landscape. **3** | Some intensity or variety in colors and contrast of the soil, rock and vegetation, but not a dominant scenic element. **3** | Adjacent scenery moderately enhances overall visual quality. **3** | Distinctive, though somewhat similar to others within the region. **2** | Scenic quality is somewhat depreciated by inharmonious intrusions, but not so extensively that they are entirely negated; or modifications add little or no visual variety to the area. **0** |
| Low, rolling hills, foothills or flat valley bottoms. Interesting, detailed landscape features few or lacking. **1** | Little or no variety or contrast in vegetation. **1** | Absent, or not noticeable. **0** | Subtle color variations, contrast or interest; generally muted tones. **1** | Adjacent scenery has little or no influence on overall visual quality. **0** | Interesting within its setting, but fairly common within the region. **1** | Modifications are so extensive that scenic qualities are mostly nullified or substantially reduced. **-4** |

munity and should be preserved because of their cultural and social significance (Lynch 1960).

Many communities and some states have programs to designate and protect scenic roads (see *Special-Purpose Ordinances,* pp. 164–65, and 6.IX.C). In order to designate them, one must decide on a system for assessing their scenic value. Such a system was developed for communities in Vermont (Ashcroft 1979).

A good way to introduce the issue of visual quality in a community is to show photographs of the community—both scenic and not so scenic—to residents and ask them to discuss their impressions of the views, their opinions on what constitutes good design, and their feelings about what resources are important to protect.

PROFESSIONAL APPRAISAL

The professional visual analysis is based on the trained eye of a landscape architect who classifies and evaluates landscapes. There is no one set of criteria uniformly used by landscape architects. Many visual analysis studies, including those conducted by the Bureau of Land Management and Forest Service, use elements of artistic composition—form, line, color, and texture—to evaluate landscapes (see illustration, p. 117).

CITIZENS' PREFERENCE SURVEYS

Appraisals using the opinions of citizens have the obvious advantage of reflecting a community's values and attitudes. Although professional assistance is advisable, particularly if the results of the survey will be used as the basis for an ordinance, community volunteers can undertake much of the work. Discussing the scenic qualities they appreciate in their community's landscape gives citizens an opportunity to increase environmental awareness.

There are many ways to solicit citizens' opinions. One method is for surveyors to take photographs of typical scenes throughout the community and then ask citizens to rate the beauty of each scene on, say, a five-point scale or to rank the photographs in order of scenic preference. The results can be mapped. To insure optimum objectivity, those conducting the survey should attempt to obtain photographs as uniform in quality and lighting conditions as possible. Obviously, how a picture is taken can have a major bearing on how a viewer ranks the quality of the scene it depicts.

CASE STUDY 8

## Cazenovia, New York: Citizens Participate in a Visual Survey

Terry LeVeque, project director of the Cazenovia Community Resources Project (CCRP), and James Palmer, a research associate at SUNY, designed a citizens' scenic preference survey for Cazenovia in 1981. Residents were asked to locate their favorite and least favorite views on a map. LeVeque then entered the combined results on a copy of the community's base map. CCRP asked twelve local organizations, selected to

Chittenango Falls, protected as part of a state park, was one of the favorite views identified in the Cazenovia visual survey.

represent the geographical, social, and age diversity of Cazenovia's population, to participate in the survey; they included the Rotary Club, the Garden Club, the Boy Scouts, the League of Women Voters, the Cazenovia Merchants' Association, the New Woodstock Historic Association, the Future Farmers of America, and the Volunteer Fire Department. A total of 170 individuals participated, representing approximately 3 percent of the town's population.

Dorothy Riester, chair of the CCRP, and LeVeque attended meetings of each organization to explain CCRP's purposes and administer the survey. They asked each person at the meetings to identify on a copy of the CCRP base map "up to ten favorite views and scenes" and "up to five least favorite views and scenes." The exercise took each participant about forty-five minutes to complete. The favorites were Chittenango Falls—a unique natural feature—and views of Cazenovia Lake. There were few negative responses, other than for a shopping plaza on the outskirts of the village, indicating a largely positive regard for the community's visual environment.

CCRP used the results to make recommendations for acquisition of scenic easements for all of the significant views and scenes, to suggest that all of the significant views be incorporated into the Cazenovia Advisory Conservation Commission's environmental review process, and to recommend enactment of design standards for commercial and other areas. Most importantly, the visual survey stimulated community interest in Cazenovia's environment by allowing residents to realize that by and large they shared perceptions on what is beautiful in their township.

VISIBILITY ANALYSIS

A useful tool in assessing the visual impact of development is to analyze what can be seen, particularly from public rights-of-way. Developers can then be asked to design their projects in such a way as to minimize their visibility.

The simplest way to determine visibility is to go to a "viewpoint"—the place from which a view is visible—and note on a map the "viewshed"—the area that can be seen from the viewpoint. Of course, vegetation must be considered when determining visibility. Viewsheds may be very different in winter than in summer if deciduous trees are present. Also, trees that would hide a development today may be removed in the future. Alternatively, there are computer programs that can display the viewshed which can theoretically be seen from a given viewpoint, using topographic information. Since the computer does not take vegetation into account, the results need to be checked in the field.

WHO CONDUCTS INVENTORY

Many landscape architects have specific training in visual assessment and can assist a community in designing a survey that fits its needs. Assistance may also be available from the Soil Conservation Service, the National Park Service, the Bureau of Land Management, or the Forest Service, all of which employ landscape architects to assess the visual impacts of proposed development or changes in vegetation on federal lands, or, in the case of SCS, on lands whose owners receive assistance. Each of these agencies has publications available on the visual assessment procedures it uses.

## C. Outdoor Recreation

Many people choose to live in rural communities because of the potential for outdoor recreation, on both public and private property. It may be helpful to map recreation resources; this may be easy in the case of publicly owned lands, but ticklish in the case of public use of private property. Owners who allow hikers, fishermen, hunters, and cross-country skiers to use their land may not wish to have the community advertise the fact through an inventory. Whether recreational uses of private property are mapped or not, the community may wish to survey the demands for recreational use of land and use this information in working out agreements with property owners for public access, easements, or acquisition. In

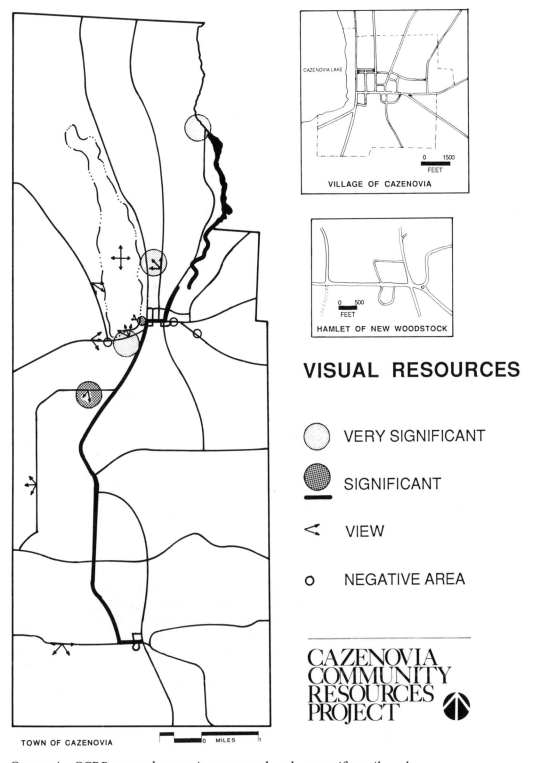

VILLAGE OF CAZENOVIA

0    1500
FEET

0   500
FEET

HAMLET OF NEW WOODSTOCK

# VISUAL RESOURCES

VERY SIGNIFICANT

SIGNIFICANT

< VIEW

o   NEGATIVE AREA

CAZENOVIA
COMMUNITY
RESOURCES
PROJECT

TOWN OF CAZENOVIA

0   MILES   1

Cazenovia, CCRP mapped recreation areas rather than specific trails and access points to private property. It also identified abandoned railroad rights-of-way. Since there was a demand for more recreational opportunities, CCRP recommended that some of these rights-of-way be ac-

*Opposite:* Cazenovia's agricultural-land ownership survey was conducted by farmers with the aid of aerial photographs. Conservation leaders were surprised to learn how much of Cazenovia's cropland is rented rather than owned by farmers, and concluded that the future of agriculture was more vulnerable than they had realized.

quired for development as trails. The Cazenovia Preservation Foundation recently purchased a right-of-way for this purpose.

## V. INVENTORYING PROBLEM AREAS

In addition to assets, most communities unfortunately have problem areas that should be identified, mapped, and evaluated. These may include dumps that may contain toxic wastes; areas that may have become polluted from rusting underground gasoline storage tanks; surface-mined land, areas underlain with abandoned mine shafts and abandoned quarries; and high-tension lines or microwave towers that mar scenery and may cause health problems (see *Special-Purpose Ordinances,* pp. 164–65).

Communities suspecting dangerous levels of air pollution from automobiles, nearby power plants, or factories may want to commission an air quality study or persuade the state agency responsible for monitoring air quality under the provisions of the Clean Air Act to investigate (6.X.D).

If noise pollution caused by industries, highways, or airports is a problem, these facilities can be monitored by measuring the noise decibel levels. Data collected in a noise study may provide the basis for controls through a local ordinance. A community may also wish to predict the noise impact of developments and require appropriate mitigation.

## VI. INVENTORYING LAND USE AND OWNERSHIP

It is helpful to map how land is used and compare land use with resources. If, for instance, the town landfill is located over an aquifer, stricter controls on its operation might be warranted. Mapping such general land-use categories as residential, commercial, industrial, agricultural, and forested is probably sufficient. A map showing current zoning at the same scale as the inventory maps allows a community to analyze whether the zoning is appropriate for the resources. For instance, if a wetland is identified in the inventory and is zoned for quarter-acre residential lots, there would be a sound justification for revising the zoning. The community may also want to map general ownership information that would show privately owned land and land owned by government agencies and nonprofit organizations. Such a map could include railroad and utility rights-of-way and properties subject to conservation easements.

Cazenovia was particularly concerned about preserving farmland; consequently, CCRP mapped farmland ownership (see illustration, p. 123). The members of the CCRP agriculture task group went to each farm to determine land use, ownership, and other data on the status of farming in the township. Task-group members showed aerial photographs to property owners and asked them to identify what land they leased and owned and the agricultural uses of each parcel.

USGS is in the process of compiling land-use and land-cover maps for the entire country at the scale of 1:250,000. Some areas are also mapped at the scale of 1:100,000. A few states, including Alaska and New York, have also mapped land use. Existing maps may be a useful point of departure, but the information on them will probably need to be checked in the field and supplemented by the community. Land use and ownership can be surveyed at the community level by volunteers. The tax assessor or the plan-

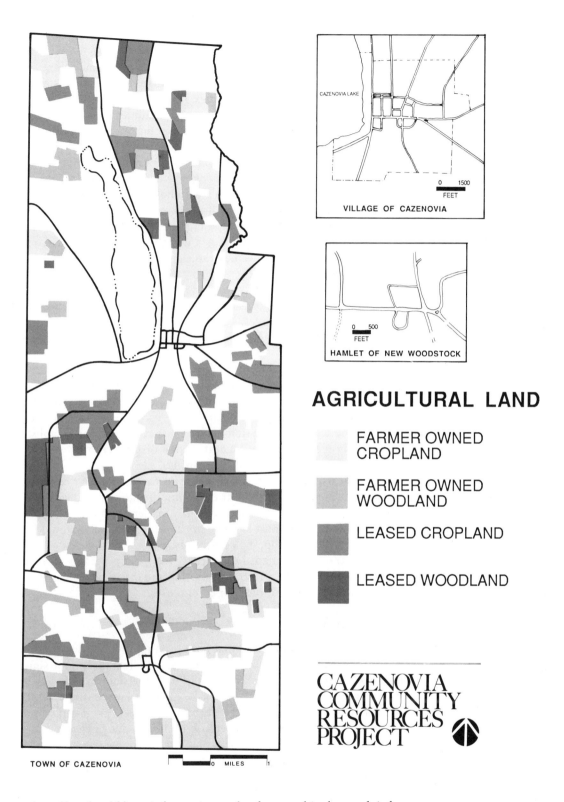

VILLAGE OF CAZENOVIA

HAMLET OF NEW WOODSTOCK

# AGRICULTURAL LAND

FARMER OWNED
CROPLAND

FARMER OWNED
WOODLAND

LEASED CROPLAND

LEASED WOODLAND

CAZENOVIA
COMMUNITY
RESOURCES
PROJECT

TOWN OF CAZENOVIA

ning office should have information on land ownership, but such information is not always easy to use. Determining the ownership of small parcels can be particularly complicated.

## Land Evaluation and Site Assessment System

*Communities wishing to evaluate cropland, forest land, and rangeland can make good use of the Land Evaluation and Site Assessment (LESA) system developed by the Soil Conservation Service. LESA incorporates the values and objectives of the communities that make use of the information. The system identifies which land has the highest potential agricultural yields, which land has the fewest limitations on development, and other factors. The LESA criteria are designed to protect farmland with the greatest production potential and farmland located within a viable agricultural area. Hardin County, Kentucky (Case Study 10), and McHenry County, Illinois (Case Study 9), are examples of communities that have used LESA.*

*On the basis of their soil characteristics, lands are evaluated and given a score ranging from the most (100 points) to the least (0 points) suitable cropland, forest land, or rangeland. A community then selects other factors to be considered in assessing the viability of the land for agriculture, forestry, or range. Each factor is assigned a maximum number of points to indicate its relative importance to the community. All of the factors (other than soil characteristics) taken together can have a total maximum score of 200. Some of the factors a community may wish to consider are*

*• Percentage of land in the area in agriculture;*
*• Economic viability factors, including the size of a farm, land ownership, and investment in such improvements as barns, equipment, and drainage systems;*
*• Impact of any change in use on the natural, agricultural, historic, recrea-*

## VII. ANALYSIS OF INVENTORY RESULTS

As surveyors collect data, they may reach preliminary conclusions on what resources should be protected. In addition to a resource-by-resource analysis, a community needs to compare resources, weigh their importance, and decide which land areas in the community should have the highest priority for protection. Areas that contain few or no resources might be recommended as the most appropriate for new development. For instance, the fact that a field is prime habitat for game birds may not in itself be sufficient grounds for disallowing new development. However, if that field is also located in an area with a seasonally high water table and is the foreground of the principal view of the community's most significant historic site, protection may become a high priority. In other cases, the presence of a single resource—perhaps a wetland, prime farmland, or a historic landmark—might be deemed sufficient to make a site inappropriate for development.

Since these decisions are rarely cut-and-dried, the biggest challenge to rural conservation leaders is often how to achieve community consensus on the need to protect resources. Various local boards and commissions will probably need to consider the findings of the environmental inventory and hold public hearings.

To aid in synthesizing the information, many communities prepare composite maps that take into account all of a community's resources and environmental constraints. Each area in the community is then evaluated for its suitability for development and other uses. Some communities develop a numerical scoring system to compare resources and establish which areas should receive the highest degree of protection (see *Land Evaluation and Site Assessment System,* pp. 124–25).

A suitability map for development, taking into account all of a community's resources, might divide the entire community into the following categories: "slight constraint" on development, "moderate constraint," and "severe constraint." The most suitable areas for development would be those with the fewest overlapping constraints.

Overlaying translucent maps or computer mapping programs may be helpful in determining where resources overlap and thus which areas may be the most and least appropriate for certain uses.

### A. Overlay Maps

Laying maps of the same scale that have been reproduced on a transparent or translucent material over one another on a light table is the simplest way to compare resources. Each map to be overlaid usually has a single resource on it. Overlay maps can be made of inexpensive tracing paper, although it tears easily and features usually become less distinct when more than three sheets are overlaid. Making maps of clear plastic Mylar, while more expensive, is a better alternative for overlay maps that will receive hard use. Graphic symbols and colored plastic cutouts can be applied to the Mylar. However, it is difficult to distinguish individual map features in an overlay of more than five sheets of Mylar.

For its overlay maps, CCRP used Color Key, a transparent plastic material developed by the 3M Company. Richard Hawks from SUNY introduced the 3M process to CCRP because it provided the ability to overlay up to fifteen maps at one time. SUNY students mapped each feature on a separate transparent Color Key sheet, and CCRP volunteers overlaid the maps to do their analyses. CCRP, the conservation commission, and the planning commission have used the maps for public education and for studying the appropriateness of certain areas for development.

## B. Computer Mapping Programs

Several computer programs have the capability to generate maps of one or more resources combined. The great advantage of computer mapping is its flexibility: new information can be added and changes made easily. The types of analyses that can be made with a computer are almost infinite, and new maps can be printed as needed. The disadvantages are the costs of acquiring the computer and the appearance of the graphics. The graphics may not lend themselves as well as conventional maps to public presentations, since they cannot be printed economically in large sizes, and some viewers may regard computer-generated maps as more complicated and beyond their capacity to comprehend.

Computer mapping basically works as follows: The area to be mapped is divided by a grid into "cells," each typically having an area of 2.5 to 10 acres. Information is entered in the computer for each resource for each cell. The more cells there are for a given area, the more precise the mapping will be and the sharper the image will be when the map is displayed.

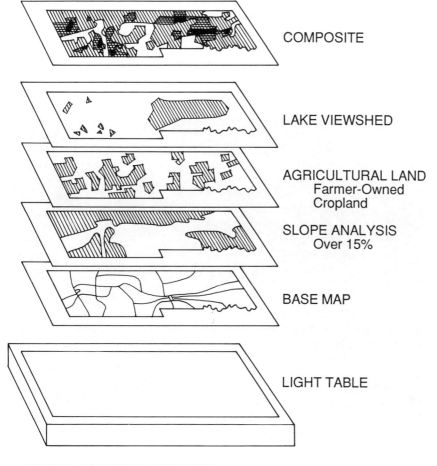

COMPOSITE

LAKE VIEWSHED

AGRICULTURAL LAND
Farmer-Owned
Cropland

SLOPE ANALYSIS
Over 15%

BASE MAP

LIGHT TABLE

*tional, and scenic resources of surrounding properties;*
*• Compatibility with local or regional plans, zoning, and other programs to protect farmland; and*
*• Presence of urban infrastructure, including water and sewer lines, roads, nearby community services, shopping, schools, and jobs.*

*After taking into account such factors, the surveyors combine the land evaluation points based on soil characteristics (up to 100) with the site assessment points (up to 200) for a total score ranging from 0 to 300. The community can then compare the relative value of all sites and set its protection policies accordingly. The SCS District Conservationist can assist a community in implementing LESA.*

*While LESA was developed to inventory and evaluate agricultural, range, and forestry resources, similar numerical rating systems can be developed for other community resources. However, such systems have their limitations. Perceptions of such resources as scenery are subjective and do not easily lend themselves to numerical ratings. Furthermore, there may not be a consensus within the community on the relative value of different resources.*

By overlaying translucent maps, conservation leaders can compare resources. This simplified depiction of an overlay consists of Cazenovia's base map and elements from the other three maps illustrated in this chapter: slope of over 15 percent, farmer-owned cropland, and the lake viewsheds (identified as one of the favorite views in the visual survey). The composite image that results from viewing the four maps simultaneously highlights the areas (the darkest) where all three constraints overlap, which are therefore the most important to protect.

## Computer Mapping

Given its high costs, computer mapping is currently used most frequently by urban governments, federal agencies, and universities. More local governments can be expected to use computers for mapping when costs are reduced, better programs are developed, and local governments acquire computers for other purposes.

### C. Reports

An inventory should not consist of maps alone. For some resources—vegetation and historic sites, for instance—maps should be accompanied by lists, inventory forms, and photographs, as appropriate. Also, a written report should accompany the maps and other data to explain how and when the inventory was conducted, who did the work, and how the results can be used. There should be an explanation of each resource map that includes the nature of the resource, the process used in identification and evaluation, sources of information, threats to the resource, potential protection techniques, and the relationship of the resource to others in the community.

The report may include recommendations that can be incorporated into a master plan or ordinance. Recommendations should appear in a distinct section of the report or as a separate document. The inventory itself should consist only of data collected in an unbiased manner.

### VIII. CONCLUSION

Although gathering information may be a group's first activity, it should not end when the early stages of a rural conservation program are completed. Rather, periodic updating and reassessment of information should continue as new events occur and new data become available.

**Mapping by computer is becoming increasingly popular. Information is entered in the computer for each resource for each area. The computer can then display an infinite number of maps comparing resources and constraints on development. This computer-generated map of Mount Desert Island in Maine, showing areas of ecological sensitivity warranting special protection, was prepared for the National Park Service, which is developing a land-protection plan for the area.**

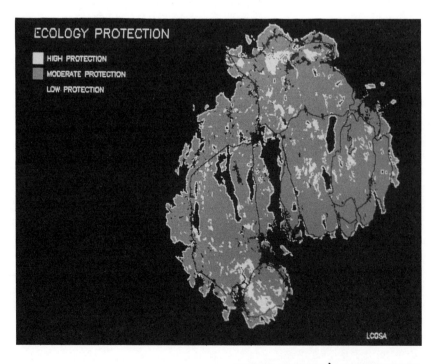

The inventory will be valuable only if it is *used*—by local governments and nonprofit organizations, and by developers and property owners. If it is unbiased and contains the right amount of information, then it should be of great use to all segments of the community and help assure rational development. The next three chapters describe the programs that local governments and nonprofit organizations can use to protect their natural, historic, agricultural, and scenic resources. These programs will be much more effective if they make use of a good environmental inventory.

# 4

# Land-Protection Techniques That Local Governments Can Use

## I. INTRODUCTION

To be successful in rural conservation, you need to become involved in local government. Through local government action, you can build official support for rural conservation and implement new protection programs. These programs might include not only ordinances governing land use, but other such activities as an environmental inventory, educational efforts, or specific projects such as the development of a park or the restoration of an old building.

In the first three chapters we have discussed the initial steps of rural conservation: identifying the issues, organizing, and inventorying resources. Once you have done this, achieving actual protection is next. This chapter and the following two provide information about public and private action that is possible to conserve land and promote good development.

Let us begin by covering some general comments about land-use management. First, the challenge in using the techniques we discuss in this chapter is to tailor them to fit your community's specific needs. The communities we cite here generally followed similar paths and examined well-known techniques in their search to address local needs. In that regard they are no different from many others. What *is* striking about these communities is that they adapted their chosen techniques to arrive at purely local innovations.

Second, beware the urban bias of much land-use planning. It can frequently favor new residential, industrial, or commercial development over maintenance of such traditional land uses as farming, ranching, or logging. Moreover, in its assumption that development will occur in most parts of a community, urban planning often fails to recognize the natural and scenic values inherent in the more open, less-developed areas of rural communities. In short, planning for a rural community is altogether different from planning for an urban one, and you should be alert to this distinction.

Third, generally speaking and depending on state law, there are few rules regarding how extensive your community's written plan should be or how much control should be built into land-use ordinances. Common wisdom in urban planning is that a comprehensive plan, with sections on economic development, housing, transportation, land use, and public services, is a prerequisite to good government. For some rural communities, however, a land-use plan may be all that is needed. With regard to land-use ordinances, the numerous regulations, extensive procedural requirements, and detailed design standards to be found in urban areas may not be needed in rural communities. Complicated land-use management systems are often difficult to administer consistently, and they may increase developers' costs, which are passed on to buyers or renters. It often makes sense to simplify review procedures and design standards to streamline an ordinance's administration, as long as it maintains sufficient control to encourage development sensitive to the environment and is consistent with requirements for due process. Developers are more likely to demand timely action, fairness, and consistency in the administration of regulations, rather than an absence of regulations altogether.

Use of most of the techniques we discuss here depends on the existence of state enabling legislation, which gives local governments the right to pass the necessary ordinances. For some of the more innovative techniques, such as transfer of development rights, your community may first need to obtain state enabling legislation. (For a discussion of lobbying, see 6.III.)

How do you become involved in local government? It may be quite simple. Local governments in areas with small populations sometimes find it difficult to find qualified people to fill all of their positions. If you have the time, energy, good ideas, and a willingness to attend meetings, you might readily be appointed or elected to office.

You cannot always get involved, however, simply by attending meetings and getting to know those who are already active. If local officials are steadfast in their opposition to rural conservation, you may need to make your views known, through publicity or by running for local office. Causing an informed and well-argued public outcry has its place in our democratic society.

## II. PLANNING

Planning should be the first step in local government action to address rural conservation. Although planning will not solve every problem that confronts a rural community, it does provide an organized approach to land use and to other areas of governmental regulation and services. Good planning, as long as it is faithfully carried out, is first and foremost a money-saving exercise. It encourages a local government to consider its future and to set its priorities for expenditures. So serious are the ramifications of designating land for new development; siting utility, water, and sewer lines; and providing roads and schools that each rural community

## Planning Defined

*The International City Management Association has defined planning as follows:*

> *The broad object of planning is to further the welfare of the people in the community by helping to create an increasingly better, more healthful, convenient, efficient, and attractive community environment. The physical as well as the social and economic community is a single organism, all features and activities of which are related and interdependent. These facts must be supplemented by the application of intelligent foresight and planned administrative and legal coordination if balance, harmony and order are to be insured. It is the task of planning to supply this foresight and this overall coordination (Smith 1979, p. 27).*

# Vernon, Vermont, Plan

*The table of contents of the comprehensive plan for Vernon, Vermont (1984 pop. 1,280), adopted by the Board of Selectmen in 1986, shows how one rural community organized its plan. Vernon's 42-page plan covers not only land use and the community's natural, recreational, cultural, and scenic resources, but also housing, transportation, economic development, and public services. Other communities might choose to include more or fewer topics, or to organize them in different ways. Note that Vernon chose to present only a small number of maps.*

should consider planning as its most important task. As an editorial in a central Pennsylvania newspaper has put it, "Any municipality on the fringes of the rapidly growing and expanding Harrisburg metropolitan area is committing community suicide if it does not have in place at least some land-use regulations."[1]

## A. What a Comprehensive Plan Is

A comprehensive plan is the community's blueprint for the future, specifying what actions should make the community a good place in which to live, work, and visit. In other words, the plan outlines what needs to be done, and how and when to do it in an organized fashion. Sometimes called a master plan, general plan, or comprehensive development plan, it is comparable to an industry's management plan or a nonprofit organization's goals and objectives (2.V.C). Planning, which conscientious officials can easily claim they perform in some fashion, and a comprehensive plan are not necessarily synonymous: the written plan is one result of a continuing planning process. The written plan serves as a public guide to public and private decision-making in order to help a community avoid costly mistakes that might occur if no plan exists. In sum, says Warren Zitzmann, a rural planning consultant, a plan "is a realistic program for describing 'where we are, where we want to go, and how we are going to get there.' "[2]

A good plan should respect natural, cultural, and scenic resources, consider the economic activities and needs of the community, and outline a course of action that is compatible with the community's traditions and settlement patterns. The plan should balance environmental protection and rural amenities on the one hand with needed residential, commercial, and industrial growth on the other, and should consider the public facilities and services the community will provide. Growth should be encouraged only in those locations where the land has the capacity for development.

The plan is usually the foundation for any of the land protections and development regulations a community may enact. Some states require local governments to have an official comprehensive plan and to update it periodically. For example, in Vermont the local plan expires every five years. In other states, the comprehensive plan is a legal document that is acceptable in court as evidence that a community's land-use controls are based on rational considerations.

A comprehensive plan should deal with both the near term (up to five years) and the future; some of its proposals should be capable of immediate implementation. A plan should have specific policies or recommended actions to support its lofty statements; otherwise, it will sit on a shelf, leaving the community to muddle along as it did without a plan.

The comprehensive plan is basically a report, generally in map and narrative form. The report summarizes the objectives, assumptions, and standards that guided the development of the plan's policies, and often includes a summary of the environmental inventory, which should precede the plan's preparation. Most plans include current data, future projections, and proposals concerning population size, demography, land use, economic activities, historic preservation, traffic, parks and open space, housing, utilities, and other pertinent aspects of a community's life and resources.

A plan need not be lengthy. In fact, some rural communities may prefer what is known as a "policy plan," in which community goals and objectives are clearly stated as a means of reviewing future development. Such a plan usually lacks specific steps that can be taken right away. On the other hand, a policy plan may prove more flexible in dealing with changing circumstances by "setting down the rules ahead of time, so that when 'x' happens, 'y' is how the community will react," as planner Dennis Gordon contends.[3]

## B. When to Develop a Comprehensive Plan

Ideally, the comprehensive plan should be developed immediately after an environmental inventory is completed, so that it is based on up-to-date information. Unfortunately, some communities have never developed a plan or are in the midst of doing one when they need to take immediate action to regulate development. In such instances, a community may need to institute basic zoning or another technique as an interim measure and follow up quickly with an environmental inventory and comprehensive plan. In states where a plan is required before regulations may be implemented, it may be necessary to impose a moratorium on development before creating a plan.

A community should not expect to rush through the planning process. Citizen involvement takes time. In the beginning, it may be desirable to hold community meetings to ask participants what things they like or do not like about their community that should be addressed by the plan. Several draft revisions may be necessary before a community reaches a consensus as to what it wants to become and before the plan becomes a document that truly meets the community's needs. The preparation of a responsive plan can take a year or more.

## C. Who Prepares the Plan

Effective planning brings citizens and officials together to develop community policies, with citizen involvement constant throughout the plan's development and final adoption. Involving as many people as possible from a broad cross-section of the community increases the chances for community understanding and acceptance. A plan perceived to have been imposed on the community, whether by an overzealous planning commission, an outside consultant, or a clique within the community, is doomed from the start. Besides encouraging better implementation of a plan, citizen involvement has other advantages. These may include saving money, if volunteers can assume some of the duties a consultant might otherwise be paid to perform; producing a better plan because local people who care are involved; and citizens' learning more about their community.

Establishing a steering committee to assist the planning commission in developing a plan can be a useful way to coordinate citizen planning efforts. A community's planning commission (or planning board) is technically responsible for preparing a comprehensive plan, but planning commissions are frequently too busy dealing with requests for zoning changes and other routine matters to spend time gathering and analyzing the necessary information. This was the case in Cazenovia, New York, for example (Case Study 6). Moreover, says rural planner Warren Zitzmann, plan-

## Development Moratoria

*A moratorium (across-the-board stoppage of development permits until a certain governmental action is completed) can buy time for a community. For example, when the community is revising its comprehensive plan or land-use controls, a moratorium helps avoid a situation where landowners rush to get permits under the old system so that they are "grandfathered," or allowed to proceed to develop under the old rules even after the new ones are in place. A moratorium may also be used to limit development temporarily in certain areas until troublesome conditions, such as traffic congestion or limited sewer capacity, are corrected.*

*A moratorium should not be used to postpone development indefinitely. Indefinite postponement amounts to procrastination at best, and deliberate foot-dragging at worst—and is likely to expose a community to numerous court challenges.*

Hardin County's Development Guidance System is based on planning that strongly emphasizes citizen participation, as evidenced by this advertisement in the *News Enterprise,* the daily newspaper in Hardin County, Kentucky (Case Study 10).

ning commissions often "need support and stimulation from citizen groups to get on with the job."[4]

Even when government officials and citizens are mutually involved in developing a plan, most rural communities without at least a part-time planning staff need the guidance of a planning consultant or a planner available from a regional or state planning agency. Few citizens have the experience or technical background on the wide variety of subjects that a comprehensive plan must cover, or the objectivity to help the community to find a balance between competing interests and inevitable personal biases.

### D. Adopting and Implementing a Plan

Once the draft of the plan is acceptable to the citizens' steering committee, it should be widely distributed. Public hearings allow for discussion and provide the planning commission with an opportunity to answer questions and encourage suggestions for revisions. A plan is often controversial, no matter how much citizen involvement is built into the process. Emotional arguments on both sides may well be as persuasive in the court of public opinion as carefully marshaled facts and arguments. The first formal hearing affords its supporters an opportunity to present the plan in the most favorable light. Later review and hearings should provide ample opportunity for as many citizens to express their views as possible.

After the town or county board has adopted the plan, no decision relating to community growth, land-use regulations, or local budget should be made without examining its impact on the goals outlined in the plan.

# Thank you Hardin County

Six years ago we asked for your help in guiding our County's future. Since then you've fueled our efforts with your ideas and aided us with your support.

This past year has been an eventful one for all of us. Since last June our joint efforts have gained widespread attention. National magazines have carried stories about our working relationship. Organizations such as the National Association of Counties, the American Farmland Trust, and the American Planning Association have awarded us their highest honors.

While all this attention is nice, the real importance lies in the fact that we did it together. Which just goes to prove what we've been saying for the past six years: citizen participation in the planning process pays big dividends — for everyone.

**Hardin County**
Planning and Development Commission

When unforeseen circumstances require a deviation from the plan, the impact of the change on other components of the plan should be anticipated and evaluated, and an amendment to the plan may be desirable.

Even the most thoughtfully prepared plans need to be updated and revised every few years. When a plan, no matter what its age, is not working as a guide to decision-making in the community, it is time to go through the planning process again. Before revising or discarding elements of a comprehensive plan, a community should determine why the original plan no longer represents the community's current needs. In general, any plan more than five years old should be reviewed to make sure it is still relevant.

## E. Partial Plans

A community may elect to plan for a single area or resource, such as wetlands, farmland, or historic sites, instead of preparing a comprehensive plan. This approach is a reasonable alternative if the need involves only one resource or a community can afford only the partial plan. All partial or functional plans should include a section of the effects that implementation may have on other aspects of the community. Partial plans are also useful in dealing with one specific area of a community. Loudoun County, Virginia, for example, developed intensive "area plans" that elaborated on the county's comprehensive plan for those parts of the county where development pressures were greatest.

A community may find that its existing plan does not address a certain issue that now concerns the community. In this case, a plan dealing with that particular issue could fill in the gaps in an otherwise acceptable comprehensive plan. Boulder County, Colorado, developed a wildlife habitat protection plan for more than nine thousand acres that has been incorporated into the county's existing comprehensive plan. Volunteers provided more than five thousand hours of research and field time to map vulnerable habitats supporting rare species. The county has implemented the plan with a variety of tools, such as management agreements (5.III.A) and the development permit process, to achieve its goal of protecting wildlife.[5]

The Guilford Preservation Alliance, a nonprofit organization in Connecticut, sponsored the development of a partial plan for historic and scenic resources in 1986. Among its recommendations: the establishment of a "visual resource overlay district" (4.IV.A), the creation of a design review board (4.V.B), the adoption of a public roadway management plan to address scenic concerns in road maintenance and improvements, and the launching of a land banking program (see *Land Banking*, pp. 184–85). Guilford's Planning and Zoning Commission endorsed the plan in 1987.[6]

## F. Spending Money Is Planning

A local government is involved in planning every time it drafts next year's budget, decides to pave a road, or authorizes the school board to renovate an old school or build a new one, even if it has no planning commission, planning department, or comprehensive plan. What has already been planned in the way of governmental expenditures can affect rural conservation—positively or negatively.

Citizens often overlook the impact that capital improvements (public facilities provided by government and paid for by public funds) can have on their community's environment. Such capital improvements as sewer

Public funds can be used to guide planning decisions in rural communities. Woodson County, Kansas, earmarked public funds for the renovation of its courthouse, built in the late nineteenth century in Yates Center and now listed in the National Register of Historic Places.

## The Constitutional Challenge: Is Zoning a "Taking" without Compensation?

*In community battles over zoning, property owners frequently invoke the so-called "takings" clause of the Constitution's Fifth Amendment, which provides that "private property [shall not] be taken for public use, without just compensation." The Supreme Court long ago ruled that the takings clause does not prohibit local governments from imposing reasonable controls on the use of land without providing compensation. Landowners, however, may still argue that a taking has occurred on the grounds either that a regulation is not reasonably necessary to protect the public welfare (that is, not a valid exercise of the "police power"), or that its effect is so extreme that it does not permit the economically viable use of land.*

*If successful, a takings challenge may result in the invalidation of a land use regulation. Under a recent Supreme Court decision, a successful challenge could also lead to a financial award to the property owner, if a regulation is found to be so extreme as to have "taken all use" of the property (First English Evangelical Lutheran Church v. County of Los Angeles, 1987). The possibility of such challenges is among the reasons that local governments are cautious in regulating land uses—even to the point of paralysis in some areas of the country.*

*According to National Trust attorney Paul W. Edmondson, however, "it is important to recognize that existing court precedent makes it difficult in the first place to prove that a land use regulation amounts to a taking" (Edmondson to authors, January 1988). For example, the Supreme Court has in several*

systems, water systems, roads, bridges, fire stations, and schools may stimulate development in the areas they serve; similarly, a lack of these facilities may deter development. Acquiring land for parks and natural areas, purchasing development rights, developing scenic trails, and implementing other rural conservation programs can become part of a community's capital improvements budget as well.

Participating in the annual planning and review of the local budget can reveal what capital improvements are planned, what they will cost, how they can be implemented, where they will be located, and what their likely or desired impact will be on the community. In some communities, it is necessary to scrutinize not only the local government's budget but also the budgets of such separate governmental entities as school boards, water and sewer authorities, or independent regional park agencies.

An increasing number of communities realize that public expenditures encourage growth and are planning for the timed allocation of public facilities to encourage concentric growth around existing settlements or are identifying urban growth boundaries beyond which public facilities and utilities will not be provided. Such measures concentrate growth where the delivery of services is most efficient.

## III. ZONING AND SUBDIVISION ORDINANCES

Rural communities vary widely in the regulations they are likely to have. Some have none, so owners can develop their property with few, if any, restrictions, although statewide regulations may pertain. Others have codes requiring building permits, observance of certain building standards, and inspection when work is completed. Many local governments require a percolation test to determine if the soils are suitable for a septic system. Other rural governments have more or less complex systems of controls that include zoning and subdivision ordinances.

### A. Zoning

Zoning divides the land under a local government's jurisdiction into districts or zones, each of which may have different requirements, in order to regulate the use of land and the placement, size, and use of buildings. Zoning is used to segregate different and incompatible uses, such as preventing industrial uses in residential subdivisions or nonfarm residences in agricultural areas.

Zoning can be used to protect environmental resources. For example, a community may limit the density of residential development in areas where soils are less suitable for septic systems or where slopes are too steep. Zoning can also be used to help a community to absorb new growth efficiently. A community may decide, for instance, to restrict all areas away from major highways to low-density residential or agricultural uses to avoid the expense of upgrading country roads to handle increased traffic and to encourage denser growth in areas where road capacities are adequate.

Zoning is often the first technique considered by someone opposed to a prison, factory, or shopping center. For others, zoning is a red flag, prompting protests of "Nobody's going to tell me what I can do with my land." Both proponents and opponents of zoning are likely to possess misconceptions about what zoning is and how it can be used. While zoning can be an effective means of regulating land development in rural areas, it is not the only technique, nor always the best technique; and used alone it is usually unsuccessful in protecting rural character.

While zoning predates planning in many rural communities, it is most effective and defensible if it implements a comprehensive plan based on an environmental inventory. Zoning usually cannot protect people or their property from existing uses: the time to establish zoning is before a problem develops.

## B. The Zoning Ordinance

A zoning ordinance usually has two parts: an explanatory text and a map showing the boundaries of each zoning district. The text should include references to appropriate state enabling legislation, legal definitions, provisions for relief in certain cases, and procedures for appeal. It should also include a carefully written statement of purpose for each category of zoning, enumerating both permitted and prohibited uses. Boundaries between zones usually follow human-made borders, such as roads, or the edges of significant natural features, such as flood plains, steep slopes, or wetlands.

A basic zoning ordinance defines residential, commercial, industrial, and agricultural uses and designates specific areas for each use. Uses in each zone can be exclusive or cumulative. Exclusive-use zones allow only those uses specified by the ordinance. Unrestricted zones allowing multiple uses are possible but do not allow for more specific regulation of uses as is possible under exclusive use. Many agricultural zones permit nonfarm activities to the extent that they are virtually holding categories for "vacant" farmland until some kind of development comes along. Such zones protect no farmland; it is therefore misleading to call them "agricultural zones." Some communities may need other special categories, such as industrial zones to permit mineral extraction or recreational development zones to regulate such uses as marinas or campgrounds. Most ordinances include a "grandfather clause" that allows nonconforming uses (existing uses that do not comply with the zoning ordinance) to remain where they are or to be phased out ("amortized") by a specified date or when the property is sold. Such amortization periods often apply to billboards and junkyards.

## C. Large-Lot Zoning

Some communities have adopted "large-lot zoning" in the hope of slowing development and preserving open space. Under such ordinances, a house may be built only if it is located on a lot that is much larger than the 1- to 3-acre minimum lot sizes typically permitted in many rural ordinances. The minimum lot size may be 10 acres in one community and 25 in another, but unless it is as large as the minimum size for a viable working farm—for example, 160 acres in McHenry County, Illinois (Case Study 9)—large-lot zoning can do more harm than good.

Although the intent may be to protect land, large-lot residential zoning may actually waste land and may increase environmental problems rather than alleviate them. Low-density development on, say, 10-acre lots often means that development will spread farther and farther into the countryside. It may require improved roads because development extends more

*cases specifically upheld land use regulations as a valid exercise of the "police power." In 1926 the Court first affirmed the constitutionality of zoning in a landmark decision concerning a zoning regulation in Euclid, Ohio (Euclid v. Ambler Realty Co.). In 1978 the Court endorsed the right of communities to adopt land use regulations to protect historic resources (Penn Central Transportation Co. v. New York City). In these decisions, the Court has made it clear that governmental controls on the use of land are not "takings" if they substantially further legitimate governmental purposes and do not deny a property owner the economically viable use of the property. While Euclid concerned zoning and Penn Central historic preservation, they are broad enough to pertain to a variety of other governmental regulations aimed at growth management.*

*No matter how remote the possibility of a successful legal challenge, municipalities should be aware of the potential costs of defending land use regulations from takings challenges—or from a variety of other legal challenges. "You have to budget for it," says the zoning administrator for Bath, Michigan, whose legal costs rose from $500 to $4,000 in 1987 in defending its 1983 ordinance (Jason Cherry, telephone conversation with author, September 1987). Only those communities conscious of the costs of doing nothing are able to contemplate the costs of litigation with any degree of equanimity. Advises Edmondson, "Close coordination with legal counsel when drafting new regulations or revising existing regulations should help ensure that the likelihood of such challenges—or at least of successful challenges—is minimal."*

Zoning map for the town of Weston, Vermont. Weston's zoning ordinance, which was adopted in 1976, includes seven categories: Conservation (C), Resource (Re), Rural Low Intensity (R), Rural Residential (RR), Village (V), Commercial (Com), and Industrial (I). In addition, there is an overlay Shoreland Zone around the pond (horizontal lines) where uses that might pollute the water are prohibited. The most restrictive zone is the conservation category, with a 5-acre minimum lot size, which is reserved for areas with "substantial physical limitations to development." Permitted uses include forestry and single-family homes. The least restrictive zone is the industrial category, with a 1-acre minimum lot size, where permitted uses include quarrying and gasoline stations. The boundaries between zones are based on such factors as property ownership, existing use, and natural features, such as the steepness of the slope.

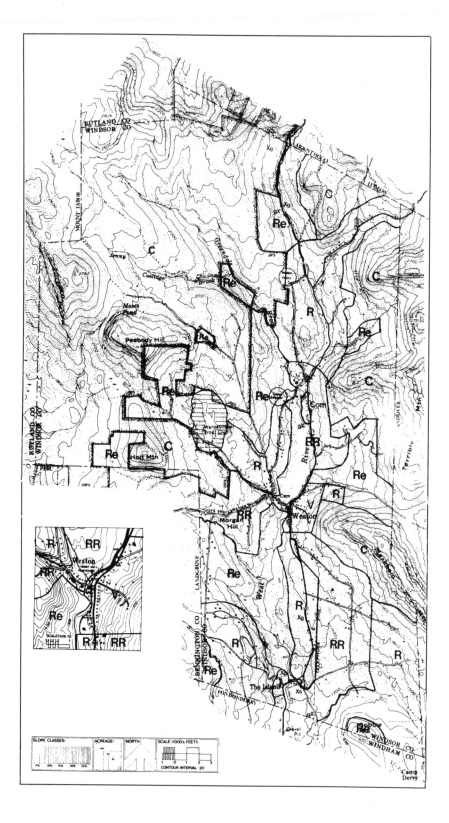

miles, as well as increased sewer, water, and other services that are costly to establish and maintain. And because it spreads development across the countryside, often in strips along roads, large-lot zoning can also hamper farm operations scattered among such "leapfrog" development and diminish the community's scenic qualities.

Large-lot ordinances are frequently regarded with disfavor by the courts, which have ruled some "exclusionary," since larger lots are expensive and thus tend to have the effect of preventing low- and middle-income residents from purchasing property. Communities considering large-lot ordinances should take care that such ordinances actually do protect environmental resources so they can withstand a legal challenge. A reasonable limit may be the minimum lot size that is able to support economically viable agriculture.

## D. Agricultural Zoning

Agricultural zoning, which limits nonfarm uses and often mandates very large, farm-sized lots, has as its aim the protection and maintenance of farm operations. Many ordinances include antinuisance clauses that protect farmers from complaints by residential neighbors about such agricultural activities as spraying herbicides or night plowing (4.VI.C). Agricultural zoning often permits the additional farm dwellings that are necessary for extended families who are living on one farm or for farm laborers. Ordinances linked to differential tax assessment provide farmers with a degree of tax relief (4.VI.A).

## Sliding-Scale Zoning

*Clarke County, Virginia, is an example of a community that has implemented sliding-scale zoning. Here are the number of units allowed for given land-tract sizes:*

| Size of Tract of Land (in acres) | Number of Single-Family Detached Dwelling Units Permitted |
|---|---|
| 0–14.99 | 1 |
| 15–39.99 | 2 |
| 40–79.99 | 3 |
| 80–129.99 | 4 |
| 130–179.99 | 5 |
| 180–229.99 | 6 |
| 230–279.99 | 7 |
| 280–329.99 | 8 |
| 330–399.99 | 9 |
| 400–499.99 | 10 |
| 500–599.99 | 11 |
| 600–729.99 | 12 |
| 730–859.99 | 13 |
| 860–1,029.00 | 14 |
| 1,030 *or more* | 15 |

*Minimum dwelling-unit lot size: 1 acre (less if lot is an existing lot of record)*
*Maximum dwelling-unit lot size: 2 acres (more if necessary for septic fields)*

A development of prefabricated houses in King County, Washington. Although the development is located on prime farmland, an increasingly scarce resource, it takes up less farmland than a large-lot subdivision of the same number of units. King County now has a program to purchase development rights in order to protect the remaining prime farmland (5.V.C).

Some communities have experimented with ways to provide farm owners with some financial gain from limited development while they engage in agriculture as a livelihood. Under some ordinances, farmers are permitted to sell off a small number of residential lots in proportion to the farm's overall acreage. In Peach Bottom Township, Pennsylvania, for example, a "sliding scale" allows one 1-acre residential lot for the first 7 acres and another for each additional 50 acres up to a maximum of nineteen lots (Keene in Steiner and Theilacker 1984, p. 16).

C A S E   S T U D Y   9

## McHenry County, Illinois: An Ambitious Agricultural Zoning Ordinance

McHenry County, Illinois, is typical of those counties in the Midwest farm belt that are facing development pressure, but its zoning ordinance is unusual: 160 acres is the minimum residential lot size in its agricultural zone. The land in McHenry County is gently rolling, its soils productive. Sixty percent of the farmland is prime, in a county where 70 percent of its 611 square miles is devoted to agriculture, mainly corn and soybeans. Agriculture is big business in the county: McHenry's farmers produced $90 million worth of products in 1983 alone.

McHenry is also typical of many rural counties facing development pressures, in this case from Chicago, 55 miles to the southeast, and from Rockford, 35 miles to the west. From 1970 to 1980, the population increased a whopping 33 percent; in 1986, the population totalled 156,489. As a result of the county's increasing population, McHenry's farmers confront many of the same problems that farmers face elsewhere in the nation. Average farm acreage prices in 1978 were five times what they were only fifteen years before, soaring as demand for developable land has grown. Farm vandalism is increasing, and the businesses upon which farmers depend are moving out of the area. Soil erosion and absentee ownership are other concerns.

What makes McHenry County unusual is the lengths to which its farmers and leaders have gone in order to protect agriculture as a business, using the planning and zoning process. In 1977 the county hired Stephen Aradas as director of the planning department. Aradas made his first priority the revision of the 1971 plan, which consisted of little more than a map with no explanatory text. Among other defects, it predicted much higher population growth than the county was experiencing, and it made no provision for agricultural preservation.

McHenry County's new *Year 2000 Land Use Plan,* written by Aradas and his staff, set goals for protecting natural areas, encouraging the preservation of open space for recreational use, promoting the protection of historic resources, and preserving agricultural areas. It recommended that farmland be protected "by allowing the limited conversion of agricultural land use only in those areas which are accessible for reasons of public safety and convenience of services, and only in those areas which are not economically viable for farming . . . , and which will not adversely affect the productivity of adjacent agricultural lands." The plan encouraged growth in the southeast corner of the county, around existing municipalities and, as needed, around smaller hamlets. Prime farmland throughout the county would be preserved, and even nonprime farmland in areas that were remote from municipal services would be protected. The county adopted the plan in October 1979.

The plan was implemented by a tough new zoning ordinance passed a month later. The county's first zoning ordinance, passed in 1949, had a minimum lot size of only 1⅛ acres. In 1974, this was revised upwards to 5 acres. McHenry's farmers soon saw, however, that this change was not enough to protect agriculture in their county, where the average farm size is 220 acres. Increasingly, 5-acre "farmettes" were being purchased by wealthy ex-urbanites interested in raising horses and enjoying country life. The 1979 ordinance created two agricultural zoning districts: A-1 with a 160-acre minimum residential lot size and A-2 with a 1-acre minimum. The best soils—about 75 percent of the farmland, or more than 200,000 acres—were zoned A-1, and the remainder became A-2. Another important provision of the ordinance is that farmers who conduct a form of agriculture that neighbors might regard as offensive—such as operating feed lots, dairying, or raising poultry—are asked to fill out an intensive-use affidavit. Once an affidavit has been filed, purchasers of nearby property cannot complain that they did not know what their farm neighbors were doing.

The new ordinance came about in an unusual way. According to Aradas, "We proposed 35 acres as the minimum residential lot size for areas zoned agricultural. However, a member of the county board misunderstood. He thought that the planning staff was saying 35 was the minimum size for a viable farm. So he proposed 160 acres as the minimum size. It was seconded and passed." When the board member realized his mistake, the rest of the board said it was too late. Of course, there were many objections, and at times emotions ran high. At first, developers did not fight the 160-acre minimum, thinking it was so ridiculous it would not stick and was therefore not worth fighting. They were wrong: more than eight years later, the 160-acre minimum lot size still holds.

A good share of the credit for getting the 160-acre zoning passed must go to Aradas's persuasive style and persistent staff. Aradas had a good relationship with the press, and at one point even hosted a radio program once a month, so he had many opportunities to get his message across. "Whatever it is you want to do, you have to get out and sell it until everyone is sick of hearing about it," says Aradas. Like other communities that have instituted strong land-use regulations, McHenry County was also spurred to act by the unfortunate examples of communities close to large metropolitan areas that had clearly lost their rural character. "We had Chicago to use as a bugaboo. We could say, 'O.K., if you want McHenry to look like Cook County, don't listen to us,' " he comments.

Farmland preservation had a great deal of support in the county. Several members of the county board and planning commission supported it from the start. The Soil Conservation Service District Conservationist and the head of the county's Farm Bureau were also supportive, testifying at many of the meetings. In 1977, the 6,500-member bureau passed a resolution in favor of farmland preservation. A local environmental group, the Defenders, was also effective in educating county residents and lobbying.

As might be expected, there have been court challenges, although, surprisingly, only two. Both times the ordinance was upheld—the last time by a unanimous decision of the Illinois Supreme Court. Prior to 1979 there had been frequent cases that went against the county, primarily because there was no good comprehensive plan to back up its zoning ordinance.

There are still challenges ahead. "Having a land-use plan adopted is only the beginning of the war," says Aradas. Development pressures are still increasing, and soil erosion is a continuing problem. While the ordinance does a good job of protecting prime farmland, there is still a large potential for sprawl because farmers remain free to build one unit per acre on nonprime soils scattered throughout the county, even though public services frequently are not available. On the other hand, since most farmers do have some nonprime A-2 land, there is less opposition to continuation of the ordinance than there might otherwise be. In fact, many farmers are better off than they were before the adoption of the 1979 ordinance. Before, they could not sell more than one lot per 5 acres. Now if a farmer wants to sell, say, ten lots, they can be concentrated on 10 acres with the rest of the land kept in profitable agriculture. Another reason why there has not been more objection to the ordinance is that although there has presumably been some loss of value in the A-1 zone, the land in 1986 still sold for $2,600 an acre, slightly more than it does in neighboring counties with similar soils but fewer restrictions.

If there is a need for more housing in an area, the zoning board of appeals entertains individual petitions for zoning changes. The rezoning requests are reviewed by the planning staff, which prepares a "plan review report" for each request. The report identifies soils and soil limitations of a site, the compatibility of the proposed use with the surrounding area, and the consistency of the use with county and municipal land-use plans, based on the Soil Conservation Service's Land

Stephen Aradas (*left*) and the SCS District Conservationist of McHenry County, Illinois, review which farmland should be protected through 160-acre minimum lot sizes.

Evaluation and Site Assessment (LESA) system, for which McHenry County was a pilot community (see *Land Evaluation and Site Assessment System*, pp. 124–25). The board of appeals then acts upon the request. It has approved several rezonings of land adjacent to existing municipalities but has held firm on more remote prime farmland.

---

## E. Regulating Subdivision

While zoning controls the use of land in the community, including the intensity of use, a subdivision ordinance governs the design of new development that is permitted, including the way it functions, such as traffic circulation or drainage. Specifically, a subdivision ordinance sets standards for the division of larger parcels of land into smaller ones, including specifying the location of streets, open space, utilities, and other improvements.

Used in concert with a zoning ordinance, the subdivision ordinance can be an important rural conservation technique. Although the word "subdivision" is often used to apply to a housing development, subdivision regulations can apply to any division of land. In fact, subdivision regulations came about to make "platting," or legal recordation of land subdivision, more orderly.

Subdivision and subsequent development affect a community's character, its natural resources, and its public services. Good design and engineering standards mandated by subdivision ordinance can go a long way to lessen the negative impacts of development, especially its visual effects, even when zoning permits intensive development. For example, regulations can mandate that strips of natural vegetation be retained or added to create buffers between residential areas and agricultural land, or can en-

Landslides can be a problem on steep slopes where vegetation is removed and inappropriate construction takes place. As this 1967 photograph of San Anselmo, California, suggests, this is not a new problem. SCS District Conservationists can advise rural communities on vulnerable areas and advise on appropriate development regulations.

## Conditional Uses, Special Exceptions, Variances, and Rezoning

*Flexibility in the administration of a zoning ordinance is sometimes desirable. On the ground, certain parcels may not conform to the size requirements for given uses, for example. Again, government officials may have their doubts about certain uses in a given zone, but when presented with a reasonable development plan that takes into account their concerns, they may find a particular use acceptable at a given location.*

*Conditional uses, special permits, or special exceptions provide flexibility by permitting a proposed use under certain conditions prescribed in the ordinance. A variance comes into play when the owner would experience a hardship—not just inconvenience or fewer profits—in complying with the ordinance, often because of the physical characteristics of the particular property. Generally, a variance is limited to dimensional, not use requirements. Rezoning actually changes the zoning category—preferably for the entire zone rather than just one parcel. The latter is called spot zoning and is frowned upon by the courts.*

*All of these means of adjustment have one great disadvantage: the danger that their indiscriminate use will erode popular support for the whole zoning ordinance. As one observer notes, "The greatest single cause for the failure of zoning to effectively guide land use development . . . has been the misuse of the variance technique" (Smith 1983, p. 109).*

courage the planting of street trees or other vegetation that will eventually help a new development blend into the rural landscape.

A subdivision ordinance usually contains a set of definitions, procedures for filing applications, approval procedures, design standards, and provisions for general administration. Subdivision of a limited number of lots, usually from two to five, may be exempted from the full approval process, especially if no new streets are involved. This avoids unnecessary administrative procedures that burden property owners and governments alike. A community should retain a measure of control, however, over even a minor subdivision to ensure that certain standards are met, since a number of small changes can add up to major effects.

An important part of a subdivision ordinance is its performance guarantees, such as an escrow account or secured bond, which ensure that development will take place only as it was approved. The guarantees permit the community to use designated funds to complete a project in the event of any default by a developer or to correct deviations from the approved plan.

A problem many communities face is platted but unbuilt subdivisions that were created when land-use controls were formerly nonexistent or weak. One rural planner in Maryland refers to the numerous unbuilt subdivisions in his county as "ghost subdivisions," a kind of "time bomb set for who-knows-when in the future," that could hurt the county's more recent efforts to improve its development standards. Some newer subdivision ordinances provide for a "sunset" which requires that if sales or construction have not actually occurred within a given period of time, the property owner must reapply for approval.

Related to subdivision regulation is the reservation of land for the creation of future roads, trails, and drainage systems at the time development occurs. This is done by designating the reservations on an "official map" adopted by the local government well in advance of development. It may also be feasible to designate land for parks, schools, or other facilities such as fire stations. At the time development occurs, a developer can be required to dedicate or sell such land to the community.

Rural communities increasingly are adopting erosion and sediment controls to combat problems related to water pollution and flooding. Such controls are sometimes enacted as part of a community's subdivision regulations; they may also be enacted separately or as part of the zoning ordinance or building code. Many are developed and enforced in cooperation with the local Soil and Water Conservation District, whose staff can assist with technical knowledge. Such ordinances may regulate site suitability, the rate and volume of storm-water runoff, the extent and duration of exposed soils during construction, and the design of construction and landscaping to reduce impervious surfaces and improve drainage. A typical requirement during construction, for example, is the use of barriers—bales of straw are common—to retain as much soil on site as possible while it is exposed to the elements. Forestry and agricultural practices that can cause excessive erosion may also be regulated (see *Special-Purpose Ordinances,* pp. 164–65).

### F. Combining Zoning and Subdivision

Since there is little reason to separate zoning and subdivision ordinances, other than that they are usually authorized by different state enabling acts, a few communities such as Medford, New Jersey, have consolidated them to create an ordinance that addresses all land development regardless of whether it involves use, lot size, design, utilities and services, or all of these. Such an ordinance may not only simplify the application process for developers and administrators, but also eliminate the possibility of incompatibility between two ordinances that may have been developed at different times by different people. Creating a new land-development code also may allow for the incorporation of the flexible land-use techniques discussed in the following section and may help to streamline the review process. Hardin County, Kentucky, for example, in educating citizens and developers about its innovative land-development code (Case Study 10), likes to cite the advantages of "one application, one fee, one approval process."

## IV. FLEXIBLE LAND-USE REGULATIONS

Several major criticisms apply to the use of traditional zoning and subdivision regulations. First of all, they may be inflexible. It is difficult to write an ordinance that covers all of the variables in development, and so a community may find that, while it may be getting technically acceptable development, it is not particularly happy with the results. Developers may be equally unhappy. A subdivision ordinance's prescribed solutions to common design or engineering problems may be more expensive than alternatives made possible by particular site characteristics. For instance, an ordinance may call for paved gutters for drainage. In relatively level areas, however, grassed swales allow for maximum absorption of storm-water runoff on site and may be cheaper. Applying for special exceptions, variances, or zoning changes to avoid inflexible standards is frequently cumbersome, especially for small projects, where such maneuvering can be burdensome for local property owners (see *Conditional Uses*, p. 142).

Another difficulty with zoning in rural areas is the assumption that different uses should be segregated. This does not always protect a community's character or its natural environment. Moreover, it may often be more convenient to rural lifestyles to permit facilities such as a grocery store or veterinary clinic to locate in an agricultural area or to intersperse some multiple family housing with single family houses. In rural areas especially, with development typically scattered over some distance, traditional zoning can create seemingly arbitrary or unnecessary exclusions of uses.

Many communities today prefer to use ordinances that offer more flexibility and more land protection. Relatively new tools such as performance zoning are being used in some communities as alternatives to traditional zoning and subdivision regulations. This section briefly describes a few of the best-known of these new techniques, which can be used alone or in combination.

### A. Overlay Zoning

Many local governments have used overlay zoning (sometimes called "critical area zoning") to protect certain resources found throughout the community regardless of zoning, such as steep hillsides or a scenic river. Overlay zoning does not affect the density or use regulations present under existing zoning; rather, it is superimposed over a community's various

## Subdivision Checklist

*In general, a subdivision ordinance establishes design and engineering standards for*

- *General design and layout of lots and buildings*
- *Streets and rights-of-way*
- *Grading*
- *Sidewalks, curbs, and gutters*
- *Drainage and storm-water runoff*
- *Street trees and street lighting*
- *Utilities*
- *Landscaping*
- *Trails and bike paths*
- *Open space and common areas*

*(Adapted from Herbert H. Smith, The Citizen's Guide to Zoning [Chicago: American Planning Assoc., 1983], pp. 149–50.)*

## Clustering

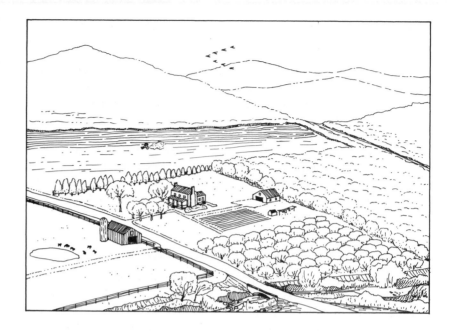

*Inevitably in some rural communities some properties must be developed for nonagricultural uses, such as housing. If development does take place, a good subdivision ordinance and a cooperative developer can assure that the results will look more like the bottom illustration on p. 145, a drawing of the hypothetical Jones farm, than the top illustration on p. 145. Of course, one could argue that there should be no development of this beautiful farm. But the premise here is that development must take place, perhaps because the farmer must sell and cannot find another farmer to buy for top dollar, and no other options for saving more of the land exist. It may also be desirable from the community's point of view that this development take place because more housing is needed and because this farm is nearest to such services as sewer and water lines and closer to other urban development than farms elsewhere in the community.*

zones, creating an additional set of requirements to be met when the special resources protected by the overlay would be affected by a proposed change. Designation and protection of historic districts and sites is a kind of overlay zoning (4.V.C). The designation and protection of shorelands is another example (see illustration, p. 136).

## B. Cluster Development

Cluster development is the grouping of buildings and lots on a small portion of a tract, which can be an effective way to allow limited development in rural areas. One of the major impacts of standard zoning and subdivision ordinances has been the creation of sprawling developments laid out with little regard for natural, agricultural, scenic, and historic resources, with little variety in design and density, and with little open space accessible to nearby property owners or the public. Cluster development allows for more flexibility. A 100-acre tract, for example, under existing land-use regulations could be divided into fifty residential lots. With a cluster provision in the zoning ordinance, usually given as an option to standard development, the developer would be able to maintain the same density of fifty units on 100 acres but offer smaller lots. The remaining land can be dedicated for agriculture through a lease with a nearby farmer, as a park under local government jurisdiction, or as recreational open space maintained by a homeowners' association. Such development may protect more of the original character of the environment and provide a more attractive setting than would a standard subdivision.

The developer's incentive to undertake these desirable things is financial. Greater flexibility in site planning, for example, means that difficult areas for building can be avoided, or natural vegetation can be retained. Other advantages include the need for fewer streets and shorter utility lines—with the added long-term benefits of reduced maintenance costs for the municipality. Some communities view clustering as a significant enough improvement over standard subdivision that they offer extra

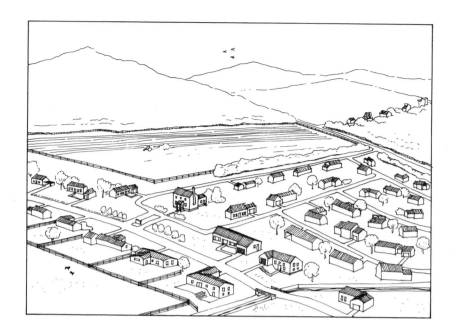

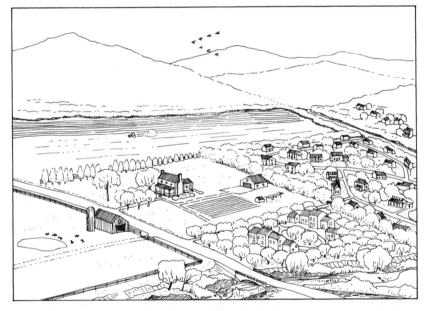

*Opposite:* The Jones farm as it is. Located on a country road, the Jones farm still embodies the distinct visual character of a late-nineteenth-century American farm. It retains its farmhouse, outbuildings, farm pond, orchard, and woodlot. Adjacent fields are still used for both cultivation and grazing. Respect for the natural environment is evident in the retention of wetlands in the foreground, vegetation along the stream, and trees on steep slopes to the right.

*Top:* Inappropriate subdivision of the Jones farm. Short-sighted development of the farm has resulted in environmental damage and destruction of much of its historic character. The original architecture of the farmhouse has been modified, and historic outbuildings and landscape elements have been removed. Development has occurred in the flood plain, and the wetland has been filled. Development along the road has reduced the farmland and gives the landscape a cluttered appearance. Construction on the steep slope not only mars the scene, but also could result in erosion.

*Bottom:* Sensitive development of the Jones farm. The same amount of development can occur without environmental degradation and loss of historic character. Traditional buildings and prime farmland can be retained, and construction on steep slopes, wetlands, and flood plains can be avoided. This development has the same number of units as the one in the illustration above, but the design is more sensitive to the environment. Ten of the units have been clustered in the former orchard. More trees have been retained in the woodlot. Although there is development on the hillside, the houses are not on as steep a slope, fewer trees have been cut, and the buildings are less obtrusive.

density as a bonus to induce a developer to choose this approach (Case Study 2).

Communities sometimes distrust clustering, however, because it can appear to be denser than ordinary development, particularly if it is poorly designed. Neighbors may also fear a loss of property values if clustering permits less expensive homes to be built, or if the open space is not properly maintained. Moreover, unless effective protections for the open land are established and enforced, through such means as conservation easements, it may not remain permanently open.

Fauquier County, Virginia, revamped its clustering requirements in 1986 to improve its protection for rural resources and to manage growth. A former limit of three new units per tract was frequently exceeded by special exception (see *Conditional Uses,* p. 142), apparently because county officials were concerned that the limit was not always reasonable and therefore not legally or politically defensible. A change to a sliding scale meant that the number of units permitted per tract was expanded (see *Sliding-Scale Zoning,* p. 137). But because county officials were more comfortable with the limits, they were more willing to limit special exceptions. The net effect, according to Virginia's Piedmont Environmental Council, was to decrease the intensity of development in the agricultural zone by at least 50 percent. Moreover, the county now requires up to 85 percent of any tract to remain open and the use of conservation easements or deed restrictions to protect the reserved lands (5.V).[7]

Planned residential development (PRD) and planned unit development (PUD) are variations of clustering. While the cluster ordinance allows variety in layout and lot size, a PRD incorporates these provisions as well as encouraging mixed housing types. A PUD allows mixed land uses and is generally applied to large-scale developments of typically 100 acres or more.

CASE STUDY 10

## Hardin County, Kentucky: Guiding Development with "Unzoning"

One example of performance zoning is Hardin County's Development Guidance System, a performance-based approach to land-use regulation that some commentators have styled "unzoning." Its development was a unique response to the county's recent history of tumultuous opposition to traditional land-use planning, after a comprehensive plan was proposed and resoundingly rejected, and a city-county planning commission was afterward dismantled.

A predominantly agricultural community—tobacco and corn are the main crops—Hardin County possesses a strong, diversified economy that includes Fort Knox. In 1987, its population totaled more than 93,000—nearly double what it was in 1950, and projected to nearly double again by the year 2020, largely as a result of growth stemming from Fort Knox, along with the county's proximity to Louisville and the convergence of several major roadways at its center. Though most residents in the county are happy to accommodate such growth, they have also become concerned about the loss of agricultural lands and determined to reduce costly sprawl.

The Development Guidance System (DGS), passed in 1984, features two innovations. First, the criteria for its point system are based on the Soil Conservation Service's Land Evaluation and Site Assessment system (LESA) (see *Land Evaluation and Site Assessment System,* pp. 124–25), the first known use of LESA for mandatory review. Second, it directly involves neighboring landowners in the public assessment of the compatibility of proposed development with its surroundings.

Anyone proposing to build on undeveloped land within the county's planned growth zone (all unincorporated areas of the county) must undergo three steps to obtain a permit: (1) a growth guidance assessment,

Pastoral Hardin County is under increasing development pressures, as evidenced by roadbuilding (*top*) and construction of new homes (*bottom*).

(2) a compatibility assessment, and (3) a plan assessment. Changes of use on previously developed sites are subject to the second and third assessments. Prohibited uses include those which would pollute air or water, or endanger archeological or historic sites.

The growth guidance assessment, based on the LESA model, is a two-part point system using assessments of soils and "amenities." The soils assessment divides the sixty-five soil series found in Hardin County into ten groups based on soil productivity and calculates the average point value per acre for a given site. The higher the final number—up to a maximum of 115 points—the more suitable are the soils for development. The calculation is weighted to discourage development of large tracts of important agricultural soils, and soils favorable for agriculture generally receive fewer points. The amenities assessment assigns points on the basis of such measurable factors as percentage of surrounding land already developed, distance to public services, and location relative to the county's "growth corridor." Points are weighted according to the importance of the various factors in the view of the county's planning commission. Location within the growth corridor, for example, is heavily weighted, even though prime soils may be lost to development as a result. "We just can't save it all in the face of our projected growth," comments the county's planning director and guiding spirit behind the system, Dennis A. Gordon. In using the LESA model, Hardin County found a reasonable way to deal with the difficulty of developing objective, measurable performance standards for locating development.

Proposals achieving 150 points or more in the growth guidance assessment (out of a possible 315) automatically advance to the next step, the compatibility assessment. Those scoring less go before the planning commission for action. Future development of a rejected site remains possible, as more points on the amenities assessment may be earned as characteristics of the area change. Gordon points out that this is a significant difference from zoning with its static maps: "Our DGS recognizes that change is inevitable, *and* it includes this inevitability in the process."

The compatibility assessment involves a required meeting of the developer and neighboring property owners, guided by the planning staff. This meeting takes place early in the review process, when changes in the developer's plans are still simple to make. Gordon notes that this "citizen participation" in local planning has proved far more positive than formal public hearings ordinarily conducted under traditional land-use regulations. "It's much easier to feel you've had an impact. Most participants have emerged as supporters of the process," he says. Through 1986, more than 1,100 people have participated in the meetings, which average less than forty-five minutes. Points of discussion at the meeting are such potential negative impacts as increased traffic, creation of unsightly views, noise, lighting problems, loss of privacy, and increased need for public services. If consensus is not reached, the planning commission may reject the proposal or make a binding decision as to what is necessary to make the proposed project compatible. The compatibility assessment guards against one of the criticisms of performance zoning, that mixed uses will create incompatibility problems. The procedure also lessens the burden of review placed on public officials as compared to other performance systems.

The final step, the plan assessment, is the point at which the developer prepares a detailed development plan meeting county specifications for streets, rights-of-way, and other aspects of subdivision and site development. Options to these standards allow reduced rights-of-way for developers planting approved trees or constructing curbs and gutters. Smaller rights-of-way mean more or larger lots, allowing the developer in turn to reap larger profits that offset the optional improvements.

In a sense, the DGS is a hybrid of elements of environmental and design review (4.V), some restrictions associated with zoning that may develop through the review (placement of signs, for example), and subdivision regulations, especially the plan assessment. But it is a hybrid with such uncommon twists as the use of LESA and a point system and

# Amenities Assessment

| Characteristics | Comments | Score 0 - 10 | Wght. Factor | Points Earned |
|---|---|---|---|---|
| 1  Size of the proposed site | | | 1.2 | |
| 2  Percent of adjacent development | | | 2.6 | |
| 3  Percent of surrounding development | | | 2.2 | |
| 4  Agricultural use and classification | | | 0.8 | |
| 5  Access road type | | | 1.7 | |
| 6  Distance to development... [A] incorporated city [B] rural community | | | 2.1 | |
| 7  Distance to public water | | | 1.7 | |
| 8  Distance to public sewerage | | | 1.5 | |
| 9  Distance to a school facility | | | 1.3 | |
| 10  Distance to a fire department | | | 1.2 | |
| 11  Distance to an ambulance station | | | 0.8 | |
| 12  Terms of ownership | | | 0.7 | |
| 13  Relation to the 'growth corridor' | | | 2.2 | |
| 14  Amenities assessment for development (add lines 1-13) | | | | |
| 15  Soils assessment for development (line 15 of Soils Assessment) | | | | |
| 16  GROWTH GUIDANCE ASSESSMENT (add lines 14 and 15) | | | | |

Hardin County's amenities assessment worksheet. The county planning staff fills out this form, plus a one-page soils assessment worksheet, using an application submitted by the developer. With all the information at hand, the developer spends about ten minutes completing the application. Note that the kinds of amenities the county seeks to assure are close to new development.

a lack of zoning districts. The various reviews associated with environmental and design review, zoning, and subdivision regulation, done separately in most communities, are combined in the DGS, with one application and one fee covering the entire process. In addition to this streamlining, the DGS mandates strict time limits for each phase, so that the entire process can be accomplished in as little as four weeks.

"So far," comments Gordon, "the greatest problem in implementation has been educating the public about the regulation's existence." Another, unanticipated problem was "erasing the specter of traditional zoning from the public's mind," he adds, even though residents have never experienced such zoning. To overcome these problems, the planning commission has placed ads in local newspapers and prepared an explanatory videotape. Letters mailed to developers and neighboring property owners explain the process and detail the role each is expected to play. All meetings begin with a discussion of the ordinance and a chance for questions.

Have sprawl and the loss of prime farmlands in the county been halted as a result of the DGS? Gordon believes that the process has slowed considerably. "In the first three years," he says, "the planning commission processed 229 applications. Of the 83 that had to undergo the growth guidance assessment, 53 were approved and 30 denied. But among the 53 approved only 363 acres were prime soils—less than 100 acres in 1986. At the end of 1985, we found that the 22 projects that were denied averaged around five miles from development or a public school, whereas the 40 that the commission approved were less than three miles away on the average. Further, the average approved site bordered roughly twice as much existing development as did a denied site." Due to publicity about the ordinance—it has won a number of national awards—it is now in its fourth printing, having been sold to more than four hundred individuals and local governments outside the county. Still another measure of the county's success is that the ordinance has proved so popular locally that in 1986 the state amended its enabling legislation, opening the door for still more flexible development regulation.

## C. Performance Systems

Performance systems attempt to address many of the criticisms of zoning and subdivision ordinances by establishing ways to examine the actual effects of any proposed development. Under performance systems the burden is placed on the developer to mitigate objectionable impacts before a building permit can be issued. Performance systems may be classified either as performance standards or as performance zoning and are generally applied through the use of a point system. *Performance standards* are applied to permitted uses in regular zoning categories in order to govern the intensity, siting, or design of a proposed development. *Performance zoning* takes performance standards one step further by reducing or eliminating the number of zones, so that, theoretically at least, any use might occur anywhere in the community.

Performance standards may govern permitted uses with respect to their impact on wetlands, vegetation, critical slopes, groundwater, traffic generation, visual impact, and numerous other criteria. In a residential zone, for example, a developer might have the option of building any type of residential unit as long as it can be demonstrated that specified natural, historic, agricultural, and scenic resources will be protected. Criteria should be based on the community's environmental inventory. Some standards can be established that must be met regardless of the overall score. For example, a community concerned about water quality may require a certain rating for impact on water quality and deny a permit if the required water rating is not met, even if the overall rating is acceptable.

Performance zoning gives developers more flexibility in locating developments and a wider range of acceptable types of development. It also confers potential for development on more land and gives landowners a more equal opportunity to capture what development the community might attract. Thus, developers, landowners, and local officials are sometimes more willing to enact stricter controls under performance zoning than they are with traditional zoning.

Under performance zoning, there are no permitted uses, except those already in place, and few, if any, prohibited uses. Such a system allows a community to know in advance exactly what any new development will look like and what its impacts on the community will be, rather than knowing only its general use category and density. When a traditional zoning ordinance is in effect, a large parcel of land that is zoned residential, for example, may be rezoned commercial at the petition of a developer planning to build a large, well-designed shopping mall that will bring new jobs and tax revenues. If the developer later decides not to build, the land usually remains zoned commercial. Depending on the way the ordinance is written, the community may find that the land receives piecemeal commercial development, with each establishment having a separate access to the highway and with other unanticipated and unwelcome impacts. This could not happen with performance zoning. Instead, each time a development is proposed for the parcel, the specific impacts of that development proposal must be examined, giving the community the opportunity to mitigate objectionable impacts. If the developer fails to build a project, a further proposal for the parcel will start from the beginning of the review process.

Performance zoning has disadvantages, since few models exist. Drafting an ordinance requires skill in developing the performance standards, so its preparation might be more difficult (and thus more costly) than the preparation of standard zoning and subdivision ordinances. The necessity of more intensive review of development proposals can be a procedural burden for any community, with or without a trained planner on staff. Performance zoning may also leave too much discretion to a planning board: its members need experience and skill in decision-making to make performance zoning effective. And finally, ironically, unless the system is well understood by the public, it may receive little support as an alternative to traditional zoning, which to many people may seem to offer certainty about what may be built where. The idea of a factory's being built near a neighborhood's "back yard," even though the factory's impacts are to be mitigated, can raise opposition when performance zoning is proposed.

## D. Transfer of Development Rights (TDR)

Using transfer of development rights (TDR), sometimes called transfer of development credits, a local government allows development rights that are assigned through zoning to one parcel to be transferred to another parcel at a different location. In this way, the right to develop a parcel of land can be separated from the land itself; both the property and the development rights remain private property and can be sold separately (see "*Bundle of Rights,*" pp. 178–79). The development rights in the area to be protected, or "sending zone," can be sold and used on a different parcel of land in an area called a "receiving zone," which has been designated as appropriate for development because it has adequate public services available or fewer resources to be protected. TDR increases the amount of development on a receiving parcel of land and eliminates or reduces the right to develop a sending parcel.

The TDR transaction has obvious advantages for the developer; the advantage to the farmer or rancher is being able to cash in on the mone-

# TDR

The transfer of development rights process in its simplest form works like this: Farmer Brown lives in an area where the county government wishes to protect and encourage agriculture. He wants to continue farming but needs cash (1). Developer Smith owns a tract in an area where the county has the resources to accommodate more development (2), and he would like to develop the tract at a greater density than allowed by the zoning ordinance, which is one residential unit per 2 acres (4). Farmer Brown's development rights are based on zoning in his area that allows one residential unit per 5 acres (3). Since his farm is 110 acres, Farmer Brown has 22 rights. He sells 18 of them to Developer Smith, reserving 1 right for his own residence and 3 rights in order to give his children land on which to build their own homes (5). Developer Smith adds Farmer Brown's 18 rights to the 38 he already owns on his 76-acre parcel, enabling him to develop 56 lots (6). The sale of rights is recorded on the deed to Farmer Brown's farm, so he can no longer build more than three new residences (although he can build new farm buildings), nor can he sell his rights again.

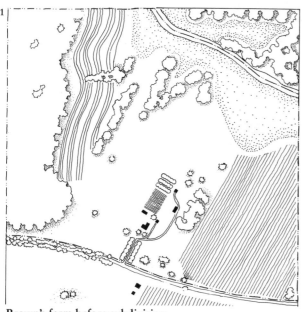

Brown's farm before subdivision

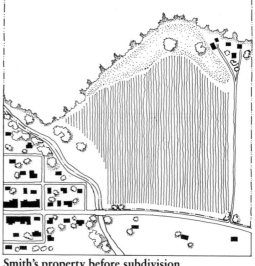

Smith's property before subdivision

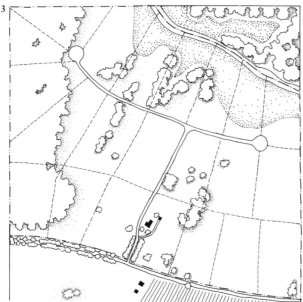

Brown's farm subdivided into 22 lots

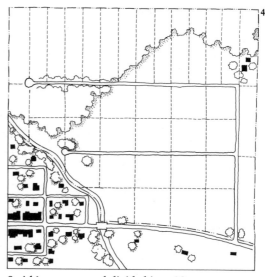

Smith's property subdivided into 38 lots

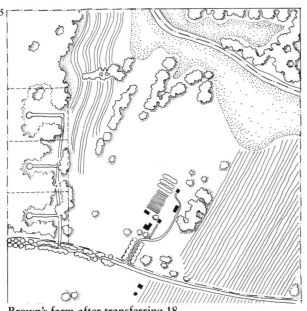

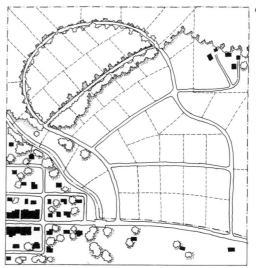

Smith's property has 56 lots after receiving 18 lots from Brown

Brown's farm after transferring 18 lots to Smith

tary value of the land's potential for development while continuing to farm or ranch. For the community, TDR permits the benefits of clustering to be extended across the community: instead of keeping land undeveloped site by site, TDR can protect large areas of the community, at little or no cost to the public, and development can be concentrated where appropriate, for savings in the cost of providing public services.

For TDR to work, there must be a healthy market for the rights, since property owners hoping to sell development rights and disappointed by sluggish sales may clamor for a return to zoning-as-usual. To initiate the TDR program in Montgomery County, Maryland, county officials reduced the allowable density for development in the farming area to be protected from one unit per 5 acres to one unit per 25 acres. This "downzoning" would not have been politically feasible if it had not been offset by allowing farm owners to sell development rights based on the old 5-acre minimum. Another problem is the resistance of residents in the receiving zone, who may oppose increased density, as has been the case with Montgomery County's program. Still another problem is that TDR programs can be complicated to administer and are difficult to explain. The few other rural TDR programs in existence are widely scattered, quite new, and generally located in communities where land values have escalated in recent years. For instance, TDR programs are in place in Monterey County, California, and Palm Beach County, Florida.

# V. ADDRESSING ENVIRONMENTAL PROTECTION, DESIGN QUALITY, AND HISTORIC PRESERVATION

The use of flexible land-use regulations answers many of the criticisms of standard zoning and subdivision. Environmental concerns and good design, however, must be incorporated into whatever controls are in place: environmental concerns at the point that development is proposed for a particular site, and design concerns at the point that the development goes onto the drawing board. How is the community to succeed in addressing both of these concerns? The answer is to create a review process with clear guidelines, flexibility, and room for good judgment by a responsible board.

For most rural communities, a modest level of environmental review and design control is administered by a planning commission, generally through subdivision regulations. In some communities, however, one or more separate boards may be responsible for environmental, design, or historic review. The powers of planning commissions and review boards may vary according to state enabling legislation. In some places, the review board must approve a proposal before the developer can proceed to a review by the planning commission or before a building permit is issued. In other communities, the board simply comments on the proposal, sometimes only at the commission's request. One liability of this extra layer of review is that it takes more time to arrive at a decision to permit or deny a development. When handled sensitively, however, review by such boards can assure that local property values and community goals for a quality environment are reinforced—a benefit for both property owners and developers. The members of such boards should be a mix of interested citizens with and without expertise in design fields. Members with training or experience may not only help spot flaws in proposals, but also suggest revisions that may not have occurred to the developer. Lay members may be able to explain design concepts to applicants without using the "jargon" of the planning and design profession and may more accurately reflect the values and concerns of the community.

## A. Environmental Review

Environmental review can be a first line of defense in protecting natural resources and farmland. A community whose development-approval process includes environmental review can require the developer to submit an environmental impact assessment specifying the resources on the site and the impacts of the planned development on those resources. Like federal and state environmental-impact statement procedures (see *Environmental Impact Statements,* pp. 208–9), environmental review does not necessarily mandate the avoidance of detrimental environmental impacts. Such review generally makes clear the choices involved, provides warning to the community that some harm to the environment will result from the development as it has been proposed, and may point the way toward some on-site mitigation of the worst impacts. In some instances, off-site mitigation may also be considered in the environmental review process—for example, the protection of three acres of wetland elsewhere in exchange for permission to disturb one acre on-site in order to install utilities. Another example of off-site mitigation might be a developer's provision of road improvements, such as widening a road or upgrading an intersection, in recognition of the added traffic burdens of the new development.

# Local Environmental Impact Statements

*Local governments can require developers to assess the environmental impacts of their proposed projects. Such an assessment need not be lengthy. Below is the form used by the town of Cazenovia, New York (Case Study 6) (courtesy Town of Cazenovia).*

ENVIRONMENTAL ASSESSMENT FORM

*Instructions:*

*a. In order to answer the questions in this EAF, it is assumed that the preparer will use currently available information concerning the project and the likely impacts of the action. It is not expected that additional studies, research, or other investigations will be undertaken.*

*b. If the answer to any of the following questions is YES, please attach a sheet explaining the potential environmental impacts associated with each and the measures to be taken to avoid them.*

*1. Will the project result in a large physical change to the project site or physically alter more than 10 acres of land?*

_____ YES _____ NO

*2. Will the project affect any known species of plant or animal life identified as threatened or endangered, or any unique or protected hunting or fishing areas?*

_____ YES _____ NO

*3. Will the project affect any known unique or unusual land forms (i.e., geological formations) or any scenic views or vistas known to be important to the community?*

_____ YES _____ NO

*4. Will the project affect any structure or site listed on or eligible for listing on the National Register of Historic Places, or any similar New York State designation?*

_____ YES _____ NO

*5. Will the project physically alter or cause any temporary or permanent contribution of sediment or other contaminant to the waters of any lake, pond, stream, or wetland?*

_____ YES _____ NO

*6. Will the project have a potentially large impact on groundwater quality?*

_____ YES _____ NO

*7. Will the project significantly affect drainage flow on adjacent sites?*

_____ YES _____ NO

*8. Is the project wholly or partially within or contiguous to any publicly owned or operated park land, recreation area, or designated open space?*

_____ YES _____ NO

*9. Will herbicides or pesticides be used?*

_____ YES _____ NO

*10. Will the project result in a major adverse effect on air quality?*

_____ YES _____ NO

*11. Is the project located in an Agricultural District?*

_____ YES _____ NO

*12. Is the project located in a Resource Management or Protection Area as identified in the* Guide for the Management of Madison County's Resources?

_____ YES _____ NO

*13. Will the project result in major traffic problems or cause a major effect to existing transportation systems?*

_____ YES _____ NO

*14. Will the project regularly cause objectionable odors, noise, glare, vibration, or electrical disturbance as a result of the project's operation?*

_____ YES _____ NO

*15. Will the project have any impact on public health or safety?*

_____ YES _____ NO

*16. Will the project affect the existing community by directly causing a growth in permanent population of more than 5 percent over a one-year period or have a major negative effect on the character of the community or neighborhood?*

_____ YES _____ NO

*17. Is there public controversy concerning the project?*

_____ YES _____ NO

**Note:** *Upon receipt of this form, the Cazenovia Planning Board reserves the right to require the applicant to complete a more detailed EAF before final project review.*

*Preparer's Name and Signature:*

_____

*Representing:* _____

*Title:* _____

*Date:* _____

# General Design Guidelines for Rural Development

*Whether a community simply offers suggested guidelines or requires design review and approval, appropriate development in rural areas should respect certain aspects of design that contribute to the community's "sense of place"—those things that add up to a feeling that a community is a special place, distinct from anywhere else. It is often difficult to identify those things precisely. The illustrations for Hanalei, Hawaii (Case Study 7), may be helpful in understanding "sense of place." Concerned citizens may find themselves at a loss for words or concepts in explaining why they find some types of change disturbing. Indeed, communities often do not realize until it is too late that approved developments should not have been built the way they were.*

*Sometimes it is useful to look at the individual elements of a landscape to help evaluate proposed changes and arrive at community value judgments about the visual impact of proposed changes. An architect or landscape architect can assist a community in reaching consensus about good design. The following discussion, while not comprehensive, raises issues that may be helpful in making design judgments. Although there can be differences of opinion on design issues, most people would agree that in each pair of drawings, below, the one on the right represents better design than the one on the left.*

***Character of Place.*** *Special features and views contribute to a rural community's visual character. New development should be avoided in such areas, but if it is inevitable, new development should be designed sensitively to minimize visual intrusions. Developing designs that protect such features as stream crossings, unique rock outcroppings, significant vegetation, or a distinct village entrance preserves the special character of a community. New development also should not block or mar scenic views, particularly those visible from scenic roads, rivers, or trails.*

*Character of place: special features.* The destruction of a hedgerow (*left*) eliminates a distinctive entrance to the town (*right*).

*Character of place: views.* A housing development sited inappropriately on a steep slope also mars a scenic view (*left*). At right, a distant orchard contributes to the agricultural character of the landscape and creates a scenic view; the housing has been constructed in a less obtrusive location in the community.

*Roads.* Many rural roads are narrow and bordered by vegetation. They generally follow old alignments developed in response to the topography and geography of the area. Designs for new roads and alterations to existing roads should keep their physical impact on the natural and historic environment to a minimum. Where possible, roads should run with the contours of the land rather than across slopes. Extensive cutting through wooded areas to provide wide shoulders or planting along road edges in open areas alters the traditional character of a rural road. Roads should be designed to accommodate the anticipated volume of traffic—including pedestrians and bicycles—but should be kept as narrow as safety allows. Narrower roads may encourage drivers to slow down.

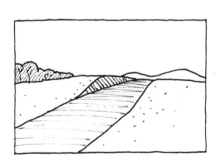 

**Roads: siting.** The road passing through the middle of an open field intrudes in the landscape (*left*); it could be less intrusive placed along the edge of the field (*right*).

**Roads: width.** Excessive cutting destroys the wooded character of the land (*left*), while a narrow clearing along the right-of-way preserves the wooded character (*right*).

**Siting Buildings.** *In most communities, rural buildings traditionally have been sited with respect for the natural environment. Where possible, new buildings should be located in a manner that is in keeping with local building traditions. New buildings and structures should be located where their construction or access does not cause substantial modification to the topography and natural resources. New buildings also should be sited in relation to each other or to existing buildings in a manner that is in keeping with siting traditions. For example, on some farms, buildings are clustered for weather protection and easy access, while on others they are scattered in order to separate diverse or incompatible functions.*

**Building Design.** *Most communities have characteristic building types that occur more frequently than others. Local building traditions usually originated in response to available building materials, climate, and the ethnic origins and occupations of residents. The one-and-a-half-story wooden cottage, for example, is characteristic of many East Coast fishing communities, while the two-story brick or stone farmhouse predominates in the German-American communities of eastern Pennsylvania. New buildings and changes to existing buildings should be compatible with the community's existing buildings. It is not necessary for new buildings to imitate a particular historic architectural style. In fact, it is usually preferable for a new building* to appear as a product of its own time as long as it is compatible in form, scale, material, and color with existing buildings.

*Roof pitches, building height, use of porches and courtyards, and building layout are some of the elements that help define the characteristic building forms of a community. If only gable and shed roofs, for example, are traditional in a community, gambrel, A-frame, or flat roofs may be visually incompatible. The size of new buildings and the proportion of such design elements as wings, porches, windows, and doors are also important in determining their compatibility with existing buildings and the natural environment. New buildings should not dwarf existing buildings; nor*

**Siting buildings: relationship to landforms and other natural features.** Extensive cutting into the hillside is unsightly and can create erosion (*left*), whereas proper siting avoids substantial modification to a landform (*right*).

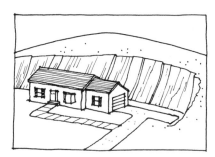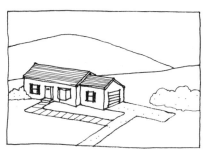

**Siting buildings: relationship to other buildings and structures.** When prefabricated agricultural structures are installed, they should supplement existing buildings, not replace them. Although the new structure (*left*) may be practical, it overpowers the existing barn. A new structure can be both practical and part of the total composition of the farm buildings (*right*).

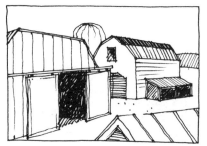

should they overwhelm nearby trees, rise above ridge lines, or tower above other landscape features. When a facility such as a school or factory needs a new building larger than the norm, it may be preferable to construct a cluster of buildings instead of one large building or to vary the heights of various parts of a single building to make it appear less monumental. Elements such as windows and doors also establish a building's porportion and can make a large building appear more compatible in scale to existing buildings if their placement is skillfully designed.

Where possible and appropriate, traditional materials and colors should be used to help new buildings be more compatible with existing buildings or complement the natural environment. Buildings with a natural color stain, for example, may blend into wooded areas more easily than those that are painted in bright colors. Roof colors can make a big difference in the visual impact of new development, with dark colors generally being less obvious.

*Building design: form.* The form and massing of the new building (*left*) does not complement the area's traditional architecture. Roof form, height, and massing can be designed so that a building is compatible with traditional community forms (*right*).

*Building design: scale.* A building typical of much new development dwarfs traditional building (*left*). A new building can be designed as a cluster of smaller parts to offer a sense of integrity to the landscape (*right*).

*Building design: materials and color.* The use of a tile roof and "Tudor" siding (*left*) seems inappropriate when compared to the materials and colors associated with a traditional Cape Cod dwelling. Complementary materials are used in the new building on the right.

# General Design Guidelines for Rural Development *(continued)*

*Vegetation.* In addition to native vegetation, most communities have vegetation that has been introduced because of the preferences of its residents or climatic conditions. In addition, most communities have characteristic ways of grouping plants. The evergreen windbreak located north of the farmhouse to provide shelter from harsh winter winds and the hedgerow along fence lines are two examples. Traditional plant species and historic planting patterns should be retained wherever possible. New species should harmonize with existing vegetation and planting traditions. Planting species that will mature to obscure significant views should be avoided. Land along streets and roads is especially visible and should be planted in a manner compatible with local practice.

*Utilities.* Utility lines are often located without regard to their visual impact on scenic and historic resources. Locations of utility lines and their rights-of-way should avoid interfering, either physically or visually, with existing trees or other vegetation, buildings, or significant views. If lines must run above ground, poles should be set either well in front of roadside trees or far enough back to avoid the all-too-common row of half trees at the edge of the road. Similarly, satellite dishes, radio towers, and other utility structures should be located so that they do not mar views. Whenever possible, such structures should be painted dark colors so that they appear less obvious.

**Vegetation.** A distinct lack of harmony with traditional plant materials and planting patterns occurs on the left, while traditional plant species and planting patterns are retained on the right.

**Utilities.** Conspicuous utilities and damage to roadside trees (**left**) compare with utilities that are screened, set back, and run below the horizon (**right**).

A good communitywide environmental inventory can provide information independent from that provided by the developer. While such an inventory is generally not sufficiently site-specific for an impact review, it can at least help the review board ask the right questions. In the best of all possible worlds, the developer pays for an independent environmental impact assessment contracted for by the review board. If the developer provides a review directly, there is the possibility that the review will paint a somewhat rosier picture than the situation warrants. Although many developers may balk at the expense, an independent assessment is worth insisting on, particularly for larger developments.

## B. Design Review

When aesthetics is an issue, "Beauty is in the eye of the beholder!" often becomes the battle cry of beleaguered property owners, accompanied by the wails of officials reluctant to become arbiters of taste. Yet, without some recognition of the desirability of good design, a community may experience a decline in its visual character, and consequently, a decline in property values and the community's ability to attract commerce and industry, including tourists. Today, says Christopher Duerksen, a land-use attorney, local governments "have great leeway in acting to protect community aesthetics" (Duerksen 1986, p. 4).

Design guidelines can illustrate what acceptable development in the community should look like and can be published by citizens' groups or governmental bodies without the need for state enabling legislation. Such a publication can encourage voluntary efforts to design new buildings and development, or alterations to old buildings, to be compatible with the existing site and surroundings. Whatcom County, Washington, for example, has a set of voluntary design guidelines for incorporating new agricultural structures into the historic dairy complexes and landscape of the Nooksack River valley (Carlson and Durrant 1985).

Design controls go a step further by requiring compliance with design guidelines, and must be permitted by state enabling legislation. Such controls are generally overseen by design review boards. The historic district commission in Nantucket, Massachusetts—with jurisdiction over the entire island, which has significant historic and natural resources—reviews and approves all new construction. Its design guidelines take into account both historic styles and a sensitivity to the landscape (Lang 1978). Some communities may wish to enact a few specific standards in their development regulations—mandatory height limits, for example—as an alternative to or a reinforcement of separate design controls.

Developing design guidelines requires sensitivity to the community's historic and environmental resources and to economic realities. Where agriculture is a business, guidelines should acknowledge the necessity of new building types and landscape changes. Guidelines should also recognize the desirability of new design, rather than rigid imitations of historic styles, in enhancing the landscape and community character.

It requires skill to create guidelines general enough to cover most circumstances that may arise and yet specific enough to protect the community's special resources and unique character. Most communities need professional assistance in developing guidelines, but residents should par-

## Visual Simulations

*If a physical change, such as a new subdivision or even a billboard, is proposed, it is often valuable to simulate what it will look like so that the community can determine its acceptability or whether modifications in the design or siting should be proposed. There are many techniques that can be used, including the preparation of drawings, computer graphics, models, and photographs that have been altered to include the new development. Photographs that have the proposed new development realistically painted in or added by photomontage are effective and inexpensive.*

ticipate as well, to ensure that design professionals are not simply codifying their own tastes. Guidelines for rural communities should not only address the aesthetics of new buildings or their compatibility within the existing built environment, but should also include guidance for site selection and the way a proposed site is to be developed. Other factors to consider include patterns of land use, access, and circulation, location of the building(s) on the parcel, utility placement, vegetation, and open space.

## C. Historic District and Historic Site Review

Historic districts and historic site review are well-established techniques for protection that apply elements of design review to significant historic resources. A local ordinance protecting a historic district or landmark, unlike the National Register of Historic Places (6.IX.B), may require property owners to obtain approval from a review board before taking any action to alter their properties through demolition, exterior alterations, or new construction. For exterior alterations, for example, synthetic sidings or a change in the size of windows may not be permitted in a locally administered district. Charleston, South Carolina, passed the first historic district legislation in the United States in 1931; today there are nearly two thousand cities and counties with locally protected historic districts.

An ancient live oak festooned with Spanish moss is found along the Ashley River at Middleton Place in South Carolina. Dorchester County protects this National Historic Landmark plantation by requiring a special permit for any development which would alter a landmark, or which "by the creation of vibration, air emissions, noise or odor" would adversely affect a landmark, or which would be visible from the landmark up to a distance of 10,000 feet. The ordinance limits development to three stories, or no taller than the top of the surrounding tree canopy (whichever is lower), and regulates removal and planting of trees and other vegetation.

The historic preservation ordinance for Loudoun County, Virginia, protects not only historic houses, but also the farm buildings that have traditionally been a part of the landscape.

*Opposite:* Photographic simulation or photomontage can help decision makers and the general public visualize a proposed development. A design professional alters a photograph to portray the visual impact of the change realistically, as was done here for a proposed high-tension line along a scenic road in Colorado. The Western Area Power Administration retained EDAW, a planning and environmental analysis firm, to do a study of the proposed project, which included this pair of "before" (*top*) and "after" (*bottom*) photographs. The photographs convinced the utility that the transmission line should not be placed near the highway.

Although there are a number of historic districts in rural small towns, only a few exist in large agricultural areas or unincorporated villages. One good example of a rural historic district is in Loudoun County, Virginia. The largest of the county's seven districts, the Goose Creek Historic District, includes about ten thousand acres of farmland. A major innovation of the Loudoun County zoning ordinance is that it provides for review of the "relationship of the size, design and siting of any new or reconstructed structure to the landscape of [a] district." The impact of new construction on a historic landscape with substantial open land has not been considered in most such ordinances, perhaps because most are based on urban models.

Another example of a locally designated rural historic district is in Birmingham, Pennsylvania. There, the district runs the length of the early-

# Special-Purpose Ordinances

Provided the state enabling legislation allows, a local ordinance can be written to protect any resource or deal with almost any problem. For example, some governments pass ordinances restricting the burning of leaves and trash to protect air quality. In fact, say two observers of rural planning, "It is not unusual for a small town or rural area to begin with a junk car ordinance, move on to a mobile home ordinance, and end up with a comprehensive plan and zoning ordinance" (Getzels and Thurow n.d., p. 55). Ordinances such as those described here can be passed separately, or may form subsections of zoning or subdivision ordinances.

**Agricultural Erosion.** Rural communities increasingly are adopting erosion and sediment controls to combat problems related to water pollution and flooding as part of subdivision ordinances (4.III.E). Close relatives of these controls are ordinances dealing with agricultural erosion, but only a few communities have dealt with this problem. Among them is Weld County, Colorado, an early practitioner of agricultural zoning as well. The county regulates the conversion of highly erodible grasslands to cropland by requiring a permit for such "sodbusting." Applicants for the permit must have a Soil Conservation Service conservation plan. Violators can be ordered to cease cultivation and sow species of grass approved by the District Conservationist. If a landowner fails to comply, the county can revegetate the area at the expense of the owner. The county can also prosecute violators (Robert Coughlin, in American Farmland Trust 1984, technical volume, pp. 29–31).

**Mining.** For surface mining of coal, sand, gravel, or other minerals, state or federal controls on coal mining, blasting, and air quality generally provide some protection to the community (6.X.B), but it is possible to enact further regulations to deal with the impacts or hazards of such activities. The location of mines, the post-mining usefulness of the land, the pace of the mining operations, and the impacts on roads are community concerns that may be addressed, primarily through zoning provisions and enforcement of vehicle codes (Curry and Fox 1978).

**Hazardous Wastes.** Disposal of locally produced hazardous wastes is another area of potential regulation in order to protect streams, lakes, and underground water supplies. While federal law deals with the worst problems (6.X.C), most households and farms generate small amounts of harmful wastes. Unregulated "small generators" (industries producing about a ton or less annually) and industries that choose on-site disposal of their wastes can also present local problems. But as one authority says, "The real chemical time bomb may be the local landfill, which often is not monitored, not required to meet strict isolation standards, reused for municipal purposes, and casually operated—and thus may be leaching toxic chemicals into the community's groundwater supply" (Martin Jaffe, "Deadly Gardens, Deadly Fruit: The Local Regulation of Hazardous Wastes," Planning, April 1981, p. 17). An ordinance can forbid deposition of hazardous wastes with regularly collected trash to help prevent contamination of landfills. This regulation can be reinforced by the establishment of special collection days at the local landfill or by contracting with a licensed waste hauler to remove hazardous materials directly from rural properties when landowners request the service.

An important related area of regulation is the siting and buffering of land uses near operating or closed hazardous waste sites. In California, for example, state law requires a 2,000-foot buffer between a waste site and neighboring land uses. The Citizen's Clearinghouse for Hazardous Wastes can provide further information.

**Air Pollution.** Although air pollution that drifts in from nearby cities or regional industrial areas may be something rural governments can do little about, they can regulate air pollution that originates in the community. Many regulate the burning of trash. A number of communities in Vermont and Colorado, especially susceptible to local pollution by their location in valleys, also regulate the use of wood stoves. The Environmental Protection Agency now limits allowable air emissions from new stoves.

**Noise Pollution.** Noise pollution is a serious problem in some communities, particularly along major highways and near airports. In some cases it is a mere annoyance; in others, it can cause hearing losses for nearby residents. Local governments can limit residents' exposure to traffic noise through zoning and subdivision regulations that limit development adjacent to major highways and by requiring vegetative buffers or deep setbacks for any development that does occur. Some communities where the problem has become acute have resorted to more expensive and sometimes unsightly options of building walls or earthen berms—or requiring that developers install them.

**Power Lines.** *Some research indicates there may be long-term health risks for people who live in the immediate vicinity of power lines and radio and television transmission towers, which produce nonionizing radiation. Moreover, quite apart from potential health problems, power lines and towers are unattractive. Local governments can limit the impacts of these installations by working with electric utilities to locate power lines away from residential areas and highly visible locations, by controlling the locations of communications towers through zoning, and by steering residential development away from existing installations. Although placing lines underground can cost several times as much as overhead transmission, some communities, such as Frederick, Maryland, have been successful in requiring utilities to place lines underground. Sometimes utilities can be persuaded to place their lines above railroad or pipeline rights-of-way, thereby reducing their combined impact.*

**Signs.** *In some communities amending local regulations with language promoting better sign control and fewer billboards may be an inexpensive and simple option for improving the community's appearance, although politically speaking, the opposition of the outdoor advertising industry can be difficult to counter.*

*Many communities regulate the size, height, number, lighting, and placement of signs both on-site and off-site. More than a thousand local governments now prohibit off-site advertising—commonly known as billboards—and still more control on-site signs. An ordinance may even, after an appropriate period of time called an "amortization period," require the removal of signs that do not meet the regulations but are already in place at the time the*

*ordinance is passed (6.IX.C). Hardin County, Kentucky, for example, prohibits all blinking signs, either permanent or temporary, and limits the size of off-site signs to a maximum of three hundred square feet and their overall height to a maximum of twenty-five feet (Case Study 10). The Coalition for Scenic Beauty can provide more information.*

**Forests.** *Just as locally valued farmland can be protected from non-agricultural development, so can productive forest lands be conserved. Delta County, one of fifteen counties in Michigan's Upper Peninsula, where more than 80 percent of the peninsula's ten million acres is forested, enacted a zoning ordinance in 1976 to protect its timber industry. The ordinance, which implemented a comprehensive plan targeting "forest and related lands," created three forest zones. The prime timber production zone provides for timber growth and harvest almost exclusively. Special permits control other development, including residences. The other two, less restrictive zones cover general resource production and open space (John C. Maurer in Society of American Foresters 1982, pp. 588–90).*

**Wildlife.** *Unfortunately, prime wildlife habitat, like prime farmland, is frequently the most desirable land in the community for development, especially in the West, where valued riparian habitat is scarce. In Adams County, Colorado, the planning department, working with the state's Division of Wildlife, mapped the distribution of endangered species, such as the peregrine falcon, and economically important species that are hunted. A composite map showed areas where develement might potentially have a high or at least moderate impact on valued wildlife.*

*Once the maps were complete, the Planning Commission adopted a review procedure incorporating consultation with the District Wildlife Manager wherever proposed development falls within those areas. In one sample case, review of a high-density mobile-home park planned for a square mile section south of a state wildlife refuge and park resulted in decreased density limited to half the section and a half square mile of dedicated open space serving as a buffer to the refuge (Dave Lovell in Sikorowski and Bissell 1986, pp. IX-47–50).*

## The Secretary of the Interior's Standards for Rehabilitation

*The federal government developed the following standards for evaluating rehabilitation work done on buildings for which owners apply for tax credits (6.IX.B). These standards can also be incorporated into local preservation ordinances.*

*1. Every reasonable effort shall be made to provide a compatible use for a property which requires minimal alteration of the building, structure, or site and its environment, or to use the property for its originally intended purpose.*

*2. The distinguishing original qualities or character of a building, structure, or site and its environment shall not be destroyed. The removal or alteration of any historic material or distinctive architectural features should be avoided when possible.*

*3. All buildings, structures, and sites shall be recognized as products of their own time. Alterations that have no historical basis and which seek to create an earlier appearance shall be discouraged.*

*4. Changes which may have taken place in the course of time are evidence of the history and development of a building, structure, or site and its environment. These changes may have acquired significance in their own right, and this significance shall be recognized and respected.*

*5. Distinctive architectural features or examples of skilled craftsmanship which characterize a building, structure, or site shall be treated with sensitivity.*

*6. Deteriorated architectural features shall be repaired rather than replaced, wherever possible. In the event replacement is necessary, the new material should match the material being replaced in composition, design, color, texture, and other vi-*

eighteenth-century Birmingham Road that lies within the township. In addition to the usual historic district review, commercial zoning for the portion of the district covering the village of Dilworthtown is tailored to its historic character. Outside the village, development innovations such as clustering are encouraged to minimize the impact of residential development. A booklet developed by the township for property owners gives the history of the district, covers design considerations for new construction and alterations, and lists procedures for obtaining a permit.

## VI. OTHER TECHNIQUES

Since this chapter has covered a considerable number of land-protection techniques and their variations, it may be helpful at this point to categorize the many powers that local governments can use for rural conservation. So far, this chapter has concentrated largely on the ability of local governments to use their power to regulate land use for the health, safety, and general welfare (including aesthetics) of the community, a power often called the "police power." Other powers of local governments can also be used to guide land-use activities. The power to tax, for example, which can be used to encourage farmland retention, is covered in this section. The power to spend and the power to acquire property are highlighted in the earlier discussion of capital improvements (4.II.F) and return in this section as aspects of agricultural districting, a hybrid approach using a variety of governmental powers. A twist to these powers is also discussed: a "hands-off" approach forbidding regulation of farm practices called a "right-to-farm" law.

### A. Taxation

Adjustments in real estate taxes can influence rural conservation. Differential taxation—also known as preferred, use-value, restricted-use, or deferred taxation, and present in all fifty states—lowers the tax burden on those lands a community wishes to protect from development. Rather than assessing these lands at their full market value, the local government assesses them at "use value." For instance, farmland close to a city might be assessed at the same rate as farmland of comparable quality remote from development pressure, instead of being assessed as land ripe for development. Since high property taxes are among the factors influencing some farmers to go out of business or sell their land for development, reduction of these taxes may encourage farmers to continue farming or to resist the temptation to sell off portions of their farms.

Used as part of a package of techniques, differential tax assessment programs may help preserve open space. Agriculture, followed by forestry, is the most frequently designated use that entitles an owner to differential tax assessment. Natural, scenic, recreational, and historical resources are named in some states' programs.

In most states, the owner who develops a property must pay a penalty for the back taxes that would have been owed if a differential assessment had been in effect, or both. Even so, differential tax assessment alone is not a long-range land-protection technique. For example, differential assessment lowers the costs of holding land for speculators, who frequently qualify for such programs by arranging for their land to be farmed. The prospect of paying several thousand dollars in back taxes is not a significant disincentive to a major development.

Another differential taxation system is called Urban and Rural Service Area Assessments. URSAA distinguishes between properties ultimately to be developed, through the extension of public water and sewer lines, and properties not targeted for development. The properties designated to receive development are taxed at a higher rate. According to two observers of growth management systems, the URSAA system "discourages speculative investment and channels development pressures into those areas which are most acceptable."[8]

Some communities have coupled deed restrictions with lower taxation. In California, for example, communities can enter into voluntary restrictive agreements with landowners, who receive lowered taxes in exchange. Perinton, New York, has created a program of voluntary short-term conservation easements tied to a sliding-scale reduction of taxes based on the number of years the easements run.

Another means of using taxing authority to achieve rural conservation is a high capital gains tax on real estate held for a short term. Vermont has found that a capital gains tax tied to the length of time the land is held helps to protect rural land from short-term speculation. Under Vermont's Land Gains Tax, owners are liable for taxes of up to 80 percent of their profit if they sell property within the first year of ownership. A sliding scale reduces the maximum tax liability to 50 percent the second year and so on downward until there is no penalty after six years of ownership. The law allows long-term farmers to make a profit on their land when they retire, but discourages speculators who want to make a quick profit. (A different kind of tax on real estate transactions, the transfer tax, is described in *Land Banking*, pp. 184–85.)

Finally, in Wisconsin and Michigan, the state income tax has been tied to local zoning in an innovative fashion. Farmland owners receive a deduction on their state income if their land is included in exclusive-use agricultural zones, which must be passed at the local level. As a result of this financial incentive, farmers heavily supported zoning. Minnesota has a similar program, in which farmers are given an unusual property tax credit of $1.50 per acre for land in exclusive agricultural zones.

## B. Agricultural Districts

By 1986, twelve states had enacted provisions for agricultural districts to help protect agriculture. These are specially designated areas where state and local governments may be limited in their ability to restrict farm practices (as described below), take farmland by eminent domain or annexation, or allow the construction of utilities. To participate, farmers sign voluntary agreements to keep their land in agriculture for a specific period of years, with the option of renewing. In some states, farmers must be part of an agricultural district to qualify for differential tax assessment or purchase of development rights (Case Study 11 and 5.V.C).

The required number of participating farmers, the amount of acreage that must be included, and the duration of time a district will exist vary from state to state. In New York, for example, an owner or owners of at least five hundred acres may apply to form an agricultural district. Public hearings and county and state approval are needed to establish a district.

*sual qualities. Repair or replacement of missing architectural features should be based on accurate duplications of features, substantiated by historic, physical, or pictorial evidence rather than on conjectural designs, or the availability of different architectural elements from other buildings or structures.*

*7. The surface cleaning of structures shall be undertaken with the gentlest means possible. Sandblasting and other cleaning methods that will damage the historic building materials shall not be undertaken.*

*8. Every reasonable effort shall be made to protect and preserve archeological resources affected by, or adjacent to any project.*

*9. Contemporary design for alterations and additions to existing properties shall not be discouraged when such alterations and additions do not destroy significant historical, architectural, or cultural material, and such design is compatible with the size, scale, color, material, and character of the property, neighborhood, or environment.*

*10. Whenever possible, new additions or alterations to structures shall be done in such a manner that if such additions or alterations were to be removed in the future, the essential form and integrity of the structure would be unimpaired. (Code of Federal Regulations, vol. 36, pt. 67.7.)*

The need for a district is reexamined every eight years. Local Cooperative Extension Service agents or Soil Conservation Service District Conservationists can provide information on a particular state's programs.

## C. Right-to-Farm Laws

Most states have laws addressing the conflicts between farmers and their nonfarm neighbors, generically called "right-to-farm laws." In general, these laws seek to protect farmers from nuisance suits by nonfarm neighbors objecting to the odors, dust, noise, or other aspects of farming they find unpleasant. The laws also prevent local governments from passing ordinances regulating ordinary farm practices. Not only farms but also food processors and related enterprises may be covered by such laws. Negligent or improper management, water pollution, or impacts on public health and safety generally are excluded from such protections.

CASE STUDY 11

# Carroll County, Maryland: Multiple Means of Protecting Agricultural Lands

Protecting farmland has been a high priority in Carroll County, Maryland, since 1978, when the county commissioners amended their zoning ordinance. Farmland preservation is carried out through three interconnected programs: agricultural zoning, voluntary creation of agricultural districts, and purchase of development rights (PDR).

A large rural county with substantial amounts of prime farmland, Carroll County is close enough to both Baltimore and Washington, D.C., to be facing considerable development pressure. In 1970, the county's population was 69,000; as of 1985, it was 109,000. Despite such growth, agriculture—principally dairy products, livestock, and corn—is still big business. In 1984, Carroll County farms and businesses supporting farms grossed more than $180 million. Sixty percent of the 291,602-acre county is devoted to agriculture, with more than 71,000 acres rated as prime farmland.

As of mid-1986, there were 180 farms protected by agricultural districts in the county, comprising more than 25,000 acres. Farmers enter agricultural districts voluntarily with approval from the county. Farms must be at least 100 acres and consist of good-quality soils. Land in agricultural districts must remain in agriculture for at least five years and cannot be subdivided, except to provide homes for the owner's children and farm laborers. Farmers in agricultural districts are protected from nuisance suits related to their agricultural activities and are eligible to sell their development rights (5.V.C) to the state upon approval by the county.

The county's agricultural districts and agricultural zoning go hand in hand. The agricultural zone, covering 189,000 acres—65 percent of the county—allows only one new dwelling unit per 20 acres, with a minimum lot size of 1 acre. Developers are encouraged to cluster any de-

Advertisements like this one on a Carroll County dairying barn add much to the cultural landscape.

Dairying is still a major business in Carroll County despite its proximity to Baltimore, Frederick, and Washington, D.C. The county has restricted subdivision within agricultural districts and acquired development rights to preserve farmland. However, much farmland has already given way to development.

velopment in the agricultural zone, so that some land on developed parcels remains permanently available for agriculture. Clustering, however, is "not as easy to accomplish as we'd like it to be," says Marlene Conaway, formerly the county planning department's agricultural preservation specialist. "It's difficult because many people who move out here want farmettes. But we have been fairly successful." She hopes that as farm owners see more clustering in use and realize that the county is committed to discouraging sprawl in the agricultural zone, more owners will be encouraged to form agricultural districts.

The "hand-in-hand" nature of the zone and the districts works both ways, however. Passing the agricultural zoning required assurances from the county that farmers would be able to form agricultural districts, thus becoming eligible to sell their development rights, and that the

Conservationists in Uniontown, Carroll County, have protected both historic buildings and the surrounding farmland that provides the setting for the village. Uniontown, which dates from 1809, is listed in the National Register of Historic Places and is protected by a county historic preservation ordinance that regulates changes to the buildings, sidewalks, and street trees. Farmers whose land surrounds Uniontown have voluntarily placed their land in agricultural districts. The owners are protected from nuisance suits and are eligible to sell their development rights to the state.

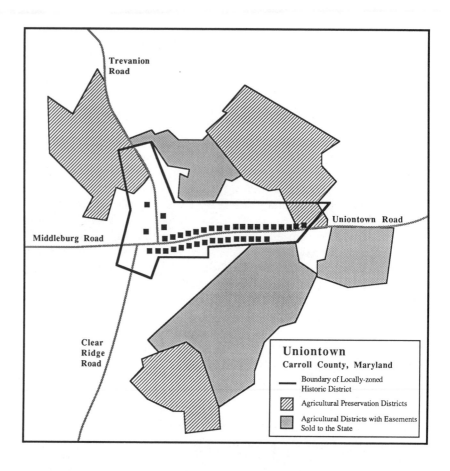

Uniontown
Carroll County, Maryland

— Boundary of Locally-zoned Historic District

⫽ Agricultural Preservation Districts

▨ Agricultural Districts with Easements Sold to the State

county would participate financially in the state's program for purchase of development rights. Each is necessary for the other to exist, says Conaway: "Zoning covers more farmland, but it's not forever: the political climate could change. If we lose the zoning, then we'd start losing districts when their time is up. The more agricultural districts we get, though, the more sure we are of maintaining the zoning," since it would make little sense to alter the agricultural zoning in areas where most farms are protected by districts, and ultimately by purchase of their development rights.

Each year since 1979, the state of Maryland has appropriated funds for the Maryland Agricultural Land Foundation to purchase development rights from farmers whose land is in agricultural districts. Counties also contribute. Carroll County has led the state in contributing to the program, appropriating close to $3 million through mid-1986 to match $7 million from the state, which has purchased easements restricting development rights on ninety-five farms, protecting 13,100 acres.

The foundation uses a bidding system to arrive at a price per acre for development rights. In 1985, Carroll County's average for development rights was $682 per acre, even though unrestricted farmland in the county sells for around $2,500 per acre. Once a farmer has notified the state of an interest in selling development rights, the foundation appraises the farm to establish its restricted and unrestricted market value. The difference between the two values is the appraised value of the de-

170

velopment rights. The farmer informs the state of his or her asking price per acre before the appraisal is done. Those offers below appraised value receive first consideration by the state, and the state cannot pay more than the appraised value.

The program has proven popular with county farmers *and* their neighbors, who are "happy to see the farms protected and their rural lifestyle maintained," says Conaway. In fact, farmers have offered more easements than the foundation can buy. County officials hope eventually to obtain easements on 100,000 acres. They believe this is the minimum amount of farmland the county must preserve to assure the continued viability of agriculture and local agribusiness.

County officials note that much of the money farmers are receiving for their development rights is being reinvested in their farms, often to buy more land or equipment. An added bonus of the PDR program is that owners of the restricted farms become very interested in soil conservation in order to maintain productivity. In fact, the foundation recently amended its standard easement to require that farms in its program implement a conservation plan. The principal problem county officials see—aside from wishing more funds were available to accelerate purchases—is that they cannot act fast enough in hardship cases. They are considering augmenting the state program by purchasing development rights directly for later transfer to the state.

## VII. DRAFTING AND ADMINISTERING ORDINANCES

In practice, most local governments adopt new regulations that are variations on those used elsewhere. By using existing ordinances as models, a community can avoid the errors or oversights that might result from drafting an original ordinance. "Plagiarism," says one rural planner, "is an asset in planning."[9] Another expert, though, cautions rural communities in this practice: "Do not assume that another community's ordinance is perfect. There are many obsolete and even illegal provisions in existing land-use regulations."[10] Moreover, a substantial amount of time may still be needed to eliminate inappropriate provisions and add those that are tailored to the community's particular circumstances. Environmental conditions vary from place to place (just think of the dry desert of Arizona versus subtropical Florida) and uses compatible in one community may be incompatible in another—hog confinements, for example, may or may not have their place.

Since land-use regulations have been used in this country for almost eighty years, there are numerous legal precedents. Even so, drafting or amending an ordinance, like creating a comprehensive plan, usually requires professional assistance, in this case often from both a planning staff or consultant and an attorney experienced in land-use law. Such professionals help to ensure that an ordinance is consistent with the state's enabling legislation, including procedures for enactment, and that it can withstand a legal challenge. As is also the case with developing a new plan, the more community involvement there is, the more useful and acceptable the product is likely to be.

A common failure among activists who have worked to get a good law enacted is to overlook how it is administered. Funds and trained staff or qualified volunteers are needed to assure the benefits of a good law. Concerned citizens should be certain that enforcement is indeed being carried out. Since many rural jurisdictions are large and have limited staff, illegal activities may all too easily go unnoticed.

Many ordinances are dependent upon citizen boards, appointed or elected, who review and approve development proposals. These boards include zoning boards, planning commissions, environmental commissions, and design review boards. In most cases, these boards are advisory only; the local governing body must approve their decisions. Obviously, it is important that a community's boards have members with few vested interests representing a broad cross-section of the community. Unfortunately, many boards dealing with land use come to be dominated by contractors, real estate agents, large landowners, and others who may profit from development. Rural conservation leaders should make the selection of dedicated board members representing the entire community a priority. "These members must also have the aptitude for careful, patient study and the ability to interrelate present decisions with their impact on the future," adds Warren Zitzmann.[11] Second only to careful selection is the importance of training these board members. Training may be available from the state's community affairs agency, a university, the Cooperative Extension Service, peer groups within the region or state, or a national group such as the National Alliance of Preservation Commissions.

## VIII. CONCLUSION

In this chapter, we have described the various techniques that your local officials can use to avoid undesirable fiscal, economic, environmental, and social impacts from changes that may loom on your community's horizon. Many of these techniques have their limitations, most notably that your next set of elected officials could dismantle them. If your community is like most, however, the problem you face is that of enacting good ordinances in the first place, since few communities have more than the bare minimum.

The next chapter covers voluntary property-stewardship techniques that can complement local government action. As in Carroll County, Maryland—where easements, voluntary agricultural districts, and agricultural zoning work hand in hand (Case Study 11)—your community may find that such voluntary techniques offer innovative ways to address the limitations of a purely governmental approach.

# Voluntary Techniques for Protecting Private Property

## I. INTRODUCTION

Having dealt with the variety of approaches to land-use management possible through governmental action, we turn now to the private sector, where experimentation and creativity, often born of desperation to save threatened properties, have resulted in a healthy ferment of ideas. Private, nonprofit historic preservation organizations have been known in this country since 1853, when the Mount Vernon Ladies' Association was established to save George Washington's home in Virginia. Nonprofit "conservancies" or "land trusts" (organizations dedicated to land conservation through ownership and encouragement of private stewardship) have been known since the founding in 1891 of the Trustees of Reservations in Massachusetts. Indeed, in the Trustees, we have an early example of an organization dedicated to both historic preservation and land conservation.

The advent of the growth pressures in the decades following World War II, combined with a dawning environmental awareness in the 1960s, spurred growth in the number of organizations formed to save land and buildings, and with that growth came innovations. "Conservation easements," for example, was a term barely known twenty years ago. Now, it is almost a commonplace idea in many urban and rural areas. Bargain sales, limited development, and management agreements are all other ideas that have sprung from organizations you will learn about here.

In this chapter we explore the range of voluntary, private techniques for land conservation you can use in working with property owners—ideas you can combine with the local government protection techniques described in Chapter 4. Indeed, the more techniques you can combine, the more flexible and widely applicable will be your rural conservation program. Planning, zoning, and other regulations broadly influence rural conservation, requiring all property owners to adhere to certain standards. Agreements with property owners can supplement such regulations by allowing you to pay particular attention to the specific resources on any one property and the objectives of the owner. Cost, permanence, coverage, and the ability to control or encourage certain uses are all considerations as you evaluate both governmental regulations and private agreements.

Although most of the techniques described in this chapter are generally carried out by nonprofit organizations, government agencies use them as well. This is particularly the case for notification, recognition, and nonbinding agreement programs (5.II), the purchase of development rights (5.V.C), and land banking (see *Land Banking,* pp. 184–85). For the sake of convenience, "organization" as it is used in this chapter refers to both private nonprofit organizations and governmental agencies.

Some techniques covered in this chapter are on the order of "handshake" agreements; others, such as easements, are legally binding. Some are perpetual, while others are only temporary. The costs of implementing and administering the various techniques vary considerably. Some involve modest sums of money or no acquisition of property rights; others may require you to make substantial expenditures and obtain assistance from accountants and attorneys. The following discussion proceeds from the least binding and most easily implemented techniques to more binding ones.

## II. NOTIFICATION, RECOGNITION, AND NONBINDING AGREEMENT PROGRAMS

A basic technique to prevent harm to important resources is a notification program. Owners who are made aware of important resources on their properties are often willing to protect them once they learn of their existence. A notification program might logically follow a comprehensive environmental inventory. The rural conservation organization simply lets the owner of a historic house, natural area, or other property know of its significance and suggests that it deserves protection. Notification generally consists of a brief letter describing why the property is significant and a follow-up visit to answer questions. Publicity is not necessary, and indeed it may be undesirable. Although entailing no actual agreement, notification can be an important first step in establishing a good relationship with a property owner; this relationship may eventually result in a permanent commitment to protecting a significant resource.

A recognition program takes notification one step further by announcing publicly that a property is significant. Recognition programs have been used by federal, state, and local governments as well as nonprofit organizations. For example, "century farms" programs established in many states honor families who have owned and farmed the same property for a hundred years or more. The federal government's National Natural Landmarks Program is another recognition program (6.IX.A).

Recognition programs work because they play on the pride of the owner, who would not want to lose face in the community by destroying a resource after having been praised for protecting it. Some organizations present plaques or certificates to owners of recognized properties. The Berks County Conservancy of Pennsylvania sells a hand-painted plaque in

Evan and Catherine Roberts (*right and left*) and two members of the Fort Collins Historical Society display a centennial farm award. Originally homesteaded in 1873 by Mr. Roberts's grandfather, the Roberts Ranch now encompasses 20,000 acres.

the shape of the county, made of cast iron in honor of early iron mining done in the region, to owners of historic buildings designated in the county. The plaque is suitable for affixing to the exterior of a building.

Although it may not be legally necessary to have an owner agree to list a property on a roster of significant properties, it is wise to do so. Some owners might resent the fact that an organization has compiled detailed information about their properties without sharing it with them; others may not want their holdings made public. To prevent hard feelings and, more importantly, to increase the owner's awareness of the significance of the property, the organization should secure the owner's permission to list the property.

A number of state governments and nonprofit organizations operate nonbinding agreement programs for natural resources, many in association with recognition programs. Property owners agree in writing to protect specified significant features of their properties and usually receive in return a plaque or certificate that acknowledges the special nature of the property and the owner's contribution to its protection. The owner's obligation to comply is strictly voluntary. The agreements are based on mutual trust, pride of ownership, recognition and appreciation of the resource, commitment to conservation, and feelings of satisfaction that participation brings. The owner can withdraw from the program at any time with advance notice, typically thirty days, and receives no financial compensation and no tax benefits.

Notification, recognition, and nonbinding agreement programs alone are not enough to insure the protection of many properties over the long run. But by using these programs initially, a group may enhance its standing in the community, make first contacts with property owners, and achieve a measure of protection. As their capability and funds allow, many rural conservation organizations move to more complex, binding agreements with property owners.

## North Carolina:
## The Natural Heritage
## Registry

A typical nonbinding agreement program is North Carolina's Registry of Natural Heritage Areas, established in 1979. It is patterned after natural heritage programs established by more than forty states, largely using state-by-state inventories created with assistance from the Nature Conservancy (3.III.E). The program has identified nearly six hundred natural areas having greatest importance to the survival of the state's

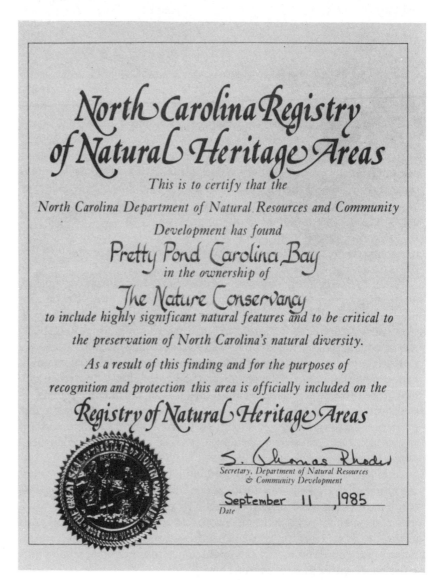

The certificate presented to landowners registering their land with North Carolina's Registry of Natural Heritage areas.

natural heritage. Across North Carolina these areas include old-growth river bottomland and swamp forests, undisturbed remnants of longleaf pine savannas, mountain bogs, mature stands of piedmont hardwood forests, and rock outcrops with unique vegetation.

One example of an endangered plant protected by the registry is Cooley's meadowrue, which grows in only a few locations in southeastern North Carolina. The plant's habitat is the open edge of pine woodlands, and the largest population grows along an electric transmission line. The landowner, a paper company, and the electric utility agreed to adopt management policies that would preserve the plant. The program's biggest project to date is a memorandum of agreement with the U.S. Air Force to protect 19,000 acres of the 46,000-acre Dare Bombing Range along the Alligator River.

After seven years, more than two hundred landowners—private, governmental, and nonprofit—have enrolled more than two hundred natural areas. Owners receive written descriptions, management recommendations, and framed certificates (see illustration). The program staff maintains frequent communications with the owners and visits the sites periodically.

---

## III. TEMPORARY BINDING AGREEMENTS

Temporary binding agreements, which are enforceable, are an approach falling between nonbinding agreements and acquisition of property or easements. By negotiating contracts with owners for a period of time, an organization can be confident that certain properties are protected at least until a specified date. During the period of the contract, the organization has time to work out more permanent protection or raise funds for acquisition.

### A. Management Agreements and Leases

Under a management agreement, a property owner agrees to care for a property in a specified manner for a set period of time, or the owner allows an organization to carry out the management. Sometimes the owner receives compensation for expenses, such as building a fence to protect an endangered plant or repairing a historic stone wall, that will help protect the property over the long term. Management agreements work well where owners have a tradition of conscientious management or at least a personal commitment to rural conservation. They are also useful in instances where an owner, such as the federal government or a corporation, is unable to lease or sell a property or donate an easement.

Occasionally it may be advantageous to lease a property to protect it from overuse or poor management. Leases entitle the lessee to control the use of a property in return for rent, which may be nominal. An owner may agree in the lease simply to forgo destructive forestry, mining, or other practices that threaten the property, or agree to allow the lessee actually to use the property for some appropriate purpose (see illustration, p. 221).

## "Bundle of Rights": What a Property Owner Really Owns

*The interest held by a property owner is called the "fee simple" interest. This interest is like a bundle of sticks, each of which represents a right associated with the property. Such rights include the right to farm, to extract minerals, to cut timber, and to do anything else with the property unless prohibited by law. These rights can be separated from the "dominant estate" and transferred to other parties as "less-than-fee interests." An easement is one such less-than-fee interest; among others discussed in this chapter are remainder interests and undivided interests.*

*In granting an easement, an owner gives up some of the rights in a property, as specified in the deed of easement (the legally recorded document); that is, the owner agrees to certain restrictions in what could otherwise be done with the property. For example, an owner can sell to a mining company the right to extract ore or give a neighbor the right to cross a field; easements covering mineral rights and rights-of-way have been in use for centuries.*

*Under a conservation easement, the owner might give up all or most of the rights associated with construction on the property—often called the "development rights"—or the rights to remove vegetation or alter building exteriors. The property owner continues to experience the rewards and responsibilities of ownership, and the property can still be sold, rented, bequeathed, or otherwise transferred while subject to the easement.*

*Easements can be condemned—that is, purchased at appraised value*

## B. Agreements Tied to Loans and Grants

Some organizations may wish to provide small sums of money in the form of loans and grants to property owners to encourage rural conservation. The Amana Preservation Foundation in Iowa, for example, gave a matching grant to the Amana Artists' Guild to reconstruct a historically accurate wooden fence adjacent to its gallery. Some organizations have provided materials for housepainting and other repairs. For instance, the Cazenovia Preservation Foundation in New York makes free paint in colors of its own choosing available to businesses in the village. It may be desirable to ask property owners to agree in writing that any work done with loan or grant funds be in accordance with certain standards and that the property's historical, natural, scenic, or agricultural integrity be maintained for an appropriate length of time.

## IV. TAX INCENTIVES

Before discussing the more permanent ways a community can protect special properties, it is useful to examine tax incentives that, along with altruism, may encourage property owners to donate all or part of their property. Present federal tax law allows both individuals and corporations to take deductions from their taxable income for gifts of property, including easements, to a nonprofit organization designated as tax-exempt by the Internal Revenue Service or to a government agency. Individuals may deduct the value of the gift up to a certain percentage of their income and spread a sizeable deduction over several years. If the gift can be divided into stages, it may be possible to spread deductions over many years. Donating a property can also reduce the value of the donor's estate at the time estate taxes must be paid. Similar savings may be available in state taxes.

Consultation with an attorney or a financial adviser is essential for anyone considering employing the charitable contribution deduction for a gift of property. Not every donation of property qualifies for a federal tax deduction. Moreover, the federal government, in an attempt to curb inflated valuations, has established specific procedures that donors must follow for appraisals. Donors of appreciated property who are subject to the federal alternative minimum tax must calculate their tax benefits under different rules.

Through tax incentives the federal government encourages gifts of property and partial interests in property that are of significant conservation value to the nation. Organizations using these tax incentives to encourage gifts should realize that, while they may not have to "pay" for the gifts, when donors receive tax deductions the public forgoes tax receipts it might otherwise collect. Thus, an organization has a responsibility to the nation's taxpayers to accept only high-quality gifts and to assure that the conservation values involved in those gifts will endure (see *Criteria for Accepting Gifts,* pp. 190–91).

For easements, a general kind of quality control is set forth in federal tax law (section 170(h) of the Internal Revenue Code). That section refers to a "qualified conservation contribution" that must meet one of several tests for "conservation purpose." Under this law, conservation purposes include the preservation of land for outdoor recreation or education, protection of "relatively natural habitat," and preservation of historically significant properties. Also a conservation purpose is served if the preservation of open space, including farmland and forest land, creates a "significant public benefit," either for the "scenic enjoyment of the general public" or "pursuant to a clearly delineated Federal, State, or local governmental conservation policy."

## V. ACQUISITION OF CONSERVATION EASEMENTS

A conservation or preservation easement is an agreement between a property owner and the holder of the easement governing treatment of the property by current and future owners. Such an agreement allows a property owner to continue owning and using a property while assuring its protection. Easements are an alternative to owning property outright or to such governmental regulation as zoning. Owning property outright may not be necessary if the owner can give it proper stewardship and if public use is not desirable; governmental regulation usually cannot be tailored to protect specific aspects of a property and cannot impose the perpetual restrictions an easement can.

Easements can protect land, buildings, or both. Although an easement may be called a "scenic," "open-space," "conservation," "facade," or "historic preservation" easement, the name has more to do with the kind of property it protects than the way it works. Easements have been used extensively across the United States, to protect buildings and their settings in rural villages such as Waterford, Virginia (Case Study 28) and Harrisville, New Hampshire (see illustration, p. 15); scenic rural areas such as Jackson Hole, Wyoming (Case Study 2), the Great River Road in Wisconsin, and the Big Sur coastline in California (Case Study 18); and farmland in such places as King County, Washington (5.V.C), and Carroll County, Maryland (Case Study 11). Easements have also been used to protect such other sensitive environmental resources as watersheds, marshes, unique geological formations, and habitats for endangered species. Use of easements, which as legal instruments date to the dawn of English common law, in this fashion is relatively new. The first conservation easement in the United States was granted more than a hundred years ago in Massachusetts. Such easements have become widespread since the early 1960s, when the IRS declared that a gift of an easement is tax-deductible.

Technically, an easement is a legally enforceable interest created by the transfer of some of the rights in the property and is recorded in local land records. Conservation easements are called "conservation restrictions" according to the law in some states. Covenants (also called deed restrictions) pertain to restrictions imposed on subsequent owners when a property is transferred, as opposed to easements, which can be created without transfer of the fee title. For organizations, covenants operate in the same fashion as easements and are commonly used with limited development and revolving funds (5.VIII). (An individual transferring a property to another owner can use a covenant instead of an easement to impose restrictions on the use and development of a property but the covenant is generally unenforceable once the transferor dies.)

Conservation easements can be either donated or sold. In most cases, nonprofit organizations obtain easements as donations and government agencies purchase them, although there is nothing that precludes the reverse.

*without the owner's consent—a power generally available only to governmental entities and public utilities. Although condemnation is used most frequently to obtain rights-of-way, it can also be used for conservation easements.*

The value of an easement for tax purposes is usually the difference in the value of the property before and after the grant of the easement (National Trust for Historic Preservation and Land Trust Exchange 1984). In addition to reducing a donor's federal and state income taxes, an easement may reduce an owner's local property taxes. This varies, of course, from state to state and from one locality to another.

CASE STUDY 13

## Blackfoot River, Montana: Protecting a Stream Corridor through Easements

The Blackfoot River in western Montana is one of the state's best trout streams. Attractive not only to fishermen but to canoeists and rafting enthusiasts as well, today the river is protected by an easement program operated by the Nature Conservancy and the state's Department of Fish, Wildlife, and Parks. The program is the product of a remarkable cooperative effort over many years to manage the growing recreational use of the river and combat increased development pressures. The overall result of the effort to protect the Blackfoot River and manage its recreational use is a model program that, with local adaptations, could protect and enhance the corridors of trails and scenic roads as well as rivers.

In the late 1960s, landowners became highly conscious of threats to their agricultural and timbering activities as recreational pressures began to mount. "Farmers got tired of getting off their tractors and running down to deal with trespassers," recalls one ranch owner along the river. Fire, vandalism, and livestock harassment were among the problems the owners faced from unwelcome visitors.

Clearly, something had to be done—but proposed federal designation of the river or county zoning did not offer satisfactory solutions to the problems of recreational use. Such ideas were also highly controversial among owners accustomed to little interference with the way they controlled their property. (The Blackfoot was considered for designation as a Wild and Scenic River in the early 1970s [6.VI.B], but due to local opposition and because local protection was under way, the U.S. Department of the Interior withdrew its request.) The landowners—a combination of ranchers, the state, the University of Montana, and a timber company—banded together with representatives of the county, state, and recreational groups in a search for answers. The first step was to find technical assistance, which was obtained from Jerry Stokes, a planner in the Denver office of what formerly was called the federal Bureau of Outdoor Recreation. A long-time observer of the project credits his "deft community organizing" as a key ingredient in its success.

What ultimately emerged from the discussions was the realization that dealing with the problems of recreational use and achieving long-term protection of the river could be done separately. The landowners

Overuse of the Blackfoot River in Montana by rafters and fishermen, among others, led to a successful cooperative effort by public and private interests to manage recreational access.

cooperated with the state in developing a recreation management plan based on voluntary short-term agreements. In these agreements, landowners dedicated land along the river for public access points that were developed and maintained by the state. The state also provided a river manager to patrol the area. While the provision of public access and the river manager might have been sufficient to deal with the problems created by recreational use, the state considered that its investment for recreation required long-term assurances that the quality of the river would be maintained—the purpose of the conservation easements.

A number of roadblocks to the use of easements existed, however. First, landowners had to be educated as to what conservation easements are and how they work. Second, until a concerted effort by interested landowners resulted in passage in 1975 of state legislation permitting their use, their legality was open to question. Third, each landowner's decision to contribute an easement was highly individual and likely in some cases to take a long time to complete.

VOLUNTARY TECHNIQUES FOR PROTECTING PRIVATE PROPERTY

181

This sign for boaters was installed by the state on privately owned, state-developed access points along Montana's Blackfoot River. The state also provides maintenance and policing.

The recreation management plan covered more than 30 miles of the river; however, easements were first sought for a 10-mile pilot segment. Each easement is tailored to the property in question. Many have special provisions for the land immediately adjacent to the river, such as restrictions on development, to complement the recreational use. Back from the river the restrictions are less stringent. Today, virtually all of the first 10-mile segment is under easement. All but one of the easements have been donated to the Nature Conservancy, which now has expanded its goal to protecting 50 miles of the river.

## A. Drafting an Easement

Unlike zoning or subdivision regulations, which generally must apply uniformly across any given area, an easement can recognize the special qualities of a single property, plus the particular needs of each property owner and the standards established by each holding organization. An easement typically begins with a statement of purpose and proceeds to restrictions stating what the owner may not do with the property. Anything not specifically prohibited remains among the owner's rights. The document also grants the organization the right to inspect the property to assure observance of the restrictions. It may also provide for enforcement procedures such as binding arbitration. Litigation to enforce an easement, of course, is always an option. The easement boundaries, determined by historical, visual, natural, political, and other factors, are also set forth in the document. All areas to be covered by the easement, and their condition, should be documented in a comprehensive inventory that includes maps and photographs. This documentation is helpful in case of disputes that may arise later.

SAVING AMERICA'S COUNTRYSIDE

Easement restrictions typically limit earthmoving, dumping, signs, utility lines, subdivision, construction, changes to existing structures, and uses made of the property. Commercial use of a residence may be prohibited, for example. Public access can be specifically granted by the owner to allow such activities as hiking or fishing, but many owners prefer to maintain their privacy. Occasionally, an organization will agree to allow an owner to reserve the right to build on a particular site or to sell off a specified portion of the property for development, where such provisions pose little risk to the resources being protected.

Because federal law governs the deductibility of gifts of conservation easements, donated easements are usually perpetual. There may be situations, however, where a "term easement" is appropriate, although it would not be deductible. For example, the Lake Champlain Islands Trust and the Vermont Land Trust (formerly the Ottauquechee Land Trust) negotiated a five-year conservation easement with the owners of a 14-acre island in Lake Champlain who wanted to experience living under the restrictions and take time to get to know the land trusts before considering a permanent commitment. The trusts have identified the important ecological features of the island and are preparing a conservation plan which all parties hope will lead to permanent protection.

## B. Who Holds an Easement

Both nonprofit conservation organizations and government at the local, state, and national level can hold easements. Federal tax regulations governing deductibility of donated easements require that the holder "have a commitment to protect the conservation purposes of the donation, and have the resources to enforce the restrictions."

An organization need not hold easements to promote them in the community if it believes others possess better resources for seeing that the easements remain viable. The Waterford Foundation in Virginia, for example, has been responsible for the acquisition of more than forty historic and

An easement held jointly by the Maryland Historical Trust and the Maryland Environmental Trust protects Lloyd's Landing in Talbot County, Maryland. The easement protects more than 1,100 acres of the Eastern Shore of the Chesapeake Bay as well as the early-eighteenth-century residence.

# Land Banking

*An old idea with a bright new name and an expanding number of successful applications, land banking is essentially a land trust operated by government and funded by real estate transfer taxes, either at the local or state level. Although Nantucket, Massachusetts, was the first to combine the name and the idea when it began its program in 1984, the state of Maryland has operated a successful statewide land banking program, Program Open Space, since 1969. The idea has a certain appeal not only because a transfer tax can yield millions of dollars even when set as low as 1 or 2 percent, but also because it creates funding out of the very reason such a program is needed: a booming real estate market. Such a tax may be more popular than other kinds of taxes, since individuals feel the bite only when they buy property.*

*By the end of 1987, the program in Nantucket (1984 pop. 5,876) had retired more than 750 acres, or 2.5 percent of the island, as permanent open space, a third of that at prices below market value. In the island's superheated real estate market— there are 340 licensed brokers— property valued at $181 million changed hands in 1987. Thus, even with the transfer tax pegged at only 2 percent, the Land Bank Commission has enjoyed a healthy cash flow, used in part to acquire property and in part toward retiring the debt on more than $11 million in bonds issued to establish the program.*

*The commission has a broad range of tools at its disposal, but has only acquired properties in fee simple. Easements on Nantucket are generally so expensive that the commission has preferred simply to pay the modest differential in price required*

scenic easements, but does not hold them. Instead, they are held either by the National Trust for Historic Preservation or one of two state agencies, the Virginia Division of Historic Landmarks or the Virginia Outdoors Foundation.

If an organization decides to hold its own easements, it may invite another organization to act as a co-holder. The Maryland Historical Trust and the Maryland Environmental Trust, for example, have jointly accepted easements over large estates with historic buildings. Each organization contributes its particular expertise in overseeing the terms of the easements: the historical trust for buildings and the environmental trust for land. In cooperative situations such as this, or as is the case in Waterford, the more organizations that are involved the more help there will be if an easement is challenged legally.

An organization should accept no easements unless there is a high degree of certainty that the organization will exist for many years. Even so, the easement document should specify one or more organizations to act as successors to the holding organization. Such organizations, of course, should be consulted beforehand. An alternative to specifying a successor is to state that the organization holding the easement has the right to appoint an appropriate successor. If successors are not specified, in the event of the organization's demise, a superior court judge or the state's attorney general would designate the next holder. The organization can further reserve the right to assign the easement later to another organization better able to administer it.

By accepting an easement, an organization accepts a continuing responsibility to ensure that easement provisions are observed. This requires periodic monitoring and communication to remind the property owner, especially a subsequent owner, of the easement's provisions. Monitoring is carried out by either on-site or aerial inspection, usually once a year. The Society for the Protection of New Hampshire Forests, for example, photographs from the air each of its properties under easement on an annual basis. Many nonprofit organizations ask for a cash donation when the easement is created, to be used for a fund to support the costs of monitoring. An organization may also need such a fund to remedy violations or defend an easement's validity in court.

## C. Purchase of Development Rights

Occasionally a community may find purchasing easements to be best, even though easements can be almost as expensive as purchasing the land outright. A few local governments have decided it is cheaper to purchase development rights than to pay for the roads, schools, and other services required by new residents if the land is subdivided and developed for housing. In this way, the land is protected, but the public bears no cost of maintenance, and the land remains on the tax rolls and in productive use. This technique has been used primarily for the preservation of agricultural lands and is usually undertaken by local and state governments, which can issue bonds or levy taxes to obtain the necessary large sources of funding. Since such easements usually pertain to rights to develop, programs involving these easements are called purchase of development rights (PDR) programs. Several states—including Connecticut, Maryland, Massachusetts, New Hampshire, New Jersey, Pennsylvania, and Rhode Island—

and a small number of counties and townships have PDR programs to protect farmland.

King County, Washington, purchased development rights in the years following 1979, when voters approved a $50 million bond issue to protect 10,000 to 15,000 acres of agricultural land, the minimum acreage needed to maintain a viable farm economy. The program divided the county's farmland into three categories, based largely on location. Top priority for purchase were development rights on lands located in urban areas, reflecting the public's desire to protect open space in the most heavily populated areas, even though rights on these lands were the most expensive to acquire. Many farmers who applied for participation were turned down; those chosen were paid an appraised value based on a standard set of restrictions, but many offered to accept still more restrictions to increase their chances for participation.

## VI. ACQUISITION OF UNDIVIDED INTERESTS IN LAND

The acquisition of an undivided interest in a property, or a percentage of ownership, gives an organization a legal interest in it, as opposed to sole ownership either of the entire property or a specific part of it. For instance, two siblings who each inherit a 50 percent undivided interest in a family farm both have the right to use the property and to divide its income accordingly. Each must share in the costs of operation and agree on its management and disposition. By acquiring an undivided interest, an organization may use its influence as a co-owner to insure that a property is managed properly, or even to negotiate a sale to a sympathetic buyer in a situation where multiple owners, often heirs, cannot agree on its disposition. The Vermont Land Trust received an 85 percent undivided interest in a 243-acre tract when the owners for tax reasons wanted to make a gift by the end of a particular year but did not have time to have the necessary surveying done. Later, the trust and the owners agreed to divide the property, with the trust taking title to 216 acres and the owners agreeing to conservation restrictions on the remainder.

## VII. OUTRIGHT ACQUISITION OF PROPERTY

In some cases, property deserving protection should be acquired outright. Some communities need additional parkland for public recreation; in other instances, a property may be of such outstanding ecological or historical importance that it can be adequately protected only through public ownership "in fee simple."

An organization may also acquire properties that can be exchanged for land with conservation value. The Guilford Land Trust in Connecticut, for example, exchanged parcels in order to protect an area surrounding a popular trail. A developer had purchased a 9-acre parcel abutting lands owned by the land trust and the state, considering it an ideal site for his own home, but the homesite was visible from the trail. When approached by the land trust about selling, he challenged it to find him a comparable property. It took nearly a year, but the trust was able to purchase an 8-acre parcel—drier, with a better exposure and also abutting land owned by the

*to buy land outright. The commission also has yet to use eminent domain—possible on a case-by-case basis with approval by local residents voting at the Nantucket town meeting. Limited development may also be possible, but more problematic, as any property acquired by the commission can be sold only with the approval of the state legislature. The commission can, however, lease property it owns. The commission has also received donations of more than $650,000 in cash and six parcels totalling over 8 acres, mirroring the public support it received at its inception, when the town meeting voted 446 to 1 to establish the commission.*

*From Nantucket, the idea of land banking has spread to Martha's Vineyard, Massachusetts, and Block Island, Rhode Island. All three programs required the special permission of their respective state legislatures. Vermont has established a statewide land bank, the Housing and Conservation Fund. Along with protecting targeted open lands, the Vermont legislation allows the use of the funds to support programs for low-cost housing. The rationale for this refinement was the acknowledgment that "banking" land for conservation purposes may remove some developable land from the community, thus causing the price of housing to rise.*

land trust but in a more private location—which proved to be a satisfactory substitute. In making the trade, the developer paid a small cost differential.

## Bandon, Oregon: A National Nonprofit Organization Does a Good Turn

Bandon, Oregon (1984 pop. 2,251), a small town and scenic harbor bordered by fir trees at the mouth of the Coquille River, was a thriving port at the turn of the century. Sailing ships, riverboats, and sternwheelers docked at the back doors of riverside businesses. The Coquille provides habitat for salmon, seals, and many bird species; Bandon's cranberry bogs make it the "Cranberry Capital of Oregon." When the Coast Guard decided to cease operating its historic station there, Bandon had to develop a creative way to acquire it, involving other publicly owned land in the community and the patient intercession of a national nonprofit organization.

Working with the Bandon Port Authority, the Trust for Public Land (TPL) undertook to save the station—a project that took six years to complete. When the port authority told the federal government of its desire to purchase the station, it learned that the property was to revert to forty heirs of the original owner. At the same time, the port authority owned land across the bay from Bandon: 289 acres of a salt marsh that biologists consider the second most productive in Oregon, and the key to a "moneyless" transaction for the port authority. Here is how it worked: (1) The port transferred the marshland to TPL; (2) TPL sold the marshland to the U.S. Fish and Wildlife Service, which will protect it permanently; (3) from the proceeds of the sale TPL paid off the forty

A view of the Bandon, Oregon, waterfront. Across the bay is a salt marsh protected by a deal among the Bandon Port Authority, the Trust for Public Land, and the U.S. Fish and Wildlife Service.

heirs to the station; (4) TPL then transferred the station and $20,000 for its renovation to the port authority. The station today houses an apartment for the port manager, a shop, an art gallery, and a historical museum.

---

Acquiring property, whether by purchase or through donation, is usually an expensive way to protect it. The costs are not limited to acquisition but include perpetual management and maintenance, unless the property is resold or leased to others who assume some of these responsibilities. In some states, nonprofit organizations must pay property taxes as well, or, if they do not, there may be local sentiment against removing a property from the tax rolls. New organizations with limited funds especially need to consider the responsibilities of ownership, even if a property could be acquired as a gift. Many organizations do not accept gifts of property unless they are accompanied by endowments that will ensure adequate maintenance.

One kind of property acquisition, however, is welcome for many organizations: receipt of "asset properties" which the organization may then sell for funds to support its operations. Although typically of little natural, historic, or agricultural value, if worthy of protection such properties can be restricted before sale. Donors of these properties generally receive a tax deduction based on the appraised value (5.IV).

## A. Rights of First Refusal and Options

To guarantee the opportunity to purchase important properties, an organization can use either a right of first refusal or an option to purchase a property. Neither technique obligates the organization to purchase the property: each simply gives it the first opportunity to buy.

By granting a right of first refusal, a property owner agrees to notify a prospective purchaser that the property is to be offered for sale and to give the purchaser the opportunity to match any *bona fide* offer, typically within ten to ninety days. A sympathetic property owner may give this right to an organization or sell it for a nominal sum. A right of first refusal should be legally recorded, which assures that the property cannot be sold unless the holder of the right is notified. Heirs can also be bound by the agreement, although intrafamily transfers often are excluded from the terms of the agreement. When the time comes to exercise the right of first refusal, the organization should have the property appraised to assure that it is not being asked to match a bogus offer.

Holding a right of first refusal usually means that the organization will be able to identify the other potential buyer and the buyer's intentions for the property. Rather than exercise its right, the organization might be able to persuade the prospective new owner to agree to one of the forms of protection discussed in this chapter. On the other hand, if the organization has reason to believe that a new owner may be unsympathetic to the idea of protecting the property, it can purchase the property if it has the funds to do so or it can raise the funds during the notice period.

An option to purchase a property usually involves paying a landowner for the guarantee that the landowner will reserve a property at an agreed-upon price for a set period of time, typically ninety days to a year. An organization can use an option to gain time, either to find a sympathetic buyer or to raise the funds necessary for purchase. Even if an organization is unsure it can afford the purchase price, it might still consider purchasing the option if the option can be transferred to another buyer who is sympathetic to conservation. The Yakima River Greenway Foundation in Washington (Case Study 27) used an option in its first transaction, the acquisition of a 40-acre parcel in the river corridor from which it takes its name. The owner was willing to make a bargain sale immediately (5.VII.C), but the organization was just getting started and had not yet received its nonprofit status from the Internal Revenue Service that would make his donation tax deductible. The option allowed the organization to publicize its intention to make the purchase in order to raise the necessary funds while waiting for its IRS ruling.

CASE STUDY 15

## Guilford, Connecticut: A Right of First Refusal Encourages a Donation

The Guilford Land Trust in Guilford, Connecticut (1984 pop. 18,474), used the concept of a right of first refusal in protecting land that the owner ultimately gave to the land trust. As part of its strategy for protecting a major wetland, the land trust approached the owner of a 54-acre parcel about selling, but he was not interested. However, the land trust persuaded him to sign a letter of intent to sell the property to the organization when he decided to dispose of it. Although a letter of intent is not enforceable (as a recorded right of first refusal is), the land trust was confident that continued contact with the owner would remind him of his obligation. Eight years later, the owner decided to donate the wetland portion of the property to the land trust and sell the high ground to a developer. The land trust was then able to persuade the owner to donate the entire property rather than sell any of it for development, through two gifts of 50 percent undivided interests five years apart (with a codicil in his will for the second gift in the event of his death). This method enabled him to take greatest advantage of the tax incentives for the donation (5.IV).

## B. Financing Property Purchases

Outright purchase is not the only way to acquire property; an organization may employ a number of creative techniques and economic incentives that may make acquisition more affordable for the buyer and more attractive to the property owner. For example, an installment sale enables the organization to spread its outlay of funds over time, and may in some cases enable the seller to spread any capital gains tax liability over several years. The Laudholm Trust in Maine, for instance, contracted to buy a large parcel in five installments (Case Study 21).

Another approach to acquiring property outright is a lease-purchase agreement, whereby the rent under the terms of the lease is applied toward an agreed-upon purchase price. An organization may find such an arrangement useful if it can afford the regular lease payments, can manage the property, and anticipates that future funding will allow it to meet the payments and management expenses. If it does not secure the future funding, it can terminate the lease-purchase agreement.

## Brattleboro, Vermont: Financing a Purchase with "Charitable Creditors"

Acquisitions of property are typically made with cash, a mortgage, a bank loan secured by other assets held by the organization, or financing provided by the property owner. There is at least one other possibility, the use of "charitable creditors" in combination with limited development (5.VIII.B). The Vermont Land Trust used this technique to protect the Rhodes Farm in Brattleboro (1984 pop. 12,081), a 144-acre dairy farm with 90 acres of cultivated land—the most in the area— considered essential to continuation of agriculture there. When the farmer was forced to put the farm up for sale to avoid bankruptcy, the trust crafted an alternative to sale to a developer.

Thirty-five individuals, many of them neighbors, guaranteed a loan of $245,000 made by a local bank toward the $295,000 asking price. (The remaining $50,000 was in the form of an assumable Farmers Home Administration loan.) A small number of the "charitable creditors" formed a steering committee to advise the land trust on subsequent disposition of the farm. The land trust then sold the open land in three parcels to two other local farmers, reinforcing their farm operations. The farmhouse and barns plus a corner woodlot and a parcel along a ridge, restricted to three residential lots, were sold separately to conservation-minded buyers found by the trust. These sales covered roughly 60 percent of the purchase price plus closing costs and expenses incurred by the land trust. The charitable creditors, plus nineteen others, donated the rest of the total cost.

Because of the success of this project and a number of others the land trust has undertaken, the land trust now maintains a confidential list of potential charitable creditors who stand ready to guarantee loans, provide interest-free loans, or make tax-deductible cash contributions for emergency projects.

## Criteria for Accepting Gifts

*The San Juan Preservation Trust is a private, nonprofit, tax-exempt organization founded in 1979 by residents who were concerned about protecting scenic, agricultural, and ecologically important lands in the San Juan Islands in Washington State. Given the multiple problems caused by tourism and population growth, and the extensive amount of land deserving protection, the trust's board of trustees agreed in 1984 to set priorities in promoting land protection. The trust accepts gifts of land and easements under the following guidelines:*

*1. The area is an important undisturbed natural area, or is adjacent to an important undisturbed natural area, or is adjacent to lands under conservation easements or is adjacent to Trust-owned property.*
*2. The property has characteristics which should be protected from development, such as scenic open space, views of water, buffer qualities, a good soil composition, or wildlife habitat.*
*3. The property is visible from public lands, public roads, public parks,*

A lease-purchase agreement, like an option, is useful whenever acting quickly without guaranteed funding is necessary. A lease-purchase agreement may be attractive to an owner who is anxious both to sell and to end responsibility for maintaining a property until the sale is consummated. The Yakima River Greenway Foundation in Washington used this technique to gain control of a key parcel for development as a park in conjunction with the county government (Case Study 27).

### C. Bargain Sale

A bargain sale, sometimes called a "donative sale," allows an organization to acquire a property partly as a purchase and partly as a gift by buying property at less than its fair market value (the price a buyer pays a seller on the open market). The seller sets a price below the appraised value of the property and considers the difference to be a gift, for which he or she can claim a charitable income tax deduction. The seller's compensation, therefore, is a combination of cash and lowered taxes.

The Big Sur Land Trust in California used a bargain sale when a scenic 3,040-acre ranch came on the market. With a conservation-minded buyer providing the financing, the trust purchased the land at a bargain—giving the owner, a developer, a tax deduction—and immediately conveyed the property to the buyer. Before the transfer, the trust added stringent restrictions on development to the deed, plus a right of first refusal and a provision for access to the land by the University of California for educational and scientific purposes. The buyer was pleased to be able to protect an important site along a famous part of the California coast and to give the trust a boost in getting established (Case Study 18).

### D. Donation

Nonprofit organizations and local governments occasionally receive gifts of property through a donation or bequest. Organizations offered such gifts should make sure they can afford the responsibility of management before accepting the property, or make sure they can sell it under the terms of the gift. Organizations should encourage potential donors to in-

**Trustee Barbara Brown surveys a property given to the San Juan Preservation Trust in Washington. The 38-acre site includes 7,230 feet of waterfront and more than met the trust's criteria for accepting gifts.**

190

form them in advance of their plans for a bequest in order to assure that it is appropriate and to discuss financial arrangements for the property's maintenance and operation.

Donations with a reserved life estate, also referred to as a life tenancy, are used by individuals who wish to continue to own and live on their property until their death or the deaths of specified heirs, at which time the property is received by a nonprofit organization or government agency. The donor is eligible to deduct the value of the gift, called a "remainder interest," at the time it is made, although the recipient will not actually take control until the donor or the donor's heirs die.

A reserved life estate may present management problems, since the owner continues to occupy the property. Although the organization has the right to see that the property is kept in the condition expected upon final transfer, a management agreement or conservation easement may help to prevent problems or misunderstandings by specifying the organization's expectations.

One example of a pending acquisition through a remainder interest is a 50-acre parcel donated to the Southern Appalachian Highlands Conservancy, which is dedicated to protecting Roan Mountain, a biologically unique massif straddling the North Carolina–Tennessee border. Remainder interests can also be purchased, as the Laudholm Trust in Maine has done. A 100-acre parcel, key to the trust's plan for acquiring land around a significant estuary, contained several summer residences that the owners were reluctant to give up, although they were willing to sell most of the property. The trust, concerned that the owners would be left free to develop the small portion in question if it could not be acquired, persuaded them to sell the entire parcel at its appraised value and then granted them a life tenancy (Case Study 21).

*or from already Trust-protected lands.*

*4. The property has important historical or current land use activity, such as forestry management, farming, public enjoyment, aquaculture.*

*5. The protection of the property would enhance the quality of life for the community.*

*6. If the property is to be accepted for resale for the benefit of the Trust rather than for preservation, the property owner shall be fully informed of that purpose.*

*7. The owner shall be made aware that the property may be transferred to another qualified recipient.*

*8. Endowment funding is necessary for the long term defense of all Trust lands. An endowment fund is established for each parcel of land accepted by the Trust. It is expected that the land donor would appreciate and participate in this essential process.*

*(Reprinted with permission from the San Juan Preservation Trust.)*

# Vernon, Vermont: Making Multiple Techniques Fit Together

Techniques for land protection are often used in combination to solve the problems presented by landowners' needs and the peculiarities of particular properties. Here is how it worked in the town of Vernon, Vermont (1984 pop. 1,280):

The owner of a 273-acre dairy farm, reaching retirement age, decided that she could no longer afford to carry the farm's debts. However, she wanted to see the traditional use of the land continued, preferably by selling the farm buildings and the 86 acres of tillable land to the young farming couple already leasing them. She also wanted to remain in her home across the road. The couple, though eager to continue as farmers, could not afford to buy the property at the time she wanted to sell.

The farm owner was fortunate to be living in a community that had previously determined it wanted to preserve its six remaining farms. In 1982, the town meeting had authorized a farmland protection program. The Vermont Land Trust was retained to work with a town committee in developing the program. The town also appropriated $50,000 as a revolving fund for projects that could pay their own way (5.VIII.C). And a project that is paying its own way, in the end, is what the land trust was able to create out of a situation others might have thought was hopeless.

The solution—which took a year to negotiate—began with a bargain sale. The town used $40,000 of its fund to purchase the open land at less than the appraised value. The cash from this bargain sale enabled the owner to discharge her debts. The couple sold a property elsewhere, enabling them to purchase the farm buildings, including a house, and a small amount of land, converting their lease payments to comparable mortgage payments. The town gave them an option to purchase the remaining open land within four years for $40,000, which would replenish the town's fund. The couple leased the land from the town in the meantime, partially offsetting the town's temporary loss of property taxes and the loss of interest on its $40,000. Upon transfer, the town will impose permanent conservation restrictions and retain a right of first refusal in the event that the couple (or their heirs) decide to sell the farm.

---

## VIII. DEVELOPING A VOLUNTARY PROPERTY-PROTECTION PROGRAM

The techniques described thus far deal with control over single properties. This section focuses on the control of multiple properties simultaneously. Nonprofit organizations are more likely to engage in multiple transactions than are local governments, since nonprofit organizations may act more quickly and with less red tape in real estate transactions. It may be useful here to distinguish between land trusts (also known as conservancies) and revolving funds as they are commonly understood. A land trust, while sometimes a nonprofit subsidiary to a "parent" organization, usually is independent and keeps at least some of its property indefinitely. A revolving fund uses the strategy of keeping funds ready to use in the event that a desirable property should suddenly become available. The reserve fund is repaid once the property is sold—that is, once it is "revolved."

Knowing what should be protected is an important aspect of developing a property-protection program. As one land trust director says, "We won't accept everything that comes along. We're not interested in loading up our inventory with meaningless property."[1] The environmental inventory, discussed in Chapter 3, should form the basis of the necessary decisions. Developing a set of general criteria in advance of such decision-making can aid the organization in accepting or denying a gift and in focusing its efforts on encouraging particular owners to donate, sell, or consider some other kind of protection.

### A. Land Trusts

Land trusts are usually established to protect areas of significant natural diversity, important recreational opportunities, or both. Some have engaged in historic preservation or farmland protection as well. A land trust holds land and other property rights for the benefit of the public and often undertakes educational, recreational, and scientific activities. As private organizations, land trusts have considerable flexibility in the way they can acquire property, especially in their ability to take risks and to act quickly to buy land before it is sold for development. Many, such as the Jackson Hole Land Trust of Wyoming (Case Study 2) and the Big Sur Land Trust described below, take care to remain neutral on community issues—as compared to the traditional activism of some environmental organizations—to guard against alienating potential donors from a cross-section of the community. This concern, however, has not prevented some land trusts from encouraging local governments to improve their land-use regulations, as the Brandywine Conservancy of Pennsylvania does (Case Study 1).

CASE STUDY 18

## Big Sur, California: A Land Trust Learns to Seize the Moment

For 75 miles south of the Monterey Bay, California's Highway 1 winds its way between the crashing waves of the Pacific and the lofty peaks of the Santa Lucia range, suspended on the steep hills and cliffs of some of the most spectacular coastal scenery in the world, Big Sur. Named "El Sur" ("the South") by Spanish explorers in the sixteenth century, Big Sur possesses one of the premier scenic drives in the nation—and one of the most harrowing—attracting more than three million visitors per year. It is also "a proud, land-loving community," in the words of one reporter. Artists and writers—Ansel Adams, Nathaniel Jeffers, Nathaniel Owings, and Henry Miller among them—settled there alongside families whose roots reach back through a century or more. It was no surprise that federal ownership was proposed to protect this spectacular area in the mid-1970s when development along much of the California coast became rampant—but it also was no surprise that such a proposal attracted the fierce (and successful) opposition of property owners deeply attached to their land.

In 1978, the Big Sur Land Trust (BSLT) was formed as a homegrown solution to the long-term problem of protecting Big Sur's magnificent scenery from excessive development. BSLT got off to a running start by finding a conservation-minded buyer for a 3,040-acre ranch that had been on the market for some time (5.VII.C). In the next ten years, the land trust protected another 1,987 acres in thirty-five transactions (mostly conservation easements) and was named as a beneficiary in three wills, protecting a further 800 acres.

The BSLT is in many ways a typical land trust: small, young, learning with each transaction, operating in an especially beloved landscape. It does enjoy several advantages: Big Sur is nationally significant, and California's Coastal Commission (6.VI.E) plus recent county planning provides a complementary governmental framework for the land trust activities. Perhaps its greatest advantage, however, is an adventurous

Big Sur, California, looking south. Although the U.S. Forest Service owns much land in the Big Sur region, nearly all of the spectacular coastal lands, from the top of the Coast Ridge to the ocean, are privately owned.

board of trustees willing to consider a wide variety of approaches to land protection.

According to Brian Steen, executive director and one-man staff for BSLT, "The board of directors has the confidence to go into a transaction knowing there are risks." For example, in one transaction, BSLT signed a sales contract to purchase 80 acres of virgin redwoods for $375,000 without the money in hand and with the imminent threat of timbering should it fail. BSLT was able to raise $40,000 in the community toward the purchase and persuaded a foundation owning adjacent land to put up the remainder in exchange for the title, which BSLT transferred with deed restrictions (see illustration, p. 196).

In its early days, the organization had to contend with community suspicions that its members were after more than simple satisfaction in

Post Ranch was a key acquisition of 437 acres (*foreground*) in Big Sur by the Trust for Public Land with assistance of the Big Sur Land Trust. It was sold to the U.S. Forest Service to protect public access to the Ventana Wilderness and the Los Padres National Forest (*background*).

seeing land preserved. "People see us doing transactions in millions of dollars and they are intimidated, refusing to believe that BSLT has only a small amount of money in the bank and no other interests in the deal except to preserve key properties," says Steen. "It's partly to do with a lack of understanding of how a nonprofit corporation works—that no financial benefits accrue to the trustees. Also, people don't understand that the trust can make money, as long as the increment is put back into our treasury and used for land preservation."

BSLT's activities are characterized by a strong respect for community and landowner concerns. For example, although BSLT lands provide visual enjoyment for everyone, BSLT avoids providing physical access to the lands it protects. Such access would create problems of liability and other headaches for the organization and neighboring landowners, who value their privacy in the face of the extensive tourism in the area. To maintain its options the organization has drawn the line in respecting landowners' wishes, however. It has refused to agree never to transfer private lands to federal ownership—an idea urged on BSLT by a vocal group of property owners who oppose federal involvement in the protection of Big Sur.

As it is for other charitable groups, fund-raising is a constant struggle, the search for steady income never-ceasing. "The spectacular nature of Big Sur leads people to assume that the area is so affluent that an effort like ours would automatically be a success," says founding board member Roger Newell, who goes on to say it is not so. Even the much-needed support from one prominent family has been a liability: "Here again, people falsely assume that because they're involved we've got it made," Newell comments. Steen adds, "Our experience bears out that a land trust needs a broad base of support in order to obtain funds and access to individuals in the community to carry out transactions."

BSLT's relations with local government have been excellent. It has helped the Monterey Peninsula Regional Park District purchase a parcel to add to its parkland inventory. One of BSLT's first projects was to conduct an environmental inventory in Monterey County; the county gov-

The Big Sur Land Trust purchased this tract of virgin redwoods in 1984.

The Henry Miller Memorial Library, a privately built home housing a collection of the famous author's books and memorabilia, was donated as a life estate by local artist Emil White (*left*) to the Big Sur Land Trust in 1981. White is shown with BSLT donor and trustee Nancy Hopkins.

ernment, along with a citizen's advisory committee drawn from Big Sur, used the geology component of the inventory in developing the Big Sur Land Use Plan required by the Coastal Commission. The plan, approved in 1986, provides for the purchase or transfer of development rights on properties in the scenic corridor where development would be visible. The BSLT has used a state grant of $100,000 to begin a program to purchase and retire the rights rather than see them transferred elsewhere in Big Sur (albeit out of sight), to help reduce the impact of expected development in Big Sur under the plan.

SAVING AMERICA'S COUNTRYSIDE

The BSLT has been opportunistic in the best sense of the word. Roger Newell believes land trusts should take calculated risks. "There's always a landowner who's sympathetic, there's frequently a philanthropic interest, and there's always the expertise around the corner—look for it!"

---

## B. Limited Development

Most land trusts are primarily concerned with the acquisition and management of property. More and more of them, however, are taking an aggressive role in influencing compatible development in their communities. Still others, concerned about the rising prices of land and the declining size of government budgets—which reduces funds available to complete "pass-through" acquisitions (5.VIII.C)—are looking for ways to lessen the costs of acquiring critical properties. "Limited development," or "compromise development," whereby land is sold for development with restrictions to protect specific environmental resources, can reduce the cost of acquiring properties while stimulating compatible development. For example, the Housatonic Valley Association in Connecticut acquired, in a bargain sale, a 37-acre tract with significant scenic and agricultural values along a tributary of the Housatonic, on which a developer could have built fourteen homes. To finance a bargain purchase at a cost of $90,000, the association created three residential building lots, plus a lot for a school. One residential lot of 25 acres included 8 acres of waterfront and 16 acres of farmland. The farmland was permanently restricted to agricultural use—enabling the leasing farmer, whose family had farmed the land for sixty years, to continue working it. Sales of the lots, which were restricted from further subdivision, brought $142,000, netting the associations's land-acquisition fund $32,000 after project costs were calculated. A similar project by the Vermont Land Trust is described in Case Study 16.

Limited, compatible development schemes can be far grander than the Housatonic Valley Association example, provided the land trust has the resources—including a leadership willing to stick its collective neck out. Colorado Open Lands used this technique to protect the spectacular 3,243-acre Evans Ranch 40 miles west of Denver. Virtually surrounded by public lands, the 116-year-old ranch could easily have been sold for development of over six hundred homesites. Instead, using a loan from a local foundation, Colorado Open Lands purchased the property for $4.5 million (2.VII). The ranch was divided into five separate ranches of 530 to 580 acres, each with a 40-acre designated homesite hidden from view. The historic ranch headquarters is shared by all of the owners as an entrance to the property and for the maintenance of the common ranching operation. Colorado Open Lands reserved a portion of the acreage to serve as an educational facility and is using funds derived from sales of the parcels, after repaying the loan, toward an endowment.

Because land trusts are in business to protect land, engaging in limited development is not without risks. "You have to be up front about what you plan to achieve and then you have to live up to those expectations," says Randi Lemmon, formerly of the Housatonic Valley Association. "An or-

## Community Land Trusts

*A small but growing number of land trusts have been established with a social thrust, and are called community land trusts. Like other land trusts, a community land trust buys property or receives it as a gift; unlike other land trusts, however, a community land trust usually intends to hold in perpetuity the land it acquires and lease it to individuals who will use the land in an environmentally and socially responsible way. Since a community land trust leases property at its use value (or below) and not at its market value, it can help low- and moderate-income residents to afford housing or farmers to afford land. The lessees can make improvements and profit from their equity in the improvements, but cannot profit from transfer of the land. Many community land trusts assist in financing such improvements, often receiving a right of first refusal to buy them if the lessee moves.*

ganization has to keep its battle plan and not say, 'Hey, we can squeeze more lots out of this.' Otherwise people will say you're nothing but a developer, sensitive maybe, but you'll lose a lot of support." Plus, he cautions, "You may be on tricky ground with the IRS if you regard limited development as just another way to make dollars"[2]—that is, the IRS may have reason to question the tax-exempt nature of the project or of the organization itself. Any land trust contemplating limited development should seek the counsel of an attorney knowledgeable about tax issues for nonprofit organizations.

Another drawback to limited development is that in general it works best financially when it results in large private homesites where buyers will pay a premium to live near preserved lands with little, if any, public access. Although the public benefits of protecting a watershed, prime farmland, or a scenic view without physical access for the public may be apparent to conservation-minded observers, many members of the general public may decry the "gentrification" of the countryside and the discouragement of low- or moderate-income housing in areas where limited development is employed. When limited development results in added public parkland or contributes to the ambiance of publicly-used recreation areas or trails, such criticism is less likely.

### C. Revolving Funds

Revolving funds are used to purchase threatened properties which are then sold to sympathetic buyers who agree to manage, develop, or restore the properties in accordance with deed restrictions. Resale of the properties, either "as is" or with improvements, replenishes the organization's funds and allows the money to be "revolved" to new projects. Tax-exempt status from the IRS enables an organization that is operating a revolving fund to sell conservation properties without being liable for capital gains taxation. A revolving fund can effectively extend an organization's financial resources and can give it the capability to act quickly in an emergency. Many funds "revolve downward," however, since restricting the rights in a property can reduce its market value to below the price paid for it. Revolving funds are most useful when a strong market exists for resale; otherwise, if some properties do not sell quickly, the revolving fund may soon become entirely committed.

Colorado Open Lands divided scenic Evans Ranch into five smaller ranches, each including an entire valley. Homesites are set away from meadows and ridge lines.

198

The Historic Preservation Foundation of North Carolina advises a number of revolving funds in small towns around the state. Note at lower left the property in the county seat of Tarboro offered by the Historical Preservation Fund of Edgecombe County.

Although a wide number of urban historic preservation organizations use revolving funds, there are few rural examples. North Carolina has several, however. The Historic Preservation Fund of Edgecombe County was the first of these, founded in 1983. Its initial project involved a frame house built in 1742 that had to be moved in order to be saved from demolition. The owner of the house and the owner of the land to which it was moved both donated their properties, enabling the fund to sell at a "profit." Funds from that sale, plus grants from a private foundation and the state, enabled the Edgecombe fund to begin negotiations with other owners of neglected rural homes in the county. As a result of local press coverage, many owners have gotten in touch with the fund seeking an alternative to simply letting the old family homestead tumble down.

Related to the idea of a revolving fund is "pre-acquisition" or "pass-through," an approach involving a partnership between a nonprofit organization and a government agency that ultimately will acquire a property. The nonprofit organization buys it, if possible in a bargain sale, in advance of an agency's ability to come up with the funds. The more flexible nonprofit organization can move quickly when a property comes on the mar-

# Deal-Making Ground Rules

*Success in the art of negotiating is vital for property conservation organizations. Regardless of who does the negotiating, there are a few ground rules that may make "making a deal" easier:*

• *Before talking to the owner, develop a profile of his or her stewardship record, approximate income, and family history associated with the property. Estimate the land's value, determine its zoning, and investigate local real estate trends.*

• *Your first contact should be a simple, friendly gesture. A brief letter or telephone call and a follow-up visit to answer questions may be sufficient to establish contact.*

• *Time your visits carefully. Avoid intensive work periods for farmers, and times of stress such as illness and death, unless the owner specifically requests the visit because the information may be helpful in making decisions during such a period.*

• *For a first visit, go with a friend, relative, or neighbor who knows the owner. The primary purpose of the first visit should be to explain the organization's interests and help you size up the owner's commitment to protection and any potential threats to the property.*

• *Be prepared to spend a lot of time with a property owner, over a number of visits—even years. Be a good listener, and be patient. Don't try to rush anyone into making a quick decision. The owner is being asked to make a decision about a property that may be the family's principal asset, that may have been in the family for generations, or that may have some other significance to the owner that you know nothing about.*

• *Always know what it is that you want to protect on a particular property; let the owner know that you are most concerned about protecting the wetland or the Greek Revival farmhouse. An owner who hesitates to protect the entire property may be receptive to protecting the part where the most critical resources are located. Don't think of the organization as saving the property: you're seeking a way for the owner to save the property. Remember that the only reason that the resource is still there is because of the actions (or inaction) of the owner.*

• *Information about the property from the community's environmental inventory, such as maps, photographs, or written narratives, may be useful in highlighting the importance of the property. As a first step, you might suggest that the owner draw the property's boundaries and point out special features on an aerial photograph.*

• *Follow up quickly. Write a thank-you note after a visit and answer any questions that were left unanswered during the visit.*

• *The setting is important. The kitchen table may be a far more successful site than a lawyer's office; holding meetings on the owner's turf reduces any sense of intimidation. If you're dealing with multiple owners, use hosts in the neighborhood.*

• *Appearances are important: dress for the occasion. Ask yourself how the landowner will interpret what you wear; casual wear, office dress, or a uniform can each be appropriate or inappropriate. "Bib overalls aren't necessary," comments one land trust negotiator in a farming area. "But I have been known to slip on a pair to help repair a combine while I talk with a farmer" (speech by Mark Ackelson, Monterey, Calif., February 1987).*

• *Strive to project confidence and build respect and trust. Be honest, positive, and open. Don't hide anything; doing so can destroy a carefully built relationship and hurt you with others. If you're not an expert, don't try to appear to be one.*

• *If an owner has difficulty understanding the options, suggest that an advisor—a relative, a friend, a family attorney—join the discussion.*

• *Take careful notes about what the owner and the family members say, and what the owner agrees to. Later, these notes may prove helpful in developing an agreement or clarifying the donor's intent once the agreement is in place.*

*(Portions of the list were adapted with the permission and assistance of Mark C. Ackelson, Iowa Natural Heritage Foundation, from his speech in Monterey, Calif., February 1987.)*

Located along Lake Champlain in upstate New York, the historic village of Essex has drawn many newcomers. As real estate values increased, the Essex Community Heritage Organization (ECHO) became concerned about the need for affordable housing. In 1984, ECHO received a state grant to purchase this property and then used its revolving fund to rehabilitate the building. ECHO later sold the building subject to an easement protecting the exterior and an agreement by the new owner to continue renting to a low-income family.

ket, and then cover its costs when it sells the property to the agency, which permanently protects it. National groups such as the Nature Conservancy and the Trust for Public Land and many local groups have used this approach in working with park agencies, the U.S. Fish and Wildlife Service, and the U.S. Forest Service (Case Study 20).

## D. Administering a Program

A successful program for voluntary land conservation may be run by volunteers, a paid staff, or both. Volunteers usually can handle simple programs and even manage an easement or acquisition program for a small number of properties. A paid staff, however, can help considerably by managing the day-to-day details and following up on negotiations. Once a program involves multiple properties, constant monitoring, and numerous transactions, paid staff is usually essential. Even with staff, however, volunteers remain important, as they can contribute their familiarity with their community and their personal acquaintance with property owners.

Consultants are needed from time to time. For example, lawyers and appraisers are essential for most real estate transactions; landscape architects may be helpful in designing the boundaries of an easement to protect scenic views; a botanist, wildlife biologist, or ecologist may be helpful if rare plant species or habitat for endangered wildlife are to be protected; and an archeologist or architectural historian may help to develop management plans protecting archeological sites or historic buildings. On occasion, simply consulting with more experienced staff members of another land trust may be useful. The Land Trust Exchange encourages this through its Peer Match Program.

Most organizations find it helpful to develop a brochure outlining their goals and objectives and explaining various protection techniques. The brochure should address the major concerns of most property owners,

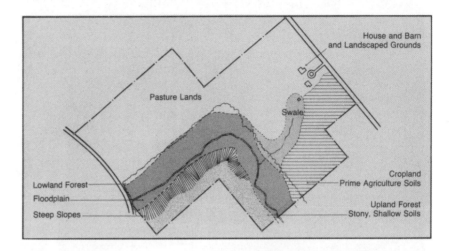

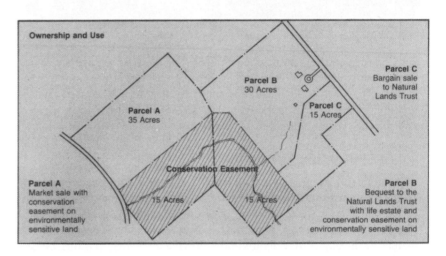

A land trust can develop a property master plan that is tailored to the characteristics of each property and the needs of its owner. Here, the Natural Lands Trust, which serves a large, three-state region centered in Philadelphia, illustrates the thought that must go into protecting an imaginary property. The *top* illustration shows a map portraying the property's features. After consulting with the owner and analyzing the property's problems and opportunities, including physical limitations and legal, market, and financial considerations, the trust develops a master plan. The plan addresses the owner's intentions with respect to ownership, *middle,* and management, *bottom.*

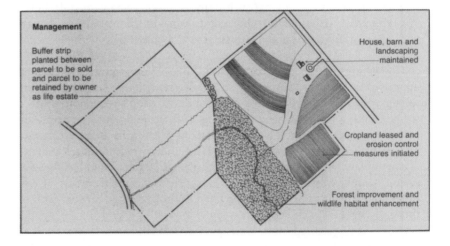

who are likely to ask: "How may I best protect the natural, historic, and scenic qualities of my property? Provide for my own and my children's future needs? Take advantage of tax deductions?"

As useful as a brochure is, it cannot substitute for personal contact. Persuading people to participate in a land protection program can require several on-site visits and many discussions. It is customary to hold discussions with a property owner over the course of several years to develop an appropriate protection strategy. Developing and implementing a protection plan for an owner not only requires a thorough knowledge of the resources to be protected and land-use and tax law, but also a great deal of patience and personal attention.

## IX. CONCLUSION

As we imply in the introduction, there is much excitement and vigor, and many creative ideas, in the nonprofit conservation movement. For rural communities, nonprofit action offers great hope for achieving protection of land and historic buildings. Perhaps the best way for you to begin is to find experienced organizations elsewhere in your state or region. You should not let the thought of emulating a well-established organization intimidate you. As these organizations have grown, so have their funding and their ambitions—from little acorns great oaks grow. Your knowledge of the potential for private action in your community can start you on the way toward duplicating the successes of others and creating successes unique to your community.

Brochure for property owners prepared by the Big Sur Land Trust of California.

# 6

# Help from the Outside

## I. INTRODUCTION

Unless a nationally significant resource is at stake, most rural conservation programs depend primarily on local initiative and financing for their success. Using the techniques described in the previous four chapters, you can go a long way toward protecting your community's natural areas, historic sites, scenic vistas, and farmland. Assistance from national, state, and regional agencies and nonprofit organizations can certainly help, however. Communities diligent in seeking outside funding, advice, and the application of state and federal regulations are generally more successful than those that try to handle all their programs alone.

Federal and state laws and programs change frequently. For example, new legislation may be enacted or existing laws amended or repealed; other laws may apply only for a certain number of years; different administrations and justices vary in their interpretation and enforcement of laws; and the amount of funding available for grants and matching requirements rarely remain constant. Also, nonprofit organizations often change their focus over the years as leaders change, funds become available, and organizational philosophies evolve. For these reasons, we cannot provide a comprehensive listing of current laws and programs; instead, we have attempted to give you ideas about the *types* of laws and programs that may be available to you and strategies your organization may use when it seeks help.

After discussing the nature of outside help and lobbying, we describe those laws and programs that are of greatest relevance to most rural communities. In the Appendix you will find basic information on all of the federal agencies and national nonprofit organizations described in this chapter. Many more, plus state agencies, are described in the National Wildlife Federation's annual *Conservation Directory*. Although our focus here is on federal agencies and national nonprofit organizations, state agencies and organizations will in many instances be more responsive. Indeed, many of the federal laws and national programs have their antecedents in innovative approaches first tried at the state level.

## II. THE NATURE OF OUTSIDE HELP

There are several varieties of environmental laws. Some prohibit actions that may be harmful to the environment or require review procedures before certain types of activities can occur; others enable state or local governments to undertake programs to protect the environment; several federal environmental laws provide partial funding to states or communities for their implementation; in some instances, such as requirements for environmental impact statements, states may have statutes paralleling the federal laws; in other instances, such as laws regulating air pollution, states may have laws that are stricter than federal regulations. Of course not all governmental programs promote rural conservation; many work against it. For instance, federal funds have often been used to finance roads, housing, and shopping centers that contribute to sprawl or take up prime farmland.

Federal agencies are as varied as the laws they administer. Many, such as the Federal Energy Regulatory Commission, are centralized, have relatively narrow mandates, and have little citizen contact. Others—notably the Cooperative Extension Service, the Farmers Home Administration, and the Soil Conservation Service—have broad mandates and are decentralized with many field offices to serve citizens and community groups. These three federal agencies are often good initial contacts for community leaders seeking help in starting a rural conservation program.

There are also numerous nonprofit environmental organizations with differing approaches. Some, such as the Natural Resources Defense Council and the Environmental Defense Fund, are primarily concerned about federal policy, legislation, and precedent-setting litigation. These organizations have the resources to offer only limited assistance to community leaders. Others, such as the Land Trust Exchange, the National Trust for Historic Preservation, and the American Farmland Trust, enthusiastically assist community projects. Organizations such as the Clean Water Action Project are narrowly focused on one issue, while others, such as the Sierra Club, are interested in a variety of issues. Many are membership organizations, such as the National Audubon Society, while others, such as the Trust for Public Land, are not. A few, such as the Nature Conservancy, protect land by acquiring and managing it; most, however, do not get involved in real estate transactions. Finally, a number of statewide nonprofit organizations, such as the Historic Preservation Foundation of North Carolina, the Iowa Natural Heritage Foundation, and the Maine Coast Heritage Trust, or chapters of national organizations, such as the National Audubon Society, the National Wildlife Federation, and the Sierra Club, may be helpful.

There are many publications on federal and state laws and programs and about the work of nonprofit organizations. Reading about programs, however, is no substitute for talking with knowledgeable officials or representatives of organizations. Most state governments have a clearinghouse that keeps track of federal programs and provides information to local governments. The Massachusetts legislature has gone a step further, establishing in 1984 the Center for Rural Massachusetts, which advises communities on controlling growth and other issues. Many other agencies and organizations have current information on the relevant laws and programs for a particular issue. For instance, if a community is concerned about protecting a river, the first organization to contact may be American Rivers. For housing programs, the Housing Assistance Council and the county office of the Farmers Home Administration are the best bet.

As for potentially harmful government action, citizen vigilance is essential. Sometimes, a public notice published in the classified section of the local newspaper is the first indication a community receives of a proposed activity that may be of concern. If volunteer conservationists in Transylvania County, North Carolina, had not seen a notice about a proposed diversion of the waters of the Horsepasture River, that stream might not be free-flowing today (Case Study 20). Fortunately, government agencies are required to publish notices for many proposed actions that affect the environment. Moreover, many agencies maintain mailing lists of individuals and organizations interested in receiving notifications of proposed activities.

## III. LOBBYING

The support of a community's congressional delegation can be invaluable. If a federal agency is not responsive, a letter to a U.S. senator or the congressional representative of the district can help. The letter should specify what information or action is requested of the agency. Elected officials usually forward letters from constituents to the appropriate agency and ask for clarification. Such letters generally receive priority handling in federal agencies. Letters to the Maine congressional delegation, for example, were essential in getting the National Oceanic and Atmospheric Administration to approve funds for the purchase of Laudholm Farm in Maine (Case Study 21). The same approach, of course, can be used with state elected representatives if state agencies are not responsive. If all else fails, a lawsuit brought against an uncooperative agency may help, as Citizens Concerned about Interstate 69 in Michigan discovered (Case Study 4).

If there is no relevant federal or state law, rural groups can consider working to enact a new law, as did the Naturaland Trust in South Carolina when it persuaded the state legislature to approve enabling legislation for easements. The Friends of the Horsepasture also persuaded Congress to request a study of the river for potential designation as a Wild and Scenic River and to appropriate funds for land acquisition.

Rural conservation leaders should keep their elected representatives informed about their activities on a regular basis, even when there is no crisis. Representatives should be invited to visit the community to learn first hand about its assets and to take part in awards ceremonies, festivals, and other events.

## IV. STATE LAND-USE REGULATION

Although the power to regulate the use of private land belongs ultimately to state governments, most regulation has traditionally been delegated to local governments. During the 1970s a number of states, faced with unprecedented growth, took direct control of certain land-use decisions. Some require local governments to prepare land-use plans; others, such as Connecticut and New Jersey, have prepared state plans and urge local governments to conform their own plans to the state's plans; still others regulate land that is considered critical, such as wetlands, flood plains, prime farmland, and coasts.

States with more comprehensive laws include Florida, Hawaii, Oregon, and Vermont. In Hawaii, all land is zoned by the state and placed in one of three categories: urban, agricultural, or conservation. Land in agricultural and conservation areas is regulated by the State Land Use Commission, and urban expansion is more contained as a result (Healy and Rosenberg 1979, p. 186).

The Vermont Environmental Control Act of 1970 (usually referred to as Act 250) provides for state review of proposed subdivisions of more than ten units, commercial development of more than one acre, and all construction above 2,500 feet in altitude. District environmental commissions, appointed by the governor, review proposed developments covered by the act. Before issuing a permit a commission must discern that a proposed development "will not have an undue adverse effect on the scenic or natural beauty of the area, esthetics, historic sites, or rare and irreplaceable natural areas." In Florida, the Environmental Land and Water Management Act of 1972 authorizes designation of "areas of critical state concern" that contain significant environmental, historical, or natural resources. If local governments do not protect these areas, the state can assume authority and regulate them. Vermont's and Florida's laws have helped to control major developments, but small-scale developments which do not come under the purview of the laws have often gone unchecked, although their cumulative environmental impact may be large (Healy and Rosenberg 1979, pp. 54 and 170).

In Oregon, the Land Conservation and Development Act of 1973 requires local governments to prepare comprehensive plans that must meet the conservation goals set by the state Land Conservation and Development Commission to protect such resources as coastal areas and farmland. The plans must delineate urban growth boundaries and designate prime farmland beyond the boundaries for "exclusive farm use," as well as provide for low-income housing.

Other states have designated certain areas as critical and have established comprehensive controls over them. For instance, New York enforces controls over 3.7 million acres of private land within the boundaries of the Adirondack Park. For more than a million acres in the park's resource-management zone, the state-zoned minimum lot size is 42 acres. New Jersey, in cooperation with the federal government, is now establishing controls over private lands in the Pinelands National Reserve. Maine's Land Use Regulation Commission plans and zones private land in the state's sparsely inhabited northern woods. Since 1980, there have been only a few new state land-use laws, including a Maryland statute to protect the Chesapeake Bay and the land around it.

Obviously, any rural community considering a plan or drafting land-use ordinances should consult with the appropriate state officials to determine the requirements state governments have imposed. State officials may also be able and willing to assist in the preparation of the plans and ordi-

## Environmental Impact Statements

*The National Environmental Policy Act (NEPA) requires all federal agencies to include in every recommendation for "major Federal actions significantly affecting the quality of the human environment," a detailed environmental impact statement (EIS) that describes:*

*(i) The environmental impact of the proposed action,*
*(ii) Any adverse environmental effects which cannot be avoided should the proposal be implemented,*
*(iii) Alternatives to the proposed action,*
*(iv) The relationship between local short-term uses of man's environment and the maintenance and enhancement of long-term productivity, and*
*(v) Any irreversible and irretrievable commitments of resources which would be involved in the proposed action should it be implemented.*

*In 1978, the Council on Environmental Quality established regulations for the application of NEPA and EIS's to the work of federal agencies. If more than one federal agency is involved, one is designated as the "lead agency." Other federal agencies and state and local governments can become "cooperating agencies." As a first step, the lead agency must prepare an "environmental assessment" for all projects that may have significant effects on the environment. This assessment provides the lead agency with the information it needs to determine whether a full EIS is needed. Federal agencies must elicit public comment in the process of making an environmental assessment.*

*If the lead agency determines that an EIS is necessary, it must involve interested parties in "scoping"—or "determining the scope of issues to*

nances. There are a number of statewide nonprofit organizations that are concerned with land-use issues. The Vermont Natural Resources Council and 1,000 Friends of Oregon, for example, have been particularly active in monitoring statewide land-use laws.

## V. THE NATIONAL ENVIRONMENTAL POLICY ACT AND STATE EQUIVALENTS

With the passage in 1969 of the National Environmental Policy Act (NEPA), as amended, the United States embarked upon a national program of environmental protection. NEPA, which states that the federal government must make it possible for the nation to "preserve important historic, cultural, and natural aspects of our national heritage," is arguably the most comprehensive and significant federal law governing the environment in the nation's history.

NEPA's key provision is the requirement that all federal agencies prepare an environmental impact statement (EIS) for proposed actions and permits that might affect the environment (see *Environmental Impact Statements*, pp. 208–9). An understanding of the EIS process is important for rural conservation leaders, since few communities are immune from federal actions. Projects undertaken by the private sector but requiring federal funds for a portion of the financing—as is the case for many large-scale construction projects—are also covered by NEPA. It is important to note that the preparation of an EIS does not stop the federal government from harming the environment. The law simply requires that the government take environmental values into account when planning projects.

Rural conservation leaders who understand the EIS process can ensure that their concerns are brought to the attention of the appropriate federal officials. For instance, farmers in Eaton County, Michigan, who were concerned about a new interstate highway that would have consumed prime farmland made good use of the EIS process to force the state highway department to change the road's alignment (Case Study 4). Conservationists should determine whether the EIS has been prepared by qualified persons, covers all of the resources the community is concerned about, is accurate, and objectively presents the alternative courses of action. If a federal agency fails to prepare an EIS, citizens' groups can seek a court injunction to halt work on a project until NEPA has been complied with.

Many states have passed their own general environmental statutes, often referred to as "little NEPAs." They require documents similar to an EIS for actions of state and local governments (not covered by the federal NEPA) that may have an impact on the environment. For projects that involve both federal and state or local funds, the impact statements are generally prepared in coordination with the federal agency.

To facilitate cross-reference, programs to deal with the following resources and problems are described in the same order as they appear in Chapter 1.

# VI. WATER AND RELATED RESOURCES

## A. Water Supply

The principal federal laws that protect water quality are the Clean Water Act of 1972, as amended, and the Safe Drinking Water Act of 1974, as amended. Both are administered by the Environmental Protection Agency (EPA), but much of its authority is delegated to state agencies when their programs are approved by EPA. The states are eligible for EPA grants to administer the acts. There are also many state water-protection laws, some of them stricter than the federal laws.

The objective of the Clean Water Act is "to restore and maintain the chemical, physical, and biological integrity of the Nation's waters." Under the act, EPA has developed national standards for water quality. The standards specify the maximum amount of each pollutant that can be discharged under given conditions. States are required to identify water-quality problems and develop plans to treat waste water. Each state must also set water-quality standards for every significant body of surface water. To meet the standards, the Clean Water Act established a National Pollutant Discharge Elimination System which requires both municipalities and industries to obtain permits from EPA or approved state agencies before pollutants can be discharged into "the waters of the United States," defined to include wetlands. The quantities of pollutants that are discharged are limited and must be monitored. Unfortunately, enforcement has generally been weak, and the act does not cover groundwater pollution, a growing concern of many rural communities.

By providing funds for sewage treatment plants, the Clean Water Act has helped to solve many problems associated with biodegradable discharges. The act has also created incentives for development in some rural areas, however, by establishing sewage treatment capacity for populations in excess of current needs. For instance, planners in Mecklenburg County, North Carolina, have found efforts at farmland retention thwarted by the presence of sewer lines that attract development. The 1981 amendment to the act ameliorated this problem by stating that, after October 1984, grants would not be made "to construct that portion of any treatment works providing reserve capacity in excess of existing needs."

While the Clean Water Act seeks to control water pollution at the source, the Safe Drinking Water Act controls it at the point of consumption. The act requires EPA to establish standards for the safe "maximum contaminant levels" for specified pollutants in water supplies. Under the act, EPA also regulates the injection of pollutants into groundwater and designates aquifers that should be protected. If EPA designates an aquifer as "the sole or principal drinking water source for an area," no federal funds can be spent on projects which would contaminate it. Although the Safe Drinking Water Act has great potential for protecting water supplies, enforcement has most often been ineffective, and very few sole-source aquifers have been designated though many exist.

The best sources of information about water pollution control are the regional offices of EPA and state agencies charged with protecting water quality. The Natural Resources Defense Council and the National Audubon Society work on legislation and litigate on clean water issues, but they do not generally get involved in local issues unless there is the poten-

*be addressed" in the EIS. To facilitate review and comment by the public, the EIS must be written in "plain English" and for most projects be limited to 150 pages of text. There are specific requirements for format and the topics to be covered. The lead agency must circulate the completed EIS to all organizations, agencies, and people affected by or interested in the project to elicit their comments. Finally, once the lead agency has made its decision, it must maintain public records stating the agency's plans for ensuring mitigation of environmental impacts.*

*For further information on the NEPA process, contact the Council on Environmental Quality. The council's annual report summarizes regulation updates.*

tial to set a national precedent. The National Demonstration Water Project, another nonprofit group, provides advice and assistance.

## Middlesboro, Kentucky:
## Yellow Creek Concerned Citizens
## Insist on Clean Water

An example of a local group that has used the Clean Water Act to curb water pollution is Yellow Creek Concerned Citizens in Middlesboro, Kentucky (1984 pop. 12,095). For years a local tanning company had dumped chemical wastes into the creek. The stench was often overpowering. Fish died and wildlife disappeared. Residents along the creek objected, but to no avail. The tannery was the major employer in town, and the city government and the courts seemed reluctant to force the company to stop polluting. A new city sewer plant, partly funded under the Clean Water Act, went on line in 1975 and received the tannery's waste, but could not adequately treat it.

For Larry Wilson, who lived nearby, the final straw was when his pigs, goats, and cattle died after drinking creek water. In July 1980, Wilson and his neighbors came together to form Yellow Creek Concerned Citizens to combat the problem. The group incorporated and elected Wilson president.

A few months later, the Environmental Protection Agency (EPA) held hearings on reissuing a discharge permit to the Middlesboro Sewage Treatment Plant. The Concerned Citizens objected, saying the city should be denied a permit until it could prove that it could effectively treat the company's waste. A number of other hearings followed. The Concerned Citizens gained membership and, more importantly, became regarded as a responsible, well-informed organization. Wilson states: "We use the old accounting principle of understatement rather than overstatement. When people start investigating what we said, most of the time they'll find it's worse than the way we stated it." The group even took its case to Washington, D.C., testifying in 1982 at congressional hearings on the Clean Water Act.

After being presented with much evidence of an alarming incidence of cancer and other diseases among residents living along the creek, local and state officials finally concluded that wells near the creek were unsafe. In September 1982, the state government and the Farmers Home Administration agreed to finance a new water system.

But the Concerned Citizens also wanted to stop the pollution itself. That November, EPA ordered the city to do a better job of cleaning up the effluent. The Concerned Citizens also pressured EPA to sue the city and the tannery for violating the Clean Water Act. The city was forced to pay $50,000 in damages. Still pending is a $31 million damage suit filed by Concerned Citizens against the city and tannery.

Members of Concerned Citizens have also gotten more involved in local politics. Member Beverly Greene and other Middlesboro citizens formed the independent Time For a Change party and put up a slate for the 1983 city council elections. Eight of their candidates won to form a new majority. According to Greene, "The tannery, aware of the changing tide and the council's determination, is at least beginning to negotiate with us. This past April [1984], tannery representatives and city council members sat down together and talked for the first time. I thought I'd never see the day that would happen." Although Greene and her allies are no longer on the city council, she believes their education campaign has paid off. Citizens are much more aware of environmental issues, and a sewer treatment plant built in 1986 has finally controlled pollution in Yellow Creek.

One observer has noted that "the same story is endlessly repeated of citizen groups believing at first that all they need do is demonstrate a serious problem in violation of the laws for somebody somewhere to do something. But typically it is shrewd political pressure, as was brought to bear in Middlesboro, that gets results."

---

## B. Rivers

Most rivers are located in more than one town or country. Consequently, efforts to protect them are usually undertaken by organizations working at the regional or state level or by an organization set up for the specific purpose of protecting a river, such as the Friends of the Staunton River in Virginia (2.IV.A).

The 1968 Wild and Scenic Rivers Act, as amended, states that it is federal policy to preserve rivers that "possess outstandingly remarkable scenic, recreational, geologic, fish and wildlife, historic, cultural, or other similar values." The law sets up a mechanism to designate sections of rivers that meet at least one of the above criteria, are relatively undeveloped, are free-flowing (i.e., are not dammed), and have good water quality.

After designation, rivers are classified as wild, scenic, or recreational, depending on the ease of access and the amount of development along them. Management plans prepared by the federal government for designated rivers are strictest for wild rivers and the most flexible for recreational rivers. Designated rivers are also protected from federally funded, assisted, or licensed dams, channelization, and other water projects. The act authorizes the federal government to acquire land or easements along their banks. As of 1987, seventy-two rivers (7,709 miles) had been designated by Congress.

There are two routes to securing a Wild and Scenic designation and two steps in each process. In one, Congress must first authorize the study of a river for its potential addition to the system. The eligibility of the river for designation is then reviewed by the Department of the Interior, or the Department of Agriculture for rivers on Forest Service land. During this time, public comment is solicited. After the studies are complete, they are submitted to Congress for legislative action on their designation. Unfortunately, fewer than one-quarter of the "study rivers" (as they are called) have been added to the system.

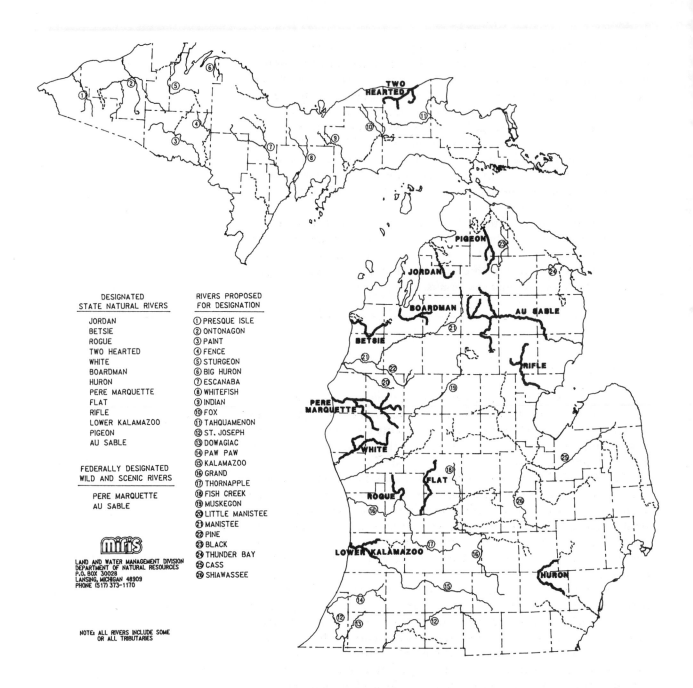

**DESIGNATED
STATE NATURAL RIVERS**

JORDAN
BETSIE
ROGUE
TWO HEARTED
WHITE
BOARDMAN
HURON
PERE MARQUETTE
FLAT
RIFLE
LOWER KALAMAZOO
PIGEON
AU SABLE

**FEDERALLY DESIGNATED
WILD AND SCENIC RIVERS**

PERE MARQUETTE
AU SABLE

**RIVERS PROPOSED
FOR DESIGNATION**

① PRESQUE ISLE
② ONTONAGON
③ PAINT
④ FENCE
⑤ STURGEON
⑥ BIG HURON
⑦ ESCANABA
⑧ WHITEFISH
⑨ INDIAN
⑩ FOX
⑪ TAHQUAMENON
⑫ ST. JOSEPH
⑬ DOWAGIAC
⑭ PAW PAW
⑮ KALAMAZOO
⑯ GRAND
⑰ THORNAPPLE
⑱ FISH CREEK
⑲ MUSKEGON
⑳ LITTLE MANISTEE
㉑ MANISTEE
㉒ PINE
㉓ BLACK
㉔ THUNDER BAY
㉕ CASS
㉖ SHIAWASSEE

miris

LAND AND WATER MANAGEMENT DIVISION
DEPARTMENT OF NATURAL RESOURCES
P.O. BOX 30028
LANSING, MICHIGAN 48909
PHONE (517) 373-1170

NOTE: ALL RIVERS INCLUDE SOME
OR ALL TRIBUTARIES

**Rivers protected under Michigan's
Natural Rivers Act.**

The second route is for rivers to be nominated for designation by state governments. The state legislature must designate the river for protection under state law and provide for its protection. Then the governor may request that the Secretary of the Interior add the river segment to the national system. Congressional approval is not required.

Twenty-nine state governments have their own river conservation programs and have designated approximately 12,000 miles of streams. Some states, such as Oklahoma and California, have strict controls on dams on designated rivers but do not regulate land adjacent to rivers. Oregon, on the other hand, regulates a corridor a quarter of a mile wide along its designated rivers (Kusler 1980, pp. 36–37). Other states, such as Minnesota,

SAVING AMERICA'S COUNTRYSIDE

have acquired land along designated rivers. Regional offices of the National Park Service assist states and communities in developing river protection programs.

## Horsepasture River, North Carolina: Halting a Plan to Divert a Scenic River

The Horsepasture River tumbles 1,700 vertical feet in just two miles as it descends from the forested eastern escarpment of the Blue Ridge Mountains. Six waterfalls along its course have long been favorites of hikers in Transylvania County. The pools below the falls are popular swimming holes. Thanks to the Wild and Scenic Rivers Act and concerted local conservation leadership, the Horsepasture should continue to be free-flowing for future generations of hikers and swimmers to enjoy.

Another fate awaited the river in 1984, when an electric power company applied to the Federal Energy Regulatory Commission (FERC) for a permit to divert most of the water to a generator.

Permission might have been granted quietly if Stuart Rabb had not read a public notice in the local paper about FERC's intention to grant a permit. At the same time, Bill Thomas, another county resident and an active member of the Sierra Club, heard about the project through a magazine article, made inquiries, and obtained a copy of the power company's application to FERC. Thomas developed a slide show on the Horsepasture and he, Rabb, and others started talking about the need to protect the river. They believed the relatively small amount of power to be generated and its cost did not warrant diminishing the spectacular power of the falls and the potential damage to fish habitat and water quality.

In April 1984, Thomas and others organized the Friends of the Horsepasture—or FROTH, as they called it for short—which quickly became an informal but effective lobbying group. They started a newsletter and within months had 800 members. On the advice of the Sierra Club, they requested a hearing with the state natural resources department and the county commissioners, held on September 24, 1984, in the local high school auditorium. Seven hundred and fifty residents showed up at the largest public hearing in the county's history.

FROTH's timing was excellent. Both Congressman James Clarke and Senator Jesse Helms were facing tough elections that November and could not afford to ignore these vocal voters. Congressman Clarke introduced legislation to have the Horsepasture studied for designation as a wild and scenic river. The "study bill" passed the House of Representatives on September 24, the very day of the public hearing. When Clarke's assistant at the meeting announced the vote, "the roof blew off the place," according to Thomas. "I still get choked up thinking about

An electric power company proposed diverting most of the water flowing over the spectacular falls of the Horsepasture River. As a result of citizen action, the Horsepasture is now protected by the Wild and Scenic Rivers Act.

Sometimes conservationists can obtain help from the Congress and federal agencies. Here Bill Thomas (*left*), chairman of Friends of the Horsepasture, shows congressional candidate Bill Hendon (*center*) and then U.S. Secretary of Energy Donald Hodel where a proposed hydroelectric plant would be located. They agreed to assist in protecting the river.

it. It was the most incredible evening I have ever spent. As soon as this great roar went up, all of the politicians jumped up in turn." Bill Hendon, the Republican candidate for Clarke's seat, was at the meeting and promised his support. An assistant to Senator Helms promised similar action in the Senate. As luck would have it, then Secretary of Energy Donald Hodel, who controlled FERC's budget, was campaigning for Hendon in Asheville two weeks later. Thomas met with Hodel, who promised his help in heading off the project.

SAVING AMERICA'S COUNTRYSIDE

Hendon and Helms won their elections and lived up to their commitments, supporting not only legislation to designate the river but also to appropriate $1 million to acquire 435 acres along the river to add to the Nantahala National Forest. Early in 1985, the Trust for Public Land (TPL), at the urging of FROTH, purchased an option on the tract from the owner. Later that year Congress passed the necessary legislation, and in February 1986, TPL purchased the land and resold it for the same price to the Forest Service. Bill Thomas and his colleagues recently established a new coalition to protect other streams in the same Jocassee watershed.

## C. Wetlands

In the past, the Soil Conservation Service assisted farmers in draining wetlands, and projects by the Army Corps of Engineers and the Bureau of Reclamation destroyed many wetlands. President Carter's 1977 Executive Order 11990, entitled "Protection of Wetlands," signaled a change in federal policy by requiring all agencies to protect wetlands.

Several federal laws, including the 1982 Coastal Barrier Resources Act (6.VI.E) and the 1985 Food Security Act (6.VII.B), now offer a degree of protection to wetlands. Section 404 of the Clean Water Act states that a permit from the Army Corps of Engineers is necessary to discharge "dredge or fill material" into wetlands. The Environmental Protection Agency can overrule the Corps and stop a permit from being issued if it will have an unacceptable effect on wetlands. The Emergency Wetlands Resources Act of 1986 requires that states acquiring land through the Land and Water Conservation Fund (6.IX.E) give priority to wetlands. Finally, the 1986 Tax Reform Act reduced incentives for draining wetlands.

In addition, many states and more than 3,000 local governments have programs to protect coastal wetlands in conjunction with coastal-zone management plans. Some also regulate or offer incentives to protect inland wetlands. Massachusetts, for instance, requires the review of proposed alterations to wetlands by municipal conservation commissions. In Oregon, property owners may receive a tax abatement on their land along streams if they join in a cooperative management plan with the Oregon Department of Fish and Wildlife.

Advice on protecting wetlands is available from the U.S. Fish and Wildlife Service (which is in the process of mapping all of the known wetlands in the United States) and from the Soil Conservation Service. The Environmental Law Institute, a nonprofit organization, has a particular interest in wetlands policy issues.

## D. Flood Plains

The National Flood Insurance Program, administered by the Federal Emergency Management Agency (FEMA), is the principal federal program to protect flood plains. FEMA works with state and local governments to map one-hundred-year flood plains (areas that have at least a 1 in 100 chance of flooding in any given year). Through the insurance program, residents in flood-prone areas can receive federally backed flood in-

## Federal Agencies Responsible for Dams

*The principal federal agencies that dam rivers are the Army Corps of Engineers, the Bureau of Reclamation, and the Tennessee Valley Authority (TVA). Though many of their projects have had unfortunate environmental consequences, each is more concerned with environmental protection than it once was.*

*The Corps of Engineers constructs dams for flood control, power, and navigation. By authority of the National Dam Inspection Act of 1972, the Corps also inventories and inspects all dams whose failure could present serious threats.*

*Providing water for agriculture in the West is the responsibility of the Bureau of Reclamation, Department of the Interior. The bureau's projects also furnish water for domestic consumption, industry, and hydroelectric power.*

*TVA is concerned with water resources in the Tennessee River watershed, which incorporates parts of seven states. In addition to providing water, flood control, and electricity from its dams, TVA advises communities on natural-resource protection.*

*All private use of rivers and streams for hydroelectric power is regulated by the Federal Energy Regulatory Commission, which reviews requests for dams and diversions and issues licenses. The 1986 Electric Consumers Protection Act requires the commission to give "equal consideration" to environmental protection.*

surance if their local government agrees to implement programs to reduce future flood risks. The local government must adopt and enforce a floodplain management ordinance or zoning and subdivision controls that meet FEMA's standards. The controls on flood ways, where flood waters are deepest and fastest, are stricter than in flood-fringe areas. Typically, flood-way land is limited to such uses as agriculture, parks, golf courses, and marinas. Construction in flood-fringe areas is often permitted if the buildings are elevated or otherwise protected. Communities that fail to adopt flood-control measures may lose federal aid for projects in floodprone areas. More than 17,500 communities have established controls meeting FEMA standards and participate in the National Flood Insurance Program. Advice on flood control is also available from the Soil Conservation Service, the Army Corps of Engineers, the Bureau of Reclamation, and the Tennessee Valley Authority. These agencies can construct dams and levees to help prevent floods, although these may cause other problems. Many states also now have laws that regulate flood plains.

### E. Coasts

The principal federal legislation protecting America's coasts is the Coastal Zone Management Act of 1972, as amended. The act declares that it is national policy "to preserve, protect, develop, and where possible, to restore or enhance, the resources of the Nation's coastal zone." Rather than impose federal regulation, the act gives incentives to states that plan and implement regulations based on the plans. The act requires "full consideration to ecological, cultural, historic, and esthetic values." The coastal zone, as defined by the act, extends over 95,000 miles and includes all beaches, estuaries, bays, wetlands, and islands along the Atlantic and Pacific Oceans, the Gulf of Mexico, and the Great Lakes.

The thirty-five coastal states and territories are eligible for grants from the National Oceanic and Atmospheric Administration (NOAA) of the U.S. Department of Commerce to develop management programs for land and water resources in their coastal zones. States with approved programs are eligible for additional grants from NOAA to implement the plans. Funds can be used to protect areas important for "their conservation, recreational, or esthetic values." Property acquisition, construction, and the rehabilitation of historic buildings are eligible activities. Federal agencies undertaking or licensing projects in the coastal zone must ensure that the projects are consistent with approved state management programs.

Many states have regulated new construction near the coast. North Carolina has one of the strictest laws, requiring new construction to be at least 60 feet behind the vegetation line. This helps to protect dunes, but does not relieve development pressure back from the beach. The California Coastal Zone Conservation Act of 1972 gave control over most construction along the state's coast and up to 1,000 yards from the coast to state and regional commissions empowered to grant or deny permits for development.

Another federal statute that protects coasts is the Coastal Barrier Resources Act of 1982. The act prohibits federal funding, including flood insurance, for projects that would result in development on specified barrier islands.

Conservationists near coasts should determine from the appropriate state government office whether any part of their community is within the designated coastal zone. In Florida and Delaware this is easy: the entirety of both states is included. For communities within the coastal zone, there are likely to be special state laws that can be used to protect coastal resources, and there may be funds designated for coastal areas that a community can use for conservation projects.

## Wells, Maine:
## Saving a Saltwater Farm

The Laudholm Trust in Wells, Maine (1984 pop. 7,988), is an example of a nonprofit organization that has taken advantage of the Coastal Zone Management Act to protect a significant natural, scenic, and historic property. To conservation leaders in Wells concerned about the protection of the Laudholm Farm, the National Estuarine Sanctuaries program sounded like a good fit. This act authorizes the National Oceanic and Atmospheric Administration (NOAA) to designate sanctuaries and provide 50 percent matching grants to states for acquisition and management. The scenic 313-acre farm, with its historic farmstead, borders an estuary and was the only large undeveloped private property left along that part of the coast.

When the farm came on the market in 1978, a group of Wells citizens got together to see what could be done to protect it. They established the Laudholm Farm Committee, but their task seemed hopeless: the owners were asking $2 million for the property and had already started to subdivide.

Then in 1980, committee members received a notice from the state planning office asking for nominations of a property that could be acquired with NOAA funds as a National Estuarine Sanctuary. The town's selectmen were supportive of nominating the Laudholm Farm so long as it would not cost the town money. After reviewing some forty applications, the state and NOAA chose the Wells site.

Three major hurdles remained: moving final approval for the project through the NOAA bureaucracy, raising the necessary 50 percent matching funds, and negotiating a sales agreement with the owners. The citizens committee got invaluable assistance in dealing with NOAA from the regional planning commission. Despite this help, final approval was slow in coming. Mort Mather, a former New York stage manager, became increasingly frustrated by the inaction: "Finally in early 1980 I said O.K., I'll have a meeting at my house. From that meeting everyone went home and wrote letters to their congressmen, to NOAA, and the editor of the paper." This did the trick. NOAA officials came up for a hearing, primarily because of the letter-writing campaign, and in 1982 awarded the first of three grants for acquisition, totaling $1.2 million.

Anticipating the federal grant, the committee members incorporated the Laudholm Trust in 1982, with Mather as president, to raise funds and acquire the property. The trust raised more than $800,000 in cash,

The Laudholm farmstead will be rehabilitated as the visitors' center for the newly created Wells National Estuarine Sanctuary.

mostly from its 2,600 members, and was given 37 acres of land plus several building lots. The state supplied $250,000.

Once acquisition was complete, the trust turned the property over to the Town of Wells, which will operate the sanctuary in accordance with a management plan negotiated among the trust, the town, the state, and NOAA. The trust will continue to raise funds for the operation of the sanctuary. The farmstead, which was recently listed in the National Register of Historic Places, will become a visitors' center.

## VII. THE LAND

### A. Soil

The federal agency responsible for soil conservation is the Soil Conservation Service (SCS). An agency of the Department of Agriculture, SCS maps soils and provides technical assistance to help individuals, organizations, and local governments to conserve soil and water resources. In cooperation with the states, SCS has established nearly three thousand Soil and Water Conservation Districts across the country. The districts generally follow county lines. Conservation districts are units of government organized under state laws and supervised by locally elected boards. Most districts have SCS District Conservationists and sometimes other staff who give advice and assistance not just to farmers but to all land users. For instance, SCS provides guidelines on controlling erosion on construction sites and information about soil limitations for housing developments.

Given its decentralization, SCS is an invaluable source of assistance to many rural conservation programs. Cazenovia, New York (Case Study 6), and many other rural communities have made extensive use of SCS, not only for help in conserving soil, but also for natural resources protection in general. SCS can best be contacted through its county offices.

## B. Farming and Farmland

In 1981 the National Agricultural Lands Study concluded that many federal programs contribute to loss of farmland. For instance, grants to build sewer lines through farmland may create an incentive for more development, and grants for highway construction may also result in farmland loss. In response, Congress in 1981 passed the Farmland Protection Policy Act. The act directs all federal agencies "to identify and take into account the adverse effects of Federal programs on the preservation of farmland" and consider alternatives that would lessen the effects.

The Congress went further when it incorporated conservation concerns in the 1985 Food Security Act. The so-called sodbuster and swampbuster provisions of the act specify that farmers who cultivate highly erodible land and wetlands could lose federal financial assistance. In the past, farmers could receive assistance regardless of the suitability of their land for agriculture. Under the Conservation Reserve Program established by the act, the Department of Agriculture (USDA) will pay farmers who agree to take highly erodible land out of crop production. Twenty-three million acres have already been placed in the reserve. Another provision of the act allows USDA to accept conservation easements in lieu of a portion of a defaulting farmer's debt to the Farmers Home Administration.

Many states have farmland protection laws that reduce taxes on farmland, establish agricultural districts, protect farmers from nuisance suits, protect them from assessments for sewers and other public improvements not related to agriculture, and make funds available for the purchase of development rights. These programs generally require local initiative, so they are described more fully in Chapters 4 and 5. Generally, the states, particularly more populous ones such as Massachusetts, have gone further than the federal government in protecting farmland.

Information on farmland retention programs can be obtained from the Cooperative Extension Service county agents, Soil Conservation Service District Conservationists, state departments of agriculture, and the American Farmland Trust.

## C. Forests and Rangeland

The Forest Service of the Department of Agriculture is the principal federal agency responsible for forest resources. It is a decentralized agency, with considerable authority given to Forest Supervisors, who prepare multiple-use management plans for national forests that incorporate public comments. In many rural communities a large percentage of the land is in national forests. In such communities it is important for conservation leaders to know their District Forest Rangers and become involved in the planning process for national forests. Also, Forest Service personnel can advise communities about protecting forests adjacent to national forests.

In addition to overseeing national forests, the Forest Service also gives help, under the terms of the 1978 Cooperative Forestry Assistance Act, to local governments, nonprofit organizations, and private landowners. In some states this assistance is offered directly by the Forest Service; in others it is offered through state agencies or the Cooperative Extension Service.

The Bureau of Land Management (BLM) of the Department of the Interior manages 170 million acres of federally owned rangeland in eleven western states. More than 21,000 livestock owners pay BLM to graze about nine million head of livestock on these public lands. Conservation leaders should contact BLM District and Resource Area Managers in order to comment on BLM's plans for rangeland. Although BLM does not provide advice on range issues off federal lands, the Soil Conservation Service, the Forest Service, and the Cooperative Extension Service have specialists on range issues who can assist community groups.

Both the Sierra Club and the Wilderness Society work to protect forest and range resources on public lands. In addition, the American Forestry Association is concerned with forest protection.

## VIII. WILDLIFE AND ENDANGERED SPECIES

### A. Wildlife

The federal agency most directly involved in wildlife protection and management is the Fish and Wildlife Service (USFWS) of the Department of the Interior. It administers more than 430 wildlife refuges across the country that include nearly 90 million acres. They provide habitat for hundreds of species on wildlife, many of which are endangered. Many refuges are located along the major flyways of migrating birds.

The Fish and Wildlife Service also evaluates the effects of development on wildlife habitat outside its refuges and offers assistance to state and local conservation programs. Expert advice on wildlife and fisheries is available from Refuge Managers and through the service's seven regional and numerous field offices. In addition, state fish and game departments can be of assistance. In the past, these offices have been primarily interested in species that are hunted or fished, but this is changing.

Numerous national and state nonprofit organizations are concerned with protecting wildlife. Three of the largest are the National Audubon Society, the National Wildlife Federation, and the Nature Conservancy; all have chapters throughout the country.

### B. Endangered Species

The Endangered Species Act of 1973, as amended, is one of the strongest environmental laws. The act gives the Secretary of the Interior, acting through the Fish and Wildlife Service, broad powers to protect endangered species and the habitat on which they depend. It also gives the Secretary of Commerce similar power to protect endangered marine species. According to the act, endangered species—"any species which is in danger of extinction through all or a significant portion of its range"—and threatened species—any species which is likely to become endangered—may be added to the U.S. List of Endangered and Threatened Wildlife and Plants. After review, the appropriate department decides whether to list the species. Once listed, an animal species cannot be removed, harmed, pursued, hunted, transported, or traded in interstate or foreign commerce without special permission. For endangered plants these provisions unfortunately apply only to federal agencies and others using federal funds.

Most endangered species are plants and invertebrate animals. Many have yet to be officially listed or protected. Here botanist Donna M. E. Ware of the College of William and Mary measures and records small whorled pogonias (*Isotria medeoloides*) in Virginia's deciduous woodlands as part of a study of the ecology of this rare native orchid. The study is an element in the U.S. Fish and Wildlife recovery plan for this endangered species. The privately owned 200-acre site is leased by the Nature Conservancy for a nominal sum.

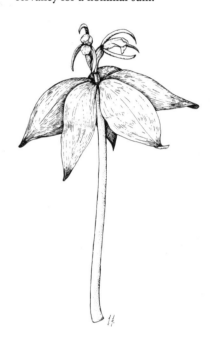

In addition to the listing of species, the law calls for the conservation of "critical habitat"—the land, water, and air a species needs for survival. Federal agencies and others using federal funds must consult with the USFWS regarding any action that might jeopardize the continued existence of a listed species or adversely affect its critical habitat. The process of determining critical habitat is similar to the one for listing species.

The principal goal of the program is to restore populations of listed species so they are no longer endangered or threatened. Recovery plans may include improved management of critical habitat and its acquisition. As of 1987, 466 endangered and threatened U.S. species were listed. Unfortunately, most scientists agree, there are many more known and unknown species that should be listed.

# IX. SPECIAL RESOURCES

## A. Natural Landmarks

The National Natural Landmarks Program was established by the Secretary of the Interior in 1962 "to identify and encourage the preservation of nationally significant examples of the full range of ecological and geological features that constitute the nation's natural heritage." Areas

Monument Rocks Natural Area in western Kansas is a designated National Natural Landmark. Composed of soft chalk capped with limestone, the rocks are striking examples of the effects of natural erosion and were conspicuous landmarks for early explorers. The private landowner is cooperating with the National Park Service to protect the landmark.

designated as landmarks represent the best examples of regional ecosystems, geologic features, and paleontologic sites, and are listed in the National Registry of Natural Landmarks. Among the approximately six hundred areas designated are Diamond Head, Hawaii; Okefenokee Swamp, Georgia; Franconia Notch, New Hampshire; and Point Lobos, California.

The National Park Service, which administers the registry, conducts inventories of natural areas to identify potential landmarks. After receiving comments from interested parties, the Park Service nominates eligible sites to the Secretary of the Interior, who confers the designation at his discretion.

The owners of the Spring Hill Ranch in Chase County, Kansas, qualified for rehabilitation tax credits when they restored the 1880s ranch for continued use. The buildings, constructed of locally quarried limestone, are listed in the National Register of Historic Places. This drawing, done shortly after the complex was built, provides invaluable documentation on the history of the ranch.

Both publicly and privately owned sites are eligible. Designation does not affect ownership of a site, nor its management and use. Nevertheless, owners of landmarks are invited to enter into voluntary, nonbinding conservation agreements with the Park Service to protect the features for which their properties have been recognized. The Park Service monitors landmarks, and federal agencies are required to take them into account when preparing environmental impact statements. The Park Service works closely with the Nature Conservancy and state natural areas programs, many of which have been established by the Conservancy in cooperation with state governments.

## B. Historic and Cultural Resources

The basic federal law protecting historic and archeological resources is the National Historic Preservation Act of 1966, as amended. The act authorized the National Register of Historic Places, made funds available to states and the National Trust for Historic Preservation, and established the federal Advisory Council on Historic Preservation.

The National Register, administered by the National Park Service, is composed of "districts, sites, buildings, structures, and objects that are significant in American history, architecture, archeology, engineering, and culture." The more than 45,000 properties in the National Register are given national recognition, which can be an incentive for their protection. The act authorizes federal matching grants for restoration of listed properties, although these funds are not currently available. An important aspect of the act is the requirement that all federal agencies consider the impact of their proposed undertakings on historic properties. There are no restrictions, however, on private owners of listed properties unless they receive federal funds or tax benefits.

Properties that are of outstanding national significance can be designated by the Secretary of the Interior as National Historic Landmarks. National Register regulations apply to these properties. In addition, the Park Service monitors the condition of landmarks and provides preservation advice to their owners.

Nominations to the National Register are usually made by state governments or, in the case of federally owned properties, by federal agencies. (The criteria used in evaluating nominations are described in *Evaluation Criteria*, p. 115.) Wherever possible, the Park Service urges the preparation of district nominations that include contiguous properties. After review by the Park Service's staff, the Keeper of the National Register enters properties in the register. Owners must be informed if their property is being nominated to the register. If they object, the property is not listed. In the case of a district, if more than 50 percent of the property owners object, the district is not listed.

At the state level, the National Register program is administered by State Historic Preservation Officers (SHPOs) appointed by the governors. The SHPOs, or their staffs, assist local governments and nonprofit organizations in preparing nominations, sometimes making funds available to assist in this work.

Under the provisions of section 106 of the National Historic Preservation Act, federal agencies must afford the Advisory Council on Historic Preservation the opportunity to comment on federal, federally assisted, or federally licensed projects that may affect properties listed or eligible for

## State Historic Preservation Officers

*State Historic Preservation Officers have the following responsibilities:*

• *To nominate properties to the National Register of Historic Places.*
• *To conduct comprehensive inventories of historic properties in the state. Inventoried properties may or may not be eligible for the National Register.*
• *To administer state registers. Many states have established their own registers that may protect properties from the actions of state and local governments. Often, as is the case in New Jersey, the nomination process is the same as for the National Register.*
• *To prepare state preservation plans.*
• *To review and give preliminary approval for rehabilitation being done for federal tax credits.*
• *To advise local governments, nonprofit organizations, and individuals on historic preservation. Many SHPOs have staff members who can visit communities to give advice. SHPOs frequently publish newsletters and conduct conferences and training programs for community preservation leaders.*
• *To advise federal agencies on avoiding or minimizing harm to National Register properties through their projects.*
• *To administer state and federal grant and loan programs, when available.*

listing in the National Register. The federal agency, the council, and the SHPO then attempt to identify ways to avoid or minimize adverse impacts. Federal agencies are required to give even greater consideration to National Historic Landmarks. In the final analysis, federal agencies are free to proceed in spite of objections by the council. Although it is the legal responsibility of the federal agency involved to inform the council of proposed actions, agencies frequently fail to do so in a timely manner. The council welcomes information from the public about potential federal projects.

Another important federal law that promotes historic preservation is the Economic Recovery Tax Act of 1981, which provides a "rehabilitation tax credit" for owners of income-producing buildings listed in the National Register or within National Register districts who rehabilitate those properties. If the rehabilitation qualifies, the owner may claim a 20 percent tax credit for the work. Numerous commercial properties, including stores and rental housing, have been rehabilitated using tax credits. Although most of the projects have been in cities, many small-town and rural properties have also been rehabilitated using the tax credits. To qualify, the building must be certified as historic by the Secretary of the Interior and the rehabilitation work must meet standards set by the secretary (see *The Secretary of the Interior's Standards,* pp. 166–67).

Sources of assistance on historic preservation are the SHPOs, regional offices of the National Park Service, regional offices of the National Trust, state historic preservation organizations, and historic preservation programs in colleges and universities.

## Rugby, Tennessee: The Corps of Engineers Does a Good Deed

Historic Rugby is an example of an organization that has prepared a nomination to the National Register and used section 106 of the National Historic Preservation Act to avoid a threat to its historic resources.

Rugby (pop. 100) was established on the scenic Cumberland Plateau of northeastern Tennessee in the 1880s by Thomas Hughes, the English social reformer and author of *Tom Brown's Schooldays.* Hughes founded Rugby as an experiment in classless cooperative living for the younger sons of English gentry. All land use in the model community was planned, with scenic areas being left in their natural state. Although crop failures, disease, and bad management soon led to the demise of Rugby as a social and economic model, the small unincorporated hamlet survived. The spectacular scenery that first attracted Thomas Hughes and the twenty-two surviving original Rugby buildings have now become a major tourist attraction.

In 1966, concerned citizens in the area established Historic Rugby to protect Rugby's historic resources and natural setting and revitalize the

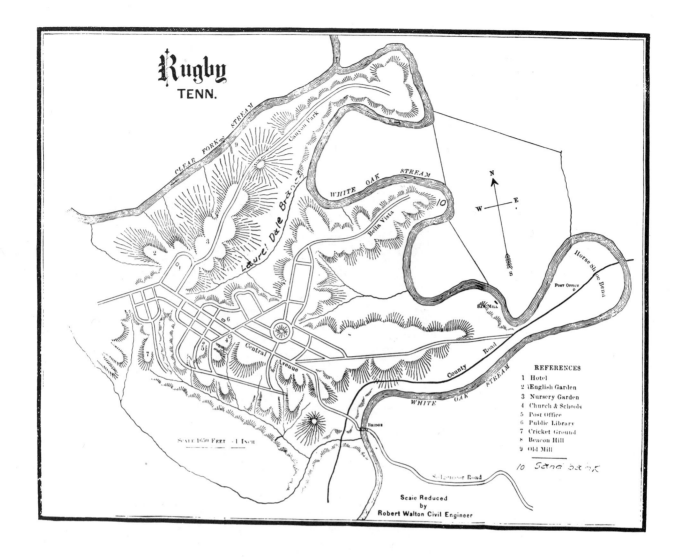

Rugby
TENN.

REFERENCES
1 Hotel
2 English Garden
3 Nursery Garden
4 Church & Schools
5 Post Office
6 Public Library
7 Cricket Ground
8 Beacon Hill
9 Old Mill
10 Sand bank

Scale 1650 Feet = 1 Inch

Scale Reduced
by
Robert Walton Civil Engineer

community. In 1972, a 900-acre Rugby Colony historic district was listed in the National Register; Historic Rugby researched and wrote the nomination. The organization has restored, reconstructed, or built nine buildings in the town. It conducts tours throughout the year and attracts thousands of visitors for its spring music and crafts festivals and its summer Rugby Pilgrimage house tours. It is the major employer in the area and a source of income for related businesses.

In the early 1960s, Congress authorized the U.S. Army Corps of Engineers to build a dam on the Big South Fork River, downstream from Rugby. Although the impounded water would not have inundated Rugby itself, it would have destroyed the spectacular Devil's Jump Gorge below the town. As a result of effective lobbying by conservationists, Congress in 1974 deauthorized the dam. In its place Congress authorized the 125,000-acre Big South Fork National River and Recreation Area, to be planned, acquired, and developed by the Corps and then turned over to the National Park Service. The first major recreation complex in the Big South Fork is now open, increasing visitor traffic to Rugby.

Rugby was established as a utopian community on the Cumberland Plateau of Tennessee in the 1880s. The village, which has retained its original street pattern, is now protected by Historic Rugby, a nonprofit organization. In 1979, the U.S. Army Corps of Engineers undertook a historic preservation plan for Rugby.

HELP FROM THE OUTSIDE

225

Rugby, a National Register of Historic Places district, is a major tourist attraction. Here visitors leave the Thomas Hughes Free Public Library, unchanged since its 1882 opening. The original 7,000-volume collection is still on the shelves.

At the request of the State Historic Preservation Officer, the Advisory Council on Historic Preservation held discussions in 1979 with the Corps on mitigating the potential adverse impacts of increased tourism on the Rugby historic district. The Corps finally agreed to fund a "Master Plan for the Development, Management and Protection of the Rugby Colony Historic Area." The planning process started in 1980 with a public meeting of Rugby residents to discuss the future of their community. According to Barbara Stagg, executive director of Historic Rugby, "The plan far exceeded our expectations and has served as a catalyst to get people in the community to sit down and start talking about our future. It has been surprising to find that on the most important issues the community seems to be in near-unanimous agreement. The planning process raised the consciousness of our residents in a way that nothing else could have. It has brought the community together and forced people to interact."

Several residents who had previously opposed the restoration effort changed their minds as a result of the planning process. A major recommendation of the plan, yet to be acted upon, was that Rugby incorporate as a town and implement zoning. Although there is no requirement that residents abide by the plan's design recommendations, several have done so voluntarily for both restorations and new construction.

## C. Scenic Areas

Scenery is protected to some extent through many federal and state laws. The National Environmental Protection Act and Vermont's Act 250, for instance, include scenery among resources to be protected. Federal agencies such as the Forest Service take steps to identify and protect scenic resources that might be damaged by their activities or the permits they issue.

Many states—including California, New York, Oregon, Virginia, and Washington—have scenic roads programs. State programs range from mere scenic designation of a particular road to controls on development along them. Scenic roads in New Hampshire are designated at town meetings. Plans to upgrade designated roads that involve removing trees or stone walls must be presented at public hearings and receive written permission from the town planning boards before "improvements" can begin.

The federal government and most states have laws regulating billboards. Lady Bird Johnson provided much of the leadership for the Highway Beautification Act of 1965, which states that "the erection and maintenance of outdoor advertising signs, displays, and devices in areas adjacent to the Interstate System and primary system should be controlled

Pine trees are cut down to clear the view of a billboard. Current federal legislation inadequately protects federally funded highways from such visual blight.

This travelers' information sign in Virginia is a simple, effective alternative to billboards and allows local businesses to advertise their presence without destroying the scenery.

in order to protect the public investment on such highways, to promote the safety and recreational value of public travel, and to preserve natural beauty." The "primary system" generally consists of U.S. numbered highways.

The law requires states to remove illegal signs and maintain "effective control" over outdoor advertising or be subject to a 10 percent reduction in their federal highway funds. In rural areas outdoor advertising should be controlled within the limits of visibility. Certain signs, such as those advertising goods or services on the premises where the sign is located, official signs, and signs in areas zoned industrial or commercial, are allowed. So are those of historic or artistic significance, such as the "Chew Mailpouch Tobacco" signs painted on barns. States are required to compensate sign owners when signs are removed.

Unfortunately, the law has not been effective. Many rural areas have been rezoned commercial or industrial at the request of billboard owners to allow for billboard construction. The cash compensation provisions make the act prohibitively expensive to implement. Some states even allow billboard owners to cut trees that block the view of their signs.

Several states—notably Alaska, Hawaii, Maine, Maryland, Oregon, Vermont, and Washington—have established strong controls on outdoor advertising that go well beyond the federal law. The Coalition for Scenic Beauty promotes sign control and assists communities in their efforts to protect scenery along highways.

## D. Outdoor Recreation

The National Park Service provides funds to the states to allow them to prepare State Comprehensive Outdoor Recreation Plans and to acquire parkland for recreation (6.IX.E). Some of the service's regional offices offer advice to local groups on recreation planning.

The Park Service also assists communities in establishing trails. The National Trails System Act of 1968, as amended, established a nationwide system of recreation, historic, and scenic trails and encourages volunteers' participation in their development and management. The legislation also encourages the conversion of abandoned railroad rights-of-way to trails. These trails often have the advantage of being accessible to urban residents, bicyclists, and the handicapped.

Congress must authorize studies to determine the desirability and feasibility of designating scenic and historic trails. Studies are generally conducted by the Park Service. The Secretary of the Interior then proposes to Congress which trails should be considered for designation. As of 1987, Congress had designated eight National Scenic Trails, totaling over 14,000 miles, and seven National Historic Trails, totaling more than 10,000 miles. Recreation trails may be designated by the Secretaries of the Interior or Agriculture, depending on which department's land is involved. In 1987 there were 772 recreation trails, totaling over 8,500 miles. Following designation, the federal agency responsible for the trail prepares a management plan. The act encourages state and local governments to protect trail portions on nonfederal land either through agreements with property owners or by acquisition.

For further information on creating trails, rural conservation leaders should contact regional offices of the National Park Service, the American Hiking Society, and the Rails-to-Trails Conservancy.

# Wisconsin: Establishing the Ice Age Trail

Trails designated under the National Trails System Act generally extend through many communities. Consequently, the organizations that have urged their designation and work for their protection tend to be statewide or regional. Many have local chapters that concern themselves with the trail in a particular county or area. The Ice Age Trail Council in Wisconsin is such an organization. Along with the Ice Age Park and Trail Foundation and numerous local trail clubs, it is making the 1,000-mile Ice Age Trail a reality.

Since the 1950s, environmentalists and hikers have worked to protect and make available to the public the scenic and ecologically varied drumlins, kames, eskers, moraines, lakes, bogs, marshes, and gorges created by the Wisconsin Ice Sheet 12,000 to 20,000 years ago. The Wisconsin Ice Sheet, which covered the northern and eastern parts of

Conservationists and hikers successfully lobbied the Congress in 1980 to establish the thousand-mile Ice Age National Scenic Trail, which follows the periphery of the former Wisconsin Ice Sheet. The trail in Wisconsin follows old stagecoach routes, traverses the land conservationist Aldo Leopold loved and wrote about in *A Sand County Almanac,* and goes by the site of the boyhood home of Sierra Club founder John Muir.

Volunteers are the backbone of most rural conservation efforts. Here Sierra Club and Ice Age Trail Council volunteers install a marker post.

the state, was the last great glacier of the Ice Age to descend into the present United States.

In 1958, concerned citizens of Wisconsin established the Ice Age Park and Trail Foundation to promote the creation of a national Ice Age glacial park. As a result of citizen lobbying, the Congress in 1971 established the Ice Age National Scientific Reserve, which protects some of the state's significant glacial features. In 1980 Congress designated the 1,000-mile Ice Age National Scenic Trail, which follows the glacier's former periphery. Although Congress appropriated no funds for land acquisition, the Park Service recently funded a full-time administrator for the trail.

Both before and since the designation, volunteers have worked to complete the trail between the publicly owned segments. In 1975, they established the Ice Age Trail Council, which is a membership organization with twenty-six county chapters along the proposed route. Chapter volunteers not only contact landowners to gain their permission to use the trail but also do much of the physical work in laying out and maintaining the trail. So far, approximately 350 miles of trail have been opened to the public for hiking and skiing.

The Ice Age Trail Foundation works to protect trail segments on private lands through the acquisition of land and right-of-way easements. In the past the foundation has relied upon donation of such lands or easements but has recently begun a trail right-of-way purchase program in several counties.

---

## E. Public Lands

The Federal Land Policy and Management Act of 1976 declared that "the national interest will be best realized if the public lands and their resources are periodically and systematically inventoried and their present and future use is projected through a land use planning process." The act further requires that "the public lands be managed in a manner that will protect the quality of scientific, scenic, historical, ecological, environmental, air and atmospheric, water resource, and archeological values."

For conservationists concerned about federal public lands, the best point of contact is generally the local manager: the Forest Supervisor, the Park Superintendent, or the Bureau of Land Management Manager. These individuals should be able to supply information about the environmental resources on the land they supervise as well as incorporate the recommendations of community leaders into their management plans. In many cases they are required by legislation to do so. Furthermore, these individuals can frequently provide assistance to community leaders in inventorying and protecting resources throughout the community. In addition, many national nonprofit organizations, including the Natural Resources Defense Council, the Sierra Club, and the Wilderness Society, have a particular interest in the protection of federal lands.

Along with addressing concerns about protecting publicly owned land, rural conservation organizations may wish to work with federal, state, or local agencies in acquiring additional land, or easements on land, that should be protected. For instance, in the 1970s conservation leaders in the U.S. Virgin Islands successfully lobbied the U.S. Congress to have Hassle Island acquired by the National Park Service. The island's lighthouse, fort, and extensive open space are now protected. In addition to its historic importance, it provides a scenic backdrop to the harbor of St. Thomas and needed space for recreation.

## Ebey's Landing, Washington: A Rural Community Cooperates with the National Park Service

Increasingly, the National Park Service, instead of acquiring new park land, is looking for strategies to protect land through easements, local regulations, and voluntary agreements. Ebey's Landing in Washington is a case in point.

Ebey's Landing National Historical Reserve was established by act of Congress in 1978 "to preserve and protect a rural community which provides an unbroken historic record from nineteenth-century exploration and settlement in Puget Sound up to the present time." Located between the Olympic Peninsula and the Washington coast on Whidbey Island, Ebey's Landing is a relatively unspoiled 17,400-acre area of prairies, uplands, woodlands, lagoons, and rural settlements. Although substantial tourism and second-home development already exist elsewhere on the island, Ebey's Landing is still characterized by a rich patchwork of fields, hedgerows, woodlots, farm complexes, fences, and roads dating from the 1850s.

The Park Service, which administers the reserve, does not plan major land acquisition; instead, it has purchased conservation easements to protect scenic and historic resources. It also advises property owners on design guidelines for the restoration of historic buildings and protection of the landscape and prepares interpretive literature for visitors. The Park Service has temporarily stationed a ranger in Ebey's Landing to assist in managing the reserve. This person works with an advisory board appointed by local officials. The federal government will eventually turn responsibility for the reserve over to a unit of local government.

Ebey's Landing National Historical Reserve is a cooperative venture between the National Park Service and the local community. Most of Whidbey Island in Puget Sound is privately owned. However, the Park Service has acquired property and easements to protect important views, including Crockett Prairie, pictured here.

Finally, local governments can apply for federal grants from the Land and Water Conservation Fund, established by act of Congress in 1964. Matching grants from the fund for the acquisition of park and recreation land are made through State Liaison Officers appointed by the governors.

## X. POTENTIAL PROBLEMS

### A. Highways

Many highway projects involve the allocation of federal and state funds. The principal federal legislation protecting the environment from the adverse effects of highways is the National Environmental Policy Act (NEPA) (6.V) and section 4(f) of the Department of Transportation Act of 1966, as amended. The latter states that "the Secretary shall not approve any program or project which requires the use of any land from a public park, recreation area, wildlife and waterfowl refuge, or historic site unless (1) there is no feasible and prudent alternative to the use of such land, and (2) such program includes all possible planning to minimize harm." The 4(f) provision makes the Department of Transportation Act one of the better federal environmental protection laws.

The federal and state agencies involved generally conduct the NEPA and 4(f) reviews simultaneously. Although each requires a separate finding, the documentation is sent out for public review bound in the same volume. The Federal Highway Administration (FHWA) is ultimately responsible for preparing the documentation and making the final determination on environmental impact, but since the agency is decentralized, it works primarily through the state highway agencies. The state highway agency and the FHWA Division Office (in the same city as the state agency) are the first points of contact for citizens. Highway officials should be contacted as early in the process as possible, preferably before they have invested a lot of time in planning a project. Formal public hearings come relatively late in the review process. By then the state agency may have invested much effort in developing alternatives and analyzing their environmental effects. Consequently officials may be reluctant to incorporate new information or perspectives.

Each year state highway agencies are required to submit a "program of projects" to the FHWA. This shopping list may be the first official notification citizens have that a highway project is being considered.

It is generally up to the state to decide how federal highway funds will be spent within the state. Most federal funds are parceled to the states according to a federal formula. In addition, there are some "demonstration projects" that are specifically earmarked in the federal legislation, often the result of pressure from a particular congressional delegation or lobby group. FHWA then oversees projects that are selected by the states or that are legislatively mandated.

Under certain circumstances federal funds can be used to preserve a scenic or historic road. The Federal-Aid Highway Act of 1987 specifically authorizes funding for the rehabilitation of bridges listed in, or eligible for, the National Register of Historic Places. The bridge over the Columbia River at Pasco-Kennewick in Washington will probably be the first project to use these funds. The act further provides that a bridge slated for demoli-

Surface-mined land can be reclaimed successfully, as this pair of photographs taken in Tioga County, Pennsylvania, illustrates. The reclamation was done under the provisions of the U.S. Department of Agriculture's Rural Abandoned Mine Program.

tion must first be offered to a unit of government or "responsible private entity" willing to preserve it. The funds that would have been spent on demolition can be applied towards a bridge's restoration. The National Trust for Historic Preservation has a particular interest in preservation and conservation issues relating to highways.

## B. Surface Mining

The Surface Mining Control and Reclamation Act of 1977 (SMCRA) established "a nationwide program to protect society and the environment from the adverse effects of surface coal mining operations." The Office of Surface Mining within the Department of the Interior administers the act. States may continue to have primary responsibility for regulating surface mining, but only if their regulations are as stringent as those required by SMCRA.

Under the provisions of SMCRA, states must identify areas that may be unsuitable for surface mining because they possess historic, natural, or other resources, or present hazardous mining conditions. SMCRA requires each state to establish a regulatory procedure for granting permits for mining activities. Permit regulations must include environmental protection performance standards based on the minimum federal standards set forth in the act. The states must conduct regular inspections of each mine and cite operators for violations of regulations. Unfortunately there are loopholes in the law, and enforcement of SMCRA has frequently been lax. The Environmental Policy Institute is the nonprofit organization most directly concerned with surface mining.

SMCRA also established the Abandoned Mine Reclamation Fund, to which all coal mine operators must pay a reclamation fee per ton of coal produced. The Secretary of the Interior distributes these funds among the states that have approved regulatory programs. These funds may be used for reclamation and restoration of land and water resources adversely affected by coal mining prior to 1977, for acquisition and filling of shafts, for acquisition of land, and for other reclamation activities. Kentucky has used some of its funds to build new water systems for people whose drinking water has been polluted by mining activities. The Secretary of the Interior may also transfer annually up to one-fifth of the fund to the Secretary of Agriculture to control erosion damage on lands mined before 1977 and to promote the conservation of soil and water resources of lands affected by mining.

## Cranks, Kentucky: Citizens Force Action on Surface Mining Law

One community that has used the Surface Mining and Reclamation Act to curb surface mining is Cranks Creek (pop. 300) in Harlan County, Kentucky, where residents were devastated by a series of floods in the 1970s that were directly attributed to extensive surface mining in the watershed upstream. Silt from the mining operation filled the stream channel, leaving nowhere for storm-water runoff to go except through people's homes. "We were flooded out seven times in three years. We were hurt worse with less rainfall each time. I've seen rocks as big as trucks bobbing on the water like balloons," stated resident Rebecca Simpson, who organized fellow residents to seek assistance.

In 1980, Simpson and her neighbors successfully sued the mine operator for $155,000 in damages. They also established the Cranks Creek Survival Center in 1982 and through it requested the assistance of the Kentucky Division of Abandoned Lands. The state placed a moratorium on surface mining in the watershed and agreed to make Cranks Creek a priority for funding from the Abandoned Mine Reclamation Fund. The state has spent approximately $2.6 million to reestablish the stream channel and to start reclamation of surface-mined land. According to one state official, "If Rebecca Simpson and her group had not been there calling and prodding, the work would not have been done as rapidly as it was."

The Cranks Creek Survival Center has not limited itself to the surface-mining issue. The organization has rehabilitated houses, distributed clothing, and cut firewood for needy families. The group is also trying to obtain a more reliable source of safe drinking water.

## C. Toxic Waste

The Resource Conservation and Recovery Act (RCRA) of 1976, as amended, governs the disposal of hazardous waste, while the Comprehensive Environmental Response, Compensation, and Liability Act (CERCLA) of 1980, as amended, provides for cleanup of abandoned waste sites.

RCRA required the Environmental Protection Agency (EPA) to institute a national program to control hazardous and solid waste from point of generation through treatment, storage, and disposal. According to EPA, approximately 11,000 firms require permits (Conservation Foundation 1982, p. 146). Companies generating waste must determine whether it is hazardous, according to criteria established by EPA. They must also utilize EPA-approved procedures for treating, storing, transporting, and disposing of waste and establish a manifest system for keeping track of it. The federal requirements are carried out at the state level by states with programs approved by EPA.

CERCLA, better known as Superfund, authorizes EPA to respond directly to the discovery of hazardous substances at uncontrolled waste sites. Costs are covered by a fund financed largely by taxes on the manufacturers of hazardous substances. The federal government, or the states under agreement with EPA, can act to recover their cleanup costs when those responsible can be identified. Unfortunately, relatively few of the identified sites have yet to be cleaned up, and once cleanup has begun, it can be extremely costly and time-consuming.

At the national level, the Conservation Foundation, the Sierra Club, and the National Audubon Society have a particular interest in legislation concerning hazardous waste. The Citizen's Clearinghouse for Hazardous Waste provides technical, legal, and organizing assistance to community groups.

## D. Air Pollution

The Clean Air Act of 1963, as amended, has as its purpose "to protect and enhance the quality of the Nation's air resources." The act gives the Environmental Protection Agency (EPA) the authority to establish national air-quality standards for specific pollutants. "Primary standards" set limits above which human health may be endangered, and "secondary standards" set limits above which other resources may be endangered. A nationwide network of monitoring stations, established by EPA, and state and local agencies monitor pollution levels. The law authorized the federal government to take action to ensure that those standards are met if state and local governments do not. Failure to comply can result in the denial of federal grants and prevent the construction of major new factories in regions not meeting the standards.

In those areas where the air is cleaner than national standards, the Clean Air Act limits the amount of new pollution. These areas are divided into three classes. Class 1 areas, which include the largest national parks and wilderness areas, can have very little pollution added. Greater increases in air pollution are allowed in Class 2 and 3 areas as long as they do not exceed the minimum national standards.

The best sources of information about air pollution programs are the regional offices of EPA and appropriate state agencies. The Natural Resources Defense Council takes a particular interest in air pollution.

## XI. RURAL DEVELOPMENT AND HOUSING

There are a number of federal and state programs designed to promote rural development and improve housing. Although much has been done in the past fifty years to alleviate rural poverty and promote community development, in recent years there has been a marked decline in funding for these programs.

### A. Rural Development

A good general source of assistance on rural development is the Cooperative Extension Service, established by Congress in 1914 as a partnership between the U.S. Department of Agriculture, state land-grant colleges, and county governments. More than 15,000 county Extension Agents and other specialists offer advice and practical education programs at the county level across the nation. Best known for the assistance it gives to farmers, Extension also promotes rural development and the protection of natural resources. Depending on their individual abilities and interests, Extension community development specialists can help a community undertake land-use and economic development planning, organize workshops, provide leadership training, and get people together to discuss community problems. Extension Agents, particularly those charged with community development, have assisted many rural conservation efforts, including the Oley Resource Project in Pennsylvania (Case Study 1).

The largest source of general-purpose federal grants to rural communities is the Community Development Block Grant (CDBG) program of the Department of Housing and Urban Development. Grants are generally made through the states to local governments for community development, economic development, public facilities, and other projects that will benefit low- and moderate-income residents. Several rural conservation organizations have received CDBG funds by making a persuasive case that their projects will benefit low- and moderate-income citizens. Historic Rugby persuaded a neighboring town in Tennessee to apply for CDBG funds to help it to restore several structures in the historic district (Case Study 22). As a result of the $456,768 CDBG grant, tourism has increased substantially and has resulted in increased employment and income in this economically depressed area.

## Federal Economic Assistance

*The following federal agencies are the principal providers of economic assistance to rural communities:*

- *Community Development Block Grant program, Department of Housing and Urban Development: Makes grants to local governments for community and economic development.*
- *Cooperative Extension Service, Department of Agriculture: Offers advice on agriculture and community development to individuals and groups.*
- *Economic Development Administration, Department of Commerce: Makes grants for the construction of public facilities such as water and sewer systems and site improvements for industries; grants to develop and implement strategies to mitigate the impacts on a community from severe economic decline or major losses of jobs; loans to businesses; and grants for economic development planning.*
- *Farmers Home Administration (FmHA), Department of Agriculture: In addition to housing programs, loans to farmers and homeowners, FmHA makes loans to nonprofit organizations and local governments for water and sewer systems and for community facilities such as fire and rescue services.*
- *Federal Highway Administration, Department of Transportation: Makes grants for constructing and rehabilitating roads, streets, and bridges.*
- *Office of Community Services, Department of Health and Human Services: Makes loans to promote rural development to alleviate rural poverty.*
- *Urban Mass Transportation Administration, Department of Transportation: Makes grants for acquisition, construction, and operation of public transportation systems in rural as well as urban areas.*

Rural America, the Center for Rural Affairs, and the Rural Coalition give assistance to rural communities and seek legislation to help rural residents.

## B. Housing

The principal federal agency that provides housing assistance in rural communities is the Farmers Home Administration (FmHA). FmHA employees serve rural communities from close to 2,000 county offices across the country. While best known for the loans it provides to assist farmers in buying and operating farms, FmHA also has programs for housing, soil conservation, water development, waste disposal, community facilities, and economic development.

Since 1950 FmHA has provided almost $50 billion in loans and grants for low- and moderate-income residents to purchase, build, repair, improve, and renovate homes. FmHA loans are often available when funding from other sources is not. FmHA also subsidizes rents and refinances mortgages for eligible families. Moreover, FmHA makes loans and grants to nonprofit organizations involved in housing. Although FmHA programs have assisted many rural Americans in obtaining decent housing, the housing has not always been well planned, and it frequently contributes to sprawl and its associated problems. Also, FmHA officials have been reluctant to use funds for rehabilitation. In addition to FmHA, the Department of Housing and Urban Development has a number of grant and loan programs for housing in rural as well as urban areas.

A leading national nonprofit organization that assists rural communities with housing programs is the Housing Assistance Council. There are also a number of statewide nonprofit organizations concerned with housing, such as Self-Help Enterprises in California and Rural Housing Improvement in Massachusetts.

CASE STUDY 26

## Cranbury, New Jersey: A Volunteer Initiative to Provide Housing

In 1963, a house occupied by farm laborers and their families in Cranbury, New Jersey (1984 pop. 2,121), burned down, leaving these long-time residents with no place to go. Twenty citizens, who had been concerned for some time about the lack of decent low-income housing in Cranbury, banded together to see what they could do to help. During the next few months they helped the families find temporary housing and raised money from neighbors to purchase and rehabilitate another building for the displaced families. The citizens eventually incorporated as Cranbury Housing Associates (CHA). Not everyone in town was pleased with CHA's efforts. Some neighbors of the building purchased were concerned that their property values would deteriorate if the project went forward. At one point CHA members, acting as individuals, sued the zoning board, claiming it was discriminating in its administration of the code. Eventually CHA obtained a building permit and enlisted volunteer help to rehabilitate the property into six units. CHA then rented the units at affordable rates to low-income families. The U.S. Department of Housing and Urban Development gave the CHA a grant to do further work on the property and subsidized the tenants' rents.

In 1964, CHA was given a lot in Cranbury and with volunteer help from a local architect designed and built a house for a low-income family. The tenant then bought the house using a Farmers Home Administration (FmHA) mortgage. In 1967, CHA helped seven low-income families purchase lots and build their own houses. Funds to purchase lots and mortgages to finance construction costs came from FmHA. CHA volunteers donated their time to help with the construction and deal with the federal and state bureaucracies. Other similar projects followed.

Over the years CHA has developed strong support within Cranbury, and the township's officials now look to the organization for assistance in protecting the community's prime farmland and historic village. Cranbury is in the middle of the fast-growing Trenton–New York corridor. The state has required all townships to provide their fair share of low- and moderate-income housing, and in 1987 the township asked CHA for assistance in meeting its obligation by building housing in areas where it will not destroy the integrity of the agricultural economy and National Register historic district. Using grants and loans from FmHA and the state, plus municipal bonds, if necessary, CHA plans to build 60 units of housing in the township in the next few years.

Much of CHA's success can be attributed to the varied skills of its members. The president is an architect; other members have skills in construction, administration, law, and social work. Reflecting on the organization's early years, board member Frank Wright says: "When you work with the housing of the disadvantaged, you become involved in their personal lives. CHA often found itself providing medical services, teaching English, chasing down birth certificates in the South, and being a personal advocate."

---

## XII. CONCLUSION

You should not let the number of laws and programs described in this chapter overwhelm you. Obviously you need to pick and choose those that make the best sense for your organization to pursue. As the case studies make clear, it is those organizations that complain, lobby, cajole, threaten, and generally refuse to take no for an answer that get results. When it comes to getting help from the outside it is the squeaky wheel that gets the grease.

This brings us to the end of three chapters on the specific ways in which rural conservation organizations can protect property. We now turn to a more general topic: Once you have decided what needs to be protected and how to go about doing it, how do you convince others in the community of the merits of your approach?

# 7

# Community Education

## I. INTRODUCTION

Education is vital to every successful conservation organization's program. If residents in your community do not appreciate the significance of prime farmland, historic farmsteads, wetland habitat, or scenic vistas, it will be difficult to establish a protection program. Not only must you educate residents about the importance of these resources; you also may need to persuade them to contribute money or property, agree to downzoning, or possibly forgo employment opportunities by keeping out an industry that would pollute. Persuading people to give up something for the common good is never easy and calls for all of the ingenuity a conservation organization can muster.

Education takes many forms. It can be formal or informal. It may consist of a media campaign, newsletters, lectures, workshops, programs for schools, special events, museum exhibits, or even a county fair or farmers' market, all of which are discussed in this chapter. Obviously many of the programs discussed in previous chapters also entail education. In fact, there is little a conservation organization does that does not involve education.

The first step in developing an education program is determining who needs to be educated about what and why. Do farmers need to be educated about a new transfer of development rights program, school children about the importance of protecting wetlands, or property owners about easements? Once an organization has identified both its audience and subject matter, it can choose an appropriate educational activity. An organization will probably conduct different activities for its board members, for government officials, for children, and for the general public.

# Yakima, Washington: Selling
# the Yakima River Greenway

"To make land conservation work, a land trust must sell its program," according to Marc Smiley, executive director of the Yakima River Greenway Foundation. "It must sell its goals to the local community that ultimately determines success or failure for the program."

The Greenway is a 10-mile, 3,600-acre river corridor in Yakima County, Washington (1984 pop. 179,479). Interest in protecting this significant scenic and recreational resource in the midst of a rapidly urbanizing area dates back to the 1960s. Finally in 1979 the county commissioners established a task force to investigate how a linear park could be established. The task force, after receiving advice from the Trust for Public Land, recommended the establishment of a private, nonprofit land trust. The commissioners accepted the recommendation, and in 1980 the Yakima River Greenway Foundation was incorporated. The initial board consisted of citizens and representatives of community groups and interested government agencies and citizens at large. The board decided that "the initial focus had to be the development of several parks and pathways that gave the community a chance to experience the values that make the entire Greenway important for protection," according to Smiley.

Over the years, the foundation has found a number of ways to publicize its program. It has organized public meetings, held fund-raising banquets, invited VIP speakers, enlisted the help of service clubs, awarded plaques to donors, had booths at state fairs, arranged rafting trips for influential officials, published a newsletter, written brochures, and prepared a slide-tape show. Contacts with the press were key. In addition to press conferences, Smiley and foundation volunteers have found time to write newspaper articles, including a regular column in the local weekly.

Many of the foundation's most successful educational projects date from a board retreat in 1984, when the members decided they needed to do a better job of getting their message out. The board established a public relations committee and prepared a public relations plan that would be updated annually. The plan included attention to press, lectures, exhibits, collaboration with civic organizations, and special events.

One of the foundation's most successful projects since the retreat has been the "Gap to Gap Relay." This annual June race includes bicycle riding, canoeing, and running along the river corridor. Corporate sponsors contribute the up-front expenses for the event. The relay teams pay registration fees for the privilege of participating. The local newspaper published an eight-page insert about the 1987 event that also served as

The Yakima River Greenway Foundation in Washington State is working to protect a 10-mile corridor between Yakima Ridge and Rattlesnake Hills, including two parks and a series of trails (dotted line) to be built along the river. The foundation's successful educational program has resulted in a committed local constituency and donations of funds, land, and volunteer labor.

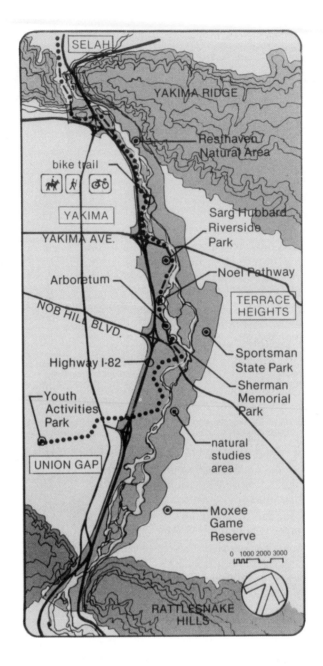

the program on the day of the race. Describing the 1987 relay, director Marc Smiley states, "Aside from the $5,000 we raised, the publicity and public use of the Greenway from this one event did more for our program than a year's worth of brochures, television programs, and newspaper articles." The relay race attracted more than 600 participants, 100 volunteers, and 1,000 spectators.

Several other Greenway educational activities are discussed throughout Chapter 7. As a result of these activities, the foundation has now raised over $2 million in private and government funds and acquired 340 acres. It has opened two heavily used parks and established a popular trail between the two.

The Yakima River Greenway Foundation's annual "Gap to Gap Relay" race includes bicycle riding, canoeing, and running. The contestants and spectators gain an appreciation of the resource, and the publicity that results has greatly increased support for conservation.

## II. NEWS MEDIA

Informing the community about activities through the local news media is one of the most effective ways of developing support. News coverage can enhance the group's credibility as well as increase its visibility. Coverage in the closest city also informs the region about the community's programs. Occasionally, residents of a nearby city who become aware of concerns will offer their services, donate funds, or help in some other way. The Amana Preservation Foundation, for example, routinely informs the media in nearby Cedar Rapids and Iowa City of its programs and as a result has received donations and drawn attendance from Amana's urban neighbors.

The interest of the news media, however, is sometimes a hindrance rather than a help. Intense, premature coverage of a proposed conservation project in a New Jersey township fanned the fires of controversy and influenced citizens to oppose the project before they learned what it could do for them. Even positive publicity can have a negative impact, especially if it results in increased visitation to a fragile area. Most archeologists, for example, avoid naming the specific locations of sites because of the danger of damage or looting. Similarly, biologists may not wish to disclose the location of endangered species. For instance, biologists in western Virginia are concerned that increased caving as a result of press publicity is disturbing the hibernation of endangered long-eared bats, causing a serious reduction in their population.

Small communities may be unable to handle the increased visitation from outsiders that may result from publicity or may fear excessive new development to accommodate visitors. Such communities may prefer not to publicize their assets. The historic village of Waterford, Virginia, has developed a happy compromise. The Waterford Foundation concentrates news coverage in the period preceding its annual Homes Tour and Crafts Exhibit. While visitors are encouraged to come to that event, there is little publicity outside the community during the rest of the year (Case Study 28).

The first steps in establishing a media program are to identify what audiences are the most important and which newspapers, periodicals, radio stations, or television programs are most likely to reach them. Although print media is more appropriate for detailed information, some people are more likely to pay attention to what they see or hear on television and radio.

# Press Releases

*Press releases should be concise and typed double-spaced. Include the following information:*

*• The name and telephone number of a contact person;*
*• The date the story should be published if the press release is sent out before the event is to be held: "For Immediate Release" indicates it can be published at any time;*
*• A brief title and a short, interesting, but objective account;*
*• Several direct quotes; and*
*• The names and titles of all persons and groups, double-checked for accuracy.*

*Accompanying photographs should be 8-by-10-inch black-and-white glossy prints, labeled on the back with the names of people and places in the photograph, date taken, and name of the photographer. Photographs that show people in action— a naturalist leading a hike, a history student interviewing an old-timer, or a soil scientist taking a sample— have more appeal than those that show only buildings and landscapes, or people lined up in a row.*

*The press release can also be accompanied by background information on the community, conservation issues, and the organization's accomplishments. It may be helpful to summarize this information in a fact sheet that can accompany all press releases.*

In addition to getting the organization's message across as part of the news, it may be possible to arrange for a public service advertisement or announcement. Most newspapers and radio and television stations offer space and time for "PSAs" to nonprofit organizations and may even help to prepare them.

Most organizations need someone to act as press coordinator or spokesperson. The Amana Preservation Foundation chose a volunteer who had experience with the League of Women Voters and other organizations to coordinate its effective public-information program. The coordinator should be well-organized and a good communicator, both in person and in writing. The coordinator needs to develop a relationship of mutual trust with reporters, since reporters are likely to get in touch with a spokesperson only if they believe they will get reliable information. Reporters have an obligation to present both sides of a story, and a spokesperson should be prepared to answer questions about opposing points of view.

A group should periodically evaluate its use of the media. The press coordinator can keep a notebook of newspaper and other clippings and a record of radio and television broadcasts mentioning the group. The group can use the notebook to determine the frequency and extent of local coverage and make judgments about what types of coverage to pursue in the future. The notebook can also be used to brief community leaders, funding sources, visitors, and others about the organization.

## A. Newspapers

Newspapers are usually the most important and available media for conservation organizations. Some rural communities have their own daily or weekly newspaper. For the many that have none, the press coordinator needs to identify the papers most people read. These may include the state's major newspaper, the paper of the closest city, or a free weekly advertiser. Developing a contact person with each newspaper is helpful: at a small paper, it might be the editor; at a large paper, one reporter might be assigned to news in a particular community.

Many newspapers welcome general interest stories that are not tied to a specific event. Others may run special supplements several times a year in conjunction with local events or particular seasons. The Oley Resource Project in Pennsylvania, for example, was covered in a special section of the *Boyertown Area Times*. In New York, the Cazenovia Community Resource Project volunteers wrote a series on rural conservation issues for the weekly *Cazenovia Republican*. It may also be possible to ask a sympathetic editor to write an editorial or for a group's leader to write a guest column.

From time to time, an organization may wish to grant an exclusive story to one newspaper. An exclusive may result in a more comprehensive article, which can be more effective than minimal coverage in several papers. Exclusives should not always be given to the same newspaper.

## B. Radio and Television

Radio is an especially good way to publicize upcoming events. Morning and late afternoon news programs appeal to many people, especially to commuters, who can find out about last night's rezoning or the upcoming

# Cazenovia Republican

Cazenovia's Oldest Industry - Established 1808

USPS 095-260

## *All About Cazenovia — — What Makes It Special?*

Don R. Callahan

*This is the first in a series of articles written by members of the Cazenovia Community Resources Project, a study assisted by the National Trust for Historic Preservation. Protection of the resources and the rural character of Cazenovia, while still accommodating growth, is the aim of the project. In this article Don Callahan, supervisor of the Town of Cazenovia, discusses Cazenovia's "quality of life."*

**By Don R. Callahan**

You have heard the axiom, "the whole is greater than the sum of its parts." In many ways this is true of Cazenovia. The ridges and rolling hills, the gorges and waterfalls, the streams and lake, the woodlots, wildlife, meadows, productive farms, historic settlements and buildings, splendid views — together these aspects are a part of what makes Cazenovia a nice place to live.

In addition to these physical characteristics, there is a sense of community that has evolved over the years. Witness the mingling of people in the streets and shops, and enjoying the parks, countryside and the lake. The number of active community organizations in Cazenovia is a good indication of the strong community feeling that exists.

Cazenovia has a good mix of people — youth, young married couples, families, farmers, tradesmen, businessmen, professionals, the retired and the elderly. We all enjoy some aspect of our surroundings, the views, the countryside, recreation, the people. Together, our environment and our community create a quality of life that is unique to Cazenovia.

These qualities, however, are disappearing in many rural communities especially those on the urban fringe.

How can we protect this quality of life as Cazenovia grows and moves into the future? This is the question that the Cazenovia Community Resources Project has been studying since June 1980 when 200 volunteers began collecting information for an extensive inventory of local resources. This article is the first in a series describing what we have learned.

The series will discuss Cazenovia from the early movements of the earth's crust which has resulted in the shape of the land, the soils, water, vegetation, and wildlife, and the large part that these resources played in the settlement of the area and the human activities which have shaped the community into what it is today.

We are all part of a system of interrelated resources. Each part of our environment determines and is dependent on other parts.

Some parts of the environment are beyond our control, such as the weather, but

we can control the kind and degree of change which occurs in the environment as a result of human activity.

As we move into an age of scarcity, we should pay more attention to local resources. Many communities have learned that growth is not necessarily synonymous with lower taxes and a better quality of life. Uncontrolled growth can often cost more in services. As a result, the wise use of resources and the consideration of the capacity of the land for certain uses is a policy more and more communities are adopting. Careful siting of housing, business, and industry can help maintain the quality of the environment and the health of the community.

We enjoy Cazenovia as it is now. But we must consider the whole in relation to the parts, we must consider the community and the environment as we grow and change so that future generations will enjoy Cazenovia as we do today.

June 23, 1982, Cazenovia Republican

---

Press coverage of conservation issues and activities is important to any conservation organization. A series of thirteen articles written by Cazenovia Community Resources Project volunteers for the *Cazenovia Republican* helped to broaden the base of support for new conservation initiatives in the upstate New York township (Case Study 6). This was the first article, written by Don Callahan, Cazenovia's Town Supervisor. Other subjects covered in the series included geology, soils, the lake, wetlands, trees, wildflowers, agriculture, architecture, and history.

---

fair while driving to and from work. Any press releases submitted to a radio station should include a brief statement that can be read over the air exactly as it is written. Radio stations often produce talk shows that can feature rural conservation issues or allow an interview with a group's leaders.

Rural stories with regional appeal can provide interesting material for television. Television stations look for action in the subjects they cover. Tree-planting or collecting litter along a highway may have more appeal than an interview with the organization's president. For instance, when the Yakima River Greenway Foundation organized a float trip for state Park Commission members, all three local television stations covered the event. The outing and the publicity helped to persuade the commissioners to continue state funding for land acquisition along the river.

COMMUNITY EDUCATION

## Photographing the Countryside

*Photographs are an important part of any community's environmental inventory and education program. They can be used to document the status of resources, to prepare publications, and to make public presentations. Photographs are essential in historic preservation surveys, for instance: they allow a community to document the current status of a historic building and monitor future alterations. The Cazenovia Community Resources Project in New York documented all of its historic buildings with photographs and prepared a popular slide show covering all of the community's resources.*

*In some cases it is worth the investment to hire a professional photographer. However, amateurs can be of great assistance in many situations.*

*Good-quality photographs can make a big difference in public presentations and publications. Here are some recommendations:*

*• Slower film yields sharper pictures, but you must guard against camera movement. Whenever possible use a tripod.*
*• Color is great for slide shows, but black-and-white is often necessary for publications. Converting color shots to black-and-white is an iffy proposition. For color photographs in publications, slides yield better results than prints.*
*• The best lighting for photography is in the early morning and late afternoon. Midday photographs tend*

**A newsletter is an effective way to communicate information promptly, particularly when there is no local newspaper. Many are published by volunteers.**

## C. Press Conferences

Press conferences sound intimidating and bring to mind images of the President sparring with reporters at the White House. But even a small organization may find it useful to hold a press conference occasionally for big announcements, such as the acquisition of a major property or the completion of a comprehensive plan. The advantage of a press conference is that it highlights the importance of the news and avoids having to tell the same story several times.

## III. NEWSLETTERS

A newsletter is an effective way to communicate information promptly, especially when there is no local newspaper. Newsletters can include such

Spring 1985 — Newsletter of the Yakima River Greenway Foundation — Vol. 3, No. 1

## Making a wish come true

*By Marc Smiley*

Supporting the Greenway has just gotten easier.

The Greenway Foundation published a Wishbook catalog just before Christmas and already the response has been tremen-

The Wishbook catalog lists more than 30 different features of the Greenway needing local support, including this picnic shelter for Sarg Hubbard Park. Pacific Northwest Bell underwrote this shelter and several picnic sites with their check for $25,000.

dous. The catalog lists most of the development needs of the Greenway, and gives interested donors a chance to pick the improvements that they want to support. In addition, it gives the Greenway some accountability, assuring that supporters know where their money is going.

The 24-page catalog is broken into three sections — In the Office, On the River, and In the Park. "In the Office" lists the administration needs of the Greenway, and the cost of supporting these program items, which include our newsletter, a computer and a pick-up truck.

The "On the River" section lists the developments outside of our two present park projects. The Pathway North, which will connect the Noel Pathway featured

in our last newsletter to the existing Selah Pathway, is just one of the features now needing support from the community. Others include a nature studies center, a footbridge and float landings

in various parts of the Greenway corridor.

The final section, "In the Park," lists the various needs within the Greenway's two newest parks — Sherman Memorial Park and Sarg Hubbard Riverside Park.

Sherman Park, completed just last year with the support of the Yakima Kiwanis Club, was the result of thousands of volunteer hours. But the features yet to come now need the financial support of the community. Signs, landscaping and further expansion are all on the list.

But the biggest feature of the Wishbook is the gem of the Greenway — Sarg Hubbard Riverside Park. Eleven pages of essentials fill the majority of the Wishbook. Prices start at a $150

contribution for the barbecue pit to $100,000 for the featured waterfall fountain that will serve as the backdrop to the amphitheatre stage of the Reflection Pond. Prices cover all costs, including shipping and installation.

The Sarg Hubbard Park project adds a special benefit to the whole package. A grant from the Inter-Agency Committee on Outdoor Recreation (IAC) matches local contributions dollar-for-dollar. In effect, this makes it possible to fund a $3,000 improvement with a local donation of $1,500. This grant covers only the Sarg Hubbard Park project and does not affect other developments.

Response to the publishing of the catalog has been tremendous. More than 30 of the catalogs have been distributed to individuals and organizations looking to fund projects within the Greenway. Contributions for the Sarg Hubbard Park development alone have been pledged or are pending on 11 of the projects.

This response has been great, but it means that some of the more visible and important features within the Greenway will soon be claimed. If you belong to a group or club that might be interested, or if you would like to support the project individually, get in touch with the Greenway. We can send a Wishbook for you to browse through at your own leisure.

Support the Greenway — and know where your support goes! Contact the Greenway office and get involved with a project that means something to everyone in the Yakima Valley — now and for generations to come.

features as photographs or drawings of local scenes, practical advice on gardening, contests to identify the individuals or sites shown in historic photographs, and a calendar of upcoming community events.

A newsletter can be an excellent project for volunteers. A printer or someone from a local newspaper can often advise on how to lay out the newsletter. Some personal computer programs can be used to prepare "camera-ready" copy and even graphics. An art teacher may be able to help with graphics or show volunteers how to use art supplies. A proof-reader, perhaps an English teacher or retired secretary, who can spot faulty grammar and misspellings is essential.

An up-to-date mailing list is important for both newsletters and other bulletins. If the list is long, a computer program that can store mailing lists, sort addresses by zip code, and prepare labels helps. Nonprofit organizations can save postage costs by obtaining bulk mail permits. Dividing the mailing list into different categories—such as members and nonmembers, residents and outsiders, local officials, donors, and press—is useful for sending out mailings aimed at particular audiences. Individuals and organizations that have helped, or are expected to help in the future, should be included, as should elected representatives and regional, state, and national organizations that may share the group's concerns.

## IV. EDUCATIONAL PROGRAMS

### A. Lectures and Slide Shows

Talks by both local leaders and outsiders are effective educational tools. The topic should be as relevant as possible to the audience. Farmers may be more interested in a talk entitled "The Economic Benefits of Agricultural Districts" than in one called "Conserving our Farmland." A talk on agricultural districts can, of course, impart a strong conservation message. It is important to select a time and place that are appropriate and convenient. To reach local realtors a luncheon meeting might be best; farmers might prefer an early morning breakfast at the local cafe.

Civic, fraternal, and other local organizations such as libraries and churches often seek new topics for their meetings. Booking speakers for these organizations is an effective way of gaining community visibility and educating a broader population about rural conservation.

Inviting a speaker from a well-known organization can attract a large audience and lend credibility to the local group sponsoring the speech. If, for instance, a State Historic Preservation Officer praises a historic farm, the group may win supporters in a fight to prevent a road widening.

Good slide shows and films may be rented or borrowed from many state and national organizations. Alternatively, an organization can develop its own slide show, videotape, or film to focus attention on its goals and programs, as well as the community's resources. Although films can be effective, they are far more expensive to produce than slide shows, and videotapes and films cannot be altered easily to take into account changing circumstances.

If an organization will be showing the same slides many times, it might consider preparing a slide-tape show. The presentation should be short enough to allow for questions and discussion within the program time. The Yakima River Greenway Foundation prepared a popular 16-minute

*to be flat in tone and lack shadows that provide good contrast.*

*• In checking the exposure, point the light meter at the most important part of the picture. Avoid pointing it at the sky.*

*• A filter that cuts haze enhances detail and emphasizes clouds. It also protects expensive lenses.*

*• Backlighted photographs, with the sun beaming into the camera, are generally to be avoided.*

*• In terms of composition, overall scenes are useful, but so are details, such as a single fern or a building cornice. Minimize distracting foreground, such as pavement, and too much sky.*

*• Use a good lab for developing. Avoid drugstores and discount shops. When ordering prints, ask for "reproduction-quality enlargements." Have color film processed by the manufacturer.*

*• Identify all photographs with the subject, location, date, and photographer.*

*• Never touch the picture area of a negative or transparency. Negatives should be stored in acid-free envelopes.*

*(Adapted from Jack E. Boucher,* Suggestions for Producing Publishable Photographs *[Washington, D.C.: The Preservation Press, 1978].)*

There is no substitute for getting a community's residents out to see the resources that need to be protected. Here a science instructor points out the many features of good wetland habitat in Kandiyohi County, Minnesota.

slide-tape show that volunteer speakers show around the community. The slides were taken by volunteers, and the narration was donated by a well-known radio station personality. According to the foundation's executive director, "The importance of the show is that it allows more of our volunteers to get involved as speakers. We know all the major issues will be covered in the show. The volunteers can then add their personal insights and messages."[1]

## B. Field Trips

Every community's environment provides a learning laboratory to explore such matters as natural resources, architectural styles, and farming methods. There is no substitute for getting people out to see the resources that need to be protected or how conservation and development can complement each other if done properly. Reading about farmland loss in a community is instructive but does not have nearly the impact of visiting a farm and learning about its operations from the farmer. After meeting with the farmer, nonfarm residents not only will better understand the importance of agriculture in their community, but may also become personally committed to assuring that the farmer they met, and his neighbors, can stay in business.

Many groups organize regular outings for their members and others in the community. An outing might consist of an hour's walk through the village historic district led by a local historian, an afternoon's nature hike in a local preserve led by the high school biology teacher, or a day's tour of farms led by the Soil Conservation Service's District Conservationist.

Each year since 1973, the all-volunteer Plymouth County Wildlands Trust in Massachusetts has organized outings focusing on particular themes. In 1982, for instance, a naturalist member of the board led a flotilla of sixty canoes to study fresh water and saline ecosystems along the North River. In other years trust members have studied the county's pinelands, bogs, farmland, and archeological sites. Members visit both properties owned by the trust and other areas important to the county's ecology and history.

In addition to sponsoring field trips, organizations can prepare booklets for self-guided tours. For example, student interns from the Yale University School of Forestry and Environmental Studies working for the Roxbury Land Trust in Connecticut prepared publications for self-guided nature walks.

## C. Workshops

Workshops can provide more detailed information than lectures, typically on subjects that have practical application. For property owners, the advantages of agricultural districts, rehabilitating an old house, or the benefits of easement donation are examples of worthwhile topics. A workshop usually includes more than one speaker, allows ample opportunity for discussion, and provides participants with instructional materials to take home for future reference. Sessions can be held over a series of evenings or on a weekend. For instance, THRIFT (Tug Hill Resources— Investment for Tomorrow), in upstate New York, sponsored two Saturday workshops to inform landowners about all aspects of forest management. Owners learned to identify trees, received guidance on woodlot management, discussed the protection of wildlife habitat, and observed sawmill operations.

Cazenovia Preservation Foundation, Inc.

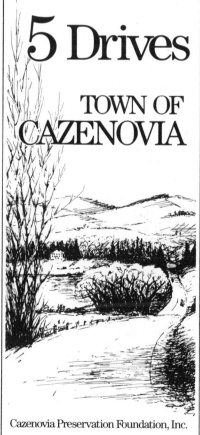

Cazenovia Preservation Foundation, Inc.

**Self-guided tour booklets encourage residents and visitors to experience the environment first-hand. Dorothy Riester wrote and illustrated these pamphlets for the Cazenovia Preservation Foundation (Case Study 6). The guides include maps and short descriptions of significant sites along the way.**

A sixth-grade class in Lakefield, Minnesota, participates in "Environmental Clean Up Day," in co-operation with the county's Soil and Water Conservation District. Projects for children increase their interest in conservation as well as that of their parents.

## D. Leadership Training

The education of leaders and potential leaders of both nonprofit organizations and local governments pays off in informed decision-making. Attending conferences, workshops, and short courses and visiting other communities that have undertaken rural conservation programs are all good ways for leaders to gain new skills and insights. Workshops designed to increase management and fund-raising skills or to provide detailed information about ecology, historic preservation, good design, or land-use law can help to improve leaders' effectiveness. For instance, a group might find that paying the registration costs for a county supervisor to attend a national conference on farmland retention may later encourage the county to take action on that issue.

In-house educational activities may be structured or unstructured, limited to selected participants such as board members or committee chairmen, or open to all members of an organization. Some organizations conduct retreats or seminars for their leaders. Collecting and making available a basic rural conservation library is a simple educational activity that all groups can conduct. The Cazenovia Community Resources Project in New York collected useful publications and placed them on a special shelf at the local library.

## E. Activities for Children

Sponsoring events for children is a good way to build and keep community awareness. An added benefit is that parents often become involved in community affairs through their children. The Amana Preservation Foundation in Iowa found that its membership increased substantially after it began sponsoring programs in the school. Students participating in the state arts council's architect-in-schools program in Rolfe, another rural Iowa community, were responsible for awakening interest in their deteriorated downtown. Students developed oral histories for each building, took

SAVING AMERICA'S COUNTRYSIDE

The Historical Society of Carroll County, Maryland, promotes its image by publishing a Heritage Calendar, financed in part by the businesses listed on each page. In addition to displaying historical prints and photographs, the calendar lists historical dates and community events.

photographs, and traced deeds as part of an exhibit on the downtown for the school fair. Another group of Rolfe students suggested improvements to building facades that resulted in a new use for a historic bank building.

Programs for children should provide hands-on experience. An occasional slide show or film is an interesting diversion from classroom work, but tours, games, and research projects that allow children to discover things on their own are generally more instructive. Every community has

*Project Seasons,* a looseleaf note-book designed and written by the Stewardship Institute (1986), consists of eighty-two environmental activities for children. The activities assist classroom teachers in teaching children to appreciate the natural and agricultural resources of the Northeast. The activities, one of which is reproduced here, are organized according to grade level, season of the year, and academic discipline. The institute also offers teacher training at Shelburne Farms, a historic estate in Vermont.

sites to visit that will interest children. Moreover, many museums and nature centers have programs specifically designed for children.

The Housatonic Valley Association in Connecticut, for instance, has made a major commitment to environmental education through its Watershed Ed project. The association helps high school teachers integrate environmental education into the curriculum. According to the executive director, a number of good environmental curriculum materials have been developed; the challenge is to get the teachers to use them and to take advantage of interesting sites for students to visit. The association provides information on published curriculum materials and about the people who are available to make classroom presentations or lead field trips. Some of the most effective presentations have been made by engineers working for industries concerned about protecting the water quality of the Housatonic River watershed. The association also conducts workshops for teachers on environmental subjects.[2]

**Title:**
*Scarecrows Are Helpful*

**Objectives:**
Students will understand the relationship farmers have with wild animals.

**Grade Level:**
3–4

**Groupings:**
Small groups of three or four

**Materials:**
(per small group) Assorted clothes, newspaper, paper bag, string, markers, paper

**Time Allotment:**
45 minutes

**Scope and Sequence:**
Introduction to plant and animal cycles, matter all around us, sensory awareness, seasonal awareness, predator/prey

**Sharpening Skills:**
Fine motor skills, classifying, hypothesizing, communicating

**Directions:**
1. Students break up into small groups and are given the materials necessary to make a scarecrow. Newspaper is the stuffing, a paper bag is the head, and the string is used to tie off the legs, arms, and neck.

2. Discuss the scarecrow's purpose. What does the scarecrow scare away? List other wild animals that are troublesome to farmers. The list might include rabbits, who eat young crop plants; raccoons, who eat poultry, eggs, and corn; mice, who eat grain; and insects, who carry disease to animals and infest crops. Make a second list of wild animals that help the farmer. The list might include bees, who pollinate crops and pasture plants; foxes, who eat rabbits; earthworms, who aerate the soil; owls, who eat mice; and ladybugs, who eat some of the bad insects.

3. Students then draw pictures showing other ways to invite or keep away wild animals from crops and livestock.

FALL/3–4

At the national level, the National Audubon Society and the National Wildlife Federation publish environmental magazines for children and supply teachers with conservation curriculum materials.

## V. SPECIAL EVENTS

An organization may have several reasons for sponsoring an event: to raise money, provide residents with a social or cultural occasion, involve members, recruit new members, obtain publicity, thank volunteers, or generate community support. Whatever the goal of the event may be, the occasion should be enjoyable. Successful events require a lot of work. Leaders need to be sure of the enthusiasm and commitment of members to ensure that the event complements and does not preempt the organization's other activities. Conducting a well-attended, well-organized, and

An information center at the annual Oley Fair in Pennsylvania was effective in giving the Oley Resource Conservation Project broad community exposure (Case Study 1). Equipped with a continuously running slide show, handouts, and volunteers who were able to answer questions, the information center provided residents with basic information about Oley's resources and the efforts to protect them. Several visitors to the booth later became project volunteers.

fun event reflects positively on the organization's ability to get things done.

While a fish fry or rodeo may work in one community, a square dance or canoe race might be more appropriate in another. Some community groups have found that reviving past events such as homecomings, harvest festivals, and parades can be successful. Events sponsored by an area's church and civic groups are useful indicators of the kinds of events that are popular. Adding special features such as a barbecue, watermelon-eating contest, or bluegrass band can enliven a routine event.

Messages reach people in a variety of ways. Some groups herald an upcoming event with promotional items such as buttons and bumper stickers. Many groups sell postcards, T-shirts, and tote bags throughout the year.

## A. Exhibits

Some organizations may prepare exhibits or arrange for demonstrations at a community event, in conjunction with a lecture or as part of a workshop. Store windows, shopping centers, and the lobbies of such buildings as banks, the county courthouse, and the town hall are good display locations.

Each year since 1983, the Yakima River Greenway Foundation has had a booth at the Central Washington State Fair. According to a board member, the 1983 booth "was decorated with plants and shrubs (loaned by a local nursery) to resemble a small park and had information posters, photographs, brochures, and a large diorama of the proposed Greenway. T-shirts and caps with the Greenway logo were offered for sale as well as silk-screened wildlife posters."[3] The annual event provides an excellent opportunity for the foundation to get its message across to area residents and recruit new members.

The simplest exhibits are often the most successful, although good lighting and attractive, high-quality graphics are essential. Not many people, for example, will read long architectural descriptions as part of a display on historic farms, but they probably will look at photographs of farmers at work, a map showing the layout of a farmstead, or a model of an interesting barn. Successful exhibits have distinct themes, such as the changing rural landscape, endangered species, the restoration of a prominent landscape, or the loss of farmland.

## B. Tours

Village walks, nature hikes, farm visits, open houses, and spring garden tours are popular. Some groups find tours profitable; others conduct them primarily for educational purposes. Refreshments using local recipes and locally produced items, audiovisual presentations, and opportunities to purchase crafts or promotional items can be incorporated into the tour agenda.

A nature walk or a village tour requires a knowledgeable leader and good publicity, but may not require a great deal of advance work for the sponsor. Tours that entail visiting private property, renting buses, or serving food, however, can require considerable planning and coordination. Occasionally, residents will not allow visitation on their property because they are concerned about liability, theft, and vandalism. The sponsoring organization may need to obtain insurance, post signs, arrange for parking, instruct visitors not to walk in certain areas or to take photographs, prepare maps, and provide rest room facilities and other services that will make the tour enjoyable for visitors and protect the community's resources.

## C. Festivals and Fairs

Many rural organizations sponsor successful festivals, fairs, and crafts demonstrations, focusing on what is authentic and appropriate to the area. These events require considerable advance planning and careful coordination. Some, such as the annual Waterford Foundation Homes Tour and Crafts Exhibit (Case Study 28), attract large numbers of outsiders and are money-making events.

# Waterford, Virginia:
# Homes Tour and Crafts Exhibit

The Waterford Homes Tour and Crafts Exhibit, in Waterford, Virginia, is one of the most successful fund-raising events conducted by a non-profit rural conservation organization. Held annually for more than 40 years, the fair started small but has expanded to the point that it generates more than $100,000 each year for the Waterford Foundation. Not only is the event a financial success, but it is also a model of community cooperation and a well-organized event that continues to be educational and entertaining year after year.

Waterford is a village of 250 residents surrounded by farmland and located 50 miles west of Washington, D.C. It began as a Quaker settlement that grew up around a mill established early in the eighteenth century on Catoctin Creek. Today the community is composed of some 100

The Waterford Foundation in Virginia was established in 1943 to protect Waterford's cultural and architectural heritage. The Patriots of Northern Virginia Fife and Drum Corps perform at the Waterford Foundation's annual Homes Tour and Crafts Exhibit. The event, which attracts thousands of people and is a major source of income for the foundation, also educates visitors about the importance of protecting the village and its rural setting.

houses, most from the eighteenth and early nineteenth centuries. The entire village, and much of the farmland that can be seen from the village, is included in a National Historic Landmark district (see illustrations, pp. 74–75).

In 1943, residents established the Waterford Foundation to protect the village's cultural and architectural heritage. Over the years it has purchased or protected both land and buildings. Today it owns more than 50 acres of land and twelve buildings. It has also arranged for sixty easements protecting more than half of the village itself and some 250 acres of open land. In 1981, the foundation hired an executive director to manage its increasingly complex programs.

The annual Homes Tour and Crafts Exhibit is responsible in large part for the positive image that the Waterford Foundation commands locally and regionally. The three-day event, which takes place throughout the village, consists of tours of historic buildings; craft demonstrations; entertainment, including performances by traditional dancers and musicians on the village's streets; and the sale of baked goods, preserves, dried flowers, crafts, and other local products. In addition to being entertained, the 25,000-plus visitors who attend each year come to appreciate the village's historic and scenic environment and the efforts to protect it.

"We really stress the educational aspects of the fair," says Constance Chamberlin, the foundation's former executive director. "The visitors are a captive audience, and in addition to giving them a good time, we make sure they go away knowing something about the significance of Waterford and the need for preservation." Every visitor receives an illustrated booklet about the history of Waterford, its historic buildings, the fair, and the foundation's preservation program.

The foundation board delegates much of the authority for organizing the Homes Tour and Crafts Exhibit to a volunteer fair chairperson. Subcommittees handle such arrangements as coordinating parking and selecting and communicating with the artisans who exhibit. The foundation has developed a manual detailing everything that needs to be done to assure a successful fair.

SAVING AMERICA'S COUNTRYSIDE

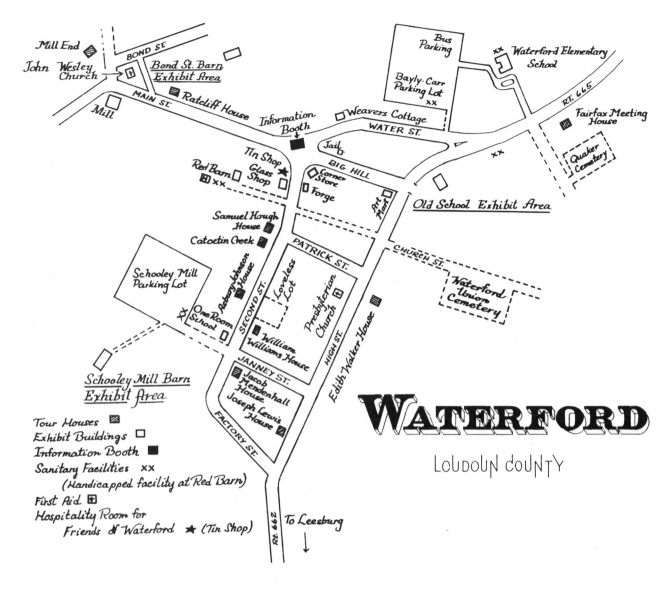

Mill End

John Wesley Church

Mill

BOND ST.

Bond St. Barn Exhibit Area

Ratcliff House

MAIN ST.

Information Booth

Tin Shop
Glass Shop

Red Barn

xx

Samuel Hough House

Catoctin Creek

Schooley Mill Parking Lot

Rickory Johnson House

SECOND ST.

One Room School

xx

Loveless Lot

William Williams House

PATRICK ST.

Schooley Mill Barn Exhibit Area

JANNEY ST.

Jacob Mendenhall House

Joseph Lewis House

FACTORY ST.

Rt. 662

To Leesburg

Bus Parking

Bayly-Carr Parking Lot

xx

Weavers Cottage

WATER ST.

Jail

BIG HILL

Corner Store

Forge

Art Mart

Old School Exhibit Area

CHURCH ST.

Presbyterian Church

HIGH ST.

Edith Walker House

Waterford Elementary School

RT. 665

Fairfax Meeting House

Quaker Cemetery

xx

Waterford Union Cemetery

# WATERFORD

## LOUDOUN COUNTY

Tour Houses

Exhibit Buildings

Information Booth

Sanitary Facilities   xx
        (Handicapped facility at Red Barn)

First Aid

Hospitality Room for
        Friends of Waterford   ★ (Tin Shop)

Although the event is sponsored solely by the Waterford Foundation, it involves the entire community and serves as the major fund-raising effort for many other community groups. For instance, civic and youth groups serve food and provide services such as parking and trash collection, for which the foundation makes a donation. Making the event a shared community experience increases community support and contributes to its overall success. Moreover, the event benefits businesses throughout the area, with many store owners, restaurants, and hotels near Waterford reporting the weekend of the fair as their best of the year.

**Visitor's map for the Waterford Foundation's Homes Tour and Crafts Exhibit. The event requires careful planning and involves volunteers from many community groups.**

Organizing a community event requires the completion of many tasks. It can seem overwhelming, but developing a budget and timetable helps to make an event run smoothly. It is a good idea to be liberal in estimating

# Recognition Ceremonies

*There are a variety of occasions for recognition ceremonies:*

• *To thank volunteers and others who have made substantial contributions;*
• *To honor outgoing board members, officers, or staff;*
• *To recognize a particular group of properties, such as century farms (farms that have been in the same family for 100 years or more);*
• *To announce a special designation such as a National Natural Landmark listing, entry in the National Register of Historic Places, or the establishment of an agricultural district;*
• *To recognize individuals who have protected their properties by some action such as donating an easement or rehabilitating a dilapidated house; or*
• *To recognize the winner of a youth essay contest or the organization's logo contest.*

expenses and conservative in projecting revenues to allow for such circumstances as a low turnout in poor weather. In general, a group should not depend on a first-time event to provide the major portion of its funding. Only well-established events such as the Waterford Foundation's Homes Tour and Crafts Exhibit are dependable, "and even we are scared to death of rain," adds its executive director.[4]

## D. Recognition and Awards Ceremonies

Occasionally, a group may elect to host an event honoring individuals or recognizing a significant property (5.II). Such events may range from a formal ceremony during which a plaque is affixed to a building, to social affairs with music, dance, and refreshments. In Pennsylvania, the Oley Resource Conservation Project planned the Oley Township Recognition Ceremony for a public presentation of the certificate designating the township a historic district listed in the National Register of Historic Places. The ceremony included representatives of the organizations that had assisted Oley in preparing the nomination, local officials, the district's member of Congress, and the state's secretary of agriculture, who praised the town's leaders for their work in protecting the community and thanked the many volunteers (Case Study 1).

As well as honoring deserving individuals, recognition and awards ceremonies call attention to the organization's goals and programs, although a potential risk is offending those not honored. Criticism can be deflected by setting clear criteria for the award, naming an impartial selection committee, and making the award annually. An organization can also spread the credit by holding a reception honoring all of the individuals who have contributed to conservation efforts in the past year. When a group does give an award, the prize need not be elaborate or expensive: a plaque, medal, photograph, or book will do. As a recipient of the Amana Preservation Foundation's Lantern Award for outstanding contributions to preservation efforts said, "It's the thought that counts; knowing that the group thinks I made a difference is reward enough."

## E. Public Service

Through public service a group can make a substantial contribution to the community and receive favorable publicity. For instance, in areas where there is an abundance of litter and clutter, a rural conservation group can perform a service by sponsoring a regular community clean-up day.

In addition to the public service a conservation organization's members can undertake, service clubs in the community may be willing to work on conservation projects. Most service clubs select community projects each year to support through fund-raisers and volunteer work. For instance, the Kiwanis Club raised over $30,000 for an irrigation system and trees for a park managed by the Yakima River Greenway Foundation in Washington. Kiwanis members also donated their time to install the irrigation system, and local businesses provided services and equipment at cost. Endorsement by a service club can significantly increase public support for a conservation organization.

Boy Scouts, Girl Scouts, 4-H Clubs, and Future Farmers of America are examples of youth organizations that volunteer their services. In Amana, Iowa, one Boy Scout directed the establishment of a "community attic"

The Garfield Farm Museum in Kane County, Illinois, is just forty miles west of Chicago. A portion of the 250-acre property is interpreted as an 1840s farm and inn. Fortunately, three of the buildings from that era survive, as have much of the correspondence and other records of the Garfield family. Here a couple demonstrates for visitors the setting of bean poles. The museum operates in conjunction with Campton Historic Agricultural Lands, Inc., a land trust that encourages the protection of farmland in the area through the donation of easements.

for discarded building materials that could be used in restoration projects. Another Scout conducted a tree-planting beautification project.

One public service that many local governments and nonprofit organizations have found popular is to publish an annual directory of local organizations and units of government that are involved in conservation or which provide community services. Such a directory can also include emergency telephone numbers, a calendar of community events, and information on municipal services. Advertising may cover much of the publication costs.

## VI. EDUCATIONAL FACILITIES

Many rural conservation organizations undertake long-term education programs that require permanent facilities such as museums, living history programs, and nature centers. These programs can be very effective but take a considerable investment of time and money and require trained staff. Often the necessary real estate can be acquired through one of the techniques described in Chapter 5.

### A. Museums

A museum may consist of a room in the county courthouse, town library, or Grange hall, or it may be something more elaborate. It may consist of a historic plantation, such as Sully in Fairfax County, Virginia, or even an entire community, such as Old Sturbridge in Massachusetts, where visitors can observe all aspects of life in an early-nineteenth-century rural New England village. In some cases the buildings are historic; in others, they are reconstructions. The buildings may be in their original locations, or they may have been moved in from the surrounding countryside, as is the case at Trail Town in Cody, Wyoming.

It is best to preserve buildings in their original settings where they can be interpreted as part of the original landscape. In some instances, however, particularly in areas where farmsteads are being abandoned or where major new developments are imminent, moving a building and re-creating its landscape may be the only alternative to demolition. Further information on museums is available from the American Association for State and Local History and the American Association of Museums.

## B. Living History Programs

Living history farms, where the public can see the farming operations of a particular period, have a special relevance for rural communities. The farm may depict the life of one family at one time in history, as does the early-twentieth-century Howell Living Historical Farm in Titusville, New Jersey; or many different farms, as does Old World Wisconsin, with its series of farmsteads reflecting the state's great ethnic diversity; or a progression through historical periods, such as Iowa's Living Historical Farms in Des Moines, with its depictions of rural life in that state from 1840 to the present. At some farms, such as Norlands in Livermore, Maine, visitors assume roles on the farm to experience first-hand the life of an earlier era. Living history farms, such as the Oliver H. Kelley Farm in Elk River, Minnesota, have also played an important role in propagating

The Finnish farmstead at Old World Wisconsin in Eagle gives tens of thousands of annual visitors a feel for Finnish heritage in America.

old animal breeds and plants that may be more resistant to disease than many of the hybrids that are used in modern agriculture. Further information is available from the Association for Living Historical Farms and Agricultural Museums.

A living history farm can become a focus for a community's conservation efforts. Protecting the countryside around the farm not only enhances the visitors' experience and the scenic beauty of the area, but also provides a model for protecting other areas in the community.

In addition to farms, rural communities can develop other living history programs. The Waterford Foundation, for instance, has developed a free program for the benefit of Loudoun County, Virginia, schools which gives third- and fourth-graders studying Virginia's history the opportunity to spend a day at the Waterford One-Room School, taking on the roles of specific nineteenth-century children. The foundation has prepared biographies of actual students who attended school there in the 1880s, which are given to the visiting children before they arrive to allow them to prepare for their roles. The foundation supplies teachers with educational kits, including activities to be conducted in the classroom before and after the visit.

## C. Nature Centers

Many rural conservation organizations, typically land trusts and local park authorities, operate nature centers, which usually include both a building with exhibits and adjacent land that is protected. The best centers relate exhibits to the surrounding environment and encourage visitors to explore that environment. Many centers have programs geared to science curricula at neighboring schools. A nature center should incorporate as many examples of the community's ecosystems as practical. As is the case with living history farms, a nature center can provide a community with a

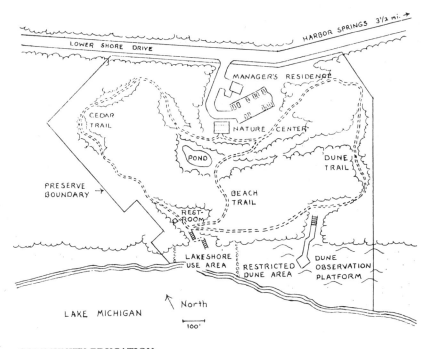

The Little Traverse Conservancy sponsors a nature center at the Thorne Swift Nature Preserve in northern Michigan near Harbor Springs. Since 1972, the conservancy has acquired more than 1,700 acres of forest, dunes, swamp, and rugged Lake Michigan shoreline. In an innovative cooperative arrangement between a private nonprofit organization and local government, the conservancy in 1982 leased the Thorne Swift Nature Preserve to West Traverse Township for an initial period of five years, for one dollar a year. The conservancy and the township jointly prepared a plan for the preserve, approved by the township board after several public hearings, and as part of that plan, built a nature center now managed by the township. In addition to the nature center, the preserve incorporates a much-needed public beach.

# Farmers' Markets

Farmers' markets have enjoyed a return to popularity in the last decade. They provide a needed incentive to keep nearby farmers in business, thereby encouraging farmland retention on the town's periphery, where it is disappearing most rapidly. Farmers' markets provide city residents with a reason to support farmland retention and rural conservation leaders with a good opportunity to cooperate with a nearby town interested in sponsoring a market.

Traditionally, most towns had markets where farmers sold their produce directly to the public. Such markets were lively places that provided both town and country people an opportunity to visit as well as to conduct business. Farmers' markets all but disappeared with the rise of the supermarket, but consumers in the 1970s and 1980s, tired of hard tomatoes, waxed cucumbers, and tasteless strawberries, have learned to appreciate farm-fresh produce. Such markets provide an outlet for farmers whose quantities of produce may not be sufficient to interest a corporate food processor or distributor.

Some farmers' markets are no more than downtown parking lots where farmers are allowed to sell from the backs of their trucks; others have stands or are located in market buildings and feature baked goods, home-cooked meals, crafts, and flowers as well as fresh produce. Some, such as the Saturday market on the square surrounding the state capitol building in Madison, Wisconsin, are seasonal, while others are year-round. Some markets are sponsored by town governments, state departments of agriculture, farmers' associations, or chambers of commerce. Others, like the twenty-four run by Greenmarket in New York City, are operated by nonprofit organizations. Greenmarket has as one of its primary purposes "to support agriculture and conserve farmland in the region." Greenmarket director Barry Benepe reports that participation in farmers' markets has made the difference between profit and going out of business for many area farmers.

A sense of permanence fosters confidence, an important ingredient for farmers and customers alike. Markets have worked best in towns such as Lancaster, Pennsylvania, that have allocated permanent space or a building for the market. It is also important to limit participation generally to vendors who are actually selling produce from their own farms. Cities such as Shelby, North Carolina, have found that farmers' markets can draw people downtown for other shopping and be a major factor in downtown revitalization.

Several state departments of agriculture—including those in California, Massachusetts, New York, and Texas—offer assistance to communities in establishing farmers' markets. The Cooperative Extension Service may be able to assist as well.

Farmers' markets not only provide city residents with fresh produce, but also help farmers on the urban fringe to stay in business. This is one of twenty-four farmers' markets operated by Greenmarket, a nonprofit organization in New York City.

focus for its rural conservation program. Further information on nature centers is available from the Association of Interpretive Naturalists and the Natural Science for Youth Foundation.

## VII. CONCLUSION

Although the purpose of educational programs is a serious one, they can and should be enjoyable and satisfying. They call for much creativity and fortunately can make use of the varied skills of many community residents. Moreover, the teamwork required in setting up such programs can be a major factor in developing an organization's esprit de corps.

# Putting It All Together

H ow do you go about applying the ideas in this handbook? Let us start with a framework for those ideas. Planners talk about following a simple process: inventory the community's resources, analyze the problems and potential solutions, and act. In life, nothing is quite so simple, however. Such complexities as personalities, culture or custom, government, and changes in land uses mean that the process is never-ending and constantly open to adjustment to account for new factors.

There is more to effective action than simply understanding the pieces of the puzzle. You need to think broadly, think in terms of coalition-building, think about the long term, and think positively. You also need to be willing to approach rural conservation creatively, in terms of solving your community's particular problems rather than offering off-the-shelf solutions. Finally, you need to be willing to take risks. Let's take up these points one by one.

***Think broadly.*** Rural conservation as we define it in the Introduction to this handbook requires that you consider all of a community's assets. In addition to its natural and historic resources, a community has other assets: its people, its government structures and officials, its organizations. Segments of the economy may have certain strengths: tourism, agricultural services, forest products, regional retailing. People may take special pride in certain aspects of the community, such as the best drinking water in the county or the best schools. Understanding these assets and figuring out how to capitalize on them requires you to think broadly.

*Think about building coalitions.* Thinking broadly includes thinking in terms of building coalitions. One well-organized group can make all the difference in helping good ideas take root; even better is broad community understanding of and cooperation toward your goals. Learn to identify mutual interests among the people, organizations, and business interests involved in your community, and learn to approach problems cooperatively, through governmental, nonprofit, and private entities—whatever will get the job done. Build multiple strengths in your community. If there is a planning void in the public sector, then develop ways to address it through nonprofit action, *and* be prepared to acknowledge and support changes in the attitude of public officials once they see the light. There is an old saying that pertains here: You can get many things done if you don't care who gets the credit.

In thinking about building coalitions, you should not lose sight of action at the regional or state level. In Michigan's Upper Peninsula, for example, fifteen counties banded together to inventory their forest lands and created resource maps that could be used by property owners. They received a grant from the U.S. Forest Service to carry out the work. For another example, the Trust for New Hampshire Lands is a broad—indeed, unprecedented—coalition of 127 businesses, foundations, conservancies, other nonprofit organizations, and government, all joined around the creation and administration of a state-sponsored Land Conservation Investment Program to protect up to 100,000 acres of "New Hampshire's most cherished natural lands" through voluntary negotiations with landowners. The trust serves as a "land agent" using the state program's $20 million trust fund, and also works with the state's communities to accomplish similar protection for locally valued lands. The Center for Rural Massachusetts and New York's $1.45 billion conservation and preservation bond issue of 1986 are both examples of innovative state legislation passed by broad coalitions. The bond act also required statewide approval by voters. A simpler example of an effective statewide coalition is in Virginia, where ten local and state conservation and preservation organizations and state agencies sponsored publication of a handbook on stewardship.

*Think about the long term.* It is all too easy to allow immediate demands to overwhelm your ability to address what is truly important—or, as another saying goes, when you're up to your ears in alligators, it's hard to remember that your objective is to cross the river. In Chapters 2 and 4 we discuss setting goals: defining for yourself, your organization, or your community what you are setting out to achieve over the long term. Plan of action, master plan, strategic goal-setting—it does not matter what you call the process or its result, and there are any number of variations in how you do it. What is important is developing a sense of who and where you are, and where you are going. Such a vision will help you to maintain the patience and persistence you will need to make the changes you believe are necessary in your community. Although your conservation work will never be complete—there is no such thing as a rural community that has achieved complete conservation—you can at least establish a framework for dealing effectively with future challenges and problems.

*Think and act positively.* This is not a mini-lecture about the power of positive thinking but rather a caution about approaching the problems in

your community in a negative manner. It may be obvious to you that your
community's planning board or nonprofit organization is ineffectual. Simply offering criticisms without constructive ideas for their solution can
easily create enemies where you most need friends. In addition, it is all too
easy to forget to consider the opinions of others; those who resist your
ideas may view your community, the problem, or possible solutions in entirely different ways. Your constructive ideas should, whenever possible,
include specific steps your organization or government officials can take,
but you must also be artful in developing community consensus in a positive way. It may well be that others do not agree that a problem exists in
the first place—which leads us to the next point.

*Be a problem-solver.* Do not let your efforts to achieve rural conservation get sidetracked by debates about solutions before you are ready. The
first level of public debate should be about whether the community has a
problem, toward developing a sense of widespread agreement among
many different interests in the community. The debate about the problem

should direct the design of any solution to be proposed. Jumping into a discussion of the merits of zoning to protect farmland, for example, may unnecessarily polarize the community. While it may seem easy to propose some kind of solution "just to get a reaction"—and, indeed, others may ask you for your ideas in order to understand your position—it is well worth resisting the temptation to advance a solution before there is consensus about the problem.

Being an effective problem-solver requires you to approach rural conservation creatively. To continue the example above, rather than simply resorting to zoning to address the problems of growth in agricultural areas, you might consider some combination of the techniques discussed in Chapters 4 and 5. Your evaluation of potential techniques plus your understanding of what your community is likely to accept should help you to combine the techniques best suited to your needs. Cost and the community's ability to implement a new technique are obviously factors to consider in evaluating potential solutions. In borrowing successful ideas from other communities, use your problem-solving approach to adapt these ideas to your community.

*Be a risk-taker.* In initiating rural conservation programs in your community, be willing to try something new. There just are not enough communities working hard at rural conservation that yours will have a neighbor it can safely emulate. You may not learn what works best in your community without trial and error, even after a careful assessment of what you want to do, how you should go about it, and what risks are involved. Among the risks are court challenges. Some communities seem immobilized by the fear of litigation, but doing nothing can have its cost too. Be ready to capitalize on your opportunities despite the apparent risks: good timing may help you carry the day. Remember that the old chestnut "nothing ventured, nothing gained" implies not only risk but also investment. Plan as wisely as you can, and then invest the resources needed to make your risk pay off. People, time, energy, money, or help from the outside are all things you may have to invest in your programs.

In rural conservation, what is "success"? As authors we seek to be like the soldier in the old European folk tale of stone soup, helping you find the answers that lie within your reach. In the story, a soldier visits a war-ravaged village and asks for food. The villagers are unwilling to share their meager stores with the stranger. He then asks for a pot, some water, and some stones, which they freely provide. Curious, they ask him what he is doing. "Making stone soup," he replies. "But it would taste better if I had an onion." Someone recalls that they might, in fact, have an onion after all. And so it goes, with villagers eagerly adding other ingredients, removing the stones, and sharing all around in the end. On one level, the tale of stone soup is about a trickster who overcame the traditional distrust of the outsider, but on another, more important level, it is about a community that discovered it could cooperate to feed its hungry citizens. Your own success may lie more in the discovery of a process that makes your community more effective in addressing its rural conservation needs than in acres or buildings permanently protected. Only you can be the judge of that success, but it surely lies in learning to make the most of what you have to work with, and in making people aware of your concerns *and* your accomplishments.

CONCLUSION

Aldo Leopold, the scientist and author who helped formulate a conservation ethic for the land, defined conservation in 1939 as a state of "harmony between man and the land." Leopold also recognized, however, that harmony is "an ideal—and one we shall never attain."[1] Yet he had faith, as we do, that in seeking that ideal, it is possible to treat the land, and the human community that is a part of the land, in the best way we can.

In conclusion, we encourage you to dream . . . a little, or a lot. What kind of out-of-the-ordinary state legislation or local ordinances would you like at your service? What makes you the maddest, or saddest, about opportunities you have lost, and what did you need to be able to seize them? (If your answer is "money," dig a little deeper.) There is strength in numbers, and salvation of a kind for those stretched thin at the local level who can discover peers nearby: Where are others like you at work, and what do you have in common? What are you doing differently, and why? If you could combine one-quarter of the ideas in this book, which ones would they be? If you had to convince outsiders to join your efforts, how would you induce them? What are your people strengths? Your other resources? Your weaknesses? Think about what is ahead for your community, your state, region, and nation. What can you achieve locally? What requires coalitions at the state or national level?

This handbook gives you some of the tools and ideas you need to refine and implement the vision of your community that *you* must develop. If we have helped you to dream about what may be possible to make your community a better place in which to live, work, and play, we have accomplished our own vision for this handbook. The rest is up to you. It is never too late, or too soon, to start.

# Sources of Assistance

## I. PRIVATE NONPROFIT ORGANIZATIONS

Those national nonprofit organizations that are most likely to be of assistance to local governments and nonprofit organizations are listed below. There are many other important national organizations doing research, lobbying for national legislation, and litigating. There are also many helpful statewide organizations. For a more complete listing of conservation organizations, see the National Wildlife Federation's *Conservation Directory* (Suggested Reading, Chapter 6). Many of the following organizations have regional and state offices. Their addresses can frequently be found in the *Conservation Directory*.

**American Association for State and Local History:** membership organization; represents history museums, archives, and historical societies; offers technical assistance. *History News,* bimonthly magazine; *History News Dispatch,* monthly. (172 Second Avenue North, Suite 102, Nashville, TN 37201)

**American Association of Museums:** membership organization; represents museum professionals and museums; offers information on programs and technical assistance. *Museum News,* bimonthly magazine; *Aviso,* monthly newsletter. (1225 Eye Street, N.W., Suite 200, Washington, DC 20005)

**American Farmland Trust:** membership organization; promotes farmland preservation and soil conservation; demonstrates preservation techniques; administers a revolving loan fund for farmland acquisition and protection; works to influence public policy; issues publications. *American Farmland,* quarterly newsletter. (1920 N Street, N.W., Suite 400, Washington, DC 20036)

**The American Forestry Association:** membership organization; promotes the intelligent management and use of forests and other natural resources; seeks to create and enlighten public appreciation of these resources. *American Forests,* monthly. (P.O. Box 2000, Washington, DC 20013)

**American Hiking Society:** membership organization; information clearinghouse on trail programs; promotes trail-building legislation; conducts training. *American Hiker,* monthly newsletter. (1015 31st Street, N.W., Washington, DC 20007)

**American Planning Association:** membership organization; monitors developments in planning, sponsors educational programs, prepares publications, and lobbies on planning issues; has committees for rural and small-town planning, historic preservation, and environmental planning. *Planning,* monthly magazine; *Small Town & Rural Planning,* quarterly newsletter; *Zoning News,* monthly newsletter. (1776 Massachusetts Avenue, N.W., Washington, DC 20036. For publications write: 1313 East 60th Street, Chicago, IL 60637)

**American Rivers:** membership organization; monitors federal and state protection legislation; provides information on developing wild and scenic river protection programs. *American Rivers,* quarterly newsletter. (801 Pennsylvania Avenue, S.E., Suite 303, Washington, DC 20003)

**The Association for Living Historical Farms and Agricultural Museums:** membership organization; encourages research, exchange of ideas, and publication on historical agriculture, rural society, folklife, and historical interpretation. *Bulletin,* bimonthly newsletter. (Room 5035, National Museum of American History, Smithsonian Institution, Washington, DC 25060)

**Association of Interpretive Naturalists:** membership organization; encourages the development of natural and historical resource interpretation skills; sponsors workshops. *The Journal of Interpretation,* semiannually; *A.I.N. National Newsletter,* bimonthly. (6700 Needwood Road, Derwood, MD 20855)

**Center for Environmental Education:** membership organization; concerned with endangered marine wildlife and its habitat; offers advice to organizations concerned with coastal wildlife sanctuaries. *CEE Report,* quarterly. (1725 DeSales Street, N.W., Suite 500, Washington, DC 20036)

**The Center for Environmental Intern Programs Fund:** five regional offices place interns with government, corporations, and citizens' groups which need short-term staff. Interns are paid by the receiving organizations and are studying at the college and graduate school levels. (68 Harrison Avenue, Boston, MA 02111)

**Center for Rural Affairs:** works to help low-income people; concerned about the well-being of small, moderate-sized, and beginning farmers; particular focus on Nebraska and neighboring states. *Small Farm Advocate,* quarterly newsletter; *Center for Rural Affairs,* monthly newsletter. (P.O. Box 405, Walthill, NE 68067)

**Citizen's Clearinghouse for Hazardous Wastes:** membership organization; provides local leaders with technical, organizing, and legal assistance. *Everyone's Backyard,* quarterly newsletter; *Action Bulletin,* quarterly. (P.O. Box 926, Arlington, VA 22216)

**Coalition for Scenic Beauty:** membership organization; promotes sign control; assists local organizations and units of government. *Sign Control News,* bimonthly newsletter. (216 Seventh Street, S.E., Washington, DC 20003)

**The Conservation Foundation:** conducts research and public education on land use, toxic-substance control, water resources, environmental dispute resolution, and other issues; Successful Communities program offers advice on controlling growth. *Conservation Foundation Letter,* bimonthly newsletter. (1250 24th Street, N.W., Washington, DC 20037)

**The Environmental Law Institute:** conducts research and prepares publications on environmental law; offers educational programs and advice on wetlands. *The Environmental Forum,* bimonthly; *The Environmental Law Reporter,* monthly; *National Wetlands Newsletter,* bimonthly. (1616 P Street, N.W., Suite 200, Washington, DC 20036)

**Environmental Policy Institute:** works to influence public policy; engages in research and litigation; information clearinghouse; special areas of concern include groundwater protection, strip mining, nuclear waste, and coastal resources. *Environmental Update,* quarterly. (218 D Street, S.E., Washington, DC 20003)

**Environmental Task Force:** membership organization; gives legal and other assistance to community organizations on pollution, hazardous waste, and other environmental issues; also refers organizations to others that can help. *Re:Sources,* quarterly; *EcoAlert,* quarterly. (1012 14th Street, N.W., 15th Floor, Washington, DC 20005)

**The Foundation Center:** service organization; good source of information on foundations, their patterns of giving, and their fields of interest; maintains offices and libraries open to the public in New York, Washington, D.C., San Francisco, and Cleveland and collections in nearly 150 cooperating libraries throughout the country; has a toll-free number (800-424-9836) for information on services and publications. (1001 Connecticut Avenue, N.W., Suite 938, Washington, DC 20036)

**Housing Assistance Council:** service organization; works to increase the availability of housing for low-income people in rural areas; administers revolving loan fund; provides technical assistance; undertakes research and training programs; publishes booklets on housing issues and programs. *HAC News,* biweekly newsletter. (1025 Vermont Avenue, N.W., Suite 606, Washington, DC 20005)

**Independent Sector:** membership organization; encourages not-for-profit initiatives; works to influence federal policy on tax and lobbying issues relating to nonprofit organizations; issues publications on how to manage nonprofit organizations. *Update,* monthly newsletter. (1828 L Street, N.W., Washington, DC 20036)

**Izaak Walton League of America:** membership organization; promotes citizen involvement in local environmental protection efforts; areas of concern include clean water, acid rain, wildlife habitat, and conservation issues relating to hunting. *Outdoor America,* quarterly. (1701 North Fort Myer Drive, Suite 1100, Arlington, VA 22209)

**Land Trust Exchange:** membership organization for land trusts and individuals; information clearinghouse; conducts educational programs, including a peer match program for land trust officials; coordinates policy development; provides technical information on tax aspects of estate planning and land conservation. *Land Trusts' Exchange,* quarterly journal. (1017 Duke Street, Alexandria, VA 22314)

**National Alliance of Preservation Commissions:** membership organization; provides information and education to members of preservation commissions and boards of architectural review. *Alliance Review,* bimonthly newsletter. (Suite 332, 444 North Capitol Street, N.W., Washington, DC 20001)

**National Association of Counties:** membership organization; seeks to improve county government and represents the interests of counties at the national level; offers educational programs and technical assistance. *County News,* bimonthly. (440 First Street, N.W., Washington, DC 20001)

**National Association of Towns and Townships:** membership organization; offers technical assistance, educational assistance, and public policy support to local government officials. *NATaT's Reporter,* ten issues a year. (1522 K Street, N.W., Suite 730, Washington, DC 20005)

**National Audubon Society:** membership organization; carries out research; education and action programs to protect wildlife and natural areas; ten regional offices and over 500 chapters. *Audubon,* bimonthly magazine. (950 Third Avenue, New York, NY 10022)

**National Demonstration Water Project:** provides advice and technical assistance on water-supply and water-quality issues to rural organizations; particularly concerned with the water needs of the disadvantaged; assistance given through affiliate organizations located throughout the country. (1111 North 19th Street, Suite 400, Arlington, VA 22209)

**National Trust for Historic Preservation:** membership organization; encourages preservation of America's historical and cultural heritage; six regional offices provide services to local organizations; Main Street Center assists downtown revitalization programs; Rural Program promotes preservation in rural communities; offers publications and educational programs. *Historic Preservation,* bimonthly magazine; *Preservation News,* monthly newspaper; *Preservation Forum,* quarterly journal for professionals and nonprofit organizations. (1785 Massachusetts Avenue, N.W., Washington, DC 20036)

**National Wildlife Federation:** membership organization; conservation education programs, with a particular focus on wildlife; thirteen regional offices and chapters in every state. *National Wildlife,* monthly magazine; *Ranger Rick,* monthly magazine for children. (1412 16th Street, N.W., Washington, DC 20036)

**Natural Resources Defense Council:** membership organization; monitors federal agencies and disseminates information to citizens; litigates and works to influence public policy; areas of concentration include air and water pollution, hazardous waste, coastal zones, and public land; publishes books and studies. *The Amicus Journal,* quarterly; *Newsline,* bimonthly newsletter. (122 East 42nd Street, New York, NY 10168)

**Natural Science for Youth Foundation:** membership organization; promotes environmental education programs; encourages establishment of nature centers; provides consulting services. *Natural Science Center News,* quar-

terly. (11 Wildwood Valley, Atlanta, GA 30338)

**The Nature Conservancy:** membership organization; encourages the preservation of natural diversity through the acquisition and protection of land that supports rare ecosystems and endangered species; has chapters in most states. *The Nature Conservancy News,* bimonthly magazine. (1815 North Lynn, Arlington, VA 22209)

**Partners for Livable Places:** membership organization; committed to improving communities' economic health and quality of life; library and clearinghouse of information on built and natural environment open to public; offers technical assistance to communities for a fee. *Place,* bimonthly magazine. (1429 21st Street, N.W., Washington, DC 20036)

**Population-Environment Balance:** membership organization advocating a stabilized population, strong economy, and healthy environment; provides information and technical assistance to communities wishing to manage growth; issues publications on growth management. *Balance Report,* bimonthly newsletter. (1325 G Street, N.W., Suite 1003, Washington, DC 20005)

**Rails-to-Trails Conservancy:** membership organization; devoted to converting abandoned railroad rights-of-way into trails for public use; advises on conversion process; assists in corridor acquisition. *Trailblazer,* quarterly newsletter. (1400 16th Street, N.W., 3rd floor, Washington, DC 20036)

**The Regeneration Project:** membership organization; encourages individual and community responsibility for community improvement; offers consulting, workshops, publications, and contacts through a computerized network. *Regeneration,* bimonthly. (Rodale Press, 33 E. Minor Street, Emmaus, PA 18098)

**Rural America:** membership organization; concerned with rural issues, particularly transportation, housing, and the needs of low-income and minority groups. *Community Transportation Reporter,* ten issues a year. (725 15th Street, N.W., Suite 900, Washington, DC 20005)

**Rural Coalition:** coalition of local and national member organizations; clearinghouse of information; forms task forces on rural issues; does research on federal legislation and policy; advises community leaders. *Update,* quarterly newsletter. (2001 S Street, N.W., Suite 500, Washington, DC 20009)

**Sierra Club:** membership organization; concerned with a broad array of environmental issues; educates on conservation; works on legislation and litigation; 57 chapters active in local conservation issues. *Sierra,* bimonthly magazine. (730 Polk Street, San Francisco, CA 94109)

**Society for American Archaeology:** membership organization; promotes interest and research in the archeology of the American continents; discourages commercialism in the archeological field; serves as a bond between those interested in the field. *American Antiquity,* quarterly journal; *Bulletin,* bimonthly. (808 17th Street, N.W., Suite 200, Washington, DC 20006)

**Society for Range Management:** membership organization; seeks to develop an understanding of range ecosystems and range-management principles; promotes public appreciation of range benefits; maintains roster of certified range managers. *Journal of Range Management,* bimonthly; *Rangelands,* bimonthly. (2760 West 5th Avenue, Denver, CO 80204)

**Society of American Foresters:** membership organization; seeks to advance the practice of professional forestry and enhance public appreciation of forest resources; maintains roster of consulting foresters. *Journal of Forestry,* monthly; *Forest Science,* quarterly. (5400 Grosvenor Lane, Bethesda, MD 20814)

**Soil and Water Conservation Society:** membership organization; concerned with wise use of land, soil, and water; educational programs. *Journal of Soil and Water Conservation,* bimonthly. (7515 N.E. Ankeny Road, Ankeny, IA 50021)

**The Trust for Public Land:** acquires and arranges for the preservation of open space to serve the needs of people; assists local land trusts through its headquarters and six regional and field offices. *TPL Update,* occasional newsletter. (116 New Montgomery Street, 4th floor, San Francisco, CA 94105)

**The Urban Land Institute:** membership organization; promotes improved land-development policy; conducts research and educational programs; publishes studies of use to planners, developers, and others involved in development. *Land Use Digest,* monthly; *Urban Land Magazine,* monthly. (1090 Vermont Avenue, N.W., Washington, DC 20005)

**The Wilderness Society:** membership organization; primary focus on wilderness, wildlife, and public lands; involved in public education, public policy, and litigation; eight field offices. *Wilderness,* quarterly magazine. (1400 Eye Street, N.W., Washington, DC 20005)

## II. FEDERAL AGENCIES

Most of the following agencies have regional offices and many have state offices. The National Wildlife Federation's *Conservation Directory* (Suggested Reading, Chapter 6) lists most of the addresses. Many have local or county offices as well, listed in the U.S. Government pages in the telephone directory. Offices closer to home may be more responsive than headquarters.

**Advisory Council on Historic Preservation:** reviews the impact of proposed federal undertakings on properties listed or eligible for listing in the National Register of Historic Places. (1100 Pennsylvania Avenue, N.W., Washington, DC 20004)

**American Folklife Center, Library of Congress:** assists local governments, nonprofit organizations, and individuals in preserving and presenting American folklife; includes recorded and manuscript collections in the Archive of Folk Culture. *Folklife Center News,* quarterly. (Washington, DC 20540)

**Army Corps of Engineers:** undertakes water projects. (20 Massachusetts Avenue, N.W., Washington, DC 20314)

**Council on Environmental Quality:** advises the President on environmental matters; oversees the implementation of the National Environmental Policy Act; prepares an annual report on the state of the environment. (722 Jackson Place, N.W., Washington, DC 20006)

**Department of Agriculture:** contains Agricultural Stabilization and Conservation Service, Cooperative Extension Service, Farmers Home Administration, Forest Service, and Soil Conservation Service. (14th Street and Jefferson Drive, S.W., Washington, DC 20250)

**Department of the Interior:** contains Bureau of Land Management, Bureau of Reclamation, Fish and Wildlife Service, Geological Survey, National Park Service, and Office of Surface Mining. (18th and C Streets, N.W., Washington, DC 20240)

**Department of Transportation:** contains Federal Highway Administration and Urban Mass Transportation Administration. (400 7th Street, S.W., Washington, DC 20590)

**Environmental Protection Agency:** undertakes federal environmental protection efforts, researches environmental problems, and administers governmental regulation programs; has ten regional offices. (401 M Street, S.W., Washington, DC 20460)

**Federal Emergency Management Agency:** administers the National Flood Insurance Program. (500 C Street, S.W., Washington, DC 20472)

**Federal Energy Regulatory Commission:** issues permits for hydroelectric projects. (825 North Capitol Street, N.E., Washington, DC 20426)

**Government Printing Office:** issues most federal publications; makes subject bibliographies available on request. (Washington, DC 20402)

**National Endowment for the Arts:** through its Design Arts Program, awards grants to individuals, nonprofit organizations, and local governments for projects that promote excellence in architecture, landscape architecture, and community design; through its Folk Arts Program, awards grants for documenting folklife traditions. (1100 Pennsylvania Avenue, N.W., Washington, DC 20506)

**National Oceanic and Atmospheric Administration, Department of Commerce:** administers Coastal Zone Management Act of 1972. (Rockville, MD 20852)

**Office of Community Service, Department of Health and Human Services.** (330 C Street, S.W., Washington, DC 20201)

**Tennessee Valley Authority:** undertakes water projects and assists conservation efforts in Tennessee River watershed. (400 West Summit Hill Drive, Knoxville, TN 37902)

# Suggested Reading

There are numerous publications on the topics discussed in this book. We have chosen to list here those that are of greatest interest to conservation leaders working at the local level.

Several publishers—the American Planning Association, the Conservation Foundation, the Johns Hopkins University Press, and Island Press, for instance—publish works of interest to conservationists. We suggest you write to them for a current listing.

Publications published by nonprofit organizations and government agencies may be ordered from those organizations. Their addresses will be found either as part of the entry or in the Appendix.

## CHAPTER 1: RURAL CONCERNS

American Farmland Trust. 1984. *Soil Conservation in America: What Do We Have to Lose?* Washington, D.C.: AFT. 133 pp.

An overview of soil conservation problems and programs for dealing with those problems. An additional technical volume, which is a compendium of background papers commissioned for the primary report, amplifies on local government, conservation district, and other programs.

———. 1986. *Density-Related Public Costs.* Washington, D.C.: AFT. 44 pp.

Sets forth a methodology for an analysis of the fiscal impacts of growth on local government revenues and costs, using Loudoun County, Virginia, as a model.

American Society of Planning Officials. 1976. *Subdividing Rural America: Impacts of Recreational Lot and Second Home Development.* Washington, D.C.: U.S. Government Printing Office. 139 pp.

Provides a national overview of the problem of recreational land development, including discussions of its environmental, economic, and social impacts and a chapter on regulating it through local, state, and federal action.

Catskill Center for Conservation and Development. 1978. *Freshwater Wetlands: A Citizens' Primer.* Arkville, N.Y.: CCCD. 26 pp. (Arkville, NY 12406)

Clark, Edwin H., II; Jennifer A. Haverkamp; and William Chapman. 1985. *Eroding Soils: The Off-Farm Impacts.* Washington, D.C.: Conservation Foundation. 400 pp.

Examines the biological and economic impacts of sediments and pollution on water quality, wildlife, and recreation. Reviews techniques for controlling erosion and government policy options.

Concern, Inc. 1986. *Drinking Water: A Community Action Guide*. Washington, D.C.: Concern, Inc. 31 pp. (1794 Columbia Road, N.W., Washington, DC 20009)

Describes water-quality issues, laws, and resources.

Conservation Foundation. 1982. *State of the Environment 1982*. Washington, D.C.: CF. 464 pp.

Reviews national trends and federal legislation concerning air quality, water resources, hazardous wastes, energy, agriculture, forestry, and land use.

———. 1984. *State of the Environment: An Assessment at Mid-Decade*. Washington, D.C.: CF. 586 pp.

Topics include toxic substances, air and water pollution, croplands, forestland, rangeland, critical natural areas, risk assessment, and risk control.

———. 1987. *State of the Environment: A View toward the Nineties*. Washington, D.C.: CF. 614 pp.

Focuses on agriculture and the environment, wildlife protection, and hazardous wastes. Five-page state-by-state environmental data summaries also available.

Conservation Foundation, Chemical Manufacturers Association, and National Audubon Society. 1983. *Siting Hazardous Waste Management Facilities: A Handbook*. Washington, D.C.: CF. 71 pp. (Order from NAS)

Discusses environmental, health, economic, and technological considerations. Summarizes federal, state, and local regulations. Describes how community leaders can become involved in the process.

Council on Environmental Quality. *Environmental Quality*. Washington, D.C.: CEQ, annual edition.

Assesses the state of the environment and summarizes recent federal environmental legislation and regulations. Highlights different topics each year.

Deetz, James. 1967. *Invitation to Archaeology*. Garden City, N.Y.: Natural History Press. 150 pp.

A brief and readable introduction to present-day archeology, explaining the field in broad terms—dating, analysis of form, space, and time, context, function, structure, and behavior—as well as its place among the social sciences.

Diamant, Rolf; J. Glenn Eugster; and Christopher J. Duerksen. 1984. *A Citizen's Guide to River Conservation*. Washington, D.C.: Conservation Foundation. 113 pp.

Dunne, Thomas, and Luna B. Leopold. 1978. *Water in Environmental Planning*. New York: W. H. Freeman and Company. 818 pp.

A comprehensive text on water supply and water quality. Covers both groundwater and surface water. Describes typical problems and solutions and contains helpful diagrams and tables.

Environmental Law Institute. *National Wetlands Newsletter*. Washington, D.C. Bimonthly.

Discusses wetland issues; describes federal, state, and local legislation; summarizes litigation; and reviews publications on wetlands.

Gordon, Wendy. 1984. *A Citizen's Handbook on Groundwater Protection*. New York: Natural Resources Defense Council. 208 pp.

Discusses groundwater pollution issues and techniques citizens can use to protect water resources. Contains helpful summaries of legislation.

Healy, Robert G. 1985. *Competition for Land in the American South: Agriculture, Human Settlement, and the Environment*. Washington, D.C.: Conservation Foundation. 333 pp.

A holistic examination of current land use, conservation issues, and the outlook for the future.

Housing Assistance Council. 1984. *Taking Stock: Rural People and Poverty from 1970 to 1983*. Washington, D.C.: HAC. 120 pp.

Describes trends for poverty, housing, public assistance, and employment. Includes census data and case studies for selected communities.

Jackson, John Brinckerhoff. 1984. *Discovering the Vernacular Landscape*. New Haven, Conn.: Yale University Press. 165 pp.

A provocative series of essays by the founder of *Landscape* magazine that explore various aspects of the everyday landscape in America, from mobile homes, to parks, to country towns. In this and other collections, Jackson attempts to foster an understanding and appreciation of the more commonplace aspects of the landscape that surrounds us.

Legator, Marvin S.; Barbara L. Harper; and Michael J. Scott, eds. 1985. *The Health Detective's Handbook: A Guide to the Investigation of Environmental Health Hazards by Nonprofessionals*. Baltimore: Johns Hopkins University Press. 256 pp.

Provides background information on toxic chemicals in the environment, advises on community organizing to deal with pollution problems, describes how to determine the extent of the problems, and suggests how to obtain help from government agencies.

MacFadyen, J. Tevere. 1984. *Gaining Ground: The Renewal of America's Small Farms*. New York: Holt, Rinehart, and Winston. 242 pp.

A look by a journalist at the problems facing farmers and the solutions to those problems. Examines creative, locally based efforts to respond to farmers' financial problems.

Maddex, Diane, ed. 1985. *All about Old Buildings: The Whole Preservation Catalog.* Washington, D.C.: National Trust for Historic Preservation. 433 pp.

A comprehensive and heavily illustrated sourcebook on historic preservation and architectural history. Contains lists of organizations, numerous quotations, extensive bibliographies, and definitions.

Meinig, D. W., ed. 1979. *The Interpretation of Ordinary Landscapes: Geographical Essays.* New York: Oxford University Press. 255 pp.

Nine provocative essays on exploring the American landscape by several of the foremost researchers of human geography and landscape history.

National Audubon Society. 1987. *Audubon Wildlife Report 1987.* Orlando, Fla.: Academic Press, Inc. 697 pp.

Describes the status of certain endangered species and gives information on federal and state programs to protect wildlife. Each annual edition features different species and agencies.

National Trust for Historic Preservation. Information Series. Washington, D.C.: NTHP.

The following titles in this series are of particular interest: *Rehabilitating Old Houses* (no. 9); *Basic Preservation Procedures* (no. 20); *Archeology and Preservation* (no. 28); *Preserving Large Estates* (no. 34); and *Saving Historic Bridges* (no. 36).

National Wildlife Federation and Environmental Action Foundation. 1977. *The End of the Road: A Citizen's Guide to Transportation Problemsolving.* Washington, D.C.: NWF and EAF. 159 pp.

Summarizes highway issues and legislation for community groups organizing over highway issues. Many of the strategies discussed apply to other environmental concerns as well. Covers such topics as tracking a project, organizing, and going to court.

President's Commission on Americans Outdoors. 1987. *Americans Outdoors.* Washington, D.C.: Island Press. 426 pp.

Describes how Americans use the outdoors, the facilities available, and the advantages of outdoor recreation. Delineates the need for local initiative, state and federal legislation, and new funding. Calls for increased protection of natural and scenic areas.

Rosenow, John E., and Gerreld L. Pulsipher. 1979. *Tourism: The Good, the Bad, and the Ugly.* Lincoln, Neb.: Century Three Press. 264 pp.

The problems posed by tourism and some of the solutions.

Sampson, R. Neil. 1981. *Farmland or Wasteland: A Time to Choose: Overcoming the Threat to America's Farm and Food Future.* Emmaus, Pa.: Rodale Press. 422 pp.

Covers the issues of farmland loss and soil erosion.

Small Town Institute. *Small Town.* Ellensburg, Wash. Bimonthly. (P.O. Box 517, Ellensburg, WA 98926)

Covers a wide range of topics of interest to rural leaders "concerned with finding new solutions to the problems facing small towns and countryside communities."

Smardon, Richard C.; James F. Palmer; and John P. Felleman, eds. 1986. *Foundations for Visual Project Analysis.* New York: John Wiley & Sons. 374 pp.

Traces history of landscape appreciation, describes the techniques for analyzing the landscape, discusses methodologies for assessing the scenic impact of new developments, and reviews laws governing scenery protection.

Stipe, Robert E., and Antoinette J. Lee, eds. 1987. *The American Mosaic: Preserving a Nation's Heritage.* Washington, D.C.: US/ICOMOS. 292 pp. (1600 H Street, N.W., Washington, DC 20006)

An excellent primer on historic preservation in the United States. Essays cover who does what at the national, state, and local levels, and "what we preserve and why."

U.S. Department of Agriculture, Forest Service. 1981. *An Assessment of the Forest and Range Land Situation in the United States.* Washington, D.C.: U.S. Government Printing Office. 352 pp.

Provides extensive information on forest, range, wildlife, fish, and water resources, both on and off federal lands.

Weber, Bruce A., and Robert E. Howell, eds. 1982. *Coping with Rapid Growth in Rural Communities.* Boulder, Colo.: Westview Press. 315 pp.

A collection of essays on growth issues in the West. Topics include demography, the impacts of rapid growth, local government options, and impact assessment.

## CHAPTER 2: INITIATING AND MANAGING A RURAL CONSERVATION PROGRAM

American Association of University Women. 1981. *AAUW Community Action Tool Catalog: Techniques and Strategies for Successful Action Programs.* Washington, D.C.: AAUW. 224 pp. (2401 Virginia Ave., N.W., Washington, DC 20037)

Provides suggestions for planning and organizing community projects. Subjects range from membership recruitment to organizing public hearings and lobbying.

Bidol, Patricia; Lisa Bardwell; and Nancy Manring, eds. 1986. *Alternative Environmental Conflict Management*

*Approaches: A Citizens' Manual.* Ann Arbor, Mich.: Environmental Conflict Project, School of Natural Resources, University of Michigan. 251 pp. (Dana Building, 430 E. University, Ann Arbor, MI 48109)

Goes beyond describing methods for dispute resolution to discuss stylistic approaches to problem-solving and teamwork that make citizens' groups more effective. Includes many worksheets and exercises.

Bingham, Gail. 1986. *Resolving Environmental Disputes: A Decade of Experience.* Washington, D.C.: Conservation Foundation. 284 pp.

Describes the first ten years of experience in the resolution of environmental disputes, analyzing factors that may affect the likelihood of success. Draws on research from 160 cases from around the nation.

Breiteneicher, Joe. 1983. *Quest for Funds: Insider's Guide to Corporate and Foundation Funding.* Special issue of *Conserve Neighborhoods,* no. 29 (March–April). Washington, D.C.: National Trust for Historic Preservation. 20 pp.

A brief, lively primer on fundraising. The "insider" is the author, who is a corporate foundation official. (Although this newsletter is no longer published, back issues can be ordered.)

Connecticut Trust for Historic Preservation. 1982. *Organizing for Historic Preservation: A Resource Guide.* New Haven, Conn.: CTHP. 48 pp. (152 Temple Street, New Haven, CT 06510)

An excellent summary of steps for organizing; especially helpful is the first chapter, on getting started, including assessing local needs, defining priorities, developing programs, and going public. Also includes sections on legal and administrative considerations for incorporation; how to design a community preservation program; and fundraising.

Firstenberg, Paul B. 1986. *Managing for Profit in the Nonprofit World.* New York: Foundation Center. 253 pp.

Proposes specific strategies to improve a nonprofit organization's financial condition through new approaches to traditional funding sources; creating income-producing programs; and maximizing returns on endowments.

Fisher, Roger, and William Ury. 1981. *Getting to Yes: Negotiating Agreement without Giving In.* Boston: Houghton Mifflin Co. 163 pp.

Discusses a method of "principled negotiation" which includes focusing on interests rather than positions and inventing options for mutual gain. Pointing a different direction from the classic "hard bargaining" familiar to realtors and attorneys, this handbook is highly recommended as companion reading to any other publications on dispute resolution.

Flanagan, Joan. 1981. *The Successful Volunteer Organization: Getting Started and Getting Results in Nonprofit, Charitable, Grass Roots, and Community Groups.* Chicago: Contemporary Books, Inc. 376 pp.

Covers the myriad details of "getting organized" in an enthusiastic, encouraging style. Highly recommended.

————. 1982. *The Grass Roots Fundraising Book: How to Raise Money in Your Community.* Chicago: Contemporary Books, Inc. 320 pp.

Filled with ideas about benefit events both small and large, plus tips on planning a fund-raising calendar and fund-raising through corporations, deferred giving, and direct mail. Includes many titles of helpful publications and sources of advice and training. Does not include discussion of raising funds from foundations and government agencies.

Gil, Efraim; Enid Lucchesi; Gilbert Tauber; and Dudley Onderdonk. 1983. *Working with Consultants.* Chicago: American Planning Association. 33 pp.

Describes how to recruit, evaluate, and contract for consulting services and how to manage a consulting project. Although written from the point of view of a public agency, it is also useful for nonprofit organizations.

Grantsmanship Center. N.d. *The Grantsmanship Book.* Los Angeles: GC. Looseleaf binder. Unpaged. (P.O. Box 6210, Los Angeles, CA 90014)

A good investment for a nonprofit organization's library. Includes articles on proposal writing, fund-raising, program evaluation, accounting, personnel management, public relations, profit-making activities, and annual reports. Reprints are also available individually and packaged by subject. The Grantsmanship Center also offers workshops on fund-raising and managing nonprofit organizations.

*Grassroots Fundraising Journal.* Knoxville, Tenn. Bimonthly. (517 Union Avenue, Suite 206, Knoxville, TN 37902)

Written specifically for small nonprofit organizations, this publication contains how-to articles on raising money from sources other than foundations and government. Articles cover such subjects as building membership, asking individuals for money, attracting large gifts, and using direct mail.

Harper, Stephen F. 1984. *The Nonprofit Primer: A Guidebook for Land Trusts.* Oakland, Calif.: California State Coastal Conservancy. Unpaged. (1330 Broadway, Suite 1100, Oakland, CA 94612)

A thorough introduction to basic legal and management considerations and fund-raising for the beginning group, as well as resource-protection strategies, although specific in some instances to California procedures. Sample documents are included.

Kahn, Si. 1982. *Organizing: A Guide for Grassroots Leaders.* New York: McGraw-Hill. 387 pp.

Written for organizers by a well-known union organizer, this is a thoughtful and sympathetic book, filled with practical tips and encouragement.

National Trust for Historic Preservation. Information Series. Washington, D.C.: NTHP.

The following titles in this series are of particular interest: *Working with Local Government* (no. 13); *Legal Considerations in Establishing a Historic Preservation Organization* (no. 14); *Private Funds for Historic Preservation* (no. 22); *Using Professional Consultants in Preservation* (no. 26); *Investing in Volunteers: A Guide to Effective Volunteer Management* (no. 37); and *Building on Experience: Improving Organizational Capacity to Handle Development Projects* (no. 39).

O'Connell, Brian. 1985. *The Board Member's Book: Making a Difference in Voluntary Organizations.* New York: Foundation Center. 208 pp.

An invaluable handbook useful not only to the board members of nonprofit organizations but also to anyone involved in managing or organizing a cooperative effort, governmental as well as nonprofit. Discussions of the qualities of leaders, strategic planning, working with committees, fund-raising, budgeting, and evaluation demystify these concerns in a warm, no-nonsense style. Includes an extensive list of references.

People for Open Space. 1986. *Using Initiatives and Referenda to Protect Open Space: A Survey and Analysis of Northern California's Experience.* San Francisco: POS. 66 pp. plus appendices. (512 Second Street, 4th floor, San Francisco, CA 94107)

Although some information is specific to California state law, case studies plus guidelines for determining objectives, drafting ordinances, and winning campaigns offer ideas for activists everywhere.

Raiffa, Howard. 1982. *The Art and Science of Negotiation: How to Resolve Conflicts and Get the Best Out of Bargaining.* Cambridge, Mass.: Belknap Press, Harvard University Press. 373 pp.

An advanced book on negotiation, recommended for those organizations who rate dispute resolution among their top priorities for program development.

Schautz, Jane W. N.d. *The Self-Help Handbook.* Rensselaerville, N.Y.: Rensselaerville Institute. 199 pp. (Rensselaerville, NY 12147)

For underfunded rural communities that need to improve or create water or wastewater systems, this book is must reading; for others, it can provide new insight into managing volunteers and approaching community projects creatively.

Susskind, Lawrence, and Jeffrey Cruikshank. 1987. *Breaking the Impasse: Consensual Approaches to Resolving Public Disputes.* New York: Basic Books. 276 pp.

Discusses both unassisted negotiation and mediation in an appealing how-to-do-it style; highly recommended for both those new to the subject and those with experience.

## CHAPTER 3: ANALYZING THE RURAL COMMUNITY

American Folklife Center. 1979. *Folklife and Fieldwork: A Layman's Introduction to Field Techniques.* Washington, D.C.: AFC. 24 pp.

Ashcroft, Mary. 1979. *Designating Scenic Roads: A Vermont Field Guide.* Montpelier, Vt.: State Planning Office. 30 pp. (Montpelier, VT 05602)

Designed to assist citizens and officials interested in protecting scenic roads and in selecting and designating the best roads.

Beatty, Marvin T.; Gary W. Petersen; and Lester D. Swindale, eds. 1979. *Planning the Uses and Management of Land.* Madison, Wis.: American Society of Agronomy. 1,028 pp. (677 South Segoe Road, Madison, WI 53711)

How to conduct resource planning, using soil surveys and other resource data.

Berger, Jonathan, and John W. Sinton. 1985. *Water, Earth, and Fire: Land Use and Environmental Planning in the New Jersey Pine Barrens.* Baltimore: Johns Hopkins University Press. 228 pp.

Declaring that "plans, to be effective, must reflect the interactions between people and their environments," the authors set out to explore "the links between people, their resources, and their use of the land" (p. xviii). A tale of empathizing with and analyzing a place and its people, with recommendations for designating "policy regions" based on the analysis. A thoughtful and important case study illustrating "human ecology" and its integration with environmental information.

Buchanan, Terry. 1983. *Photographing Historic Buildings.* London: Her Majesty's Stationery Office. 108 pp. (Order from PRG, 5619 Southampton Drive, Springfield, VA 22151.)

Covers the techniques for both exterior and interior photographs.

Clark, John. 1976. *The Sanibel Report: Formulation of a Comprehensive Plan Based on Natural Systems.* Washington, D.C.: Conservation Foundation. 305 pp.

A case study from Sanibel Island, Florida, showing how the "carrying capacity" of a natural system (i.e., its ability to support development) can be determined and then used in formulating a comprehensive land-use plan (included in abridged form).

Deetz, James. 1967. *Invitation to Archaeology.* (See entry for Chapter 1.)

Eastman Kodak Company. 1987. *Kodak Index to Photographic Information.* Rochester, N.Y.: EKC. 27 pp. (Rochester, NY 14650)

Kodak publishes useful books and pamphlets on many aspects of photography. This free index lists several on landscape photography.

Fraser, Elisabeth A., and Anne F. Morris. 1980. *Getting It All Together: The Application of Environmental Information to Land-Use Planning.* Mendham, N.J.: Association of New Jersey Environmental Commissions. 323 pp. (Box 157, Mendham, NJ 07945)

The environmental resource inventory is described in lay terms for use by community groups in carrying out studies of their environmental resources.

Lynch, Kevin. 1960. *The Image of the City.* Cambridge, Mass.: MIT Press. 194 pp.

This pioneering work in landscape architecture and urban studies is of interest to rural conservation leaders as well. Lynch explores what the city means to the people who live there and what planners can do to make the city's image more vivid and memorable. The same principles can be applied to rural communities. Includes appendices that are useful for visual inventories.

Marsh, William M. 1978. *Environmental Analysis: For Land Use and Site Planning.* New York: McGraw-Hill Book Company. 292 pp.

An excellent description of the techniques for inventorying and mapping natural resources. Specific information on slope, soils, drainage, vegetation, and flood plains.

McAlester, Virginia, and Lee McAlester. 1984. *A Field Guide to American Houses.* New York: Knopf. 542 pp.

A comprehensive handbook on architectural styles. There are numerous regional and state guides as well. The state historic preservation office (6.IX.B) can advise which ones are best.

McClelland, Linda F.; J. Timothy Keller; Genevieve P. Keller; and Robert Z. Melnick. Forthcoming. *Guidelines for Identifying, Evaluating, and Registering Rural Historic Landscapes.* National Register Bulletin no. 30. Washington, D.C.: U.S. Department of the Interior, National Park Service.

McHarg, Ian L. 1969. *Design with Nature.* Garden City, N.Y.: Doubleday. 198 pp.

A pioneering work of essays and case studies that stresses the need for environmental design in harmony with the natural conditions of an area. Explains en-

vironmental inventories and the use of maps to analyze the suitability of land for development.

Smardon, Richard C.; James F. Palmer; and John P. Felleman, eds. 1986. *Foundations for Visual Project Analysis.* (See entry for Chapter 1.)

Steiner, Frederick. 1981. *Ecological Planning for Farmlands Preservation.* Chicago: American Planning Association. 122 pp.

A comprehensive guidebook to help communities determine what agricultural land to preserve. Details how to analyze natural resources and existing land uses. Summarizes farmland preservation techniques used at the federal, state, and local levels and describes five local preservation programs.

Sullivan, George, ed. 1981. *Discover Archaeology: An Introduction to the Tools and Techniques of Archaeological Fieldwork.* New York: Penguin. 288 pp.

Includes a chapter on historical archeology with lengthy listings of sources of information.

Town of Cazenovia, N.Y. 1984. *Land Use Guide: A Report of the Cazenovia Community Resources Project.* Cazenovia, N.Y.: Town of Cazenovia. 87 pp. (7 Albany St., Cazenovia, NY 13035)

Good example of one rural community's analysis of its resources and recommendations for their protection.

U.S. Department of the Interior, National Park Service. 1985. *Guidelines for Local Surveys: A Basis for Preservation Planning.* National Register Bulletin no. 24. Washington, D.C.: USDI. 112 pp.

Warren, Roland L. 1965. *Studying Your Community.* New York: Free Press. 385 pp.

Suggests the questions one should ask in gathering information about one's community.

## CHAPTER 4: LAND-PROTECTION TECHNIQUES

The American Planning Association is an excellent source of a wide variety of printed materials, from its magazine *Planning* to its Planning Advisory Service (see below) to its publications. Often written for professional and urban audiences, and too numerous to list, APA's publications are nonetheless valuable references.

American Farmland Trust. 1986. *Density-Related Public Costs.* (See entry for Chapter 1.)

———. 1987. *Planning and Zoning for Farmland Protection: A Community Based Approach.* Washington, D.C.: AFT. 58 pp.

Although based on research performed in Michigan, this booklet is applicable across the nation. Briefly covers the "why" of saving farms and farmlands, simple planning principles, and comparisons of agricultural zoning techniques, including sample regulations. Includes a "community profile worksheet" and a step-by-step summary for getting started.

———. 1984. *Soil Conservation in America: What Do We Have to Lose?* (See entry for Chapter 1.)

American Planning Association. Planning Advisory Service Reports. Chicago: APA.

Many titles in this series are of interest, including *The Administration of Flexible Zoning Techniques* (no. 318); *Appearance Codes for Small Communities* (no. 379); *The Cluster Subdivision: A Cost-Effective Approach* (no. 356); *Mechanics of Sign Control* (no. 354); *Performance Controls for Sensitive Lands: A Practical Guide for Local Administrators* (nos. 307 and 308); *Preparing a Historic Preservation Ordinance* (no. 374); *Regulating Mobile Homes* (no. 360); *State and Local Regulations for Reducing Agricultural Erosion* (no. 386); and *Working with Consultants* (no. 378).

———. *Small Town and Rural Planning.* Manhattan, Kans.: Division of Small Town and Rural Planning, American Planning Association, quarterly. (Department of Regional and Community Planning, Kansas State University, Manhattan, KS 66506)

Covers the activities, interests, and policies of a spunky segment of the American Planning Association membership that demanded its own working group.

Brower, David J.; Candace Carraway; Thomas Pollard; and C. Luther Propst. 1984. *Managing Development in Small Towns.* Chicago: American Planning Association. 176 pp.

This excellent small handbook is a land-use regulation encyclopedia, discussing 36 planning tools and how each can be adapted to manage growth in rural areas.

Carlson, Christine, and Steven Durrant. 1985. *The Farm Landscape of Whatcom County: Managing Change through Design.* Seattle: University of Washington. 38 pp. (Department of Landscape Architecture, JO-34, University of Washington, Seattle, WA 98195)

Extensively illustrated with photographs, this brief set of design guidelines for dairy farms is one result of a visual resources project conducted by a local group with assistance from the University of Washington and many others. The first of its kind, it recognizes the economic realities of prefabricated agricultural structures from loafing sheds to silos.

Clark, John. 1976. *The Sanibel Report: Formulation of a Comprehensive Plan Based on Natural Systems.* (See entry for Chapter 3.)

Coughlin, Robert E., and John C. Keene, eds. 1981. *The Protection of Farmland: A Reference Guidebook for State and Local Governments.* Washington, D.C.: U.S. Government Printing Office. 284 pp.

This report of the federal government's National Agricultural Lands Study reviews land-use controls appropriate for agricultural preservation and makes a number of useful recommendations for effective action. Companion volumes give case studies.

Curry, William J., III, and Cyril A. Fox, Jr. 1978. *A Role for Local Governments in Controlling Strip Mining Activities.* Pittsburgh: Western Pennsylvania Conservancy. 53 pp. (316 Fourth Avenue, Pittsburgh, PA 15222)

Covers regulation of surface mining by zoning and performance controls and control of road use and blasting. Includes model ordinance provisions.

Doherty, J. C. 1984, 1985. *Growth Management in Countryfied Cities.* Vol. 1, *Change and Response;* Vol. 2, *Six Perspectives.* Alexandria, Va.: Vert Milon Press. 102 pp. and 158 pp. (Box 332, Alexandria, VA 22313)

Readable, instructive companion volumes on the problems of rural areas experiencing growth management problems. Volume 1 reviews rural growth management in general. Volume 2 gives case studies for planning efforts in six rural communities.

Duerksen, Christopher J., ed. 1983. *A Handbook on Historic Preservation Law.* Washington, D.C.: Conservation Foundation and National Center for Preservation Law. 523 pp. plus appendices. (Order from Conservation Foundation.)

Provides a complete history of preservation law and prescribes the elements of a comprehensive local preservation program, including how to draft and administer an ordinance. Also covers state and federal law, including general constitutional questions related to development controls, and economic incentives for preservation. As preservation law is a "leading indicator" of the lengths to which communities may regulate development and design, this is an especially useful text for attorneys interested in land-use law.

———. 1986. *Aesthetics and Land-Use Controls: Beyond Ecology and Economics.* Chicago: American Planning Association. 45 pp.

An extremely valuable description, with clearly written legal analyses, of design review both within historic areas and outside them, protection of scenic roadways and vistas, preservation of trees on public and private property, and regulation of signs, billboards, satellite dishes, and communication antennas. Includes sample ordinances.

Getzels, Judith, and Charles Thurow, eds. N.d. *Rural and Small Town Planning.* Chicago: American Planning Association. 326 pp.

Although ostensibly for the professional planner, this excellent reference is also useful for local officials and citizens. Sections on zoning and development permit systems, subdivision regulations, and infrastructure planning cover concepts discussed in this chapter.

Godschalk, David R.; David J. Brower; Larry D. McBennett; Barbara A. Vestal; and Daniel C. Herr. 1979. *Constitutional Issues of Growth Management*. Chicago: American Planning Association. 476 pp.

Discusses and illustrates the general legal principles of due process, "taking," regional welfare, equal protection, and the right to travel. A good reference for those who need this level of detail.

Hendler, Bruce. 1977. *Caring for the Land: Environmental Principles for Site Design and Review*. Chicago: American Society of Planning Officials (now American Planning Association). 94 pp.

A discussion of principles for planning new construction and subdivisions, including consideration of visual impact. Extensively illustrated, this book is an extremely useful aid to reviewing development proposals.

Jackson, Gary W.; Leonard C. Johnson; and James L. Arts. 1981. *Controlling Runoff and Erosion from Land Development Projects: Some Institutional Tools*. Publication no. G3132. Madison, Wis.: University of Wisconsin—Extension. 38 pp. (Agricultural Bulletin Building, 1535 Observatory Drive, Madison, WI 53706)

Covers the different kinds of ordinances into which a community might incorporate erosion and sediment controls, with sample ordinances, and discusses key points for effective administration.

Kusler, Jon A. 1980. *Regulating Sensitive Lands*. Cambridge, Mass.: Ballinger Publishing Co. 248 pp.

Examines state and local policies for resource conservation, including methods of defining sensitive lands, performance standards, and regulatory programs aimed at such resources as wetlands and coastal areas.

Lang, J. Christopher. 1978. *Building with Nantucket in Mind: Guidelines for Protecting the Historic Architecture and Landscape of Nantucket Island*. Nantucket, Mass.: Nantucket Historic District Commission. 128 pp. (Town Building, Broad Street, Nantucket, MA 02554)

Extensively illustrated guidelines demonstrate a sensitivity to both scenic and architectural qualities of a historic landscape.

Mandelker, Daniel R., and William R. Ewald. 1988. *Street Graphics and the Law*. Chicago: American Planning Association. 207 pp.

Discusses the legal basis for the regulation of signs and how to design appropriate street signs for businesses. Includes an annotated model ordinance and extensive illustrations.

Marsh, Elizabeth Redfield. 1981. *Cooperative Rural Planning: A Tug Hill Case Study*. Watertown, N.Y.: Temporary State Commission on Tug Hill. 147 pp. (State Office Building, Watertown, NY 13601)

The story of the creation of a cooperative planning board by nine sparsely settled townships in the Tug Hill region of western New York, by a sympathetic observer. Among other ideas tailored to the needs of rural communities, this book details the use of a "circuit rider"— a professional or volunteer who provides technical assistance to multiple local governments by attending meetings, setting up training sessions, answering questions, and coordinating outside assistance.

National Trust for Historic Preservation. Information Series. Washington, D.C.: NTHP.

Several titles in this series are of interest, including *Working with Local Government* (no. 13) and *The Development of Rural Conservation Programs: A Case Study of Loudoun County, Va.* (no. 29).

Palmer, Arthur E. 1981. *Toward Eden*. Winterville, N.C.: Creative Resource Systems. 417 pp. (Winterville, NC 28590)

A detailed case history spanning ten years of planning in Medford, New Jersey, which was based on an environmental resources inventory and which resulted in a combined zoning-subdivision law. Includes numerous supporting documents.

Porter, Douglas R.; Patrick L. Phillips; and Terry J. Lassar. Forthcoming. *Flexible Zoning: How It Works*. Washington, D.C.: Urban Land Institute.

A study of how innovative zoning techniques have been implemented in seven communities. Includes recommendations for local governments that are considering implementing such techniques.

Sargent, Frederick O. 1976. *Rural Environmental Planning*. South Burlington, Vt.: Published by the author. 199 pp. (330 Spear Street, South Burlington, VT 05401)

Excellent handbook for rural planning commissions and citizens. Among topics covered are agricultural planning, protecting lake and river basins and other natural areas, and recreational planning, as well as planning for aesthetics and growth control. Chapters on public surveys, inventorying, and social and economic impacts of rural planning are especially useful.

Schiffman, Irving. 1983. *Alternative Techniques for Controlling Land Use: A Guide for Small Cities and Rural Areas in California*. Davis, Calif.: Institute of Governmental Affairs, University of California. 98 pp. (Davis, CA 95616)

Describes 21 land-use management techniques, listing potential benefits and limitations, interrelationships with other techniques, and references. Especially valuable for its short descriptions of how to streamline land-use review regulations, as well as for its discussions of capital-improvement programming, fiscal-impact analysis, and urban-area boundary designation.

Schretter, Howard A. 1977. *Zoning the Countryside: What's Wrong with It and an Alternative Approach*. Athens, Ga.: Institute of Community and Area Development, University of Georgia. 83 pp. (Athens, GA 30602)

Describes a simplified approach to rural zoning that combines conventional zoning in established or rapidly changing areas, performance-based regulation of unique natural or man-made conditions in special areas, and minimum development standards for all other areas.

Sikorowski, Linda, and Steven J. Bissell, eds. 1986. *County Government and Wildlife Management: A Guide to Cooperative Habitat Development*. State Publication Code DOW-R-M-1-86. Denver: Colorado Division of Wildlife. Unpaged. (6060 Broadway, Denver, CO 80216)

Although written for Colorado's District Wildlife Managers, anyone interested in wildlife habitat protection will find this hefty manual useful. Describes both state support and local ideas for habitat protection and includes 22 case histories.

Small Town Institute. *Small Town*. (See entry for Chapter 1.)

Smith, Herbert H. 1979. *The Citizen's Guide to Planning*. Chicago: American Planning Association. 198 pp.

Covers the duties of the planning commission, the comprehensive plan, planning through the capital budget, and community improvements, the relationship of planning to zoning, and citizen action.

———. 1983. *The Citizen's Guide to Zoning*. Chicago: American Planning Association. 242 pp.

A concise manual explaining the philosophy, constitutionality, and administration of zoning. Reviews the role of citizens, explains the variance procedure, and briefly examines emerging techniques.

Society of American Foresters, Working Group on Land-Use Planning and Design. 1982. "Land-Use Planning." *Journal of Forestry* 80 (September): 579–602. (A reprint of the eight land-use planning articles can be ordered from the society.)

Eight articles of this issue of the *Journal of Forestry* are devoted to helping foresters understand and participate in land-use planning. A useful resource for communities seeking to improve their forest planning, which the first article notes is "ignored or downplayed in most local planning efforts." Focuses on forests under multiple private ownership.

Solnit, Albert. 1987. *The Job of the Planning Commissioner*. Chicago: American Planning Association. 198 pp.

A readable introduction to planning and zoning intended for citizens serving on planning boards in California. Contains useful ideas for board members elsewhere on such subjects as board ethics, environmental considerations, and group dynamics.

Southern Environmental Law Center. 1987. *Visual Pollution and Sign Control: A Legal Handbook on Billboard Control*. Charlottesville, Va.: SELC. 36 pp. (Order from the Coalition for Scenic Beauty.)

A "how-to" manual for obtaining a strong local ordinance for sign control, including recommended provisions. Also discusses federal and state controls and issues in local and constitutional law.

Steadman, Stan, ed. *The Western Planner*. Soldotna, Alaska: Published by the author, bimonthly. (P.O. Box 3405, Soldotna, AK 99669)

An independently published newspaper with many articles of interest to a rural constituency. The editorial board also sponsors an annual meeting.

Steiner, Frederick. 1981. *Ecological Planning for Farmlands Preservation*. (See entry for Chapter 3.)

Steiner, Frederick R., and John E. Theilacker, eds. 1984. *Protecting Farmlands*. Westport, Conn.: AVI Publishing Co. 312 pp.

Provides an overview of farmlands protection, including public involvement and legal issues, and a discussion of local approaches, including three case studies.

Thomas, Ronald L., Mary C. Means, and Margaret A. Grieve. 1988. *Taking Charge: How Communities Are Planning Their Futures*. Washington, D.C.: International City Management Association. 85 pp. (ICMA, 1120 G Street, N.W., Washington, DC 20005)

Describes the common themes of successful planning efforts where the initiative has shifted from "professionally-dominated back rooms" (p. 7) to a communitywide process. Includes case studies.

Vranicar, John; Welford Sanders; and David Mosena. 1982. *Streamlining Land Use Regulation: A Guidebook for Local Governments*. Chicago: American Planning Association. 74 pp.

Discusses more than 35 techniques for simplifying the administration of ordinances to guide and control development.

Yaro, Robert D.; Randall G. Arendt; Harry L. Dodson; and Elizabeth A. Brabec. 1988. *Dealing with Change in the Connecticut River Valley: A Design Manual for Conservation and Development*. Amherst, Mass.: Center for Rural Massachusetts. 183 pp. (CRM, University of Massachusetts, Amherst, MA 01003)

Text and excellent graphics describe conventional and creative alternatives for development on eight rural properties (similar in approach to illustrations on p. 144–45). Contains case studies on protecting land and "town character" for two rural municipalities. Includes model language for ordinances on open space protection, sign control, and site plan review.

## CHAPTER 5: VOLUNTARY TECHNIQUES FOR PROTECTING PRIVATE PROPERTY

Adirondack Land Trust. 1987. *Developing a Land Conservation Strategy: A Handbook for Land Trusts.* Elizabethtown, N.Y.: ALT. 38 pp. (P.O. Box D-2, Elizabethtown, NY 12932)

A straightforward book about developing criteria for land conservation projects. In addition to providing a simple discussion of inventorying and mapping natural and scenic resources, it covers ways to narrow the focus through geographic and ownership considerations, critical resources, or themes such as corridors or valleys.

Barrett, Thomas, and Putnam Livermore. 1983. *The Conservation Easement in California.* Covelo, Calif.: Island Press. 173 pp.

Although specific to California, this is a sound reference for attorneys and professional land trust staff everywhere. Includes sections on drafting an easement and alternative techniques.

Brenneman, Russell L., and Sarah M. Bates, eds. 1984. *Land-Saving Action.* Covelo, Calif.: Island Press. 249 pp.

Contains 35 articles, covering the operations of conservation organizations (including useful discussions of criteria for acquisition and management); the technical details of certain aspects and kinds of conservation transactions; federal taxation; and concerns of individual property owners.

Diehl, Janet, and Thomas S. Barrett. 1988. *The Conservation Easement Handbook: Managing Land Conservation and Historic Preservation Easement Programs.* Alexandria, Va.: Land Trust Exchange and Trust for Public Land. (Order from LTE)

Gathers the best of theory and practice in conducting an easement program, including developing criteria, drafting an easement, gathering base-line data, monitoring observance of restrictions, and ensuring perpetuity. Includes model conservation and historic preservation easements.

Fisher, Roger, and William Ury. 1981. *Getting to Yes: Negotiating Agreement without Giving In.* (See entry for Chapter 2.)

Harper, Stephen F. 1984. *The Nonprofit Primer: A Guidebook for Land Trusts.* (See entry for Chapter 2.)

Historic Preservation Foundation of North Carolina and Young Lawyers Division of the North Carolina Bar Association. 1987. *Handbook on Revolving Funds for Nonprofit Historic Preservation Organizations.* Raleigh, N.C.: HPFNC and YLDNCBA. Unpaged. (Order from HPFNC, P.O. Box 27644, Raleigh, NC 27611)

Describes a revolving fund, including acquisition methods, leasing, rehabilitation, loan programs, incorporation, and the responsibilities of the organizers and staff. Also covers selecting and marketing properties, dealing with prospective buyers, fundraising, and easements. Includes sample documents.

Hoose, Phillip M. 1981. *Building an Ark: Tools for the Preservation of Natural Diversity through Land Protection.* Covelo, Calif.: Island Press. 221 pp.

Examines conservation techniques used to protect the habitats of rare or endangered plant or animal species. This basic reference discusses state natural heritage inventories, management agreements, leases, rights of first refusal, and environmental review, as well as easements and other methods.

Institute for Community Economics. 1982. *The Community Land Trust Handbook.* Emmaus, PA: Rodele Press. 230 pp. (Order from ICE, 151 Montague City Road, Greenfield, MA 01301)

Describes the community land trust model, including organizing, acquisition, financing and management, and case studies. Promotes cooperative ownership of land for farming or housing.

Johnson, Andrew L., and Michael G. Clarke. 1982. *A Handbook for the Landowner: The Use and Protection of Privately Held Natural Lands.* Philadelphia: Natural Lands Trust. 32 pp. (1616 Walnut Street, Suite 812, Philadelphia, PA 19103)

Contains a good discussion of the process of analyzing and creating a master plan for an individual property, complete with drawings (see illustrations, p. 202); includes several illustrations of limited development and many case studies of Natural Lands Trust transactions.

Land Trust Exchange. 1985. *For the Common Good: Preserving Private Lands with Conservation Easements.* Sixteen-minute color film; also available in video. Can be purchased or rented from the sponsor.

Designed to educate public officials about the public benefits of conservation easements, this entertaining movie is also popular with landowners and the public. Includes on-location case studies and interviews in Freeport, Maine, along the Blackfoot River, Montana, and beside the Chesapeake Bay.

———. 1985. *National Directory of Local and Regional Land Conservation Organizations.* Bar Harbor, Maine: LTE. 131 pp.

Lists more than 500 organizations by state and provides a profile of land trusts that summarizes the scope of their conservation activities.

Lemire, Robert A. 1986. *Creative Land Development: Bridge to the Future.* Lincoln, Mass.: Published by the author. 176 pp. (Order from Massachusetts Audubon Society, South Great Road, Lincoln, MA 01773)

Describes how natural-resource protection can be integrated with land development to build balanced communities. Case studies of limited development projects are included.

Meder-Montgomery, Marilyn. 1984. *Preservation Easements: A Legal Mechanism for Protecting Cultural Resources.* Denver: Colorado Historical Society. 165 pp. (Colorado Historical Society, Colorado State Museum, 1300 Broadway, Denver, CO 80203)

A thorough discussion of easement program concerns, preservation or otherwise, with appendices going well beyond the usual reproduction of legislation and easement documents to include, for example, reproductions of an easement inspection report form and an analysis of long-term inspection costs. Especially nice is a blow-by-blow case study of program considerations for the Colorado Historical Foundation.

Montana Land Reliance and Land Trust Exchange. 1982. *Private Options: Tools and Concepts for Land Conservation.* Covelo, Calif.: Island Press. 292 pp.

Includes more than 80 papers covering such topics as marketing land preservation, management implications of land stewardship, tax incentives, traditions of private land protection in various parts of the nation, and limited development.

National Trust for Historic Preservation. Information Series. Washington, D.C.: NTHP.

The following titles in this series will be of particular interest: *Establishing an Easement Program to Protect Historic, Scenic and Natural Resources* (no. 25); *The Development of Rural Conservation Programs: A Case Study of Loudoun County, Va.* (no. 29); and *Routes of History: Recreational Use and Preservation of Historic Transportation Corridors* (no. 38).

National Trust for Historic Preservation and Land Trust Exchange. 1984. *Appraising Easements: Guidelines for the Valuation of Historic Preservation and Land Conservation Easements.* Washington, D.C.: NTHP. 68 pp.

Written by experts knowledgeable about both easements and appraisal to provide basic guidance on appraisal procedures for organizations, appraisers, and advisors to property owners.

Small, Stephen J. 1986. *The Federal Tax Law of Conservation Easements.* Bar Harbor, Maine: Land Trust Exchange. Unpaged.

The definitive guide for attorneys, including an invaluable interpretation of the Internal Revenue Service's regulations governing gifts of conservation easements and copies of all relevant documents.

———. 1988. *Preserving Family Lands: A Landowner's Introduction to Tax Issues and Other Considerations.* Boston, MA: Published by the author. 47 pp. (Powers & Hall Professional Corporation, 100 Franklin Street, Boston, MA 02110)

An easy-to-read handbook about land-saving options; an excellent generic text for attorneys and land trust members new to the process as well as property owners.

Snyderman, Lois; Samuel N. Stokes; and A. Elizabeth Watson. 1988. *Virginia's Heritage: A Property Owner's Guide to Resource Protection.* Richmond, Va.: Department of Conservation and Historic Resources. (221 Governor Street, Richmond, VA 23219)

One of several "landowners' options" books written for various states, this one includes an extensive discussion of the state's resources and threats plus examples of transactions completed in the state.

U.S. Department of the Interior, National Park Service. 1986. "Easements." Chapter 8 of *Planning Process Guideline.* National Park Service Document NPS-2. Washington, D.C.: USDI. 64 pp.

Covers in detail the many issues in drafting an easement, including a list of questions to be asked of the landowner to help prevent future management problems. Also covers developing an administrative plan for an easement property and analyzing the cost-effectiveness of easement acquisition versus outright ownership. Highly useful for any easement program.

Ward, Wesley T., ed. 1987. *Land Conservation Methods and Their Tax Advantages: A Guide for Massachusetts Landowners.* Essex, Mass.: Essex County Greenbelt Association and Trustees of Reservations. 40 pp. (ECGA, 82 Eastern Avenue, Essex, MA 01929)

A thorough, but brief and clearly written explanation of the tax benefits of land protection. Includes an excellent section on choosing the best protection strategy. Should be of use beyond the state of Massachusetts.

Whyte, William H. 1968. *The Last Landscape.* Garden City, N.Y.: Doubleday. 428 pp.

Eminently readable; refreshing insight though published two decades ago. Primer on the issues, techniques, and planning alternatives in open space, landscape, and environmental protection.

## CHAPTER 6: HELP FROM THE OUTSIDE

In addition to the following publications, there are many booklets and brochures published by federal agencies on the programs and laws they administer. They are too numerous and change too frequently to list here. You should, however, contact the agencies that interest you to obtain those currently available.

American Association of University Women. 1981. *AAUW Community Action Tool Catalog: Techniques and Strat-*

*egies for Successful Action Programs.* (See entry for Chapter 2.)

Ashcroft, Mary. 1979. *Designating Scenic Roads: A Vermont Field Guide.* (See entry for Chapter 3.)

Concern, Inc. 1986. *Drinking Water: A Community Action Guide.* (See entry for Chapter 1.)

Conservation Foundation. 1982. *State of the Environment 1982.* (See entry for Chapter 1.)

———. 1987. *State of the Environment: A View toward the Nineties.* (See entry for Chapter 1.)

Conservation Foundation, Chemical Manufacturers Association, and National Audubon Society. 1983. *Siting Hazardous Waste Management Facilities: A Handbook.* (See entry for Chapter 1.)

Coughlin, Robert E., and John C. Keene, eds. 1981. *The Protection of Farmland: A Reference Guidebook for State and Local Governments.* (See entry for Chapter 4.)

DeGrove, John M. 1984. *Land, Growth, and Politics.* Chicago: American Planning Association. 454 pp.

Describes land-use laws and how they were adopted in California, Colorado, Florida, Hawaii, North Carolina, Oregon, and Vermont.

deKieffer, Donald E. 1981. *How to Lobby Congress: A Guide for the Citizen Lobbyist.* New York: Dodd, Mead and Company. 241 pp.

Topics include developing an action plan, writing letters, dealing with congressional staff, testifying, the press, demonstrations, what to do if things go wrong, and deciding whether professional assistance is needed.

Diamant, Rolf; J. Glenn Eugster; and Christopher J. Duerksen. 1984. *A Citizen's Guide to River Conservation.* (See entry for Chapter 1.)

Duerksen, Christopher, J., ed. 1983. *A Handbook on Historic Preservation Law.* (See entry for Chapter 4.)

Environmental Law Institute. *National Wetlands Newsletter.* (See entry for Chapter 1.)

Firestone, David B., and Frank C. Reed. 1983. *Environmental Law for Non-Lawyers.* Ann Arbor, Mich.: Ann Arbor Science Publishers. 282 pp.

Describes key federal laws, typical state and local laws, and the legal remedies available to citizens.

Gordon, Wendy. 1984. *A Citizen's Handbook on Groundwater Protection.* (See entry for Chapter 1.)

Government Institutes, Inc. 1987. *Environmental Law Handbook.* 9th ed. Rockville, Md.: GI. 608 pp.

Intended for both attorneys and lay audiences. Covers the National Environmental Policy Act and federal laws relating to water, air, noise, toxic substances, pesticides,

and marine protection. Gives information on their legislative histories and how they are applied.

Healy, Robert G., and John S. Rosenberg. 1979. *Land Use and the States.* 2d ed. Baltimore: Johns Hopkins University Press. 284 pp.

An overview of state land-use laws. Contains case studies of California, Florida, and Vermont.

Hubler, Kathryn, and Timothy Henderson, eds. 1985. *Directory of State Environmental Agencies.* 2d ed. Washington, D.C.: Environmental Law Institute. 275 pp.

Basic data on responsible agencies and citations to relevant legislation.

Kusler, Jon A. 1980. *Regulating Sensitive Lands.* (See entry for Chapter 4.)

———. 1983. *Our National Wetland Heritage: A Protection Guidebook.* Washington, D.C.: Environmental Law Institute. 168 pp.

A good description of techniques and laws that can be used to protect wetlands.

National Audubon Society. *Audubon Wildlife Report 1987.* (See entry for Chapter 1.)

National Trust for Historic Preservation. 1986. *A Guide to Tax-Advantaged Rehabilitation.* Washington, D.C.: NTHP. 20 pp.

An explanation of federal tax incentives for the owners of income-producing properties listed in the National Register of Historic Places.

———. Information Series. Washington, D.C.: NTHP.

The following title in this series is of particular interest: *Routes of History: Recreational Use and Preservation of Historic Transportation Corridors* (no. 38).

National Wildlife Federation. *Conservation Directory.* Washington, D.C.: NWF, annual edition.

Lists private organizations and government agencies at the national and state levels that are concerned with conservation. Briefly describes each organization and names its key officials.

National Wildlife Federation and Environmental Action Foundation. 1977. *The End of the Road: A Citizen's Guide to Transportation Problemsolving.* (See entry for Chapter 1.)

Steiner, Frederick R., and John E. Theilacker, eds. 1984. *Protecting Farmlands.* (See entry for Chapter 4.)

U.S. Department of Agriculture, Forest Service. 1981. *An Assessment of the Forest and Range Land Situation in the United States.* (See entry for Chapter 1.)

U.S. Department of Agriculture, Office of Rural Development Policy. 1985. *Rural Resources Guide: A Directory* of *Public and Private Assistance for Small Communities.* Washington, D.C.: U.S. Government Printing Office. 564 pp.

Provides brief information on a wide variety of resources for communities concerned about such issues as economic revitalization, water supply, transportation, and housing.

## CHAPTER 7: COMMUNITY EDUCATION

Brigham, Nancy, with Ann Raszmann and Dick Cluster. 1982. *How to Do Leaflets, Newsletters, and Newspapers.* New York: Hastings House Publishers. 144 pp. (Order from P.E.P. Publishers, P.O. Box 289, Essex Station, Boston, MA 02112)

Buchanan, Terry. 1983. *Photographing Historic Buildings.* (See entry for Chapter 3.)

Eastman Kodak Company. 1987. *Kodak Index to Photographic Information.* (See entry for Chapter 3.)

Flanagan, Joan. 1981. *The Successful Volunteer Organization: Getting Started and Getting Results in Nonprofit Charitable, Grassroots, and Community Groups.* (See entry for Chapter 2.)

———. 1982. *The Grass Roots Fundraising Book: How to Raise Money in Your Community.* (See entry for Chapter 2.)

National Trust for Historic Preservation. Information Series. Washington, D.C.: NTHP.

The following titles in this series are of particular interest: *Preservation Education: Kindergarten through Twelfth Grade* (no. 23) and *Public Relations for Local Preservation Organizations: Press Relations, Public Education, and Special Events* (no. 24).

Stewardship Institute. 1986. *Project Seasons.* Shelburne, Vt.: Shelburne Farms. Looseleaf binder, unpaged. (SF, Shelburne, VT 05482)

A classroom teachers' aid to environmental learning exercises for children in kindergarten through sixth grade in the Northeast.

# Notes

## CHAPTER 1: RURAL CONCERNS

1. Author-date citations in the text refer to works found in the suggested readings for the chapter in question.

2. Timothy E. Wirth, as quoted by T. R. Reid, "From Spuds to Scenery: West Shifts Economic Focus," *Washington Post,* 12 February 1987.

3. Richard Lingeman, *Small-Town America: A Narrative History, 1620 to the Present* (New York: G. P. Putnam's Sons, 1980), p. 493.

4. U.S. Department of Agriculture, *Using Our Natural Resources: 1983 Handbook of Agriculture* (Washington, D.C.: U.S. Government Printing Office, 1983), p. 450.

5. Ibid., p. 24.

6. Arabic and roman numerals in parentheses are cross-references to relevant chapters (arabic numerals), sections (roman numerals), and, where applicable, subsections (capital letters) in this volume.

7. As quoted by Kathy Hoke, "County Water Supply Unsafe," *Daily Progress* (Charlottesville, Va.), 1 April 1984.

8. USDA, *Using Our Natural Resources,* p. 238.

9. Peter Steinhart, "The Edge Gets Thinner," *Audubon,* November 1983, p. 98.

10. Ibid., p. 101.

11. All three examples from ibid., p. 97.

12. Economic Research Service, USDA, *Foreign Agricultural Trade of the United States* (Washington, D.C.: ERS, 1987), p. 30.

13. Figure for 1985, from Economic Research Service, USDA, *Measuring the Size of the U.S. Food and Fiber System,* ERS AER, no. 566 (Washington, D.C.: ERS, 1987), p. 2.

14. National Agricultural Statistics Service, USDA, *Agricultural Statistics, 1986* (Washington, D.C.: NASS, 1986), p. 382; Bureau of the Census, *Historical Statistics of the United States* (Washington, D.C.: BC, 1975), p. 457.

15. The 1986 figure is from NASS, *Agricultural Statistics, 1986,* p. 370. The 1880 figure was 134 acres: Bureau of the Census, *Historical Statistics,* p. 457.

16. John McCormick, "The Once and Future Barn," *Newsweek,* 9 July 1984, p. 12.

17. USDA, *The Second RCA Appraisal,* draft (Washington, D.C.: USDA, 1987), pp. 3-8 to 3-12.

18. Bureau of the Census, *1982 Census of Agriculture* (Washington, D.C.: BC, 1984), 1, pt. 51:4.

19. USDA, *Using Our Natural Resources,* p. 136. Of this percentage, 18% are national forests, and 9% other public ownership.

20. U.S. Department of the Interior and others, "1982–1983 Nationwide Recreation Survey" (Unpublished, 1985), p. 18.

21. James P. Ludwig, Ecological Research Services, Bay

City, Mich., telephone conversation with author, February 1988.

22. USDA, *Using Our Natural Resources,* p. 397.

23. Stephen U. Lester, Citizens' Clearing House for Hazardous Wastes, to author, 5 February 1986.

## CHAPTER 2: INITIATING AND MANAGING A RURAL CONSERVATION PROGRAM

1. Joseph M. Keyser, "Backyard Landsaving: Building a Coalition," *New American Land,* September–October, 1987, p. 50.

2. Jane W. Schautz to author, 21 August 1986.

3. P. K. Pettus, former member of the Virginia Conservation Council, speech, Washington, D.C., 14 June 1980.

4. Ibid.

5. Kim McAdams, "Public Survey Leads to New Trust," *Land Trusts' Exchange,* Summer 1983, p. 8.

6. Ibid.

7. Telephone conversation with Constance Chamberlin, August 1986.

8. Phoebe L. Hopkins, speech, Louisville, Ky., October 1982.

## CHAPTER 4: LAND-PROTECTION TECHNIQUES

1. "Unrestricted Growth Threatens Rural Areas" (editorial), *Harrisburg* (Pa.) *Patriot-News*, 21 September 1987.

2. Warren Zitzmann to author, October 1986.

3. Dennis Gordon to author, 5 November 1986.

4. Zitzmann to author, October 1986.

5. Dave Hallock, "Boulder County Makes Room for Wildlife," *Planning,* September 1984, pp. 12–14.

6. Guilford Preservation Alliance, *Master Plan for Preservation and Scenic Conservation* (Guilford, Conn.: GPA, 1986).

7. Piedmont Environmental Council, "Fauquier Leads Virginia in Rural Protection," PEC, *Newsreporter,* May 1986, pp. 1–30.

8. Eugene T. Ruane and Robert J. Gray, *Community Responses to Population Growth and Environmental Stress: A National Inventory of Local Growth Management Strategies* (Washington, D.C.: Population-Environment Balance, Inc., 1987), p. 26.

9. Kat Imhoff to author, 6 October 1986.

10. Zitzmann to author.

11. Ibid.

## CHAPTER 5: VOLUNTARY TECHNIQUES FOR PROTECTING PRIVATE PROPERTY

1. Telephone conversation with Randi S. Lemmon, November 1986.

2. Ibid.

## CHAPTER 7: COMMUNITY EDUCATION

1. Telephone conversation with Marc Smiley, July 1986.

2. Telephone conversation with Ralph H. Goodno, Jr., July 1986.

3. "A Brief Historical Synopsis of the Yakima River Regional Greenway" (undated), p. 4.

4. Telephone conversation with Constance Chamberlin, June 1986.

## CONCLUSION

1. As quoted and analyzed in Charles McLaughlin, "Aldo Leopold's Land Ethic, 1887–1987," *Iowa Natural Heritage,* Winter 1987, p. 4.

# Sources for Case Studies

The following numbers refer to case study numbers.

1. Work and visits of A. Elizabeth Watson, 1980–84. Quotation from Phoebe L. Hopkins in letter to author, October 1987.

2. Visits of Samuel N. Stokes, 1984.

3. Adapted from Art Roche, "Heritage Trail," *Iowa Natural Heritage,* Fall 1986, pp. 7–9 (including quotation), with further reference to Pat Nunnally, "Iowa's Heritage Trail," *American Land Forum,* March/April 1987, pp. 23–27, and telephone conversations of A. Elizabeth Watson with Doug Cheever, 1988.

4. Telephone conversations of Samuel N. Stokes with Frederic L. McLaughlin, 1986.

5. Adapted from Randi S. Lemmon, "Land Conservation Via Mediation Planning," *Land Trusts' Exchange,* Summer 1985, pp. 8–9.

6. Work and visits of Samuel N. Stokes, 1980–85.

7. Work and visits of Robert Z. Melnick, J. Timothy Keller, and Genevieve P. Keller, 1986–87.

8. Based in part on Terry Ryan LeVeque and James F. Palmer, *Cazenovia's Visual Resource* (Cazenovia, N.Y.: Town of Cazenovia, 1983).

9. Visit of Samuel N. Stokes, 1985.

10. Dennis A. Gordon, "The Power of the Point System," *Planning,* December 1984, pp. 15–17; NASDA Research Foundation Farmland Project, "Hardin County,

Kentucky, Directs Rural Growth without Zoning," *Farmland Notes* (published by NASDA), May 1986, p. 2; and A. Elizabeth Watson's conversations and correspondence with Dennis A. Gordon, 1986–87.

11. Visit of Samuel N. Stokes, 1985, and telephone conversation of A. Elizabeth Watson with Marlene Conaway, 1986.

12. Telephone conversations of A. Elizabeth Watson and Samuel N. Stokes with Charles E. Roe, 1986.

13. Visits of A. Elizabeth Watson and Samuel N. Stokes, 1984–85.

14. Visit of J. Timothy Keller, 1984.

15. Telephone conversation of A. Elizabeth Watson with Carolie Evans, 1986.

16. Telephone conversations of A. Elizabeth Watson with William H. Schmidt, 1986.

17. Ibid., and William H. Schmidt, "Everyone Wins: More Saved than a Farm," *Journal for Constructive Change,* Spring 1984, pp. 23 ff.

18. Visits of A. Elizabeth Watson, 1985–86. Quotation in first paragraph from Wendy Grissim Brokaw, "Homegrown Preservation," *Monterey Life,* April 1982, p. 34.

19. Michael Staub, "We'll Never Quit It!" *Southern Exposure,* January–February, 1983, pp. 42–52 (quotation in third paragraph); Beverly Greene, "Middlesboro: Perseverance Pays Off," *ruralamerica,* September–October 1984 (quotation in sixth paragraph); and telephone con-

versation of Samuel N. Stokes with Ben Drake, 1986 (quotation in last paragraph).

20. Telephone conversations of Samuel N. Stokes with Bill Thomas and Kathleen A. Blaha, 1985.

21. Telephone conversations of Samuel N. Stokes with Mort Mather, 1985–87.

22. Telephone conversations of Samuel N. Stokes with Barbara Stagg, 1985–87.

23. Telephone conversations of Samuel N. Stokes with Gary Werner, 1985–87.

24. Visit of J. Timothy Keller, 1984.

25. Mary Beebe, "State Plans Reclamation Project for Cranks Creek," *Mountain Life and Work,* September 1981, pp. 9–11 (first quotation), and telephone conversations of Samuel N. Stokes with Simpson and state official who asked not to be identified, 1985 (second quotation).

26. Telephone conversations of Samuel N. Stokes with Frank A. Wright and Mark A. Berkowsky, 1985–87.

27. Telephone conversations of Samuel N. Stokes with Marc Smiley, 1985–87.

28. Visits of Genevieve P. Keller, J. Timothy Keller, and Samuel N. Stokes, 1980–87.

# Figure Credits

# Notes about the Authors

**Samuel N. Stokes** is a consultant on land conservation and historic preservation. He advises rural communities on the protection of natural and historic resources and writes and lectures on the subject. From 1976 to 1984, he worked for the National Trust for Historic Preservation, first as the director of the Trust's Mid-Atlantic Regional Office and later as the director of the Rural Program, which he designed and initiated. In 1983–84 he was a Richard King Mellon Fellow at the Yale School of Forestry and Environmental Studies. Before working for the Trust, Mr. Stokes helped implement a cooperative Smithsonian–Peace Corps environmental program, administered a famine-relief program in Africa, was the first Peace Corps director in Benin, and served as a Peace Corps Volunteer in the Ivory Coast. He has a B.A. in history from Yale University.

**A. Elizabeth Watson** is the special assistant to the secretary of the Department of Environmental Resources in Pennsylvania and works on public-land, environmental-protection, and water-resource issues. From 1985 to 1987 she served as liaison for the Land Trust Exchange in Washington, working with Congress, federal agencies, and national organizations on conservation and taxation issues. She was executive producer of an award-winning film on conservation easements, *For the Common Good.* As the field representative of the National Trust's Rural Program from 1979 to 1984, Ms. Watson gave assistance to numerous communities and was the author of several monographs on conservation. She previously worked for the Trust's Preservation Press. Ms. Watson holds a master's degree in regional planning from the Pennsylvania State University.

**J. Timothy Keller,** ASLA, and **Genevieve P. Keller** are principals in the planning and design firm of Land and Community Associates of Charlottesville, Virginia, and Eugene, Oregon. They advise nonprofit organizations and government agencies on environmental design, land planning, and historic preservation. They are coauthors of several publications, including two National Register Bulletins written for the National Park Service: *How to Evaluate and Nominate Designed Historic Landscapes* and *Guidelines for Identifying, Evaluating, and Registering Rural Historic Landscapes* (forthcoming). In addition to writing and speaking on these subjects, Mr. Keller has taught landscape architecture at Iowa State University. Mrs. Keller serves on the Governor's Commission to Study Historic Preservation in Virginia and is president of the Preservation Alliance of Virginia. In 1987, the Kellers received the Department of the Interior's Public Service Award in recognition of their significant contribution to historic preservation in the United States. Mr. Keller holds a master's degree in landscape architecture from the University of Virginia. Mrs. Keller holds a master's degree in architectural history from the University of Virginia.

# Index

Association for Living Historical Farms and Agricultural Museums, 261, **270**

Association of Interpretive Naturalists, 263, **270**

Audio-visual productions, 247–48

Bandon, Oreg., 186–87

Bargain sale, **190**, 197, 199

"Barn Again," *41*

Barns and outbuildings: design guidelines for, 158, 161; illustrated, *41, 50, 52, 56, 60, 169;* in rural historic districts, *163;* threats to, *10, 39–40*

Barrier islands, 24, 216

Base map, 96–99, *125*

Benepe, Barry, 262

Bequest, 188, 190–91, 193

Berks County Conservancy (Pa.), 53, 56, 174–75

Big South Fork National River and Recreation Area, 225

Big Sur Land Trust (Calif.), 67, 190, 193–97, *203*

Billboards, 165, 227–28

Birmingham Township, Pa., 163, 166

Bishir, Catherine W., 1

Bishop Hill, Ill., 38–39

Blackfoot River, Mont., 180–82

Block Island, R.I., 185

Blue Ridge, 213

BLM. *See* Bureau of Land Management

Bonds: for housing, 239; for land banking, 184; in New York, 265; as performance guarantees, 142; for purchase of development rights, 184, 185

"Boom and bust" communities, *16, 17*

Boulder, Colo., xvii, 133

Boundaries: defining, 74, *74–75;* in easements, 182; in historic landscapes, *112–13;* in zoning, 135, *136*

Brandywine Conservancy (Pa.), 55–56

Brattleboro, Vt., 79, 189

Brazoria County, Tex., 74–75

Bridge rehabilitation, 233–34

Brown, Barbara, *190*

Budget, 76, 133–34, 135

"Bundle of rights," 178–79

Bureau of Land Management (BLM): forest land, 32; public land, 44–45; rangeland, 34, 220; scenic resources, 117, *117,* 120

Bureau of Reclamation, 215, 216

Burlington, Vt., 15

Cade, Norma, *65*

California: 12, 19, *21,* 38–39, *141,* 153; coastal protection in, 193, 196, 216; farmers' markets, 262; housing in, 238; river protection in, 212; scenic roads in, 227; toxic waste in, 164; voluntary property restrictions for tax reductions, 167

Callahan, Don, 92, *245*

Camp fire, *78*

Capital gains tax, 167, 189, 198

Capital improvements, impacts on environment by, 133–34

Carroll County, Md., 168–71, *251*

Cascade County, Mont., *25*

Cazenovia Advisory Conservation Commission (N.Y.), 93, 94, 109–10, 120, 125

Cazenovia Community Resources Project (N.Y.) (CCRP), case study of, 89–94; consultants, 95; environmental inventory, 86, 88; and environmental review, 155; and farmland, 121–22, *122;* library, 250; mapping by, 96, 98, *100–101,* 104, 124–25; and National Trust, xix–xx, 90–92; photographs by, 246; and planning, 88; professional volunteers, 78; publicity, 244, *245;* and recreational resources, 120–22; and scenic resources, 118–21; and water resources, 105, 107; and wetlands, *106;* and wildlife, 110

Cazenovia Lake (N.Y.), *103,* 105

Cazenovia Planning Commission (N.Y.), 125

Cazenovia Preservation Foundation (N.Y.), 90, 92, 94, 98, 178; tour booklets, *249*

*Cazenovia Republican* (N.Y.), 93–94, 244, *245*

CCRP. *See* Cazenovia Community Resources Project

Center for Environmental Education, 270

Center for Environmental Intern Programs Fund, 82, **270**

Center for Rural Affairs, 238

Center for Rural Massachusetts, 206, 265

Century farms, 174, *175*

Chamberlin, Constance, 256

Champlain, Lake (Vt.), 183

Channelization, **21–22**, 211

Charitable contribution. *See* Donation

Charitable creditors, 189

Charleston, S.C., 162

Chase County, Kans., 222

Cheever, Doug, *65*

Chesapeake Bay, 12, 207

Chester-Sassafras Foundation (Md.), 74

Citizen participation. *See* Public participation

Citizen's Clearinghouse for Hazardous Waste, 164, 236, **270**

Citizens Concerned about I-69 (Mich.), 68–71

Clark, Story, 61

Clarke, James, 213

Clarke County, Va., 137

Clean Air Act, 236–37

Clean Water Act, **209**, 210–11, 215

Climate, 110–11

Clustering, 143–46, 158; examples of, *60–61,* 168–69; historic design, *113;* and TDR, 153

Coalition for Scenic Beauty, 165, 228, **270**

Coalitions, 265

Coastal Barrier Resources Act, 215, 216

Coastal Zone Management Act, 216–18

Coast Guard, U.S., 186

Coasts, xv, 24, 190–91, *190,* 193–97, 216–18

Codicil, 188

Collins, Dennis, 84

Colorado, 17, *162–63,* 164, 165; Boulder, xvii, 133; historic preservation in, *85, 175;* tourism in, *12, 13*

Colorado Open Lands, 58, 83, 197, *198*

Colorado River, 18

Columbia River (Wash.), 233

Community Development Block Grant, 54, **237**

Community land trusts, 198

Community needs assessment, 74–76, *77*

Community services: grants for, 237; planning and budgeting for, 129, 131, 133–34; problems in rural areas, 11–12, *17;* in suitability analysis, 125, 148, *149;* and taxation, 167

Compatible development, 147–48, 197

Compensation "taking," 134–35

Comprehensive Environmental Response, Compensation, and Liability Act, 236

Comprehensive plan, 129, 130–34; in McHenry County, Ill., 138; by states, 207. *See also* Planning

Compromise development. *See* Limited development

Computer mapping, *126*

Conaway, Marlene, 169, 170, 171

Condemnation, 178–79, 185

Conditional uses, 142

SAVING AMERICA'S COUNTRYSIDE

Designed by Susan P. Fillion
Composed by Brushwood Graphics, Inc., in Sabon display and text
Printed by the Maple Press Company, Inc., on 55-lb.
Glatfelter Offset paper